# Environment and Development in the Caribbean

# Environment and Development in the Caribbean

## Geographical Perspectives

**Edited by**
David Barker and Duncan F. M. McGregor

The
# PRESS
**University of the West Indies**

● Barbados  ● Jamaica  ● Trinidad and Tobago

The Press, University of the West Indies
1A Aqueduct Flats, Mona, Kingston 7, Jamaica W.I.

CATALOGUING IN PUBLICATION DATA

Environment and development in the Caribbean : geographical
    perspectives / David Barker and Duncan F.M. McGregor, eds.

    p. cm.

Papers presented at the British-Caribbean Geography Seminar,
held in the Department of Geography, University of
the West Indies, Mona, August 1992.

Includes bibliographical references.
ISBN 976 640 007 5
1. Sustainable development – Caribbean Area – Congresses.
2. Envrionmental policy – Caribbean Area – Congresses.
3. Environmental impact assessment – Caribbean Area – Congresses.
4. Man – Influence on nature – Caribbean Area – Congresses.
5. Tourist trade – Environmental aspects – Caribbean
Area – Congresses.
I. Barker, David.   II. McGregor, Duncan, F.M.
III. British-Caribbean Geography Seminar (1992 : Mona, Jamaica).
HC79.E5E68 1995                        333.7    dc–20


Book and cover design by Prodesign Ltd, Jamaica
Text set in 10/13 Optima with Futura display

# Contents

List of Figures                                                                viii

List of Tables                                                                  xi

Preface                                                                        xiii

Acknowledgements                                                               xvi


## Introduction

**Chapter 1:** *Duncan F. M. McGregor and David Barker*
A Geographical Focus for Environment and Development
in the Caribbean                                                                3

## Coastal Zone Resource Management

**Chapter 2:** *Leonard A. Nurse, Kenneth A. Atherley and Leo A. Brewster*
The Impact of Thermal Effluent Discharge on the Barbados
Southern West Coast                                                            21

**Chapter 3:** *Neil E. Sealey*
Bahamian Blue Holes: Windows on the Past, Resources for the Future             35

**Chapter 4:** *Peter R. Bacon*
Wetland Resource Rehabilitation for Sustainable Development
in the Eastern Caribbean                                                       46

## Tourism and Development Planning

**Chapter 5:** *Lesley France and Brian Wheeller*
Sustainable Tourism in the Caribbean                                           59

Contents

**Chapter 6:** *Klaus de Albuquerque and Jerome L. McElroy*
Tourism Development in Small Islands: St Maarten/St Martin
and Bermuda                                                          70

**Chapter 7:** *Frank L. Mills*
The Cost of Housing in a Tourist Economy:
The US Virgin Islands                                                90

## Natural Hazards and Disaster Management

**Chapter 8:** *Jeremy McA. Collymore*
Disaster Mitigation and Cost-Benefit Analysis:
Conceptual Perspectives                                             111

**Chapter 9:** *Alison J. Reading and Rory P. D. Walsh*
Tropical Cyclone Activity within the Caribbean Basin
since 1500                                                          124

**Chapter 10:** *Rafi Ahmad*
Landslides in Jamaica: Extent, Significance
and Geological Zonation                                             147

**Chapter 11:** *Russell J. Maharaj*
Evaluating Landslide Hazard for Land Use Planning:
Upper St Andrew, Jamaica                                            170

## Land Resources and Development Planning

**Chapter 12:** *Duncan F. M. McGregor*
Soil Erosion, Environmental Change and Development
in the Caribbean: A Deepening Crisis?                               189

**Chapter 13:** *Fatima Patel*
Coastal Development and Geomorphological Processes:
Scotland District, Barbados                                         209

**Chapter 14:** *Patrick E. Williams*
Drainage and Irrigation Projects in Guyana:
Environmental Considerations                                        233

## National Parks In Jamaica: Problems And Prospects

**Chapter 15:** *David C. Smith*
Implementing a National Park System for Jamaica:
The PARC Project                                                    249

**Chapter 16:** *L. Alan Eyre*
The Cockpit Country: A World Heritage Site?                    *259*

**Chapter 17:** *David Barker and David J. Miller*
Farming on the Fringe: Small-Scale Agriculture on the
Edge of the Cockpit Country                                    *271*

*Index*                                                        *293*

*Contributors*                                                 *302*

# List of Figures

**1.1** The Caribbean Basin Showing Principal Territories
Covered in this Volume                                          *12*

**2.1** Location of Study Area                                  *23*

**2.2** Schematic Representation of Volumetric Beach
Changes at Barbados Light & Power Company (1987-1989)           *25*

**2.3** Schematic Representation of Volumetric Beach
Changes at Barbados Light & Power Company (1989-1992)           *28*

**2.4** Schematic Representation of Mean Surface and
Bottom Temperature in Relation to Distance from
Outfall at Barbados Light & Power Plant                         *32*

**3.1** Location of Fracture Controlled Blue Holes in South Andros   *37*

**3.2** Variation of Salinity, Carbon Dioxide Partial Pressure,
and Aragonite, Calcite and Dolomite Saturation in
Evelyn Green's Blue Hole, South Andros                          *38*

**3.3** The Flank-Margin Model of Cave Formation                *39*

**3.4** Distribution of North Andros Blue Holes used in Hydrological Study   *40*

**3.5** Summary of the Circulation of Saline Waters in a Carbonate Platform   *41*

**3.6** Schematic Diagram Illustrating the Distribution and
Rates of Diagenesis within a Bahamian Platform                  *42*

**4.1** Location of Islands in Wetland Survey of Eastern Caribbean, 1991   *48*

**6.1** Butler's Model of Hypothetical Evolution of a Tourist Area   *72*

**6.2** Bermuda Visitor Arrivals (1949-1991)                    *76*

**7.1** Tenure and Vacancy of Households                        *93*

**7.2** Vacant Housing Inventory, 1990                          *98*

**8.1** The Optimal Level of Hazard Mitigation *118*

**9.1** Subregions of the Caribbean: Historical Data *126*

**9.2** Decadal Frequency of Cyclones in Ten Subregions of the Caribbean *127-130*

**9.3** Grid Map of the Caribbean: Charted Data *130*

**9.4** Decadal Frequency of Cyclones, 1870s–1980s, per 5° Grid Square *133*

**9.5** Decadal Frequency of Hurricanes 1900s–1980s, per 5° Grid Square *135*

**9.6** Spatial Variations in Intensity Patterns for Five Selected Grid Squares *137-138*

**9.7** The Origin of Cyclones in the North Atlantic *139*

**10.1** Geographical Distribution of Major Landslides in Jamaica Based on the Events Listed in Tables 10.1 and 10.2 *154*

**10.2** Geology of Jamaica with Eight Landslide Zones *155*

**11.1** Location Map for Upper St Andrew *171*

**11.2** Geological Units in Upper St Andrew *173*

**11.3** Landslide Inventory Map of Upper St Andrew *177*

**11.4** Geotechnical Map of the Study Area *178*

**11.5** Landslide Susceptibility Map for Upper St Andrew *181*

**12.1** Jamaica: Location Map *192*

**12.2** Relative Soil Loss from Different Crop Types, Bellevue *195*

**12.3** Clarke & Hodgkiss 1974 Estimate of Topsoil Erosion in Yallahs Catchment *197*

**12.4** Global Temperature Rise, Averaged Figures 1880-1988 *199*

**12.5a** Combined Surface Temperature Anomalies from Long-term Average *200*

**12.5b** Sea Surface Temperature Anomalies from Long-term Average *201*

**12.6** Surface Temperature Anomalies for the Americas: 1981-1990 with Respect to 1951-1980. Isolines in °C *202*

**12.7** Decadal Incidence of Hurricanes and Tropical Cyclones *203*

**13.1** The Study Area *210*

**13.2** Principal Locations in the Study Area *211*

**13.3** Geology of the Study Area *213*

**13.4** Intensity of Geomorphic Change *218*

**13.5a** Land Use in the Study Area, 1951 and 1982 *221*

**13.5b** Land Use in the Study Area, 1991                                          *222*

**13.6** The Geomorphological Response of
the System to its Various Components                                               *226*

**13.7** Susceptibility to Geomorphic Change                                        *229*

**14.1** Drainage and Irrigation Projects in Guyana                                 *236*

**14.2** MMA Project Catchment Area                                                 *238*

**15.1** Location of Blue and John Crow Mountains
National Park in Eastern Jamaica                                                   *253*

**16.1** The Cockpit Country and Environs                                           *260*

**17.1** Cockpit Country in its Regional Context                                    *272*

**17.2** Geology of the Study Area                                                  *277*

**17.3** Geomorphology of the Study Area                                            *278*

**17.4** Patterns of Encroachment within the Study Area                             *280*

# List of Tables

**2.1** Power Generation Capacity and Thermal Effluent Volumes for
Selected Years, Barbados Light and Power Company     *23*

**2.2** Results of Current Direction (Dye Injection) Tests     *27*

**2.3** Mean Sulphide, Dissolved Oxygen and Conductivity Values for
Eight Sampling Sites at Brighton North     *30*

**4.1** Mangrove and Associated Wetland Sites in the Eastern Caribbean Islands     *47*

**4.2** Mangrove Community Types and Associated Ecosystems in the
Eastern Caribbean Islands     *49*

**4.3** Goods, Services and Attributes Derived from Caribbean Wetland Systems     *50*

**4.4** Causes of Degradation of Coastal Wetlands in the Eastern Caribbean     *51*

**4.5** Selected Examples of Wetland Enhancement by Low Cost
Rehabilitation Methods     *54*

**6.1** Basic Indicators for Bermuda and St Maarten/St Martin     *74*

**6.2** Selected Tourism Indicators     *75*

**6.3** Bermuda Visitor Arrivals by Mode of Arrival, 1970-1991     *77*

**6.4** St Maarten/St Martin Visitor Arrivals by Mode of Arrival, 1970-1991     *79*

**7.1** Selected Indicators of Economic Growth     *92*

**7.2** Tenure of Housing Units, 1990     *95*

**7.3** Real Estate Sales, 1970-1989     *96*

**7.4** Regression Analysis of Median Rent     *100*

**7.5** Regression Analysis of Median Home Value     *101*

**8.1** Comparison of Selected Economic Indicators for Dominica,
Fiscal Years 1978-1983     *116*

**9.1** Categories of Cyclones in the North Atlantic Region      *140*

**9.2** Circulatory Factors Which May Influence
Cyclone Activity in the North Atlantic      *141*

**10.1** Some Major Slope Movements in Jamaica, Including
Fatalities, Injuries, and Economic Costs      *150-151*

**10.2** Prehistoric/Undated Landslide Events with Volume in Excess
of 1mm$^3$      *152*

**10.3** Geological, Structural, Geomorphological and Landslide
Characteristics of Eight Landslide Zones in Jamaica      *158-161*

**11.1** Characteristics of Each Geotechnical Unit      *176*

**11.2** Types and Frequencies of Mapped Landslides      *179*

**11.3** Slope Failures Recorded for Different Lithologies      *180*

**11.4** Slope Failure Record for Each Slope Category      *180*

**11.5** Engineering-Geologic Characteristics and Slope Failure
Record for Each Landslide Susceptibility Class      *182*

**12.1** Soil Profile Characteristics, Bellevue, Jamaica      *193*

**12.2** Published Estimates of Soil Erosion, Jamaica      *194*

**13.1** Index Properties of Some East Coast Soils      *216*

**13.2** Geomorphological Process Types      *218*

**13.3** The Percentage Areal Extent of Process Types for
Different Slope Steepness      *227*

**13.4** The Percentage Areal Extent of Process Types for
Different Material Groups      *227*

**13.5** The Percentage Areal Extent of Process Types for
Different Land Uses      *228*

**13.6** Hazard Classes      *230*

**13.7** Predicted Hazard Classes for Different Land Uses      *230*

**15.1** Responsibilities and Institutions within PARC      *250*

**15.2** Components of the PARC Project and Associated Agencies      *250*

**17.1** Farm Fragmentation: Number of Separate Plots per Farmer      *282*

# Preface

The year 1992 marked the 500th anniversary of European contact with the Caribbean, and also the date at which the European Community became a single economic market. Whether reflecting on the past or examining the prospects for overseas trade, the central issue facing the Caribbean region and its people as the 21st century approaches is how to achieve sustainable development — prosperity and growth without undermining or indeed crippling the resource base.

Perhaps because of the scale involved, the Caribbean region receives far less attention from the world at large than other developing areas. Yet, the economic and environmental problems facing the Caribbean's island micro-states are quite different to those of larger developing countries, though no less urgent to the people and governments of the region. On Caribbean islands the relationship of people to their environment is much more immediate and dramatic than in many temperate regions of the world, such as western Europe. Fragile ecosystems are at risk from natural hazards — a hurricane or a flash flood can have a disastrous proportionate effect on an island economy. No less serious are the long-term effects of deforestation and land degradation on the limited cultivable land, or of pollution and deterioration of coastal resources on the tourist industry.

The importance of focusing simultaneously on human systems and environmental systems in the equation which binds together people, resources and sustainable development cannot be understated. Geography's most enduring paradigm has been its focus on how people interact with their environments. Associated with this is a concern for how people use (or misuse) resources.

Many disciplines, such as zoology and botany, and economics and sociology, continue to make significant contributions to research on environment and development. Newer fields like environmental chemistry are particularly innovative in advancing knowledge, for example, in tracing the complex causal mechanisms by which pollutants affect the environment. However, if a broad view of environment and development is needed, especially with environmental planning and policy in mind, geography has much to offer. Geography provides a bridge between the natural and the social sciences, and a perspective which can help unravel the complex ways in which economic, social, cultural and political systems (human processes) interact with natural systems (physical processes).

At the present time, the opportunities for geographers from the UK and the Caribbean to meet, share ideas and initiate collaborative research are limited — only a few joint research programmes are currently in place. The meeting from which the present volume has derived, the British-Caribbean Geography Seminar, was held in the Department of Geography at the Mona campus of the University of the West Indies in August 1992. It was instrumental in bringing together, for the first time, a specialist group of geographers from the UK and the Caribbean. The meeting was conceived along the lines of the successful "Overseas Seminars", promoted by the Institute of British Geographers. The meeting was sponsored by the Commonwealth Foundation, the British Council, and the Institute of British Geographers. The Commonwealth Foundation provided funding for several participants from the Eastern Caribbean and also part-funding for a UK participant, and assisted financially in the production of this volume. The British Council sponsored the co-organizer of the meeting, and several of the UK participants received funding from the British Academy.

The meeting provided an opportunity for professional geographers from the different anglophone Caribbean states (and from both inside and outside tertiary institutions) to meet each other and their UK counterparts; and facilitated interaction between Caribbean and UK university geography departments in providing a forum for the presentation of research, and informal discussion of collaborative research opportunities. The interdisciplinary nature of the seminar was reinforced by contributions, both formally and in discussion, from scientists and social scientists across a wide spectrum of disciplines.

A total of 27 papers was presented at the British-Caribbean Geography Seminar. This volume contains 16 of those papers, suitably revised and improved for this publication. Most of the remaining papers from the meeting have already been published in a special issue of the journal *Caribbean Geography* (volume 3, no. 4, September 1992).

The organizers of the inaugural British-Caribbean Geography Seminar are planning a follow-up seminar, to be held at Royal Holloway, University of London, in August 1995.

*David Barker*

*Duncan F. M. McGregor*

# Acknowledgments

The editors would like to thank a number of institutions and individuals for their assistance and support in facilitating both the British-Caribbean Geography Seminar (held at the University of the West Indies, Mona, Kingston, 1992) and the production of this volume. The Commonwealth Foundation provided funding to enable several participants from the Eastern Caribbean to attend the meeting; part-funded the attendance of a UK participant; and provided financial assistance in the production of this volume. The British Council sponsored the co-organizer of the meeting, and the Institute of British Geographers provided seed money to cover some of the administrative costs of the Seminar. Study and Travel Grant Funds from the University of the West Indies, Mona enabled one of the editors to visit the UK twice during the editorial process.

At various times, Carolyn Graham, Dawn Cyrus, and Kathy Roberts all assisted by keying-in individual chapter files, often at short notice. Many of the maps and diagrams published in this volume were re-drawn by Justin Jacyno from originals supplied by the various authors.

*David Barker*
*Duncan F. M. McGregor*

# Introduction

Chapter 1

# A Geographical Focus for Environment and Development in the Caribbean

Duncan F. M. McGregor and David Barker

This volume illustrates and highlights how geographical research is being applied to address key environmental problems in the Caribbean region. It demonstrates ways in which geographers and other scientists in cognate disciplines can assist in conceptualizing, identifying and monitoring such problems in a variety of areas of decision making and policy concerned with environmental planning, economic development planning and resource management.

The general purpose of this chapter is to introduce the work of geographers engaged in research on environment and development in the region. We suggest three areas where a geographical perspective is important in the Caribbean region: economic development and its geographical context; environmental risk and environmental change; and human impacts on island environments. We also indicate useful research contributions which have been made by geographers in each of these areas. In the second half of the chapter, we discuss the rationale behind the inaugural British-Caribbean Geography Seminar, which was held in Kingston, Jamaica in 1992, a meeting designed to allow geographers and researchers in related fields an opportunity to present their current research in the field of environment and development. The essays in this book are based on a selection of papers presented at that meeting and, in the last of part of this chapter, we briefly introduce each of these contributions.

## Economic Development and Geographical Context

The ebb and flow of colonial power, the rise and fall of the plantocracy, the significant legacy of slave and indentured labour, the economic hegemony of the major industrial powers, and enduring island insularity are well documented and important factors in the shaping of the modern day perspectives of Caribbean people. These factors are some of the traditional foci that social scientists have used in analysing the process of economic development and economic dependency. Belatedly, Caribbean social scientists are beginning to recognize that an island's geography, ecology and environment also play a significant role in shaping the path of economic development [Girvan 1991]. The geographical underpinnings of the region's historical struggle for economic development are very clearly brought out in Bonham Richardson's recent work [Richardson 1992].

Geography has long recognized that interactions between economic development and environment are reciprocal; each shapes the other, whether it be in nurturing the history of a people, fashioning the evolution of a cultural landscape or in the channelling of patterns of economic activity. Paul Vidal de la Blache, the pre-eminent French geographer, once observed that when a country acquires a specific character it becomes "as a medal cast in the likeness of a people" [Vidal de la Blache 1927]. In the contemporary world, as countries face up to the challenges of the 21st century, the two faces of that medal are clearly the prospects for their environment and their economic development.

A geographical approach allows for synthesis. Thus, environment and development may be considered together: how are human activities affected by an island's physical conditions, and how can human activities, in turn, modify an island's physical and environmental processes? This approach is valid for a variety of geographical scales: the farm, or business establishment (*micro*); the village, town, or city and their hinterlands (*meso*); and the national level, or larger grouping of territories (*macro*). At each scale a number of geographical factors may be considered: the nature of the human and physical resource base; its location in relation to particular environmental and physical variables; and its location in relation to particular economic, social, political and cultural circumstances.

There is a dimension to the relationship between environment and development, however, that strikes right at the heart of many of the persistent economic problems facing modern Caribbean nations: the *geography* of small islands. Thus, limited physical size of land area, island topography, fragile tropical ecosystems, limited renewable and non-renewable resources, limited amounts of flat, arable land and restrictions to the carrying capacity of land at particular levels of technology are specifically *geographical* factors that have constrained the process of economic development for an individual country.

Thus, *economic sensitivity*, due to limitations of size, a restricted resource base, and relative isolation (leading to a greater relative dependence on high-cost transport systems than continental areas), is a significant factor in small island development. In what was eloquently described by Michael Manley [1987] in the Jamaican case as "up the down escalator", the limited capacity of the small island to produce and to consume restricts the potential of the small island state to generate internal finance and capital markets, and increases sensitivity to wider economic fluctuations. Dependence on external aid seems to be almost an inevitable fact of economic life. The relationship with an existing or former colonial power frequently becomes central to the island's economic survival. Economic dependency is thus firmly rooted in small island size, as well as in chronic out-migration of the young and able, and in undiversified economies.

At the global scale, tropical climates, location in a hurricane belt and in a seismically active region, proximity to industrial North America, overseas migration and vibrant familial connections with Caribbean diaspora in the UK, Canada and the USA are just a few of the specifically *geographical* factors into which the islands of the region are locked, and which have an impact upon their struggle for sustainable development.

## Environmental Risk and Environmental Change in the Caribbean

Caribbean islands have a high degree of sensitivity to natural events and to human-induced environmental change. They are also widely characterized by degrees of environmental degradation ranging from significant to extreme. High energy climatic environments, with seasonal hurricane activity and extreme rainfall events, allied to high natural weathering rates, create a fragile landscape. Environmental sensitivity is exacerbated by human use of the land, and resource depletion of all kinds is a persistent feature of the Caribbean environment [see for example, Eyre 1989a].

The key to recognizing environmental pressure points is often an understanding of the equations between sensitive natural systems, limited natural resources and expanding population. Jeffrey [1982] for example, argues cogently that natural disasters are not events which can be separated from the broader issues of development, since economic change can create vulnerability to natural disaster. She shows in the case of the Dominican Republic how the development of large-scale commercialized agricultural production has created such vulnerability by reducing or restricting the resource base of sectors of the population.

Physical hazards are an ever-present fact of Caribbean life. Hurricanes are perhaps the most violent natural events to affect the Caribbean with some regularity. Recent examples include Hurricane Gilbert which devastated Jamaica in 1988 [Eyre 1989b; Barker & Miller 1990]; Hurricane Hugo which swept across the northeastern Caribbean islands in 1989, bringing wanton destruction and damage to Montserrat and the Virgin Islands, as well as St Kitts and Nevis; and Hurricane Andrew which, in 1992, hit The Bahamas and south Florida. Such catastrophic events can cause loss of life, and serious damage to property and agriculture on land through wind, storm surge, coastal flooding and onshore saline intrusion. At the national level, these disasters have a damaging impact on island economies [Barker 1993], and especially the agriculture sector [Williams 1988].

Earthquakes are commonplace in the Caribbean; eight major ones in the last 200 years have caused an estimated 16,000 deaths. Since the major earthquake which devastated Kingston in 1907, there has been a deficit in earthquake energy release in the region. This is more a cause for concern than complacency, as the rapid urbanization of the Caribbean in recent decades has led to significant population concentrations in relatively high-risk zones where tremors are frequent. Perhaps Kingston (population 650,000), located on an alluvial fan called the Liguanea plain, is the best example in the English-speaking Caribbean. Moreover, post-1965 urban redevelopment of Kingston's downtown central business district is sited on infill — reclaimed waterfront land which has an inherently high risk of failure (liquefaction) under earthquake shock conditions [Hudson 1989]. There is also the possibility of the coastal areas fringing Kingston harbour, including the dormitory settlement of Portmore (population 100,000) being inundated by tsunami should there be nearby offshore earthquakes. San Juan, Puerto Rico, is another example of a similarly sited, highly urbanized and vulnerable location [Molinelli 1989].

Volcanic activity is a further ingredient in the cocktail of environmental risk in the Caribbean, particularly in the Windward and Leeward Islands [Shepherd 1989]. Tectonic activity is high around the rim of the Caribbean Basin; the eastern island chains roughly coincide with the arcuate Atlantic border of the Caribbean tectonic plate. For example, Dominica is estimated to have one of the densest concentrations of active volcanoes in the world [Robson & Tomblin 1966]. About one-third of all West Indian eruptions are violent. The most recent eruption was Soufrière in St Vincent in 1979, but the most spectacular and destructive post-Colombian event was the Mt Pelée eruption of 1902 in

Martinique which resulted in an estimated 30,000 deaths. This particular eruption added a frightening new term to the disaster lexicon — the *nuée ardente* or glowing avalanche — and ironically provided an important impetus for the advancement of modern volcanology.

Rapid mass movements are a natural consequence of the high rainfall, high weathering rates and steeply sloping terrain encountered throughout the Caribbean islands. For example, DeGraff [1991] has reviewed landslide activity in Dominica, St Vincent and St Lucia. Slope failure is mostly triggered by the effects of seasonal heavy rainfall and by individual storm events such as hurricanes, tropical depressions or earthquakes. Loss of life can occur and damage to crops, houses and disruption to communications are an ever-present drain on resources. Economic losses are severe [DeGraff et al. 1989] especially the recurrent costs of repairing roads [Naughton 1984].

There is little systematic long-term data on erosion rates under natural and agricultural conditions in the West Indies, yet soil erosion has been rampant in the region for centuries [Watts 1987; Barker & McGregor 1988]. Pioneering work carried out by Sheng [1972; 1981] at Smithfield Experimental Station in northwest Jamaica has been reported in the literature, and is highly regarded internationally. Yet the ongoing work at Smithfield has not been widely disseminated in Jamaica, results are largely confined to internal memoranda, and there appears to be little diffusion of innovations beyond the immediate vicinity of the Station. The few short-term studies which have been carried out suggest, however, that soil erosion is a continued problem on agricultural hillslopes [McGregor 1986; 1988]. Land degradation is an inevitable consequence, throughout the region. The degree of degradation is regarded as effectively irreversible in the worst cases, as exemplified by the recent US Agency for International Development (USAID) "Targeted Watershed Management Project" on the slopes of Pic Macauya, Haiti [Paskett & Philoctete 1990].

These environmental hazards rarely operate independently. The linkages between slope failure and soil erosion, for example, are well established in theory, if not accurately quantified in practice. Interaction of physical and human factors is also critical, notably in research into land degradation, where the extreme event can exacerbate a trend of increasing land degradation, but where the underlying cause is overuse or inappropriate use of the land itself.

Coastal zone degradation is perhaps the most complex environmental risk to assess, because it is the focus of many forms of human activity [Archer 1985; Hudson 1989] and notwithstanding the possible direct impact of hurricanes. Coastal zone flooding, too, is a result of a suite of environmental and human factors which may be difficult to disentangle. This point is illustrated by Collymore and Griffith [1987], in a case study of coastal flooding in Speightstown, Barbados.

Set against this background, the threat to the region posed by global warming must be taken seriously. Although conflicting hypotheses bedevil the recently emerging literature, it seems possible that the Caribbean over the next century will be affected by greater seasonality, with fewer but potentially higher-magnitude rainfall events, and by increasing sea surface temperatures leading to changing and possibly intensifying hurricane tracks.

## Human Impacts on Island Environments

The obvious visible manifestations of the impact of human activities on island environments are the modifications to natural landscapes. The geographer David Watts [1987] has documented this process in detail for the Eastern Caribbean, and provides a number of alarming historical examples which illustrate that Europeans misused natural resources through deforestation and over-exploitation in the Caribbean from the earliest post-Colombian times. At the small scale of an island ecosystem, environmental systems can be altered, sometimes irreversibly, by insensitive resource mismanagement.

The historical development of agriculture in the Caribbean region is a good example of the interaction of political economy and island environments which has not only created typical Caribbean rural landscapes, but has persisted to influence contemporary agricultural development and exacerbate *environmental stress*. Thus, the emergence of structural dualism in the agricultural sector led to export-led, large-scale plantation agriculture pre-empting the best land, forcing small farmers to occupy and cultivate marginal hillside land for food crops [Mintz 1974]. Entrenched rural poverty is widespread throughout the region [Beckford 1972; Barker & Spence 1988]. Further, agricultural dualism has a geographical dimension. It has created a landscape signature for many of the mountainous Greater Antilles and the Windward Islands, whereby the larger farming enterprises (like sugar cane) tend to be located on the flatter, alluvial, fertile coastal plains whilst small-scale mixed farming is relegated to areas which are often marginal to sustainable agriculture [Barker 1989].

A contemporary consequence of persistent agricultural dualism is that increasing population pressure, combined with the limited supply of good agricultural land, leads inevitably to severe environmental stress on land resources, particular in interior hillside farming areas [Barker 1989]. The legacy of inappropriate use of land resources in Caribbean islands with mountainous interiors is not only land degradation, restricted agricultural production and rural poverty, but increasing levels of vulnerability to flooding in the coastal plains. Rivers that drain the inland interior regions may carry so much water in a flood event (exacerbated by increased surface runoff through deforestation) that coastal zones are inundated; hence closing one of the circles of environmental risk sketched out in the previous section. For example, serious flood events have occurred a number of times in Jamaica in recent years — 1979, 1985, 1986, 1991 and 1993 — and prime areas of sugar cane and bananas have been hard hit. The increased incidence of flooding in these cases is directly related to poor land use practices and deforestation of the upper reaches of rivers such as the Rio Minho or Rio Cobre as much as to the high rainfall event itself.

Not all hillside farming methods have a negative impact on the environment, and careful appraisal of particular agronomic practices in relation to the site characteristics of individual cultivated plots are needed. Historically, there has been an increasing awareness of the inherent rationality of indigenous agricultural knowledge and techniques in the tropics. An early example was the re-evaluation of intercropping, originally frowned upon by colonial agricultural scientists more familiar with the farming techniques of temperate latitudes. Like their counterparts in other tropical regions, Caribbean geographers have stressed in their research the economic and ecological benefits of some of the techniques used by small farmers. Good examples are the work on kitchen gardens [Brierley 1976; 1991] and food forests [Hills & Iton 1983; Hills 1988]. Essentially, these particular components of Caribbean small-scale agriculture are traditional forms of agroforestry [McGregor & Barker 1991] and thus have considerable potential for land management, in combating soil erosion and in providing an economic return to farmers.

Tourism development is another area of concern that illustrates how human economic activities can have significant impacts on environmental processes on Caribbean islands. The phenomenal growth of tourism in many territories in the last 30 years has had positive effects on island economies but, in some cases, has also exacerbated inappropriate resource exploitation, leading to further degradation of islands' ecosystems. Many of the worst effects of resource exploitation, and the related increases in environmental risk, are to be found in the coastal zone, where tourism activities are concentrated. For example, tourism is now Barbados' principal source of export revenue. Barbados already has the highest population density in the Caribbean, making it difficult environmentally to cope with the additional demands on resources, especially water supply. Major problems, made worse by tourism, though tourism itself was not the original cause, include destruction of shallow-water corals, bacteriological contamination and nutrient enrichment of coastal waters, and beach depletion possibly linked to reef deterioration [Archer 1985].

## Environment and Development in the Caribbean: The British Caribbean Geography Seminar 1992

The overall contributions of geography and geographers to research and education in the Caribbean region, and to the region's growing and increasingly popular environmental movement, have not as yet been well documented or properly assessed. Though significant, it was felt by the authors of this volume that more could be done to disseminate the results of geographical research and to provide opportunities for links to be forged with geographers both within and outside the region [see, for example, Barker 1986; Barker 1990].

For many years, the small number of professional geographers in the Caribbean region's universities (University of the West Indies, University of Guyana, University of Puerto Rico, University of the Virgin Islands, Université Antilles-Guyane, together with the College of The Bahamas) has undertaken research on the region's environment and development problems. Though significant, the research has been relatively low key, poorly funded, and without access to the technology and resources with which modern university geography departments are equipped. Moreover, research efforts have been fragmentary, reflecting the difficulties of coordinating activities and communicating results across the region.

The first locally produced geography graduates from the University of the West Indies arrived on the job market in 1969. Since then, UWI geography graduates have been widely employed throughout the Commonwealth Caribbean, notably in various planning agencies in the fields of urban planning, disaster management, tourism planning, watershed management, agriculture and rural physical planning, resource development, and housing and transport. Some of these individuals now hold very senior positions, but even young professionals in government service make important contributions to decision making and policy. However, the results of their research and other activities are not widely disseminated outside their respective territories and they are often unaware of recent developments in applied geographical research. Further, their basic training in geography often goes unrecognized or is subsumed by more specialized training at the postgraduate level. Collectively, like many geographers worldwide, they share Gould's [1985] enigmatic reluctance to identify with their own discipline. Thus, one strong motivating factor behind this collection of essays was the desire to bring the contribution of Caribbean geographers more sharply into focus in the region.

On the other hand, there is growing interest in the Caribbean amongst geographers in British universities. Over the last ten years, an increasing number of articles and books on the region have been published by British geographers [Watts 1987; Potter 1989]. UK-based geographers have access to more sophisticated technical resources than their Caribbean counterparts. However, their ability to conduct effective research is constrained by the short periods they are able to work in the region and limited personal contacts, particularly in the initial stages of research [Barker 1986].

As a result of some of these undercurrents, the editors of this volume organized the first British-Caribbean Geography Seminar which was held at the University of the West Indies, Mona Campus, in August 1992. The chapters included in this collection represent a selection of these papers, modified for publication in book form. The chapters are grouped into five major themes: coastal zone resource management, tourism and development planning, natural hazards and disaster management, land resources and development planning, and problems and prospects for the development of national parks in Jamaica. Figure 1.1 indicates the principal territories covered by the research presented in this volume.

The coastal zone is one of the most critical pressure points of the Caribbean landscape, and coastal zone resource management will assume an appropriately important role in future resource sustainability considerations. Leonard Nurse, Kenneth Atherley and Leo Brewster illustrate the importance of pre-project evaluation of the environmental impacts of coastal developments. They examine the effects of Barbados' lone electricity generating plant on the adjacent coastal zone. Rapid changes in coastal hydrodynamics, accelerated beach erosion, and changes in water quality deleterious to marine organisms are among the damaging effects of this plant. As the authors point out, post-project mitigation is a costly exercise, environmentally as well as financially.

Neil Sealey describes the background to the archaeological and scientific investigations of the famous blue holes of The Bahamas. He indicates the importance of these features for present day island hydrology, and the necessity for properly regulated policy for their protection and for their development as a major tourist attraction. Peter Bacon shows from his extensive research into the status of Eastern Caribbean wetlands, that many wetlands are in a degraded condition. Wetlands are frequently reclaimed without regard to longer-term sustainability, with losses of hydrological, ecological and potential economic value. Investment in site rehabilitation could significantly improve their contribution to economic development.

Three papers on tourism and development planning underline the critical role of tourism in the economic profile of many Caribbean states. Lesley France and Brian Wheeller commence this section by examining the feasibility of truly sustainable tourism in the Caribbean context, and question the idealistic premises on which sustainable tourism are based. They argue that thus far, ecotourism is

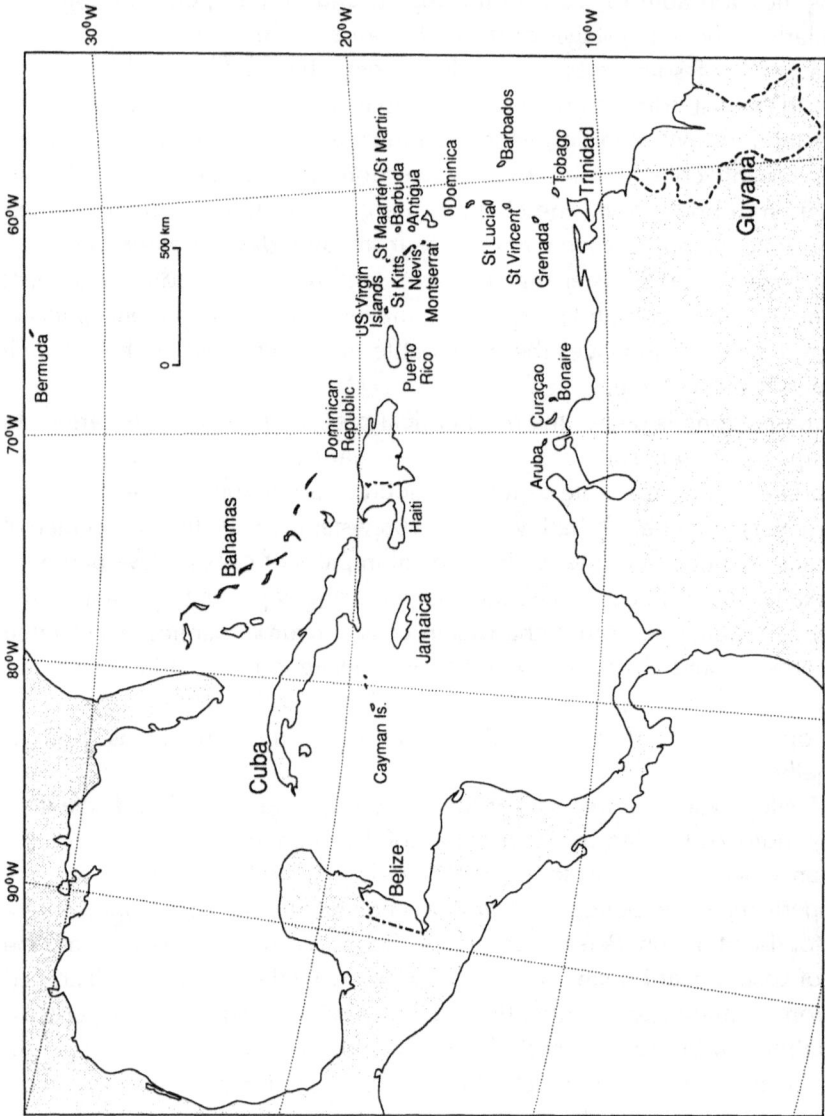

*Figure 1.1* The Caribbean Basin showing principal territories covered in this volume

essentially a recent addition to existing marketing strategies, especially for countries like Belize and Dominica which are relatively new entrants to the tourist industry.

Klaus de Albuquerque and Jerome McElroy, using Butler's model of resort development, point to the dangers, as well as the benefits, of tourism through a comparative analysis of St Maarten/St Martin and Bermuda. Development controls in St Maarten/St Martin are weak, and the tourist industry appears to be in a downward spiral of deteriorating environment and facilities. On the other hand, Bermuda, with its strong development controls, has maintained its status as an important up-market tourism destination. Frank Mills concludes this section and focuses on the impact of tourism on the housing market in the US Virgin Islands. His analysis pivots around the fact that as tourist numbers have grown since the Cuban Revolution, some mainland tourists return to the Virgin Islands to buy second homes. The increased demand has pushed the price of houses beyond the reach of the islanders themselves. The unpalatable irony is that despite soaring house prices, there is plenty of unoccupied accommodation, held on a speculative basis.

Natural disasters are an ever-present fact of Caribbean life. Jeremy Collymore points to the necessity for resources to be focused on the development of mitigation strategies, rather than continual assistance for response and recovery. His paper explores the problems of providing the necessary quantitative information on which to base mitigation strategies. Alison Reading and Rory Walsh examine historical patterns of cyclone activity, and identify periods of peak hurricane activity and periods when they were relatively infrequent. There have been geographical shifts in hurricane patterns too; over time, the favoured tracks of cyclones shifted westwards and southwards and, more recently, eastwards, into the open Atlantic.

Two papers deal with landslide hazard. Rafi Ahmad examines the historic record of landslide incidence in Jamaica, and relates the pattern of landslide activity to geological zones. He also shows how the cumulative direct and indirect effects of landslides on the Jamaican economy are a significant and ongoing cost, and suggests mitigation strategies appropriate to each of the type situations where landslides commonly occur. Russell Maharaj examines in detail the nature of landsliding in St Andrew parish, Jamaica. Through extensive and detailed examination of landslide types, he is able to identify the range of conditions under which landslides occur, and the specific types of features which commonly arise. This detailed information is an essential precursor to proper recognition of landslide hazard, and thence to appropriate mitigation strategies.

The fragility of Caribbean environments, and their sensitivity to resource exploitation, is illustrated by three papers under the general heading of land resources and development planning. Duncan McGregor, in exemplifying the

Caribbean-wide problem of land degradation, points to the lack of basic empirical data on soil erosion in Jamaica. The potential influences of global warming on the extent and importance of soil erosion, and hence on land degradation, are discussed, and research strategies briefly outlined. Fatima Patel shows, for the Scotland District of Barbados, how land use has a radical impact on the sensitivity of the natural landscape to geomorphological processes. Her assessment of the potential geomorphological response to development, and associated land use change, identifies particular developments which will almost certainly lead to high risk of geomorphological hazard.

In contrast, Patrick Williams focuses attention on Guyana, which has a long history of development projects concerned with coastal drainage and irrigation for agriculture. He examines a number of environmental and developmental issues arising from the drainage of wetlands in the vicinity of the Berbice river, for rice and sugar production. Though much larger in scale than development projects on the English-speaking Caribbean islands, Guyana's experience offers a number of lessons for the region.

Finally, concerns for conservation, and the embryonic development of national parks in the region are illustrated by three papers on Jamaica. David Smith presents a progress report on efforts to establish the national park system. The first national park was established in 1992 under a project entitled Protected Areas Resource Conservation (PARC), funded by the US Agency for International Development and the Government of Jamaica. Community involvement is a key feature of the project, but enforcement of environmental laws is proving difficult.

The last two papers examine the future of the world-famous Cockpit Country region of Jamaica, an area proposed as a national park in the future. Alan Eyre deplores the lack of enforceable protection and the present rate of deforestation in the Cockpit Country Forest Reserve. In a passionate plea for protection, he points to the environmental qualities and scientific potential of the area, and the potential benefits to the nation of promoting Cockpit Country for World Heritage Site listing. David Barker and David Miller examine the impact of small-scale agriculture on the northern margin of Cockpit Country and show how the pattern of encroachment is significantly controlled by the physical landscape. Farmers have an accurate perception of microclimates, and many would farm there if access was improved. The geographical integrity of the forested area should be preserved and the temptation to improve access into the Cockpits for tourists (and, inadvertently, farmers) should be resisted.

## Prospect

At the present time there is a wave of environmentalism flowing across the Caribbean Basin. The pioneering environmental research of several departments of the UWI's Faculty of Natural Sciences, together with the work of organizations such as the Caribbean Conservation Association, has been augmented by a growing number of professional Environmental Consultants engaged in environmental impact assessments and environmental audits. The ranks of well established, environmentally based groups like the Jamaican Geographical Society, the Trinidad and Tobago Geographical Association, the Barbados Geographical Society, the Natural History Society of Jamaica and the Geological Society of Jamaica have been swollen by newer, more activist NGOs and ENGOs. For example, during the last five years over 35 such new groups have been formed in Jamaica alone, many of them following the successful lead of PEPA (Portland Environmental Protection Association). A number of these groups are now in a position to capitalize on the influx of project oriented, environmentally related funds which are available from international sources.

Though the wave of environmentalism in the region has not reached storm surge proportions and has not yet touched many sectors of the population or business people, the tide has certainly reached the shores of government and policy makers. The authors trust that the appearance of this volume is a timely reminder to all concerned with environment and sustainable development in the region that geography has a key role to play in applied research.

A follow-up meeting is planned for August 1995 to be held at Royal Holloway, University of London. The papers to be presented there will report on the continuing research, by geographers and other scientists and social scientists, on the topics covered in this volume.

### References

Archer, E. 1985. "Emerging environmental problems in a tourist zone: the case of Barbados". *Caribbean Geography* 2: 44-55.

Barker, D. 1986. "Core, periphery and focus for geography?" *Area* 18: 157-60.

Barker, D. 1989. "A periphery in genesis and exodus: reflections on rural-urban relations in Jamaica". In *The Geography of Urban-Rural Interactions in Developing Countries*, edited by R.B. Potter and T. Unwin, pp 294-322. London: Routledge.

Barker, D. 1990. "Towards regional conferences and a regional association for Caribbean geographers in the 1990s". Paper presented at Caribbean Studies Association Meeting, Port-of-Spain, Trinidad & Tobago (May), 22-26.

Barker, D. 1993. "Dualism and disasters on a tropical island: constraints on agricultural development in Jamaica". *Tidjschrift voor Economishe en Sociale Geographie* 84: 332-40.

Barker, D., & D.F.M. McGregor. 1988. "Land degradation in the Yallahs Basin, Jamaica: historical notes and contemporary observations". *Geography* 73: 116-24.

Barker, D., & D.J. Miller. 1990. "Hurricane Gilbert: anthropomorphising a natural disaster". *Area 22: 107-16.*

Barker, D., & B. Spence. 1988. "Afro-Caribbean agriculture: a Jamaican maroon community in transition". *Geographical Journal* 154: 198-208.

Beckford, G.L. 1972. *Persistent Poverty: Underdevelopment in Plantation Economies in the Third World.* Oxford: Oxford University Press.

Brierley, J.S. 1976. "Kitchen gardens in the West Indies, with a contemporary study from Grenada". *Journal of Tropical Geography* 43: 30-40.

Brierley, J.S. 1991. "Kitchen gardens in the Caribbean, past and present: their role in small farm development". *Caribbean Geography* 3: 15-28.

Collymore, J.McA. & M.D. Griffith. 1987. "Flooding in Speightstown: towards a flood management strategy". In *Proceedings of a Meeting of Experts in Hazard Mapping in the Caribbean,* edited by D. Barker, pp 117-25. PCDPPP/ODP/UWI Geography Department.

DeGraff, J.V. 1991. "Determining the significance of landslide activity: examples from the Eastern Caribbean". *Caribbean Geography* 3: 29-42.

DeGraff, J.V., et al. 1989. "Landslides: their extent and significance in the Caribbean". In *Landslides: Extent and Economic Significance,* edited by E.E. Brabb & B.L. Harrod, pp 51-80. Rotterdam: A.A. Balhema.

Eyre, L.A. 1987. "Jamaica: test case for tropical deforestation?" *Ambio* 16: 336-41.

Eyre, L.A. 1989a. "The Caribbean environment: trends towards degradation and strategies for their reversal". *Caribbean Journal of Education — Special Issue on Environmental Education: Global Concern and Caribbean Focus* 16: 13-45.

Eyre, L.A. 1989b. "Hurricane Gilbert: Caribbean record breaker". *Weather* 44: 160-64.

Girvan, N.P. 1991. "Economics and the environment in the Caribbean: an overview". In *Caribbean Ecology and Economics,* edited by N.P. Girvan, & D.A. Simmons, pp xi-xxiv. Barbados: Caribbean Conservation Association.

Gould, P. 1985. *The Geographer at Work.* London: Routledge & Kegan Paul.

Hills, T.L. 1988. "The Caribbean peasant food forest: ecological artistry or random chaos?" In *Small Farming and Peasant Resources in the Caribbean,* edited by J.S. Brierley & H. Rubenstein, pp 1-28. *Manitoba Geographical Studies* no.10, Winnipeg: University of Manitoba.

Hills, T.L. & S. Iton. 1983. "A reassessment of the 'traditional' in Caribbean small-scale agriculture". *Caribbean Geography* 1: 24-35.

Hudson, B.J. 1989. "Waterfront development and redevelopment in the West Indies". *Caribbean Geography* 2: 229-40.

Jeffrey, S.E. 1982. "The creation of vulnerability to natural disaster: case studies from the Dominican Republic". *Disasters* 6: 38-43.

Manley, M. 1987. *Up the Down Escalator: Development and the International Economy, a Jamaican Case Study.* London: Andre Deutsch.

McGregor, D.F.M. 1986. "Assessment of soil erosion hazard in the Upper Yallahs Valley, Jamaica". *Caribbean Geography* 2: 138-43.

McGregor, D.F.M. 1988. "An investigation of soil status and land use on a steeply sloping hillside, Blue Mountains, Jamaica". *Singapore Journal of Tropical Geography* 9: 60-71.

McGregor, D.F.M. & D. Barker 1991. "Land degradation and hillside farming in the Fall River basin, Jamaica". *Applied Geography* 11: 143-56.

Mintz, S.W. 1974. *Caribbean Transformations.* Baltimore: Johns Hopkins University Press.

Molinelli, J. 1989. "Earthquake vulnerability study for the metropolitan area of San Juan, Puerto Rico". In *Proceedings of a Meeting of Experts in Hazard Mapping in the Caribbean,* edited by D. Barker, pp 77-85. Kingston, Jamaica: PCDPPP/ODP/UWI Geography Department.

Naughton, P.W. 1984. "Flood and landslide damage-repair cost correlations for Kingston, Jamaica". *Caribbean Geography* 1: 198-202.

Potter, R.B. 1989. *Urbanization, Planning and Development in the Caribbean*. London: Mansell.

Paskett, C.J. & C-E. Philoctete. 1990. "Soil conservation in Haiti". *Journal of Soil and Water Conservation* 45: 457-59.

Richardson, B.C. 1992. *The Caribbean in the Wider World 1492-1992: A Regional Geography*. Cambridge: Cambridge University Press.

Robson, G.R. & J.F. Tomblin. 1966. *Catalogue of the Active Volcanoes of the World, Including Solfatara Fields*. Naples: IAF.

Shepherd, J.B. 1989. "Earthquake and volcanic hazard assessment and monitoring in the Commonwealth Caribbean: current status and needs for the future". In *Proceedings of a Meeting of Experts on Hazard Mapping in the Caribbean*, edited by D. Barker, pp 50-60. Kingston, Jamaica, PCDPPP/ODP/UWI Geography Department.

Sheng, T.C. 1972. "A treatment-oriented land capability scheme for hilly marginal lands in the humid tropics". *Journal of the Science Research Council of Jamaica* 3: 93-112.

Sheng, T.C. 1981. "The need for soil conservation structures for steep cultivated lands in the humid tropics". In *Tropical Agricultural Hydrology*, edited by P. Lal and E. R. Russell, pp. 357-72. New York: Wiley.

Vidal de la Blache, P. 1927. *Geographie Universelle*. Paris: Armond Colin.

Watts D. 1987. *The West Indies: Patterns of Development, Culture and Environmental Change since 1492*. Cambridge: Cambridge University Press.

Williams, M.C. 1988. "The impact of Hurricane Allen on the St Lucia banana industry". *Caribbean Geography* 2: 164-72.

# Part 1

# Coastal Zone Resource Management

Chapter 2

# The Impact of Thermal Effluent Discharge on the Barbados Southern West Coast

Leonard A. Nurse, Kenneth A. Atherley and Leo A. Brewster

## Introduction

### Background to the Study

Following construction of the Bridgetown Port in 1961, noticeable accretion has occurred at beaches immediately to the north of the harbour, especially within the Brandons-Brighton Bay area. Indeed, so dramatic has been the silting up of the bay that at low tide, mean water depth some 50m offshore is a mere 2m. However, from about the latter half of 1986 it was becoming evident that severe erosion was occurring at northern Brighton, adjacent to the outfall of the Barbados Light and Power Company Limited. Some of the overt manifestations of erosion included the exposure of incipient beach rock, the undermining of vegetation (*Hippomane mancinella*, *Coccoloba uvifera*, *Ipomoea pes-caprae*), landward migration of Mean High Water Mark, and a marked reduction in average beach width. In the absence of any signs of reversal of the trend, the Coastal Conservation Unit embarked on a programme of intensive monitoring at the site in November 1987.

Beach recession along this particular stretch of coastline was clearly anomalous, occurring as it did within a cell which had accreted almost uninterruptedly since the early 1960s. Moreover, the changes tended to be highly localized, as the central and southern segments of the cell showed no signs of accelerated erosion. In fact, so rapid was the retreat at the site of the power plant, that by early 1988, an entire line of mature vegetation had disappeared and most of the company's coastal installations were threatened. On 17 June 1988, the Coastal Conservation Unit received an application from the Barbados Light and Power Company Limited, seeking permission to construct five boulder groynes and a backshore revetment, to protect its property. Under the circumstances, the Coastal Unit recommended approval of the application, but with certain conditions attached. One such condition was that the applicant could be required ". . . to modify or remove the structures at the applicant's own expense", if it was determined that negative impacts were being triggered at adjacent properties. Engineering works commenced in February 1989, and the Coastal Conservation Unit has been monitoring the site continuously since then.

At the same time, many residents and beach users were becoming concerned about what they perceived to be undesirable changes in water quality seaward of the main outfall. Since Brighton is a popular recreational beach for many locals, complaints of dangerous currents and foul odours and proliferation of algae at the site, warranted urgent, systematic investigation. Thus, an analysis of the quality of the thermal effluent discharged from the power plant, and its impact on nearshore waters, formed an integral part of the study.

### A Brief History of the Power Company

The Barbados Light and Power Company Limited is located on the southern west coast of the island, at the north limb of the Brandons-Brighton Bay cell, less than two kilometres north of Bridgetown (Figure 2.1). The plant commenced operation at this site in 1964, and over the years has been forced to upgrade facilities and increase its power generation capacity to meet the country's needs. Output of electricity rose from an estimated 150 million kWh in 1965 to approximately 330.6 million kWh in 1980, reaching 539.3 million kWh in 1990. This increasing production has necessitated corresponding increments in water for cooling the company's turbines. The volume of thermal effluent discharged from the cooling towers increased from 60 million imperial gals/day in 1976 to 75.9 million gals/day in 1989 (Table 2.1). It therefore became clear, from an early stage in the investigations, that both the rate and volume of discharge of effluent were critical forces driving beach and oceanographic changes at the site.

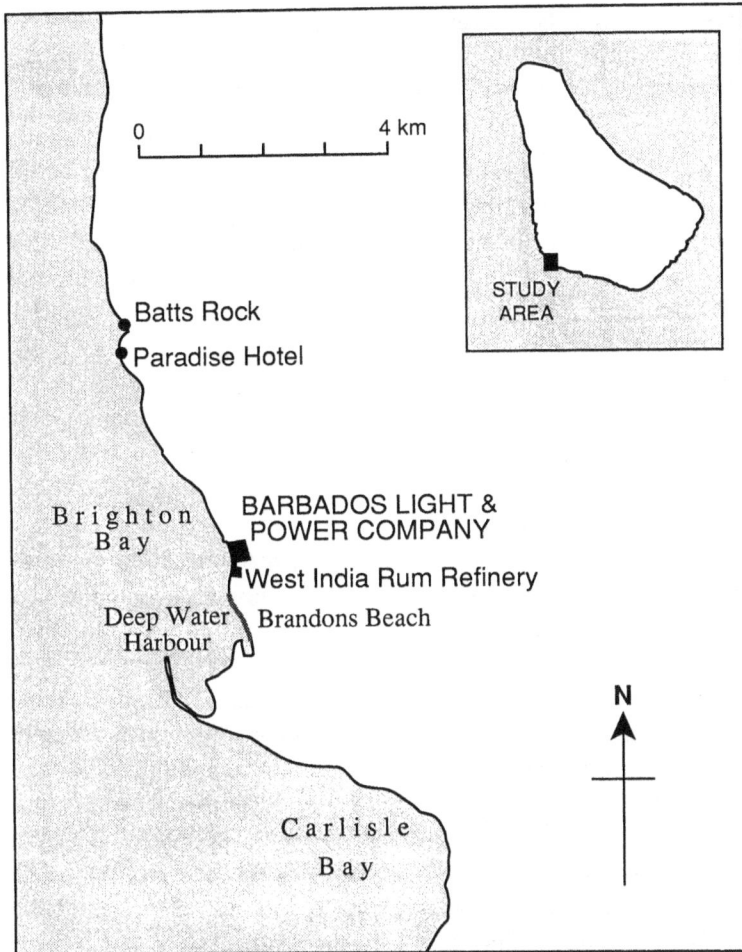

*Figure 2.1.* Location of study area.

*Table 2.1* Power Generation Capacity and Thermal Effluent Volumes for Selected Years, Barbados Light and Power Company

| Year | Power (kWh) | Year | Discharge (million gals/day) |
|------|-------------|------|------------------------------|
| 1965 | 150.0 | 1976 | 60.0 |
| 1980 | 330.6 | 1982 | 67.9 |
| 1985 | 388.7 | 1987 | 75.9 |

Note: *The years quoted are those for which reliable records exist.*
Source: *Barbados Light and Power Company Limited.*

# Changes in Beach Volume

## Period Preceding Construction of Shoreline Protection Works

Shortly after the erosion accelerated, three beach profiles were established and carefully surveyed at predetermined intervals, between November 1987 and February 1989. During this time, there was severe beach loss at all profile sites. The percentage change in beach volume was -82%, -63% and -47% at Profiles 1, 2 and 3, respectively (Figure 2.2). Actual net sediment loss amounted to 14.6m$^3$, 10.7m$^3$ and 27.4m$^3$, representing beach recession rates of approximately 1.0m$^3$, 0.7m$^3$ and 1.8m$^3$ per month respectively, over a period of fifteen months.

Excessive rates of continuous erosion, such as exemplified above, are indeed abnormal along low-energy coasts. Scour of this magnitude occurs only during high energy events, such as "winter swells" and tropical storms; and even then these phenomena do not persist beyond a few days, after which beach recovery tends to be fairly rapid. It therefore appeared reasonable to conclude that beach changes experienced at northern Brighton were being generated by some persistent factor, the impact of which was cumulative over time [Nurse 1990].

This phenomenal rate of recession could be placed in clearer perspective by comparing erosion rates here with figures for other segments of the west coast, over the same period. For instance, mean annual percentage change at Flats Village, Barbados Beach Village, Sandy Lane and Read's Bay further north, was -9.0%, -14%, -14% and -16%, respectively [Atherley 1989]. These were the most rapidly receding beaches on the island's west coast (apart from Brighton north) and, in all cases, reduction in sediment volumes was appreciably lower than at any of the three profiles near the power plant.

## Impact of Thermal Effluent Discharge on Beach Changes

As indicated above, the spectacular reduction in beach sediment volumes at Brighton north cannot be explained solely in terms of wave energy conditions operating at the site since 1987. While there was no indication that this segment was subjected to greater wave energy than elsewhere along the west coast, all other evidence pointed in the direction of the power plant's thermal effluent discharge. Further analysis of Table 2.1 would demonstrate that the rate of discharge increased from 2.5 million gals/hr in 1976, to just under 3.2 million gals/hr in 1989, representing an increment of some 21 percent over the period. The volume of water discharge becomes even more striking when one considers that:

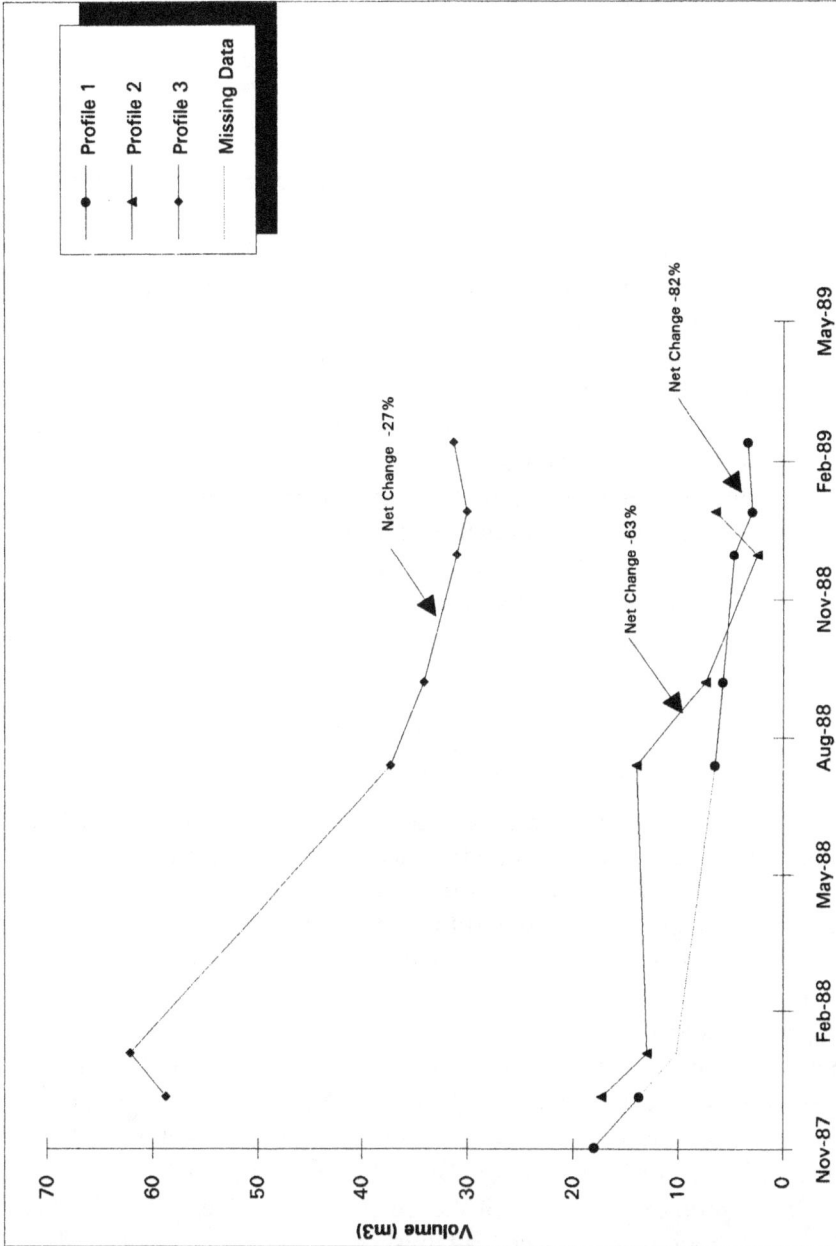

*Figure 2.2* Schematic representation of volumetric beach changes at Barbados Light and Power Company (1987-1989)

(a) the same discharge point has continued to be used despite the plant's expansion;

(b) the outfall drain is relatively small in size, approximately 4m x 2m;

(c) in 1989 the volume of water discharge was 2.5 times greater than the island's mean daily water consumption (approx. 29 million gallons).

Given the volume and rate of discharge from the outfall, it is not surprising that the speed of the seaward moving surface current often exceeded 58cm/sec, and during most field trials was seldom less than 50cm/sec. The result has been the formation of a "permanent" scour channel in front of the outfall. For the most part the channel is kept free of sand, since most of the fine sediment is moved seaward in suspension, until the force of the current diminishes. There was also random spit development and movement, both on the north and south of the scour channel, the location of which depended on current speeds and predominant wave conditions. One local coastal engineer referred to the channel as an "invisible groyne".

Therefore, there can be no doubt that the rate of discharge of thermal effluent from the outfall has disrupted "normal" sediment transport processes, and has had a negative impact on the beach sediment budget at Spring Garden. This additional "sink" has led, over the years, to a reduction of sand within the beach and nearshore systems, manifesting itself as marked, strongly localized erosion.

**Beach Recovery Following Construction of Groynes**

To reduce erosion along the coastline, a series of five short groynes (each 5m long) and 280m of boulder revetment was erected by Barbados Light and Power. The groynes were added to the revetment at the insistence of the Coastal Conservation Unit to expand the measures from merely an erosional prevention concept to beach enhancement as well. The benchmarks used to fix Profiles 1 and 2 were lost during construction, leaving only Profile 3 intact. Beach volumes at Profile 3 for the period 1989 to 1992 are given in Figure 2.3. It is immediately noticeable that there has been slow recovery at this site, with sediment volume increasing from 28.7m$^3$ in August 1989 to 34.3m$^3$ in February 1992. The overall net change of +5.63m$^3$ gives a mean monthly rate of increase of 0.19m$^3$/month, over the last two and a half years.

In order to monitor the effect of the groynes on the beach stabilization process, four new profiles were established within the groyne cells in December 1989. Sediment accumulation within the groyne sub-cells has been considerably more rapid (with the possible exception of Groyne 4) than along Profile 3, further south and only 3m north from the thermal outfall. An examination of Figure 2.3 would reveal that, when compared with Profile 3, actual accretion was two times greater at Groyne 1 (11.3m³), and more than one and a half times greater at Groyne 2 (9.4m³) and Groyne 3 (39.m³) versus 5.63m³. Even in the case of Groyne 4, where accretion was slower, the net increase still exceeded that at Profile 3 by some 17 percent.

It is clear from the field data presented that the presence of the groynes has halted the erosion trend at the site. Indeed, since the erection of the structures, beach accretion has been virtually continuous at all Profile sites, even though the rate of recovery has not been spatially uniform. Generally, the rate of accretion within the groyne cells appears to decrease in a northerly direction, with distance from the thermal outfall. Thus, Groyne 1, the southernmost structure, experienced the greatest net percentage change (+93%), while Groyne 4, the northernmost site, recorded the smallest net percentage change (+39%), among the groyne sites (Figure 2.3). Net percentage volumetric change at Groynes 2 and 3 is in conformity with this trend. This spatial variation can be explained by the general direction of the main littoral current. While the littoral current and sediment transport are not unidirectional, the net direction of movement is towards the north. This is quite evident from Table 2.2 which shows the results of dye injection tests conducted on eight beach profiles, survey dates being between March 1990 and December 1991. Hence, with a dominant, northerly littoral current, a faster rate of sand accumulation would be expected at "updrift" structures than at "downdrift" sites. Consequently, more rapid accretion should only be expected at Groyne 4 after "updrift" cells have filled out, thereby permitting adequate sediment bypass to occur.

Table 2.2   Results of Current Direction (Dye Injection) Test

| Date | Groyne 1 | Groyne 2 | Groyne 3 | Groyne 4 |
|---|---|---|---|---|
| 90-03-09 | N | S | S | N |
| 90-08-01 | S | N.N.D. | N.N.D. | N |
| 90-09-18 | S | N | N | N |
| 90-12-17 | N | N | N | N |
| 91-03-07 | N | N | N | S |
| 91-06-07 | N | N | N | N.N.D. |
| 91-09-03 | N | N | S | N |
| 91-12-05 | S | N.N.D. | S | N |
| % N | 62.5 | 62.5 | 50.0 | 75.0 |
| % S | 37.5 | 12.5 | 37.5 | 12.5 |
| % N.N.D. | 00.0 | 25.0 | 12.5 | 12.5 |

Note: N = Northward movement; S = Southward movement; N.N.D. = No net direction.

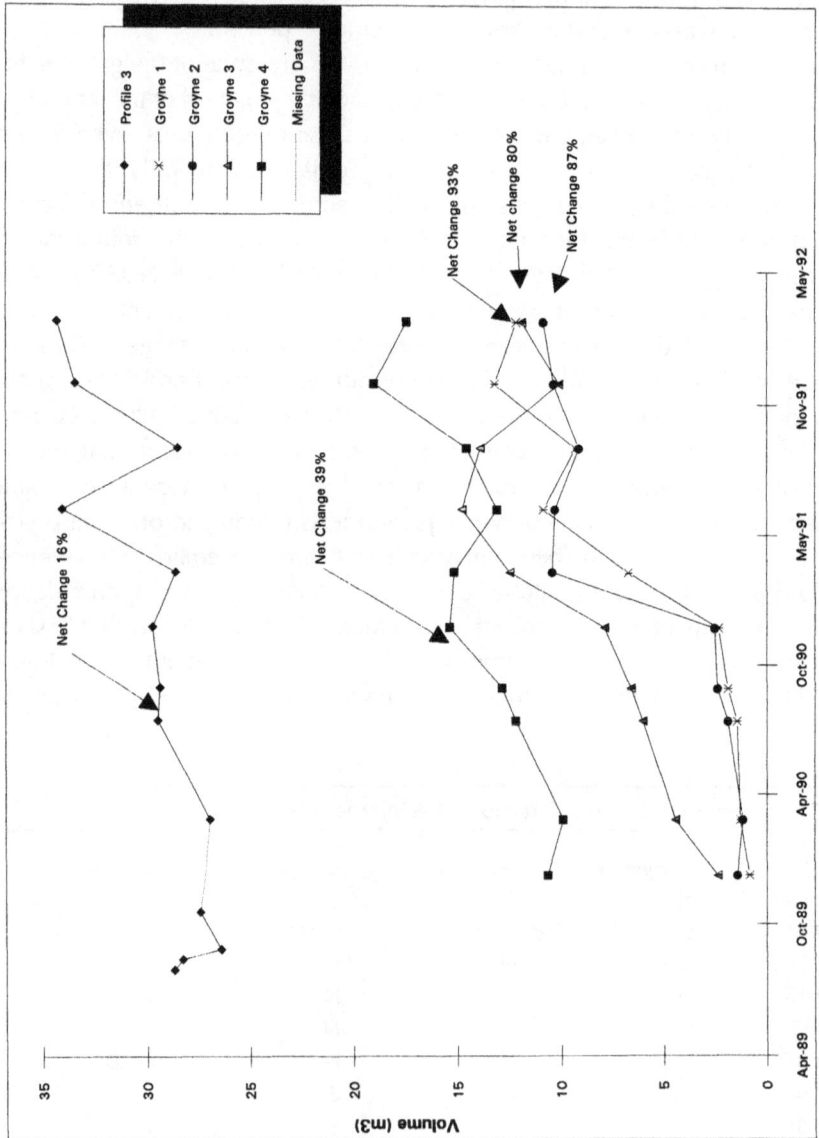

*Figure 2.3* Schematic representation of volumetric beach changes at Barbados Light and Power Company (1989 - 1992)

Contrastingly, the very low rate of accretion at Profile 3, post-1989, is primarily a function of proximity to the outfall, located a mere 3m north from the point of discharge. The rapid surface current (at times greater than 50cm/sec), created by the volume of thermal effluent discharged, carries much sediment seaward in suspension, beyond the immediate nearshore zone. This process has serious implications for the beach sediment budget, since it could lead to a reduction in available sand for natural beach building. The extent to which this sand becomes "lost" to the beach is controlled by a combination of forces, chief among which are:

(a) the distance the sand is carried out of the nearshore zone;

(b) the efficiency of onshore sediment transport mechanisms in returning the sand to the beach.

The effectiveness of the latter process is likely to be diminished in the present circumstances since the velocity of the usual onshore current generated by wave motion is, on average, 8-18cm/sec — much less than that produced by discharge from the outfall. Thus, recovery at Profile 3 would be very slow, as this site falls directly within the sphere of influence of the thermal outfall, discharging at a rate greater than 3 million imperial gals/hr.

While the groynes have been instrumental in returning some measure of stability to the beach at Spring Garden, it must be emphasized that sediment volumes still appear to be nowhere near pre-1987 levels. This observation is strongly supported at Profile 3, where measured beach volumes were some 58.74m$^3$ in December 1987, but only 34.33m$^3$ in March 1992. It is contended that former sediment volumes will only be restored naturally, when a more efficient method of effluent disposal is implemented.

## Effect of Discharge on Water Quality

### Methods

In order to assess the impact of discharge on coastal water quality, eight sampling locations were chosen, one inland at the manhole, five within the nearshore zone and two offshore. The period of monitoring lasted for one month (February 1990), sampling once every two weeks. Water samples were collected in autoclaved polythene bottles, allowing minimum aeration at the time of collection. Chemical analyses were undertaken for nutrients ($NO^{3-}$), sulphide ($S^{2-}$), dissolved oxygen (DO) and conductivity (mmhos). Temperature profiling was also conducted to identify the boundaries of the thermal plume.

Surface temperatures were measured using a portable temperature/dissolved oxygen meter in depths not exceeding 2m. For temperatures at depths greater than 2m, a protected reversing thermometer was employed. The advantage of this method is that temperature measurements and water samples from different depths could be collected simultaneously.

Prior to deciding on sampling locations, it was necessary to establish the extent of the thermal effluent plume. This was accomplished by running a series of regular, offshore transects (50m apart), parallel to the shore, until temperature readings became constant [Brewster & Wilson 1990].

## Results and Discussion

Test results indicated that $S^{2-}$, DO, conductivity and temperature were influenced strongly by the thermal discharge. For example, while nutrient levels ($NO^{3-}$, $PO^{2-}_4$) in the nearshore area were high, samples collected at the mouth of the thermal outfall were low in nutrients. Further random testing showed that the high concentrations were primarily the result of terrestrial runoff, issuing from an adjacent storm water sewer. Thus, the discussion which follows focuses on those variables on which thermal effluent appeared to have a most direct impact.

### Sulphide

$S^{2-}$ concentrations were consistently high at the mouth of the outfall and at the manhole, with values between 7.5mg/l and 7.7mg/l (Table 2.3). These were also the locations where the smell and taste of $S^{2-}$ in the water were strongest. The general spatial variation was not unexpected. Sulphide concentration is of critical concern since it is highly soluble in water as $H_2S$ and $S^{2-}$, and its unpleasant odour creates a nuisance factor. Thus, even in low level concentrations, sulphide is still a continuous low level source of pollution which can be toxic to marine organisms.

Table 2.3    Mean Sulphide, Dissolved Oxygen and Conductivity Values for Eight Sampling Sites at Brighton North

| Site | Sulphide (mg/1) | Dis. Oxygen (mg/1) | Conductivity (umhos) |
|---|---|---|---|
| Manhole | 7.5 | 1.3 | 37.3 |
| Thermal outfall | 7.7 | 3.8 | 30.7 |
| Breaker zone | 1.6 | 4.3 | 32.7 |
| South breaker zone | 1.7 | 7.7 | 39.6 |
| North breaker zone | 1.7 | 7.7 | 39.6 |
| 100m from outfall | 1.6 | 6.7 | 40.8 |
| Offshore 1 (South) | 2.4 | 7.2 | 42.2 |
| Offshore 2 (North) | 2.0 | 7.4 | 40.6 |

## Dissolved Oxygen

DO levels for most nearshore stations tended to be similar to concentrations detected at the two offshore reference locations, averaging between 6.7 mg/l and 7.7mg/l. It is noteworthy that highest values were recorded in the zones of maximum mixing, that is, just north and south of the breaker zone. Contrastingly, DO concentrations were very low at the thermal outfall and manhole where mean values were 3.8mg/l and 1.25mg/l, respectively (Table 2.3). Where nutrient levels are high, low DO provides ideal anaerobic conditions for bacterial growth and algal blooms. These would in turn increase stress levels on critical ecosystems such as coral reefs, by reducing water transparency and therefore light penetration, vital for continued reef system survival.

## Conductivity

While conductivity at most sites compared favourably with values derived for the reference stations (between 39.6 and 41.3mmhos), figures were significantly lower (30.7mmhos) at the thermal outfall (Table 2.3). This reflects the presence of the large volume of brackish thermal discharge, whose salinity is appreciably lower than that of seawater (31%). Reduced salinity (18%-20%) could become an additional stress factor for certain marine organisms, both plant and animal, which inhabit nearshore waters and are dependent on higher levels of salinity.

## Temperature

The surface temperature of nearshore bathing waters for the Barbados west coast typically ranges between 26°C-28.5°C, while the temperatures at the offshore reference stations (8m deep, 1.85km offshore) were constant at between 26°C-26.3°C. Naturally, highest elevated temperatures were recorded at the manhole and at the thermal outfall, where surface values averaged 33.3°C and 33.6°C, respectively. Bottom temperature values at the outfall and manhole were similar to those recorded at the surface. Not unexpectedly, there was a detectable spatial gradient, with a gradual reduction in temperature with distance seaward of the outfall (Figure 2.4). The seaward boundary of the plume varied in time according to tide and current direction, but extended between 250m and 300m offshore.

A major concern arising from the presence of the elevated temperatures, is the reduction in the capacity of sea water to absorb oxygen [Brewster & Wilson 1990]. With less available oxygen, the water becomes less capable of supporting most aquatic species. In other circumstances, species diversity and balance could be affected, as those species with a greater tolerance for high temperatures would proliferate. The problem assumes greater proportions in

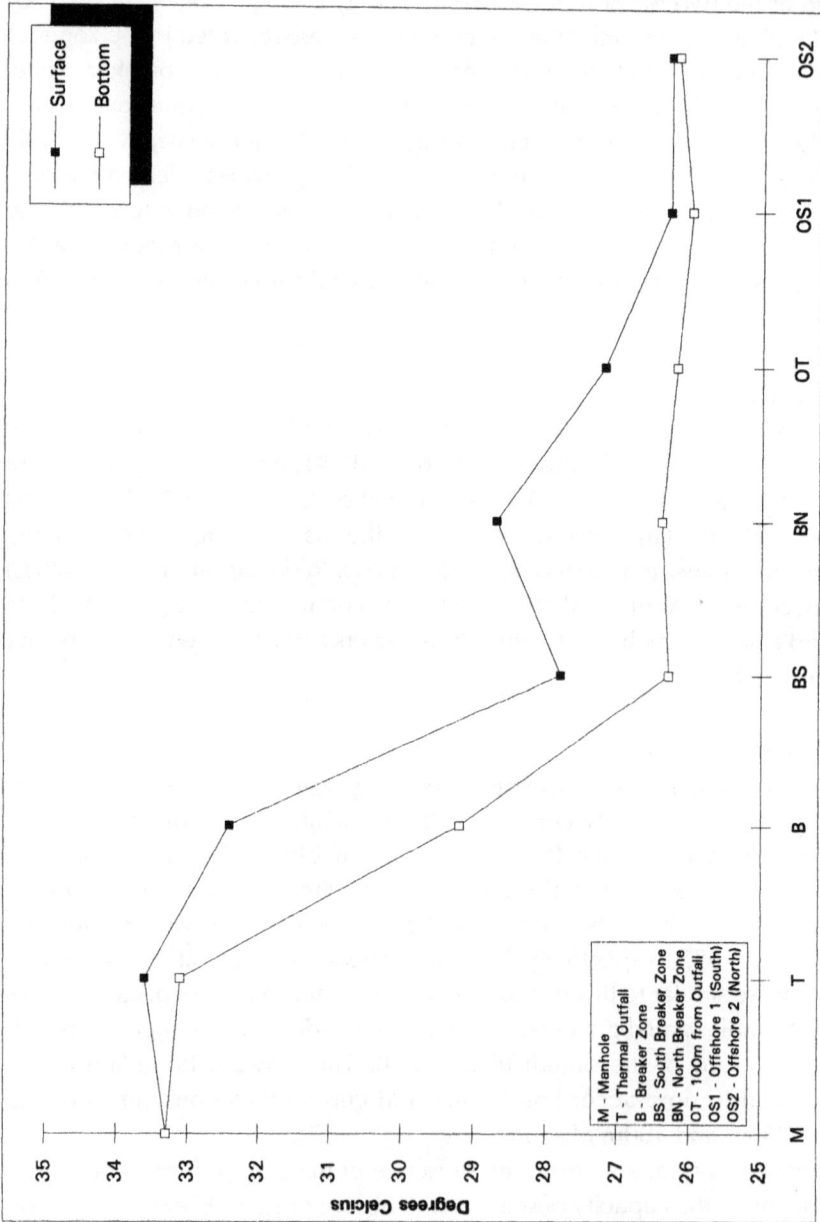

*Figure 2.4* Schematic representation of mean surface and bottom temperature in relation to distance from outfall at Barbados Light and Power Plant

the Tropics where the ambient water temperature is already frequently close to the "thermal death point" of many marine organisms [Berry et al. 1974; Clark 1986]. Hence, this critical threshold could be exceeded with any further elevation in temperature. Most marine fauna find difficulty surviving increases of 3°C and 5°C for prolonged periods, and sponges, molluscs and other crustacea often succumb to temperatures nearing 40°C.

Corals can be quite sensitive to fluctuations in temperature, so that what may appear to be quantitatively small changes (for example, as little as 3° and 5°C) can have a significant impact on the viability of some species. It is therefore not entirely surprising that there is now a virtually dead reef directly offshore from the outfall, near the edge of the thermal plume. A recent reef survey at the site has indicated that there are only four major species of hard coral with a mean percentage coverage of only 32%, three species of algae with a mean percentage coverage of only 1.5% and approximately 14 species of fish with a mean diversity of only six [Bellairs Research Institute 1989], clearly indicating a poor level of species diversity in general. This could also have severe implications for the eventual stability of the beach, as the reefs not only provide sand but also reduce the erosive impact of incident waves on the shoreline.

## Highlighting the Need for Anticipatory Planning

The foregoing discussion emphasizes the need for careful planning of coastal developments which may have detrimental consequences on nearshore dynamics. It is evident that the Barbados Light and Power plant was established without any serious environmental scoping or consideration of the likely impact which could be triggered by the inevitable discharge of thermal effluent. While it is true that environmental impact assessments were not required in the 1960s when the plant was first built, there has been significant subsequent expansion within recent times, in an era when the need for such evaluations is widely accepted. Understandably, the plant has expanded over the years in response to growing national needs; however, this attempt to satisfy market demands for power has clearly not been accompanied by corresponding strategies for mitigating the undesirable environmental impacts of expansion.

Now that the beach and the nearshore system at Brighton north have been stressed beyond critical thresholds, the power company has been mandated by Government to implement appropriate mitigation expeditiously. This will require further detailed investigative work at the site, before an appropriate method of reducing the rate of discharge can be implemented. Government has recommended a number of alternatives, which the power company is currently investigating at great cost. The tragedy is that both the damage to the shoreline and high cost of the mitigative process could have been avoided if a thorough environmental assessment had been undertaken early in expansion of the plant. In this way, the cost of mitigation and subsequent monitoring would have been "factored in" as part of overall expansion costs.

The Barbados Light and Power Company Limited has already contracted the services of a firm of British consultants to undertake the work. While the cost to the company has not been publicly revealed, it is estimated that consultancy costs (that is, for scientific surveys and engineering design) could be in the vicinity of US$150,000 and US$200,000. The actual cost of implementing an appropriate design cannot at this stage be estimated, as the design can vary substantially depending on the method chosen for controlling the rate of discharge.

Finally, at least one positive result has emerged from this "bad" experience. The company is about to expand further, and has now accepted that the carrying capacity of the present site is close to being exceeded. An application for a new site has been submitted to the planning agencies, and the company has already hired a Canadian consulting group to undertake a full environmental impact assessment.

## References

Atherley, K.A. 1989. "Analysis of beach change on the Barbados coast". Technical Report. Coastal Conservation Unit, Government of Barbados.

Bellairs Research Institute. 1989. "Community descriptors (1987) for nearshore and offshore reefs on the south and west coast of Barbados". Report prepared for Government of Barbados (September).

Berry, et al. 1974. *Land Use, Urban Form and Environmental Quality*. Chicago: University of Chicago Press.

Brewster, L., & J. Wilson. 1990. "A preliminary assessment of nearshore water quality near the Barbados Light and Power outfall, Spring Garden". Technical Report, Coastal Conservation Unit, Barbados (March).

Clark, R.B. 1986. *Marine Pollution*. Oxford: Oxford University Press.

Nurse, L.A. 1990. "Beach changes near the outfall of a power generation plant: Barbados Light and Power site, Spring Garden". Technical Report. Coastal Conservation Unit, Barbados, (February).

Chapter 3

# Bahamian Blue Holes: Windows on the Past, Resources for the Future

Neil E. Sealey

## Introduction

The blue holes of The Bahamas have long generated popular interest, and are characterized in local folklore as the homes of various monsters; as being of unfathomable depth; and being mysteriously connected to the sea. Serious investigation began when George Benjamin first saw the inland and offshore blue holes of Andros in the late 1950s. Over the next 15 years Benjamin and others such as Archie Forfar and Jacques Cousteau dived many of these blue holes, and by 1971 had discovered as much as could be expected with the technology available [Benjamin 1970; Palmer 1989:5-43]. However, it was not for another 15 years that scientific investigation of the blue holes was to resume and advance, largely due to the work of Robert Palmer [Palmer 1985; 1989].

Blue holes are not unique to The Bahamas. They are found in the adjacent areas of south Florida and the Turks and Caicos Islands, and in Belize and the Yucatan peninsula. They may be considered as flooded solution holes of Pleistocene age, formed variously by surface and underground solution, and collapse into caverns [Jennings 1985: 228-30]. Although many are circular at the surface, they may be of many shapes due to structural control, such as with the cleft openings of South Andros. They occur on low-lying rockland (up to +5m) or on shallow offshore banks (down to -10m), and do not usually exceed 130 metres in depth, although Dean's blue hole in Long Island has been explored to 202 metres, the deepest known [Wilson 1994]. In some cases, notably in Andros and Grand Bahama, they contain fresh water in their upper levels where they have intercepted the freshwater lens.

The earliest studies were essentially descriptive and aimed at divers and caving enthusiasts, and much of the current work is still produced for this market [Palmer 1986; 1991; Palmer, McHale & Hartlebury 1986; Farr & Palmer 1984]. Despite this, the significance of the blue holes was not lost on geographers and geologists interested in dating the recent past in The Bahamas [Dill 1977; Gascoyne, Benjamin et al. 1979; Gascoyne 1984; Sealey 1985]. As well as absolute dating of speleothems, the sea level history could be deduced from cave stalactites by interpreting the varying layers of secondary calcite, marine encrustation, and the depth of marine boring. Smart [1984] anticipated the direction of much of the later work with his limited study of the hydrology of the inland blue holes, but the great upsurge in purely scientific investigation dates from the large multipurpose Andros Project led by Palmer in 1987.

## The Andros Project and the Archaeology of Blue Holes

The Andros Project had several components, and was directed at a succession of blue holes developed along a major fault running from Mangrove Cay southward across South Andros until it entered the sea near Mars Bay, itself the site of a major blue hole (Figure 3.1). Diving, filming, and geological, hydrological and biological research were all included and, on arrival in The Bahamas the possibility of finding cultural remains was also discussed. In nearby Florida the value of blue holes (usually called *cenotes* or sinks in Florida) had long been recognized and some extensive underwater archaeological excavations had been carried out [Clausen et al. 1979]. Skeletal material had been found in blue holes in Grand Bahama and the Turks and Caicos Islands [Keegan 1982], but it had always been disturbed or removed before archaeologists could visit the site. As the South Andros blue holes were mostly unexplored, it was felt that special care should be taken while they were being dived. For many years Andros had been considered uninhabited by Lucayans (the Bahamian name for the Caribbean Taino people who settled the islands) [Goggin 1939] but, recently, evidence of settlement has come to light [Keegan & Sealey 1988]. Most Lucayan settlements had a coastal location, but in Andros in particular these seem to have suffered from erosion, presumably during hurricanes. However, the large number of blue holes near the coast encouraged belief that more evidence could be found as the Lucayans were known to have favoured both blue holes and dry caves as burial sites [Keegan 1982].

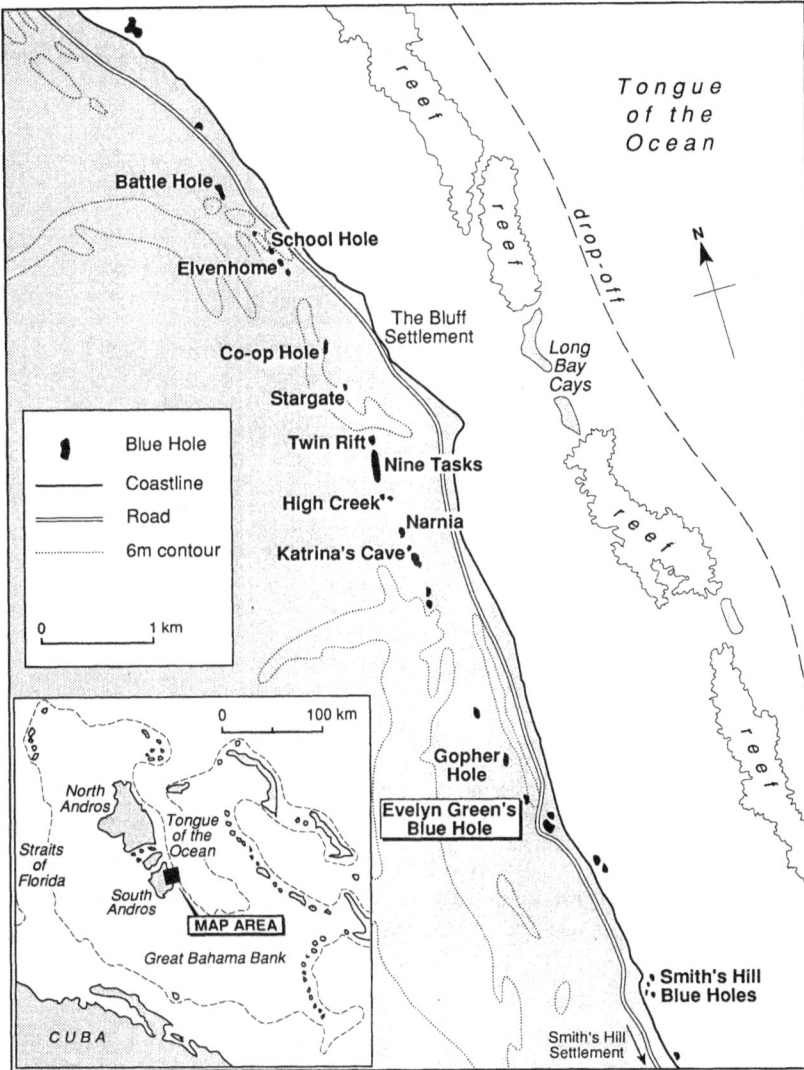

*Figure 3.1* Location of fracture contolled blue holes in South Andros

Geographically, the Andros Project proved especially productive. For example, systematic variations in chemical characteristics at different water depths have been measured by Smart et al. [1988] for Evelyn Green's blue hole, South Andros (Figure 3.2). Examination of the rock walls during the Andros Project showed excessive corrosion of the limestone in the mixing zone between fresh and saline water. Smart and Whitaker [1988] have shown that in the mixing zone the water is chemically undersaturated with respect to

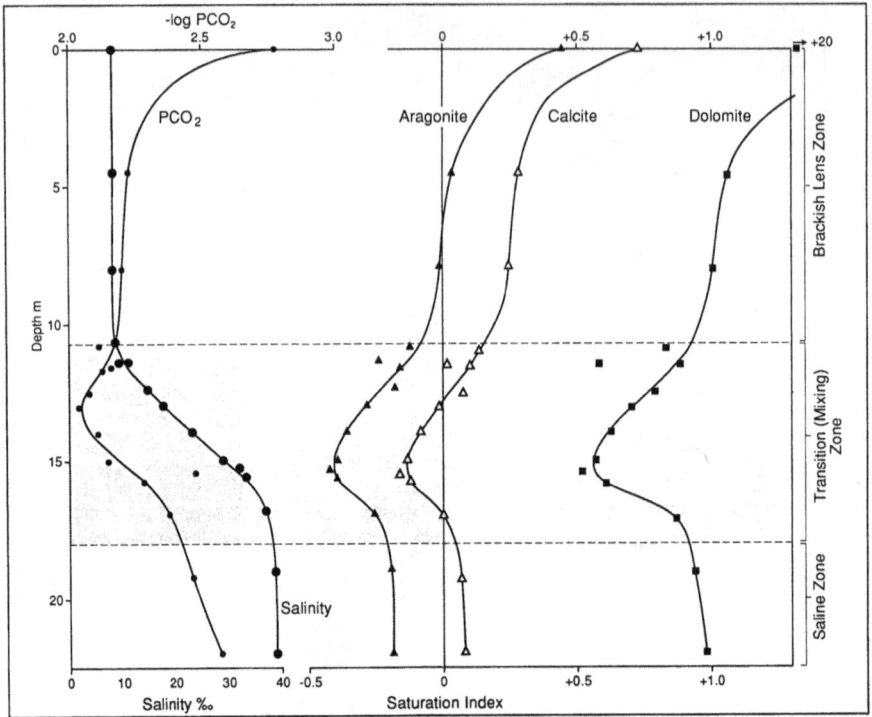

*Figure 3.2* Variation of salinity, carbon dioxide partial pressure, and aragonite, calcite and dolomite saturation in Evelyn Green's Blue Hole, South Andros

calcite and this causes a pervasive dissolution of wall rock (in the range 0.4 percent to 0.8 percent per 1,000 years), such that large pieces of rock may be broken off by hand. Bacterial oxidation of organic matter and sulphate reduction are important in this process [Smart & Whitaker 1988; Smart, Dawans & Whitaker 1988].

Subsequently, Mylroie and Carew utilized the above processes to account for the formation of caves and conduits in what they termed the Flank Margin Model of Cave Formation [Mylroie & Carew 1988; 1990]. This model is represented schematically in Figure 3.3. It shows dissolution along the water table and in the mixing zone. These combine to produce large phreatic chambers at the margins of the freshwater lens. At the same time, Smart and Whitaker pursued the opportunity to investigate island hydrology and transferred their operations to North Andros (Figure 3.4), where communications were better and the distribution of blue holes was geographically more favourable [Whitaker & Smart 1990; Whitaker 1992]. Their research showed active circulation of ground water under the island, flowing in an easterly direction, but surmounted by a flow of slightly higher salinity driven by reflux.

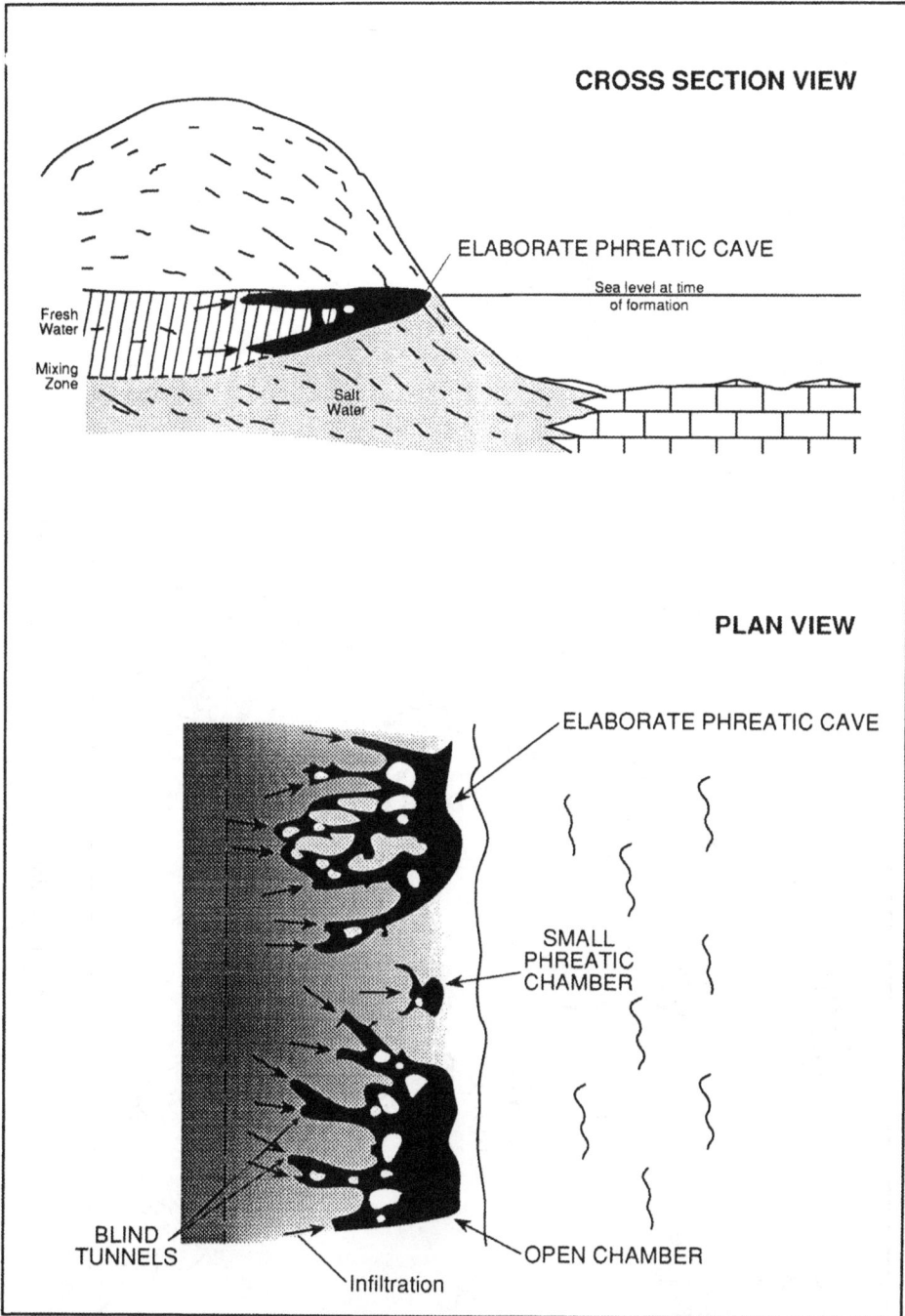

**CROSS SECTION VIEW**

ELABORATE PHREATIC CAVE

Sea level at time
of formation

Fresh
Water

Mixing
Zone

Salt
Water

**PLAN VIEW**

ELABORATE PHREATIC CAVE

SMALL
PHREATIC
CHAMBER

BLIND
TUNNELS

OPEN CHAMBER

Infiltration

*Figure 3.3* The Flank-Margin Model of Cave Formation

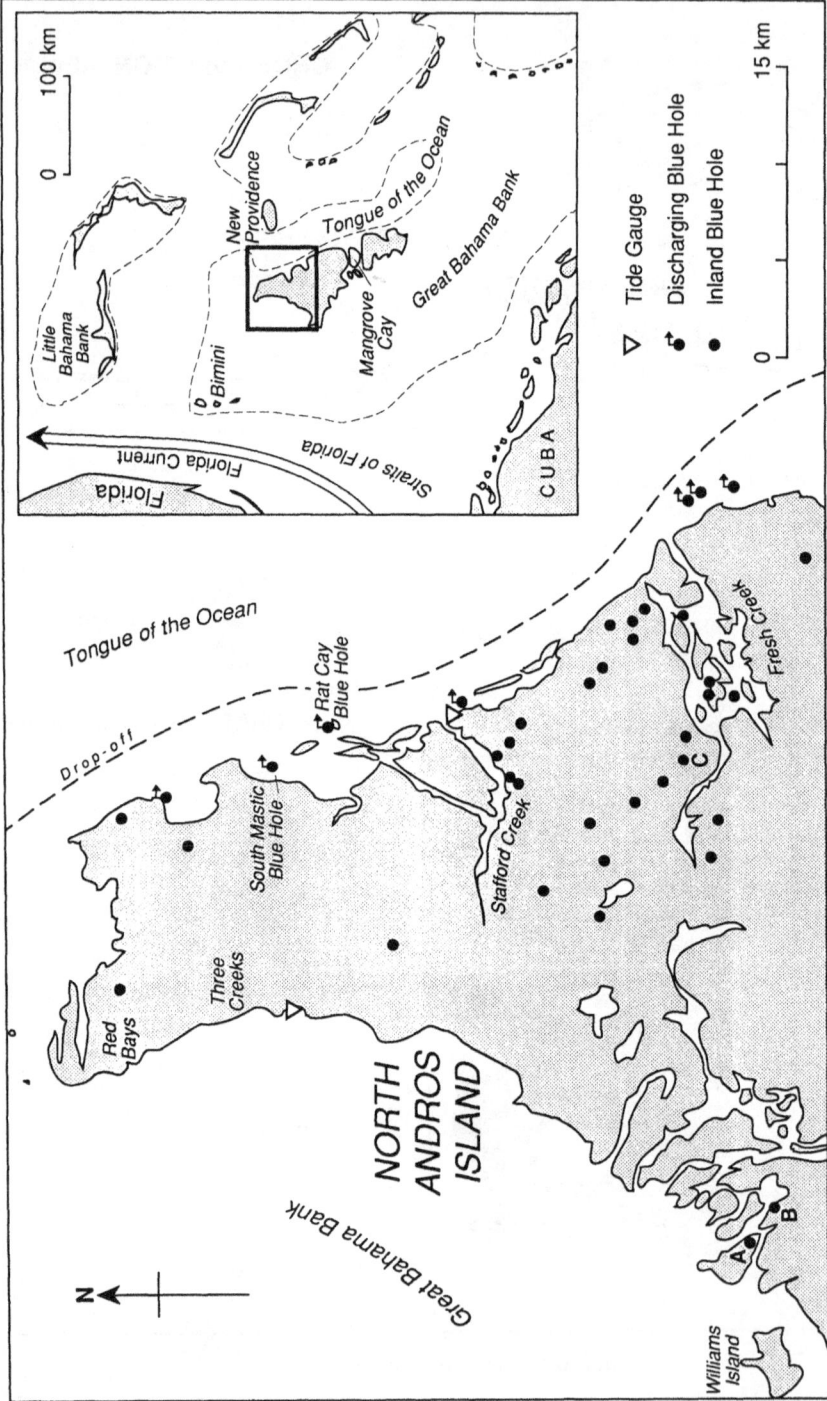

*Figure 3.4* Distribution of North Andros blue holes used in hydrological study

This is the movement of a more saline and therefore denser body of water, downward and outward. The high level of evaporation over the shallow Great Bahama Bank west of Andros generates this reflux (Figure 3.5).

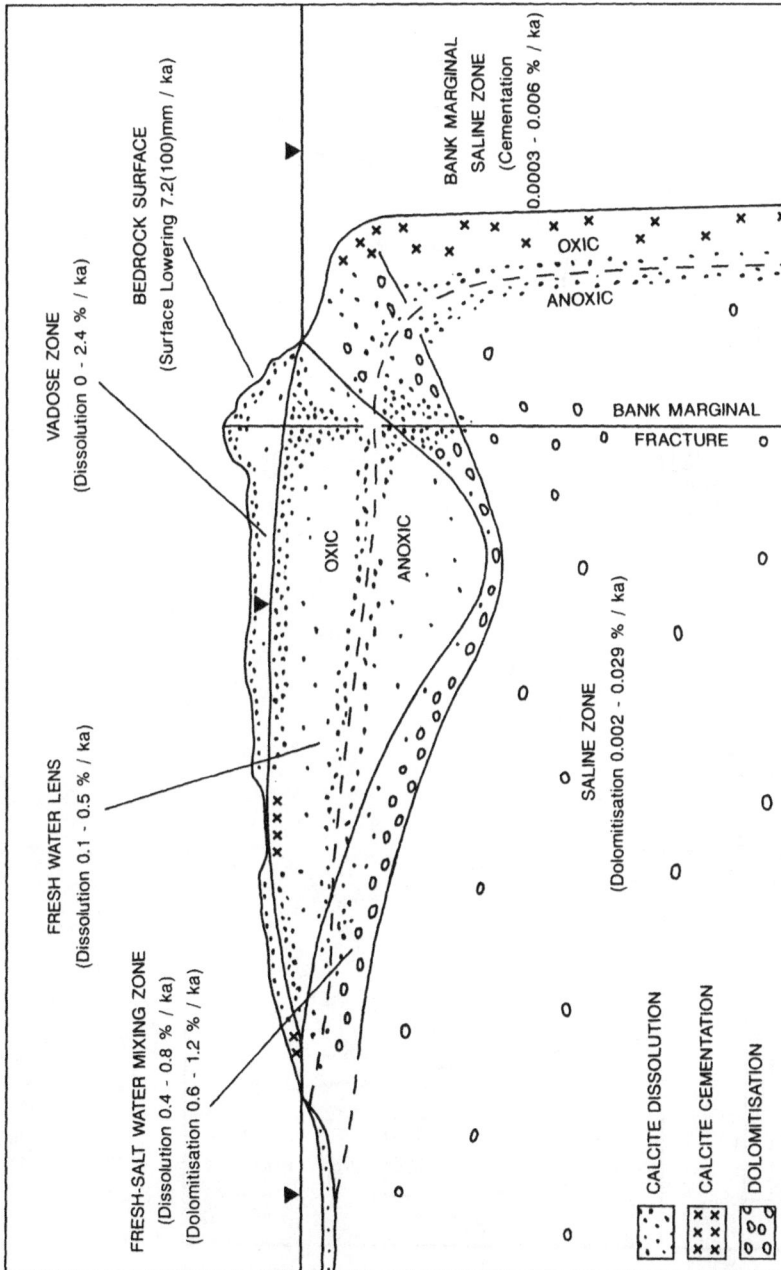

*Figure 3.5* Summary of the circulation of saline waters in a carbonate platform

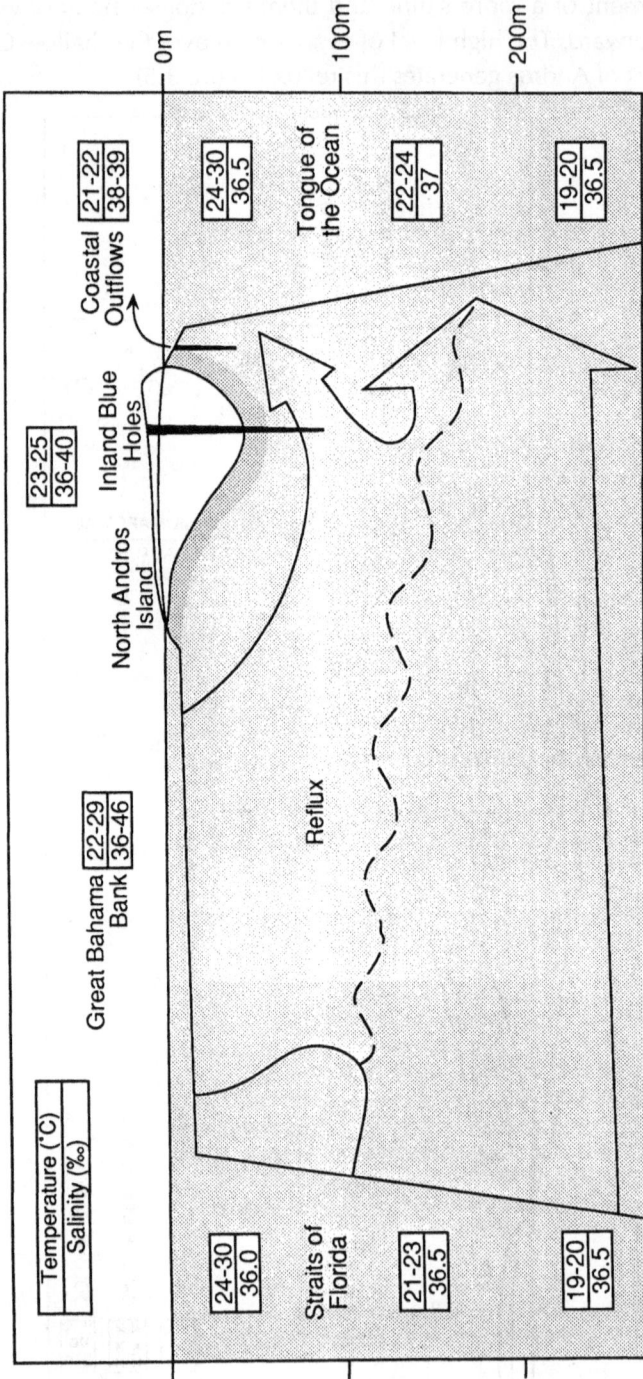

Temperature (°C)
Salinity (‰)

| | | |
|---|---|---|
| 23-25 | 36-40 | |

| | |
|---|---|
| 22-29 | 36-46 |

Great Bahama Bank

North Andros Island

Inland Blue Holes

Coastal Outflows

| 21-22 | 38-39 |
|---|---|

| 24-30 | 36.5 |
|---|---|

Tongue of the Ocean

| 22-24 | 37 |
|---|---|

| 19-20 | 36.5 |
|---|---|

Reflux

Straits of Florida

| 24-30 | 36.0 |
|---|---|

| 21-23 | 36.5 |
|---|---|

| 19-20 | 36.5 |
|---|---|

0m

100m

200m

*Figure 3.6* Schematic diagram illustrating the distribution and rates of diagenesis within a Bahamian platform

Whitaker combined the studies on dissolution and hydrology into a broader consideration of the geochemical processes at work underground, and produced a model of diagenesis for carbonate platforms [Whitaker 1992]. She concluded that in the freshwater zone dissolution is dominant with surface lowering averaging 7mm/year, but increasing to 100mm/year in "banana" holes (soil-filled solution holes). In the mixing and saline zones dolomitization is prevalent in the pore spaces (Figure 3.6).

No significant cultural remains were seen in any of the more than 40 blue holes explored in South Andros until very near the end of the expedition. While diving in a blue hole now named Sanctuary, Robert Palmer identified human remains and retrieved one skull for examination. This skull proved to be Lucayan and became the basis for the later Project Sanctuary [Palmer 1989: 132, 140-42].

## Project Sanctuary and the Cultural Significance of Blue Holes

In the years following the Andros Project increasing surface evidence of Lucayan habitation in Andros came to light, and in 1991 it was decided to return to Sanctuary blue hole and retrieve, under strict archaeological control, the human remains that Palmer had found in 1987. Improved diving technology in the form of heliox rebreathers made this much more feasible, allowing two one-hour dives to one hundred feet each day. In addition, as the rebreathers were closed systems, there were no exhaust bubbles to disturb cave debris and reduce visibility.

In all, a total of 12 further skulls and other skeletal remains were recovered, packaged in the same blue hole water, and sent to the Florida Museum of Natural History in Gainesville for expert analysis. The initial reports confirmed that all the remains were Lucayan and comprised eleven males, four females, and a young child. The adults were mostly in their mid 30s, but two were in their 40s. Analysis showed that there were remains from 16 separate individuals, and on revisiting the site this was immediately confirmed when three more skulls were discovered. No evidence of the cause of death has yet been found, and carbon dating has still to be carried out. As well as human remains the skulls of a turtle and a boar were found, these being of historic age, and the skulls of two Lucayan "barkless" dogs known as *arco*. The site is of great archaeological significance as it is intact, large and has yielded the greatest number of Prehistoric bodies and the only Prehistoric dogs ever found in The Bahamas [Sealey 1991].

# The Future of the South Andros Blue Holes

South Andros is sparsely populated (under 2,000 persons, or about 8/km$^2$) and relatively undeveloped. It has an airport and several small hotels, and tourism is the main economic activity. The offshore diving is excellent and a dive centre is likely to be added to the largest hotel within the next year. The future use of the blue holes is therefore something which must be decided very soon.

Traditional use, or misuse, has been limited to swimming and dumping litter, although this only applies to the few holes near settlements. As a result of the Andros and Sanctuary projects and the considerable publicity they have generated, public attention has now been focused on the blue holes. In addition, the tourism infrastructure has been improved, and diving is destined to be a key attraction. Unless specific blue holes are targeted for various purposes, their value as scientific sites will be rapidly destroyed. It is the way in which this is to be done that now requires consideration. Some blue holes, such as Stargate at the Bluff, could well be developed for recreational cave divers. It has good access, is large, and extremely attractive. Most of it is safe for accompanied divers, and other areas could be netted off.

Sanctuary and a few other blue holes have great scientific interest. Although their location has been kept secret, this secrecy cannot be maintained easily. Designation as sites of great scientific or historic interest by the international community is probably the next step. However, at the present time this can hardly be a high priority for funding or legislation in the short term, and the problem remains of how to protect these sites for further research.

## References

Benjamin, G.J. 1970. "Blue holes of The Bahamas". *National Geographic Magazine* 11, no. 360.
Clausen, C.J., et al. 1979. "Little Salt Spring, Florida: a unique underwater site". *Science* 203: 609-14.
Dill, R.F. 1977. "The blue holes – geologically significant submerged sink holes and caves of British Honduras and Andros, Bahama Islands". *Proceedings 3rd International Coral Reef Symposium*. Rosentiel School of Marine and Atmospheric Science, University of Miami, Florida, May, 237-42.
Farr, M., & R. Palmer. 1984. "The blue holes: description and structure". *Cave Science* 11: 9-22.
Gascoyne, M. 1984. "Uranium Series Ages of Speleothems from Bahamas Blue Holes and their Significance". *Cave Science* 11: 45-49.
Gascoyne, M., G. J. Benjamin, et al. 1979. "Sea level lowering during the Illinoian glaciation: evidence from a Bahama blue hole". *Science* 205: 806-08.
Goggin, J.M. 1939. "An anthropological reconnaissance of Andros Island, Bahamas". *American Antiquity* 5: 21-26.
Jennings, J.N. 1985. *Karst Geomorphology*. Oxford.

Keegan, W.F. 1982. "Lucayan cave burials from the Bahamas". *Journal of New World Archaeology* 5: 57-65.

Keegan, W.F., & N.E. Sealey. 1988. "A preliminary archaeological survey of the Fehling site [AN-1], Andros, Bahamas". Florida Museum of Natural History, Miscellaneous Project Report no. 40.

Mylroie, J., & J. Carew. 1988. "Solution conduits as indicators of late quaternary sea level position", *Quaternary Science Reviews* 7: 55-64.

Mylroie, J., & J. Carew. 1990. "The flank-margin model for dissolution cave development in carbonate platforms". *Earth Surface Processes and Landforms* 15: 413-24.

Palmer, R. 1985. *The Blue Holes of The Bahamas.* London: Jonathan Cape.

Palmer, R. 1986. "Ecology beneath the Bahama banks". *New Scientist*: 44-48.

Palmer, R. 1989. *Deep into Blue Holes.* UK: Unwin Hyman.

Palmer, R. 1991. "Vestiges of a lost civilisation in the blue holes of The Bahamas". *Geographical Magazine* 18: 8-1.

Palmer, R., M. McHale, & R. Hartlebury. 1986. "The caves and blue holes of Cat Island". *Cave Science* 13: 71-78.

Sealey, N.E. 1985. *Bahamian Landscapes*, UK: Collins Caribbean.

Sealey, N.E. 1991. "Project Sanctuary". *Tribune* (13 & 14 November), 7-8; 12-13.

Sealey, N.E. 1994 *Bahamian Landscapes.* 2d ed. Nassau, Bahamas: Bahamas Media Publishing.

Smart, P.L., & F.F. Whitaker. 1988. "Controls on the rate and distribution of carbonate bedrock dissolution in The Bahamas". In *Proceedings of 4th Symposium on the Geology of The Bahamas*, Bahamian Field Station, San Salvador, Bahamas, 313-21.

Smart, P.L., J.M. Dawans, & F.F. Whitaker. 1988. "Carbonate dissolution in a modern mixing zone". *Nature* 335: 811-13.

Whitaker, F.F. 1992. "Hydrology, Geochemistry and diagenesis of modern carbonate platforms in The Bahamas", PhD diss., University of Bristol.

Whitaker, F.F., & P.L. Smart. 1990." Active circulation of saline groundwaters in carbonate platforms: evidence from the Great Bahama bank". *Geology* 18: 200-03.

Wilson, W. L. 1994. "Morphometry and hydrology of Dean's blue hole, Long Island, Bahamas". *Bahamas Journal of Science* 2: 10-14.

Chapter 4

# Wetland Resource Rehabilitation for Sustainable Development in the Eastern Caribbean

Peter R. Bacon

## Introduction

One of the major characteristics of insular Caribbean resources and environments is their degraded condition; the result of long periods of unregulated use, over-exploitation and neglect. Much of the development planning that is carried out in the region and the assessment of development potential is based, therefore, on resource systems that are functioning below optimum.

The poor status of many environments and their natural vegetation and fauna not only weakens the case for conservation but gives the impression that many types of natural resource use are not sustainable. The current condition of the natural resources is likely to be a poor indicator of their economic potential and should not be used as the main basis for decision making. Existing stressors and previous site history should be taken into account, as should the need to return resources to a productive condition before further exploitation can take place.

A study of coastal wetlands in the Eastern Caribbean is presented as evidence of degraded resource status and to suggest how investment in site rehabilitation could significantly improve their contribution to economic development.

## The Case Study

In late 1991, a survey was conducted of mangrove forests and associated wetland ecosystems in 9 insular Caribbean states, comprising 16 individual islands (Figure 4.1); the survey was part of the regional sector of the Tropical Forestry Action Plan and was sponsored by the Commission of the European Communities.

The survey was carried out on wetland sites throughout the whole latitudinal range of the Eastern Caribbean, in Windward and Leeward Islands and in islands of different sizes and degrees of development (Table 4.1). The coastal wetlands under consideration were quite varied ecologically, with some 10 mangrove community types and 7 associated habitat types identified (Table 4.2). Regionally, the areal coverage by wetlands was small, with the largest sites in Trinidad, which has approximately 7,000ha of well developed mangrove forest, and an additional 1,800ha spread through the other islands (Table 4.1). A major objective of the survey was to assess the available forestry resources and other values of the wetlands in the context of the island

Table 4.1   Mangrove and Associated Wetland Sites in the Eastern Caribbean Islands

| Country | No. of sites | Approx. area (Ha) |
|---|---|---|
| Antigua | 36 | 559 |
| Barbuda | 9 | 616 |
| Barbados | 8 | 10 |
| Dominica | 10 | 10 |
| Grenada | 24 | 149 |
| Grenada Grenadines | 4 | 67 |
| Montserrat | 4 | 4 |
| St Kitts | 8 | 71 |
| Nevis | 8 | 8 |
| St Lucia | 18 | 157 |
| St Vincent | 4 | 2 |
| St Vincent Grenadines | 13 | 48 |
| Trinidad | 38 | 7020 |
| Tobago | 11 | 100 |
| **Total** | **195** | **8821** |

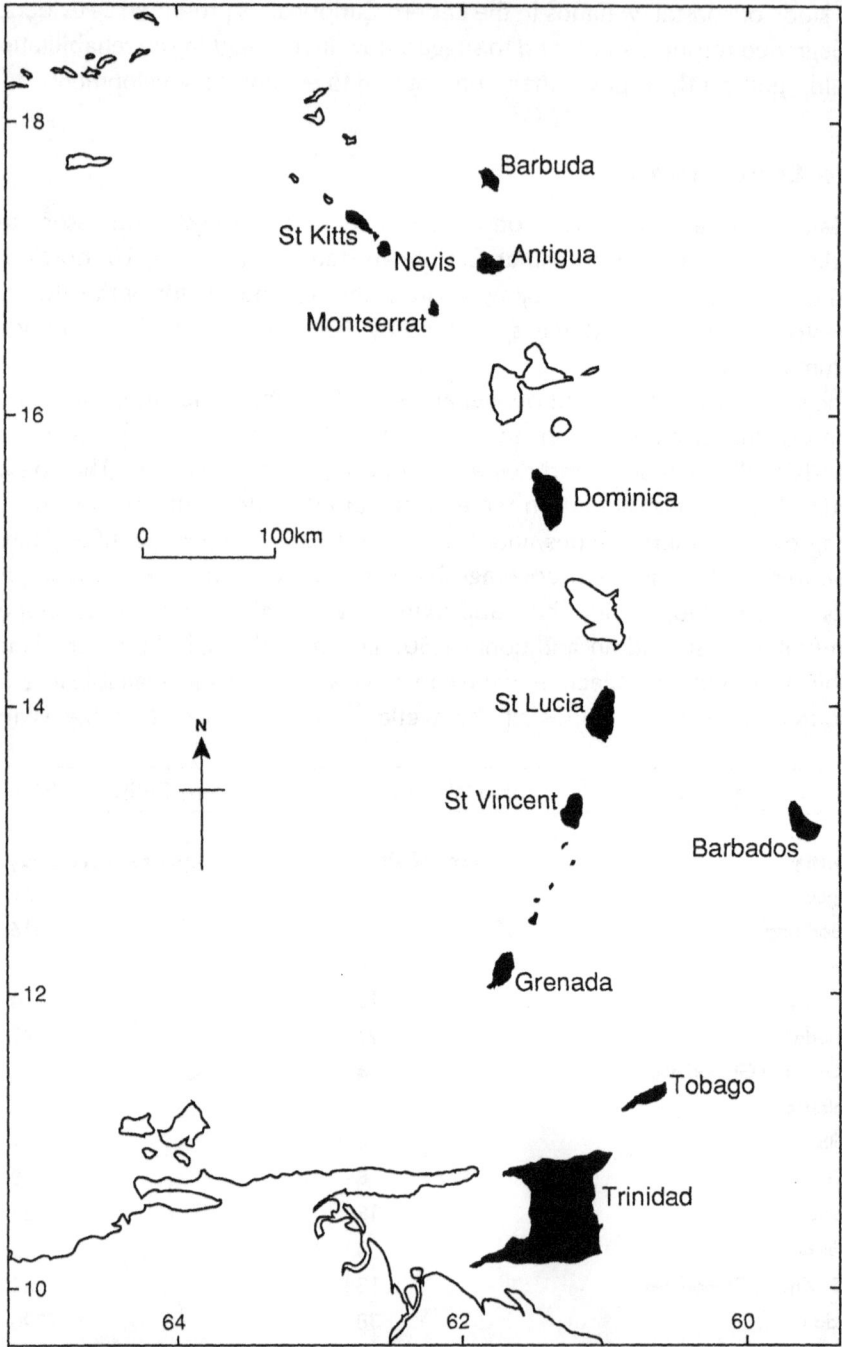

*Figure 4.1* Location of islands in wetland survey of Eastern Caribbean, 1991

**Table 4.2** Mangrove Community Types and Associated Ecosystems in the Eastern Caribbean Islands

### 1. Mangrove Community Type

**A. Estuarine systems**

| | |
|---|---|
| 1. Estuarine *Rhizophora* | Estuarine/river mouth sites dominated by Red Mangrove. |

**B. Fringe systems**

| | |
|---|---|
| 2. Fringe *Rhizophora* | Areas dominated by Red Mangrove fringing open coasts or bays. |

**C. Basin systems**

| | |
|---|---|
| 3. Basin *Rhizophora* | Red Mangrove occupying pond margins or depressions not connected directly to the sea. |
| 4. Basin *Avicennia* | Black Mangrove occupying low-lying areas, depressions, not connected directly to the sea. |
| 5. Basin *Laguncularia* | White Mangrove occupying pond margins or depressions, or behind barriers separated from the sea. |
| 6. Basin Mixed Mangrove Forest | Areas containing more than one mangrove species behind beach barriers or in depressions not connected directly to the sea. |

**D. Scrub systems**

| | |
|---|---|
| 7. Scrub *Rhizophora* | Very short, but mature, Red Mangrove forest, with trees showing poor trunk development. |
| 8. Scrub *Avicennia* | As above, with Black Mangrove. |
| 9. Mixed Scrub Mangrove | As above, with mixed Red and Black Mangrove. |
| 10. Scrub *Conocarpus* | As above, with Button Mangrove. |

### 2. Associated Habitats

| | |
|---|---|
| **E. Salt Pond** | Saline or hypersaline water bodies not connected to the sea. |
| **F. Salina** | Areas with hypersaline soils, frequently dry with a crust of algae, subjected to seasonal inundation; unvegetated. |
| **G. Salt Marsh** | Areas dominated by low, salt tolerant herbs; frequently interspersed with scrub mangrove. |
| **H. Freshwater Marsh** | Areas dominated by aquatic freshwater herbs, either rooted or floating. |
| **I. Swamp Forest** | Areas dominated by trees with adaptations to permanent or seasonal inundation by fresh water; either on river banks or in swampy depressions. |
| **J. Littoral Woodland** | Low, often scrub-like trees bordering the coast or on beach barriers; adapted to salt spray and sea breezes. |
| **K. Strand and Dune** | Herbaceous plant communities occupying back-beach and/or sand dune areas. |

*Table 4.3*   Goods, Services and Attributes Derived from Caribbean Wetland Systems

**GOODS (COMPONENTS, RESOURCES)**

1. Mineral resources (salt)
2. Energy resources (peat)
3. Water supply
4. Forest resources (woody biomass, fuelwood, charcoal)
5. Agricultural resources (food, fibre, aquaculture)
6. Forage resources (grasslands, grazed plants)
7. Fishery resources (finfish, crabs, shellfish)
8. Wildlife resources (game birds, mammals, crocodilians)

**SERVICES (FUNCTIONS)**

1. Groundwater recharge/discharge
2. Flood and flow control
3. Shoreline stabilization/erosion control
4. Sediment retention
5. Nutrient retention
6. Water quality maintenance
7. Storm protection/windbreak
8. Support to neighbouring ecosystems (e.g. coral reefs)
9. Recreational/educational opportunity
10. Water transport

**ATTRIBUTES**

1. Biological diversity
2. Uniqueness & cultural heritage
3. Scenic/landscape value

Source: *Adapted from Barbier [1989]*

economies. Wetlands have traditionally provided a range of goods and services in the Caribbean (Table 4.3) and are widely recognized internationally for their important ecologic and economic roles [Maltby 1986; Scott & Carbonell 1986; Barbier 1989]. It was hoped that the survey would identify both the direct and indirect values associated with the wetland systems in the islands and quantify these as far as possible.

Of the 195 sites investigated, some 47 percent showed evidence of serious resource degradation resulting from human impact and all sites showed some damage. A range of impacts was identified, the most important of which are indicated in Table 4.4. These included [Bacon 1991]:

Table 4.4   Causes of Degradation of Coastal Wetlands in the Eastern Caribbean

| Island | No. of sites | Types of human impact | | | | | % of sites |
|---|---|---|---|---|---|---|---|
| | | LF | CL | RE | DR | EF | |
| Antigua | 36 | 9 | 1 | – | 3 | 1 | 39 |
| Barbuda | 9 | 2 | 3 | – | – | – | 56 |
| Barbados | 8 | 1 | 4 | – | 2 | 1 | 100 |
| Dominica | 10 | 1 | 3 | 1 | – | – | 50 |
| Grenada | 24 | 4 | 6 | – | – | – | 42 |
| Carriacou | 3 | 1 | 1 | – | – | – | 67 |
| Saline Island | 1 | – | 1 | – | – | – | 100 |
| Montserrat | 4 | 1 | – | – | – | 1 | 50 |
| St Kitts | 8 | 2 | – | – | 2 | 1 | 63 |
| Nevis | 8 | 1 | 1 | – | – | – | 25 |
| St Lucia | 18 | 3 | 5 | – | – | 2 | 56 |
| St Vincent | 4 | 2 | 1 | – | – | – | 75 |
| Mustique | 2 | – | 1 | – | – | – | 50 |
| Union | 11 | 2 | 4 | – | – | – | 55 |
| Trinidad | 38 | 5 | 3 | 2 | 6 | 3 | 50 |
| Tobago | 11 | 2 | – | – | – | – | 18 |
| **Total** | **195** | **36** | **34** | **3** | **13** | **9** | |

Key to Symbols:
LF = Landfill or solid waste disposal; RE = Reclamation for agriculture; DR = Drainage alteration; EF = Effluent pollution

Note: Record does not include sites completely destroyed. Record only applies for severe impact
Source: Bacon [1991]

(a) landfill and solid waste dumping;

(b) vegetation clearance, particularly unregulated cutting for timber or charcoal production;

(c) reclamation for agriculture, including some fish pond construction;

(d) alteration of natural drainage patterns, particularly by roadways or flood diversion schemes;

(e) pollution by factory and domestic effluents.

A feature not included in Table 4.4 was modification of the catchment areas of the wetlands, which influences their hydrology and sedimentation processes. In addition, in the majority of cases, the hinterland had been developed /altered right up to the edges of the inundated areas, leading to isolation of the wetlands from terrestrial ecosystems.

Severely degraded sites were observed in all islands visited; 12 of the 16 islands had more than half their sites showing damage. The percentage of degraded sites was very high in some islands; for example, Barbados (100%), St Vincent (75%) and St Kitts (63%).

Furthermore, the statistics were derived from existing sites and no attempt is made here to present historical records for wetlands which have been cleared or filled in completely, although it is known that many wetland sites have been "reclaimed" [Hudson 1983; Bacon 1987]. Wetland destruction has been serious in some islands, such as Barbados where loss of more than half the original wetland sites is documented following expansion of the tourism sector [Williams 1990].

The quantity and quality of goods and services derived from wetlands was low in almost all cases; to the extent that wetland products were not included in any national accounts. The survey itself had been included in the Tropical Forestry Action Plan as an afterthought, because mangroves were no longer considered to be "production forests" in the Caribbean. The only site actively managed for charcoal production, at Man Kote in St Lucia, was found to be unable to support the members of the cooperative without supplementary fuelwood inputs [Walters & Burt 1991]. Only three sites supported commercial tourism activity and these were important also as nature reserves [Ramdial 1975; James 1980; Mussington 1983].

In summary, the survey suggested initially that one of the characteristic natural ecosystem types of the Caribbean islands, the coastal wetlands, was likely to contribute little to future economic development.

## Discussion of the Case Study

Some of the implications of using the current status of the wetland sites in assessing economic development potential are outlined below.

(a) As wetland sites become degraded, and less productive, the perception that they are "wasteland" increases. They are seen then as suitable sites only for dumping of wastes or for clearance for more productive activities. This leads to further deterioration of the sites and negative perceptions of once valuable resources.

(b) During environmental impact assessments of development proposals influencing the coastal zone, e.g. resort or marina construction, the socio-economic gains from a proposed use of the site are likely to be weighed against those derived from degraded natural systems; with a predictable outcome that the estimated value of the natural system is not competitive. Too frequently, developers fail to see the potential for incorporating wetland systems in resort and residential area design, because they perceive the degraded status as the norm.

(c) There is an obvious anomaly between the low value attached to wetlands in the islands and the increasing international attention being paid to wetlands conservation. Wetlands play an important role in fisheries, forestry, recreation and tourism, water quality control and landscape/scenic appreciation in many other countries. These benefits are rarely utilized in the insular Caribbean, despite the need for greater food and materials production and the expanding tourism sector. Considering the general paucity of other resources, particularly in the Lesser Antilles, the neglect of any one potential resource type is cause for concern.

## Resource Management

In a second phase, the wetland survey [Bacon 1991] considered what each wetland site could be used for, if attention were paid to site rehabilitation and management. In every island, opportunities were recognized for an increase in mangrove forest production (stakes, timber, charcoal); for the improvement of wildlife habitat (for educational and recreational purposes); and for the incorporation of wetland habitat (ponds, lagoons and creeks) in landscaping to enhance residential areas and tourist venues. Site rehabilitation would include such activities as removal of landfill or waste deposits, re-vegetation and channel clearance. It would be based on records of the geographical extent of former wetlands and resources used at the subsistence level, in an attempt to reverse the effects of negative human impact.

Related efforts were already in progress in some islands. For example, in Montserrat, the National Trust recognized the importance of the small wetland at Fox's Bay, only 2.4ha in extent and one of only four sites containing mangroves in the island. The site was acquired in 1979, cleaned up and made accessible to the public under management as a nature reserve [Margetson 1991]. The site had quickly become a tourist attraction and recreation area for nationals, as well as a prime bird-watching location. The uniqueness of the site, in a resource poor island, was an important factor in generating interest in its management. Its contribution to biodiversity on Montserrat and to the island's tourism product was greater than had been expected when the degraded site was first investigated.

Other examples of sites which would benefit from active management are listed in Table 4.5. Rehabilitation would be low cost, using proven methodologies [Kusler & Kentula 1990], and would be likely to show benefits in a relatively short time; as was found to be the case at Fox's Bay in Montserrat. The costs could be borne largely by the private sector, because of

*Table 4.5* Selected Examples of Wetland Enhancement by Low Cost Rehabilitation
Methods

| Island | Site Name | Rehabilitation Method and Objective |
|--------|-----------|-------------------------------------|
| Antigua | Hanson's Bay | Dyking and restriction of town dump, replanting of mangroves to screen waste site; clean up of a prime bird-watching site for tourism; contain leachate from dump site to protect estuarine environment. |
| Barbuda | Bull Hole | Clean up of minor solid waste dumping; silviculture of trees to improve scenic character and wildlife viewing; site of prime scientific interest as an "inland mangrove", therefore of potential value in tourism diversification. |
| Barbados | Graeme Hall | Re-establishment of tidal flushing by repair of sluice system; clean up of forested areas; improvement of trails and provision of picnic sites to create a recreational area around the island's largest inland water body. |
| Dominica | Cabrits | Vegetation management including some replanting to diversify interest features in Cabrits National Park. |
| Grenada | Levera Pond | Clean up and replanting of mangroves; management of charcoal cutting; improvement of access; sustainable yields of timber and charcoal, in conjunction with park development. |
| St Kitts | Gt Salt Pond | Engineering modification to reflood old salt workings; replanting of mangroves; to upgrade quality of this major feature of Southeast Peninsula National Park. |
| St Lucia | Choc Bay | Containment of abandoned dump site; opening of Choc River mouth; planting on banks and edges of dump site; to stabilize dump and improve aesthetic quality of a river mouth between major resort sites. |
| St Vincent | Carenage | Replanting of damaged mangroves; clean up of stream channels; to improve site in the middle of an important recreational area. |
| Trinidad | Point Lisas | Replanting of mangroves on landfill; for coastal protection, stabilization and scenic improvement. |
| Tobago | Bon Accord | Removal of solid waste; replanting and mangrove management; to improve scenic quality near a resort; to maintain ecological linkages between mangroves and neighbouring reefs. |

the benefits to be derived by the resorts or residential areas; although the island governments should be involved because of the benefits to be derived from greater forest production and opportunities for diversification of the tourism product.

## Conclusions

The case study suggests that rehabilitation of a site to improve its quality and productivity should precede assessment of its value. In so far as planning for sustainable development in the insular Caribbean depends on the quality of the available resource base, it is critical that the base be evaluated correctly.

In the case study described, where more than half the resource is degraded, rehabilitation is an obvious starting point for resource management effort. Wherever feasible, a projection should be made for the value of a wetland site and/or its resources when returned to a functional optimum, rather than basing this calculation on its current status.

The same is almost certainly true of other resource types, such as upland forests and coral reefs. It makes little economic sense to base estimates of sustainable yield of forest products on current outputs from the remaining heavily exploited stands on degraded hillsides, or of dive tourism or fisheries development potential on reefs which are heavily stressed by eutrophication and excess siltation. A general principle to be derived from this brief discussion is that the rehabilitation of the major natural resource types appears to be a prerequisite for sustainable development planning in the insular Caribbean.

### References

Bacon, P.R. 1987. "Use of wetlands for tourism in the insular Caribbean". *Annals of Tourism Research* 14: 104-17.

Bacon, P.R. 1991. "The status of mangrove conservation in the CARICOM islands of the Eastern Caribbean". Report to the Commission of the European Communities, Brussels.

Barbier, E.B. 1989. *The Economic Value of Ecosystems: Tropical Wetlands.* London: International Institute for Environment and Development.

Hudson, B.J. 1983. "Wetland reclamation in Jamaica". *Caribbean Geography* 1: 75-88.

James, A.A. 1980. "Freshwater swamps and mangrove species". Forestry Division, Ministry of Agriculture, Dominica.

Kusler, J.A., & M.E. Kentula. 1990. *Wetland Creation and Restoration: The Status of the Science.* Washington: Island Press.

Maltby, E. 1986. *Waterlogged Wealth.* International Institute for Environment and Development. London: Earthscan Books.

Margetson, F.A.L. 1991. "Wetlands of Montserrat". In *Wetlands Management in the Caribbean and the Role of Forestry and Wetlands in the Economy.* Puerto Rico: Institute of Tropical Forestry.

Mussington, J. 1983. "A survey of the Codrington lagoon system (Codrington, Barbuda)". Eastern Caribbean Natural Area Management Program and the Government of Antigua.

Ramdial, B.S. 1975. "The social and economic importance of the Caroni Swamp in Trinidad and Tobago". PhD diss. University of Michigan.

Scott, D.A., & M. Carbonell. 1986. *A Directory of Neotropical Wetlands*. Cambridge: Conservation Monitoring Centre.

Walters, B.B., & M. Burt. 1991. "Community based management of mangrove and fuelwood resources: a case study of the Mankote-Aupicon project, St Lucia, West Indies". Caribbean Natural Resources Institute, St Lucia.

Williams, K.A. 1990. "The wetlands of Barbados – a disappearing resource". BA thesis, University of the West Indies, Mona.

# Part 2

# Tourism and Development Planning

Chapter 5

# Sustainable Tourism
# in the Caribbean

Lesley France and Brian Wheeller

## Introduction

Recently, there has been a growing awareness, together with a belated acknowledgment on behalf of the tourist industry itself, of the problems caused by the negative impact that has invariably accompanied tourism growth. Tourism clearly brings some benefits to the recipient regions and obviously also benefits the tourists themselves. However, though sometimes the scapegoat for other negative forces, there is a catalogue of catastrophic impacts that provide graphic evidence of tourism's destructive power. In the global arena, the magnitude and intensity of effects are exacerbated by the current tourist invasion into many developing countries. Environmental destruction is prevalent, cultural differences most marked, and social tensions heightened by the rapid flood of tourism from the alien industrialized nations into the developing world.

There is the general misapprehension that these costs are somehow only, or primarily, associated with mass tourism. The individual tourist or small group of tourists is not identified for criticism, nor is travel — travel and the traveller are beyond reproach. It is popular mass tourism that is regarded as the villain of the "peace". A school of thought has evolved that appears to be based on the premise that changing the demands of mass tourism would somehow provide the solution to the negative impacts of tourism. There is now substantial, verbose rhetoric in support of this new "alternative" as a prerequisite to any tourism planning and development [Owen 1991; Ruschmann 1992]. What is required, it is argued, is a more caring, "aware" form of tourism industry, small-scale developments which are ecologically sound, local integration, seasonal and geographical spread of demand, and a more aware tourist, well versed in the ethics of travel. The pace of any development should be steady, controlled, sympathetically planned and managed and, of course, sustainable [Wheeller 1991].

A wide range of definitions of sustainability exists, though the most widely accepted is that advanced in the Brundtland Report [World Commission on Environment and Development 1987: 43]: "development that meets the needs of the present without compromising the ability of future generations to meet their own needs". In a narrow sense, it would be possible to achieve ecological sustainability by excluding or restricting people, as in wilderness areas, although in developmental or social terms this could be catastrophic. Another possibility would be to permit a small group of people to benefit while attaining a relatively high degree of ecological sustainability. Such a group could be connected to government, or be an elite involved with a specific development project. This might involve a visit to an up-market hotel, or a luxury safari that has changed the surrounding area very little but which brings satisfaction and financial rewards to small groups of wealthy tourists and the elite owners of tourist facilities, for example, as is the case in Costa Rica and with gorilla safaris in central Africa. The small number of beneficiaries have power or money or both and are therefore able to gain access to resources such as land.

An alternative third view of sustainability that has a political economic standpoint can set notions of equity, for example, or the reduction of poverty, alongside considerations of ecological maintenance. This is very much more difficult to achieve because it contains far greater contradictions. The challenge is to achieve a compromise between ecological sustainability and sustainable lifestyles for the majority of the population. The problem here is the underprivileged group including the poor, the elderly, children and women. Some of the ensuing dilemmas can be found in examining issues concerning national parks, in which tourism, conservation and benefits/costs to local people create immense planning and management difficulties. Such problems have become especially apparent in some national parks in East Africa.

Perhaps the only satisfactory approach is to agree on priorities but, realistically, can this be achieved? For example, is the main aim to satisfy the needs of the tourists — in which case, are the needs of others regarded as unimportant? Alternatively, is it a question of the conservation of the physical environment being of paramount concern — with the needs of people considered to be of lesser importance? Or is the principal focus the improvement of the situation for the disadvantaged and powerless who are likely to lose through the action of the market? At different stages, particular countries or areas may theoretically vary their priorities.

Different stances could be adopted: the first stage perhaps could be a tourist visit to a remote area involving very small numbers (for example, expeditions or small safaris), such that the area remains unchanged and tourist satisfaction is high. If operated either by an external (possibly multinational) organization or by a local elite, any economic benefits are unlikely to filter down to the local community and improve the lifestyles of those in most need.

A second possibility might involve small-scale, local guest-houses providing accommodation in a little modified, physical and social environment whose quality is so low that demand is minimal. Nevertheless, the original environment is sustained and any economic benefits that do accrue go to relatively poor people, or to people who would otherwise lose out as a result of tourism developments.

Another scenario could involve a large tourism enterprise in which considerable numbers of local people are employed. In terms of the poorer, unskilled members of society this would undoubtedly involve low paid, menial work. All people in the area would not necessarily benefit by obtaining jobs, and the environment may be destroyed in the process.

A further option might be small-scale, locally managed tourism enterprises that may spread benefits more widely throughout the local community, as has happened, for example, in the Lower Casamance scheme in Senegal and ecotourism developments in Belize. Through compromise, a measure of satisfaction of a variety of sustainable aims could be achieved.

In each of these scenarios the trickle down or prolonging effects would need to be considered, assuming that they could actually be measured in the first place. Certainly, in any strategy the emphasis could theoretically be placed on a number of these tactics and, through time, that emphasis could change.

Ideally, sustainable ecotourism should provide satisfying jobs and carefully planned economic growth. Decisions should be made locally and democratically; benefits should be diffused through the community; traditional values should be maintained and the natural environment should not be abused. The "traveller" is preferred to the tourist; the independent specialist operators are more acceptable than large firms; indigenous village accommodation is preferred to multinational hotel chains. All these features basically involve small versus mass. Unfortunately, the chasm between what (perhaps) the perfect situation should be and what the situation actually is, or is likely to be, remains vast. The ideals of sustainable ecotourism remain essentially just that: utopian myths divorced from the harsh constraints of reality. True, there are many examples of small-scale alternative successes but these should not be cited (deliberately or inadvertently), as evidence that tourism as a whole can in a physical sense be sensitively controlled. There is a distinction, often conveniently ignored, between planning for an individual tourism project at the micro-level and macro considerations. The essence of the success of ecotourism at the micro-level is an effective control of numbers of tourists in line with a particular project's carrying capacity. Clearly this cannot be successful at the macro-level where, on the one hand, the problem is that the massive global growth in the numbers of tourists is out of control and is increasing at an accelerating rate. Yet, on the other hand, the suggested solutions of slow, small-scale steady development demand much greater control.

## Tourism and the Caribbean

The Caribbean is currently at a crossroads in the development of tourism. Development that may be regarded as sustainable varies with the physical and social characteristics of the country or area concerned. It is worth reviewing briefly the existing situation in order to provide the context for a consideration of the influences and opportunities available to Caribbean countries. A simplistic approach might be to divide these countries into groups relating to the numbers of visitors they receive, the type of tourist and the level of organization of the industry within them. Four distinct groupings are readily identified.

1. The first group comprises countries in which tourism is largely undeveloped. Such places are visited by small numbers of adventurous travellers using scheduled services or yacht facilities. Generally, these are the less accessible islands and include St Vincent and Dominica.

2. In the second category of countries, visitor numbers demonstrate a distinct level of growth and overseas operators are beginning to have a presence, promoting "up-market" forms of tourism. Anguilla and the British Virgin Islands are examples of these still fashionable destinations that so far remain the haunts of the adventurous.

3. A relatively large group of countries that have experienced rapidly growing visitor arrivals comprise the third group of countries. Multinational firms within these territories are heavily involved in the construction and running of hotels and the provision of infrastructure, and through the presence of tour operators, the mass market is beginning to discover these destinations. Examples here include Aruba, Martinique, St Kitts and Nevis, and St Lucia.

4. The last group of countries is characterized by the maturity of tourism development; which is achieved through large numbers of visitor arrivals, the existence of a well organized industry in which tour operators play a significant role, a range of types of accommodation and a large and diverse support sector. The mass market has become well established at these destinations. Included in this group are islands such as Antigua, The Bahamas, Barbados and Jamaica [France 1991].

To an extent, the possibilities for different forms of future tourism evolution are dependent upon the level of development already experienced. Ecotourism, seen as an exciting prospect by many countries, may not be such a realistic proposition in the more developed parts of individual islands where mass package tourism has emerged and dominates. These geographical areas show evidence of irreversible change as charter air travel and the tour operators have organized large numbers of visitor movements from North America and Europe. However, such change should be viewed in context because not all Caribbean countries have experienced tourism development on virgin land. Once natural environments have been modified, tourism development can be sustainable for generations, as the experience of many successful resorts demonstrates. The critical factor in this respect is the ability to continue to satisfy the demands of tourists without changing the character or scale of the resort, or of the destination created.

This is a task fraught with difficulties and requires a measure of planning to permit its successful implementation. On a small scale, the plans to promote tourism on Nevis for example, involving the use of the island's historical and architectural features, the planned restoration of sugar mills and the creation of a botanical garden, follow such guidelines. The plans incorporate the use of physical and cultural assets and attempt to bring long term community benefits through the modest expansion of a thriving economic activity. At the same time the host population is consulted to ensure that a measure of local participation will maximize the use of the island's restricted resources [*Travel Trade Weekly* 1992].

In Jamaica, the increasing importance of the environment was acknowledged by the appointment of a Minister to balance tourism needs with environmental protection through the creation of a joint ministry. It is anticipated that as a result of this move more emphasis will be placed on the development of ecotourism, with concomitant dangers. Initiatives already launched include the establishment of a marine park in the Montego Bay area [*Travel Trade Gazette* 1992; and see Smith, this volume] and, in 1992, a temporary stop was placed on developments along the

South Coast until the results of a study on the likely impact of tourism on the environment are known (though see later).

While these efforts are limited in scope, they are indicative of a greater commitment to sustainability, recognizing the value of existing environments whose long-term survival is important and where the scale and pace of development need to be in keeping with the nature of the area [Owen 1991]. But the question may be posed: is the commitment real or merely convenient rhetoric? Similar efforts to acknowledge the role of the environment and the importance of utilizing resources to ensure that their future existence is not threatened are behind the moves to clean up the coastline on the Cayman Islands [*Travel Trade Weekly* 1992] and selected underwater areas around Grenada [*Travel Trade Gazette* 1992b].

Closer involvement of local people in environmental protection and in the development of conservation strategies that could provide a base for the launch of ecotourism is evident on a number of islands. Canadian financial support is being provided in Grenada in an attempt to create more tourism opportunities through the development of environmental projects. Similar schemes exist in the other Windward Islands, such as Dominica, St Vincent and St Lucia. Ultimately the aim is that of promoting greater regional cooperation. Such developments are in their early stages, but the initial local response appears good [*Travel Trade Gazette* 1992c]. In Montserrat, the introduction of environmental education projects has been taken a step further and has been extended from local people to include tourists. In the Montserrat case, United Nations funding will lead to the improvement of popular attractions, among which will be a new visitor centre and botanical gardens.

In some Caribbean islands, as is often the case with destinations where per capita income levels are low, in addition to government and overseas financial aid there is considerable involvement by multinational companies, with a consequent loss of local control [France 1991]. However, the tourism industry has been established in the region for some considerable time and experiments (notably in Jamaica) with the local ownership of institutions like the all-inclusive SuperClub hotels have introduced a "greener" element in the system. Local ownership is supposedly one of the essential criteria that defines green or alternative tourism, and this is certainly a feature of the SuperClub chain. Yet the chain is an international group whose profits may be repatriated back to Jamaica from other countries in the Caribbean, where the hotels are located.

One may question further whether it is possible for such dense commercial clusters to be described as "green". They have undoubtedly brought irreversible change; they are large rather than small in scale, and they are indubitably energy intensive. Yet they satisfy the demands of visitors and, if they provide the Caribbean dream created and marketed so vociferously by the tourist industry, do they not focus change into manageable ghettos that generate income, provide employment, and yet are capable of restricting and confining large numbers of tourists into small parts of the environment? Further, this type of development limits the extent of land required for tourism purposes.

The converse would be an attempt to spread tourism more thinly but more widely both across the islands and within any specific territory. Efforts to limit the spatial extent of tourism have been mooted in an effort to avoid just such a situation. One example comes from Jamaica, where the Negril Chamber of Commerce has been seeking to stop the spread of low, wide, sprawling buildings by suggesting that construction should be limited to two-thirds of any plot [*Travel Trade Weekly* 1992]. Restrictions are also being considered in relation to another major form of mass tourism that has been growing in popularity in the Caribbean in recent years: cruise shipping. A number of countries are looking into the possibility of following Bermuda's lead in limiting cruise vessels' access in order to protect their increasingly overloaded infrastructure [*Travel Trade Gazette* 1992c]. Cruise lines are trying to pre-empt a debate on ecological impacts by briefing clients on suitable behaviour when they go ashore, and by calling at "private-owned" islands in order to relieve pressure on certain destinations.

## Development of Ecotourism

While the major tourist "honeypots" continue to enjoy considerable success there is, at the same time, a small but increasing demand for "green" holidays in the Caribbean. Holiday firms based in the United Kingdom, like "Explore" and "Cox and Kings", are merely responding to market pressure when they offer packages such as a botany tour of Dominica [*Travel Trade Gazette* 1992c]. It is partly in response to this surge of interest in the environment within many of the main tourist originating countries that ecotourism has been adopted enthusiastically by a number of Caribbean countries, particularly those where tourism development is in its infancy. They view ecotourism as an approach to green or alternative tourism that is a viable way forward. As a preliminary to a more widespread adoption (and here, of course, is the inherent danger) lists of resources for ecotourism development have been drawn up [Caribbean Tourist Organization 1991]. Essentially, these consist of inventories of the flora and fauna, together with details of national parks and protected areas that might attract adventurous and specialized visitors. But the essence of many of these lists is that they consist of species in need of protection rather than exploitation. The real danger of such potential exploitation can be seen in some parts of the Caribbean region. In Cuba, for instance, with the recent expansion of tourism, the island's spectacular wildlife is used to lure simultaneously the "caring" ecotourist and also the hunting and fishing fraternity.

Few islands have the structures to market their facilities themselves and would need to depend on external institutions whose major motive is profit rather than the careful and restricted development of vulnerable resources. For many of them, greater numbers of tourists imply greater profits. Once control over development is lost, the rate, scale and direction of change tends to lie outside the influence of a country. Further, it is likely that the imposition of stringent government restrictions would be likely to result in the abandonment of the destination by the tourist industry.

The first steps on this downward slide can be viewed in Belize, where ecotourism is widely accepted as an appropriate form of development. Although small-scale development is a preferred option, 90 percent of coastal development is under foreign ownership. However, there are no plans to restrict foreign land ownership since overseas investment is needed [Cater 1992]. As the number of visitors choosing ecotourism in Belize increases, there is no doubt that similar infrastructural demands to those of more traditional forms of tourism will result. Although regarded by many as a lesser evil than mass tourism, ecotourism is likely to be coordinated by firms based in the visitors' country of origin, and the repatriation of profit made by such firms back to the countries in which they are based will reduce the benefit to local populations and to the host country. Perhaps under such circumstances ecotourism could more realistically be named "ecocolonialism".

One attempt to retain control in the hands of Caribbean institutions is via CHARMS, the Caribbean's own computerized hotel reservations systems service operated by Cable and Wireless in conjunction with the Caribbean Hotels Association. One hundred and ninety-eight hotels in 28 Caribbean countries agreed to participate in this scheme, which began on 31 December 1992, alongside a number of multinationals such as Hilton International and Ramada Resorts International [*Travel Trade Weekly* 1992]. This type of cooperative venture will hopefully both reduce the high costs of marketing and increase understanding among member states, ostensibly permitting the easier monitoring and control of tourism patterns.

## The Ecotourism Debate

Ecotourism and sustainability are being manipulated by the industry and by the official tourist lobby to sell the product. There is considerable intellectual debate and convenient confusion as to what precisely are the principles of ecotourism and as to which of these principles are being applied. In tourism, this debate on sustainability has evolved rapidly over the last decade as perspectives and nomenclature have changed. Seminal works in the mid 1980s [Krippendorf 1987; Murphy 1985] led to a spate of articles and books advocating the ethics of the new tourism and urging tourists to behave "correctly" [Bramwell 1991; Anscombe 1991; Wood & House 1991]. In turn, these have prompted a number of critiques which question the validity of sustainable tourism on both intellectual and practical grounds [Cazes 1989; Butler 1990; Pigram 1990; Wheeller 1991;1992a]. For many practitioners, however, these dilemmas do not seem to exist. While exhortations that green is good (or God) are continually being made, responses depend on business assessment of the extent to which green issues influence their own particular market. The philosophy being adopted is simple — if it can be employed to sell the product then use it. Interpretations of just what constitutes good management policies inevitably vary. However, much of the current evidence suggests that ecotourism is, for many involved in the industry, just another marketing ploy. See for example, Wheeller [1992b].

Real fears of this process are evident in recent debate surrounding plans to open up tourism to undeveloped areas of Jamaica. The Minister of Tourism and Environment was reported as stating that "We are examining opening up the South Coast of the country to tourism. It is a different type of product. We are looking at small-scale, ecologically sensitive development in the area" [*Travel Trade Gazette* 1993]. However, concern has been expressed in Jamaica that development in this area will be anything but small-scale and that growth could take the form of some resorts on the north coast of the island. This is an example of an as yet unresolved question in the ecotourism debate.

Given the dynamism for growth inherent in tourism, can a product like ecotourism remain small-scale if it is successful? Obviously those advocating the development of ecotourism argue that its very success depends on its smallness and exclusivity; that, therefore, it is imperative for its own continued survival and success that its scale remains small — that it is in the industry's own interest to preserve and enhance the small-scale product of ecotourism. Those with a somewhat more pessimistic, but, perhaps, realistic point of view are painfully aware of the intense pressure for continued growth and spatial expansion of tourism [Wheeller 1991]. Indeed, in the same article [*Travel Trade Gazette* 1993], satisfaction is expressed with Jamaica's current five-year development plan (1990-95). It is hoped that visitor arrivals will increase from 1.3 million to 1.7 million over the period and that foreign exchange will increase from US$677 million to US$974 million. A new major advertising campaign in Europe is underway to help ensure this "success". Part of the campaign is based on the imagery of native flora and fauna and concomitant vague notions of ecotourism. Combine this with the introduction of cheap air fares from London to Jamaica from 1993, and the inherent problems of control are obvious. This is symptomatic of tourism development — always a demand for more. There seems little to suggest that if ecotourism is "successful" it will be effectively controlled. Indeed the more successful it is the more likely it will be "copied". Rather than a danger of killing the goose that lays the golden egg, it is more a matter of success breeding success.

A point worth raising at a general level in the ecotourism debate is the question of which particular environment is being considered — the global or the specific. The ecotourist (and indeed the ecofirm) so concerned ostentatiously to behave sensitively in the endangered destination environment, generally is not so concerned about the danger to the overall environment he/she causes in actively reaching the destination. Here, convenience takes precedence over conscience — a car to the airport and a jumbo jet are hardly paradigms of virtue in the environmental stakes.

## Conclusion

In the Caribbean, as is the case elsewhere, ecotourism is very much in vogue, and is playing an increasing role in the tourism development debate. Ecotourism does indeed provide an answer. Unfortunately, it is an answer to the wrong question. Rather than effectively tackling the alarming complexities of tourism impact, what ecotourism is actually achieving is the considerably easier task of answering the question: how are we to cope with the criticisms of tourism impact, while, of course, enabling the tourism industry to continue to develop? It has been frighteningly successful at accomplishing this. There are many unresolved problems with ecotourism/sustainable tourism both at the philosophical level, but more importantly, at the practical, organizational level. Certainly, any development of this "nature" should be treated with extreme caution. This paper, while acknowledging the desire and need for development, hopes to serve as a warning that the problems associated with tourism development will not be solved simply by the adoption of ecotourism. Those regions restructuring their existing tourism or developing new areas should not be readily seduced by the myth of green tourism, which may be little more than a growth policy masquerading behind the pseudo respectability of a green mantle. The critical factor in the "success" of any ecotourism development is effective control of numbers. Side-stepping the practical difficulties of actually implementing such a policy, the ultimate choice remains, of course, a complex political decision.

# References

Anscombe, J. 1991. "The gentle traveller". *New Woman* (June): 51-53.

Bramwell, B. 1991. Shades of green tourism". *Leisure Management* (February): 40-41.

Butler, R. 1990. "Alternative tourism: pious hope or Trojan Horse?" *Journal of Travel Research* (Winter): 40-45.

Cazes, G. 1989. "Alternative tourism: reflections on an ambiguous concept". In *Towards Appropriate Tourism*, edited by T. Singh, F. Go and L. Go. pp 117-26. Frankfurt: Lang.

Caribbean Tourism Organization. 1991. *Eco-Tourism. A CTO Market Guide.* Barbados: Caribbean Tourism Organization.

Cater, E. 1992. "Profits from paradise". *Geographical Magazine* 64: 16-21.

France, L. 1991. "An overview of tourism in the Caribbean". Newcastle: Centre for Travel and Tourism, in association with Business Education Publishers Limited.

Krippendorf, J. 1987. *The Holidaymakers* London: Heinemann.

Murphy, P. 1985. *Tourism: A Community Approach.* London: Routledge.

Owen, R.E. 1991. "Strategies for sustainable tourism". Paper presented at International Conference on Tourism Development, Trends and Prospects in the 90s. 16 September, Kuala Lumpur.

Pigram, J. 1990. "Sustainable tourism, policy considerations". *Journal of Tourism Studies* 2: 2-9.

Ruschmann, D.V.M. 1992. "Ecological tourism in Brazil". *Tourism Management* (March): 125-28.

*Travel Trade Gazette.* 1992a. "Jamaica". (30 January): 80-84.

*Travel Trade Gazette.* 1992b. "Caribbean report". (6 February): 39-44.

*Travel Trade Gazette.* 1992c. "Caribbean report". (14 May): 46-52.

*Travel Trade Gazette.* 1993. "Caribbean report". (4 February): 33.

*Travel Trade Weekly.* 1992. "Caribbean close-up". (4 March): 47-48.

Wheeller, B. 1991. "Tourism's troubled times". *Tourism Management* (June): 91-96.

Wheeller, B. 1992a. "Is progressive tourism appropriate?". *Tourism Management* (March): 104-05.

Wheeller, B. 1992b. "New wave tourism". *Insights* (May): 41-43.

World Commission on Environment and Development. 1987. *Our Common Future* (Brundtland Report). Oxford: Oxford University Press.

Wood, K., & S. House. 1991. *The Good Tourist.* London: Mandarin.

Chapter 6

# Tourism Development in Small Islands: St Maarten/ St Martin and Bermuda

## Klaus de Albuquerque and Jerome L. McElroy

## Introduction

In several earlier papers [McElroy & de Albuquerque 1991; 1992] it was argued that the current mass market style of tourism being pursued in many small Caribbean islands (less than 300,000 population and 800km$^2$) is not sustainable in the long run. First, there is a structural disequilibrium between the open, large-scale throughput nature of the international tourism economy and the closed, fragile, insular ecosystem [McElroy, 1975]. To maximize their short-term profits, heavily invested international hotel chains, resort developers, airlines, cruise lines, and tour operators promote the kind of high volume, high density tourism that threatens the very natural amenity base that attracts the tourist in the first place.

Second, island policy makers are often captive of the psychology of annually rising visitor volumes, and unaware or uninterested in the long-term consequences of aggressive short-term tourism promotion. This is partly due to the fact that the benefit-cost sequence of tourism impacts provide poor signals for effective long-range policy making. While the direct foreign exchange and employment benefits of visitor spending are quite real and visible in the short run, the environmental, economic and sociocultural costs accumulate slowly and generally only become clearly apparent long after costly major infrastructure and large development projects have been completed [Stough & Feldman 1982].

Third, tourism is a dynamic socio-economic and physical process that is not well understood [Dann & Cohen 1991]. As a result, tourism research is often uneven in quality and an imperfect guide for designing long-term strategies for sustainability [Dann 1988]. There is as yet no universally accepted model of tourism development, although the concept of *resort cycles* or the *tourism destination life cycle model*, as we have chosen to call it, comes closest to this.

The most thoroughgoing and oft-quoted model of the evolution of a tourist destination is Butler's [l980] resort cycle formulation, wherein resorts pass through a series of predictable stages from low to high tourism density along an S-shaped curve (see Figure 6.1). Patterned loosely after the product life cycle concept, the stages are as follows:

(a) an initial *exploration stage,* characterized by small numbers of more adventurous tourists;

(b) an *involvement* stage, with more visitors and with locals providing facilities specifically for tourists;

(c) a *development stage,* characterized by rapid growth in visitor arrivals, accommodation, and the heavy penetration of the industry by outsiders;

(d) a *consolidation stage,* where the growth rate in arrivals declines but the numbers continue to increase, the number of total visitors often exceeds the resident population, and there is now some local opposition to tourism;

(e) a *stagnation stage,* where capacity levels have been reached, there is surplus bed capacity, and a heavy reliance on conventions and other forms of organized mass tourism; and

(f) a *decline stage,* where the resort becomes a "veritable tourist slum", visitor numbers decrease rapidly and many tourist facilities are converted to non-tourist use. A destination in decline may experience *rejuvenation,* but Butler suggests that this is a less likely outcome.

Wall [1982] notes that the resort cycle is not one cycle but many cycles because the types of visitors change over time [Cohen 1972], as do the residents' attitudes towards tourism [Doxey 1976], the origin of investment, and the resort landscape. In a recent empirical test of Butler's model, employing over a dozen indicators of tourism intensity, McElroy and de Albuquerque [1991] confirmed three basic life cycle stages for Caribbean small island tourism:

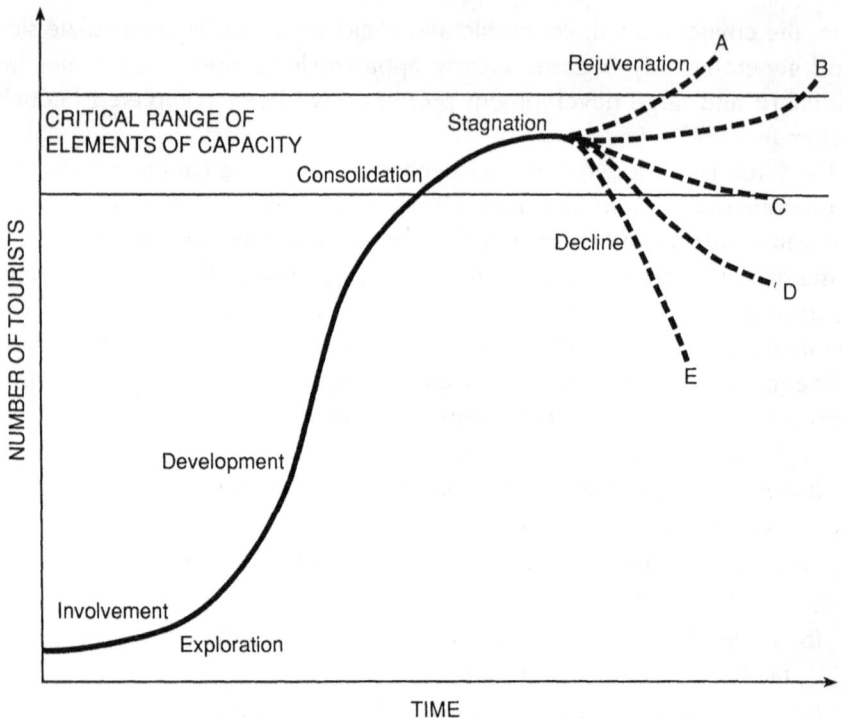

*Figure 6.1* Butler's model of hypothetical evolution of a tourist area
Source: *Butler [1980]*

(a) a newly emerging low density style (Stage I);

(b) an intermediate style characterized by rapid expansion in hotels and visitor arrivals (Stage II); and

(c) a mature stage typified by slow growth or no growth, high visitor densities and the prevalence of man-made attractions (Stage III).

## Scope of the Present Study

The present study focuses on two small islands, Bermuda and St Maarten (Dutch)/St Martin (French), located near the upper end of Butler's S-curve and identified by the authors [McElroy & de Albuquerque 1991; 1992; de Albuquerque & McElroy 1992] as "mature" (Stage III) destinations. It is destinations such as these that are at their most critical juncture, for as Butler [1980: 9] suggests "stagnation" is more likely to lead to "decline" than "rejuvenation" because the rejuvenation stage "will never be reached without a complete change in the attractions on which tourism is based".

Another possibility of sustaining tourism at manageable levels, not considered by Butler, also exists. However, this requires having in place the kinds of policies/planning mechanisms and the necessary local political will and community consensus to mitigate some of the more serious environmental and sociocultural costs of mass tourism. The weight of recent evidence suggests that achieving an environmentally and socioculturally compatible high impact style of tourism is exceedingly difficult at best, given the overgrowth propensities of international tourism.

The central concern in this paper is to explore the alternatives for Bermuda and St Maarten/St Martin suggested by the destination life cycle model. Of particular concern is the predicted decline stage of the model and how Bermuda and St Maarten/St Martin might best stave off the Caribbean Tourism Organization director's worst-case scenario — "derelict tourist facilities, littered beaches and a countryside and resident population that cannot return to its old way of life" [Holder 1988: 121].

## Bermuda and St Maarten/St Martin

Although Bermuda is in the Atlantic, it physically resembles a Caribbean island, and Bermudians have long had contact with the region, particularly with Jamaica and Barbados where many Bermudians were educated. Being further north, Bermuda experiences a much cooler winter and consequently its tourist season is from April through October.

Bermuda and St Maarten/St Martin have roughly similar size populations, with St Maarten/St Martin being larger in land area and having a lower population density (Table 6.1). Dutch St Maarten occupies the southern part of the island and is 41.4km$^2$, while French St Martin is larger and covers 54.4km$^2$. Bermuda's population has grown very slowly since 1970 (average annual rate of 0.6 percent). By contrast, St Maarten's population grew at an estimated average annual rate of 7.1 percent between 1972 and 1992. In fact, since 1972, the population of St Maarten/St Martin has more than tripled.

Bermuda is considerably more affluent, with a per capita Gross Domestic Product (GDP) more than double that of Dutch St Maarten. Both islands are very heavily tourism dependent with visitor spending contributing roughly 85 percent of GDP. As mature Caribbean small island destinations, both islands have roughly similar tourism styles — see McElroy & de Albuquerque [1992] — large hotels, high average daily visitor densities, shorter stays, and significant cruise ship traffic (Table 6.2). Bermuda has a much higher dependence on the North American market (92 percent of visitors) and experiences greater seasonality (Table 6.2). There are some noticeable differences in the tourism product offered by both islands. Bermuda is noted for

**73**

*Table 6.1*   Basic Indicators for Bermuda and St Maarten/St Martin

| Indicators | Bermuda | St Maarten/St Martin |
|---|---|---|
| Population (1991) | 58,460 | 60,739[a] |
| Land Area (km$^2$) | 55 | 96[b] |
| Population Density (per km) | 1,063 | 646 |
| Per Capita GDP (US$, 1989) | 23,000 | 10,893[c] |
| Average Annual Population Growth Rate (%, 1970-1990) | 0.1 | 7.1[c] |

Notes:
a: *Does not include illegal immigrants conservatively estimated at between 12,000-16,000. Population data for St Maarten are for 1992 and for St Martin, 1990.*

b: *Simpson's Bay Lagoon occupies 11.7km$^2$ thus effectively reducing the land area to 84km$^2$.*

c: *Data are for St Maarten only for 1972 to 1992. The population of St Martin grew by an average annual rate of 11.6 % between 1982 and 1990.*

Source :
*Bermuda Department of Statistics [1992b]*
*Caribbean Tourism Organization [1990]*
*INSEE [1992]*
*Netherlands Antilles Central Bureau of Statistics [1993]*

its manicured English country quaintness, its beautiful vistas, pink sand beaches, historical architecture, orderliness, quiet and safety, while St Maarten/St Martin is known for its duty-free shopping, its restaurants, and its casinos. In other words, Bermuda's attractions are primarily natural while St Maarten/St Martin's are mostly man-made.

## Tourism Development in Bermuda and St Maarten/St Martin

### Bermuda

Bermuda's tourism traces its genesis to 1884 when Princess Louise, the daughter of the Queen of England, visited the island and extolled its charm and beauty [Brown & Riley 1992]. Not long after, steamship service to New York was inaugurated and wealthy New Yorkers began monthly trips to "the English tropics" [Manning 1979]. Between the world wars, tourism growth spurted as a result of heavy resort investment by the local landed aristocracy. The various celebrities, writers and photographers that visited the island also proclaimed it as a visually beautiful and quaintly English insular society, creating an image of Bermuda as a vacation paradise for the well heeled. Over the years this image

Table 6.2   Selected Tourism Indicators

| Indicator | Bermuda | St Maarten/ St Martin |
|---|---|---|
| Average Annual Growth, 1980-1990 (%) | | |
| Total Visitor Arrivals | -1.1 | 12.5 |
| Air Arrivals (stayovers) | -1.3 | 10.1 |
| Cruise Arrivals (daytrippers) | -0.5 | 15.9 |
| Cruise Visitors as a % of Total Visitors (1990) | 20.6 | 47.7 |
| Per Capita Visitor Expenditure (US$, 1991) | 7,766.0 | 4,990.0 |
| Average Length of Stay (nights, 1987) | 6.5 | 4.8 |
| % Staying in Hotels (1989) | 68.0 | 66.0 |
| Average Annual % of Growth in Hotel Rooms (1980-1990)[a] | 0.7 | 7.1 |
| % Rooms in Large Hotels (100+ rooms, 1989) | 67.0 | 64.0 |
| No. of Hotels with 100+ Rooms (1989) | 7.0 | 8.0 |
| Hotel Occupancy Rates (%, 1988) | 60.5 | 55.0 |
| Stayover Market Share — % from US/Canada (1989) | 92.0 | 58.0 |
| Index of Seasonality (1986-1990)[b] | 1.4 | 1.19 |
| Average Daily Visitor Density per 1,000 pop. (1989)[c] | 132.0 | 128.0 |
| Average Daily Visitor Density per Sq. Km (1989)[d] | 141.0 | 82.0 |

Notes:
a. Data are for 1980-1989
b. The seasonality index for Bermuda was computed by taking the number of stayovers from April through September (Bermuda's high season — the season actually extends through October) divided by the numbers of stayovers during October through March. Seasonality for St Maarten was computed by taking the stayovers during the winter season (December through May) divided by stayovers during the summer (June-November).
c. [(Number of stayovers x average stay) + Number cruise]/(pop. x 365)
d. [(Number of stayovers x average stay) + Number cruise]/(km x 365)

Source
Bermuda Department of Statistics [1992a; 1992b]
Bermuda Department of Tourism [1991]
Caribbean Tourism Organization [1987; 1990; 1992]

was carefully cultivated, maintained and marketed, and it persists today in the eyes of most visitors and tourism industry personnel.

In the immediate post-World War II period, with the addition of five new steamship lines and the construction of a modern airport, Bermuda was positioned for a transition to mass market tourism. Figure 6.2 shows the growth in Bermuda's tourism from 1949 onwards. Declines in the number of tourists arriving by steamship were marked between 1949 and 1966, but these were paralleled by increases in the number of visitors by air and in the number of cruise ship passengers (daytrippers). Between 1949 and 1980 total visitor arrivals increased elevenfold as a result of large-scale foreign investment in hotels and expanded cruise ship traffic. The year 1980 remains the best year for

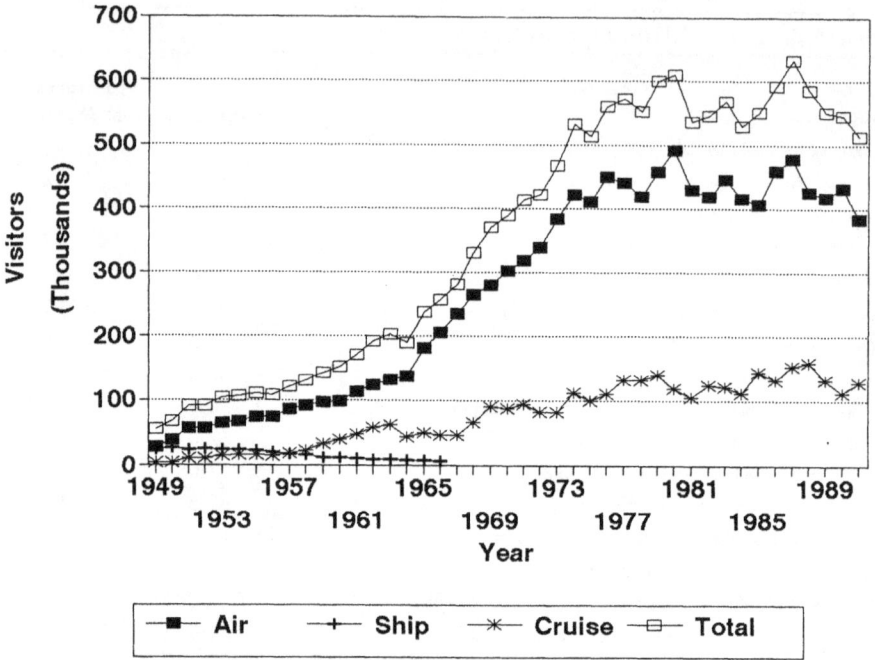

*Figure 6.2*   Bermuda visitor arrivals (1949 – 1991)

Note: *After 1966 ship arrivals were negligible and are repoted with cruise arrivals.*
Source: *Bermuda Deptartment of Tourism [1991]; Bermuda Department of Statistics [1992a]*

air arrivals and 1988 for cruise arrivals. With the exception of 1986 and 1987, air arrivals have declined, with 1991 arrivals down by more than 100,000 from the high in 1980 (Table 6.3).

Cruise arrivals have shown a downward trend since 1988. This downward trend in arrivals continued through 1992, with total arrivals at 505,503, down almost 8,000 from 1991 and 40,000 from 1990 [Bermuda Department of Statistics 1993]. Although a hotel phasing policy, which was in effect until 1993, limits capacity to 10,000 beds, hotel bed capacity peaked at 9,677 in 1987 and since then over 1,000 beds have been lost through the closure of 3 large resort hotels and a few guest-houses, and also because some housekeeping cottages and apartments have been taken off the short term visitor rental market for the more lucrative long-term, residential market. Employment in the hotel industry has also shown parallel declines, from highs of 5,634 and 5,515 respectively in 1980 and 1987 to a low of 4,048 in 1992 [Bermuda Department of Statistics 1993]. Interestingly, the percentage of non-Bermudians in the hotel industry rose from 21.7 percent in 1980 to 31.1 percent in 1989 [Bermuda Department of Tourism 1991].

Table 6.3   Bermuda Visitor Arrivals by Mode of Arrival, 1970-1991

**Visitor Arrivals**

| Year | Total[a] No. | % Change | Air (Stayovers) No. | % Change | Cruise (Daytrippers) No. | % Change |
|------|------|----------|------|----------|------|----------|
| 1970 | 387,742 | – | 301,604 | – | 86,138 | – |
| 1980 | 608,951 | 57.1 | 491,035 | 62.8 | 117,916 | 36.9 |
| 1981 | 534,705 | -12.2 | 429,260 | -12.6 | 105,445 | -10.6 |
| 1982 | 543,332 | 1.6 | 419,154 | -2.4 | 124,178 | 17.8 |
| 1983 | 566,410 | 4.2 | 445,564 | 6.3 | 120,846 | -2.7 |
| 1984 | 528,154 | -6.8 | 416,744 | -6.5 | 111,410 | -7.8 |
| 1985 | 548,664 | 3.9 | 405,761 | -2.6 | 142,903 | 28.3 |
| 1986 | 591,156 | 7.7 | 458,954 | 13.1 | 132,202 | -7.5 |
| 1987 | 630,296 | 6.6 | 476,859 | 3.9 | 153,437 | 16.1 |
| 1988 | 584,283 | -7.3 | 425,915 | -10.7 | 158,368 | 3.2 |
| 1989 | 548,134 | -6.2 | 416,812 | -2.1 | 131,322 | -17.1 |
| 1990 | 545,257 | -0.5 | 432,706 | 3.8 | 112,551 | -14.3 |
| 1991 | 512,197 | -6.1 | 384,046 | -11.2 | 128,151 | 13.9 |

Note:
a. Totals for 1980-1989 include passengers who arrived by cruise ship but departed by air.

Source :
Bermuda Department of Tourism [1991]; Bermuda Department of Statistics [4th Quarter 1991, 1992a].

## St Maarten/St Martin

Tourism in St Maarten/St Martin is, in comparison to Bermuda, relatively new. Published documentation of the industry's origins and evolution is essentially nonexistent. Although Samson [l989] traces St Maarten's tourism development to 1960 following the closure of Cuba, St Maarten did not take off until 1970. At this time St Maarten was in Butler's involvement stage or what McElroy and de Albuquerque [1991; 1992] have labelled a "low density emerging stage" (Stage I). The town of Philipsburg (St Maarten) had a few hotels — Pasanggrahan (St Maarten's oldest inn, formally the governor's guest-house), Seaview Hotel, Great Bay Beach Hotel, and several guest-houses. There were a couple of guest houses on Simpson's Bay, and a few small hotels and guest-houses in Marigot on the French side.

Risdon's Cafe, Risdon's Drive-In, and a Chinese restaurant on Back Street were the three most popular eating places for locals. For the small but growing number of tourists there were a few French restaurants in Marigot (Grand Case was still a sleepy village without a restaurant), an Italian restaurant and the West Indian Tavern, a Philipsburg landmark built in 1830 on the site of an old synagogue. Night-life was restricted to two clubs and a handful of bars, the most popular of which was Oraanje Cafe on Front Street in Philipsburg. St Maarten/St Martin was truly a friendly, uncrowded and relatively undeveloped island in 1970. It was dominated by a handful of local families, the most important of which were the Wathey family on the Dutch side and the Fleming family on the French side.

The construction of the 600 room Mullet Bay Resort in 1969/1970 represented a decisive turning-point in orienting the island's small-scale, informal, and loosely organized tourism industry onto a new growth trajectory. On the heels of Mullet Bay a number of new resorts appeared on Maho Bay, Cupecoy Bay, Bay Longue, Baie Rouge, Baie Orientale, Oyster Pond and Pointe Blanche. While some of these (La Samana, Oyster Pond Hotel) were decidedly upscale, Mullet Bay had set the trend towards tapping the mass market. By the end of the 1970s, hotel construction was at a breakneck pace and in a three-year period (1979-81) close to 600 new rooms were added. The decade of the 1980s ushered in a virtual free-for-all in tourism construction, lured by very generous tax and other concessions (for example, government assistance in financing projects, subsidized water and power). Any semblance of rational planning soon disappeared, the permitting process was routinely bypassed, and building codes were not enforced. Indeed, the absence of controls led to a construction boom unparalleled in the region.

To fuel the demand for construction workers and for workers in the tourist industry, large numbers of workers were recruited from other islands. With the exception of Antilleans (from Curacao, Aruba, Saba, and St Eustatius) and workers from elsewhere in the French West Indies, most of the workers were illegal. Some of these came from nearby English-speaking islands, but the vast majority were from the Dominican Republic and Haiti, two of the poorest countries in the region.

The number of hotel rooms in St Maarten more than doubled in the boom decade of the 1980s, from 1,670 in 1980 to over 3,500 in 1990, figures which actually understate activity on the island because they exclude the French side where much of the growth occurred after 1986. A considerable amount of the growth on both sides of the island was in the form of time shares/vacation ownership with the trend towards time-shares being set by Pelican Resort in the mid 1980s.

Table 6.4 shows the enormous growth in visitor arrivals between 1970 and 1990 that accompanied this burgeoning construction. Air arrivals more than doubled between 1970 and 1980 and increased by over 2.5 times between 1980 and 1990. After virtually 20 years of uninterrupted growth in air arrivals, 1991 saw a slight decline. The greatest growth occurred in cruise ship arrivals, which increased by almost 500 percent between 1980 and 1990. Lured by *de*

*Table 6.4*   St Maarten/St Martin Visitor Arrivals by Mode of Arrival, 1970-1991

| | | | **Visitor Arrivals**[a] | | | |
|---|---|---|---|---|---|---|
| | **Total** | | **Air (Stayovers)** | | **Cruise (Daytrippers)** | |
| **Year** | **No.** | **% Change** | **No.** | **% Change** | **No.** | **% Change** |
| 1970 | N/A | | 100,000 | | N/A | |
| 1980 | 310,125 | | 204,655 | 104.7 | 105,470 | |
| 1981 | 296,807 | -4.3 | 190,453 | -7.0 | 106,354 | 0.1 |
| 1982 | 306,217 | 3.2 | 213,352 | 12.0 | 92,865 | -12.7 |
| 1983 | 336,309 | 9.8 | 263,267 | 23.4 | 73,042 | -21.3 |
| 1984 | 430,275 | 27.9 | 317,575 | 20.6 | 112,700 | 54.3 |
| 1985 | 543,192 | 26.2 | 397,517 | 25.2 | 145,675 | 29.3 |
| 1986 | 710,101 | 30.7 | 396,208 | -0.3 | 313,893 | 115.5 |
| 1987 | 840,669 | 18.4 | 451,544 | 14.0 | 389,125 | 24.0 |
| 1988 | 930,666 | 10.7 | 479,740 | 6.2 | 450,926 | 15.9 |
| 1989 | 975,726 | 4.8 | 503,704 | 5.0 | 472,022 | 4.7 |
| 1990 | 1,079,345 | 10.6 | 564,371 | 12.0 | 514,974 | 9.1 |
| 1991 | 1,050,252 | -2.7 | 548,038 | -2.9 | 502,214 | -2.5 |

Note:
a. Data for 1980-1985 represent arrivals at hotels. Arrivals for St Maarten/St Martin are understated since they do not include the small numbers of arrivals at Grand Case airport and Marigot Harbour on the French side.

Source :
*Caribbean Tourism Organization [1987; 1990; 1992]*

*facto* duty-free shopping (there are no customs duties on St Maarten/St Martin) the number of cruise ship calls increased dramatically. In the short space of 10 years, St Maarten became the fourth most popular cruise ship destination in the Caribbean, after the region's traditional historical leaders, Puerto Rico, The Bahamas and the US Virgin Islands.

## Current Conditions

### Bermuda

Bermuda entered the 1980s with a very healthy tourism industry and with a reputation for providing a good quality product. However, by 1984 it became apparent, to use Butler's terminology, that tourism had stagnated and was in danger of declining. A reassessment of tourism policy led to a "changing of the guard at the Department of Tourism in 1984", the relaxing of some more stringent policies along with a new marketing campaign [Brown & Riley 1992].

The industry also began to examine its pricing policies and started offering its visitors more options. Increases in visitor arrivals in 1985 to 1987 would appear to have vindicated these policies, but these same years also saw parallel visitor increases in many Caribbean small island destinations.

The decline in tourism arrivals Bermuda has experienced since 1987 is quite perplexing in light of the high level of satisfaction visitors to Bermuda have registered in periodic exit surveys. In 1989, 62 percent of the visitors rated the island as one of the best possible vacation destinations and 73 percent said they were likely to revisit in the next two years, with these two figures being at their highest levels since 1980 [Bermuda Department of Tourism 1991]. Actual repeat visitation stood at 43 percent in 1989, an enviable level in comparison to other island destinations and the highest level since 1980. The only significant negative comment charted in the exit surveys concerned the high cost of a Bermuda vacation (up from 8 percent in 1980 to 37 percent in 1989). Concerned about the perception of Bermuda as an expensive destination, the Department of Tourism commissioned a major study to determine Bermuda's comparative position in terms of perceptions of the value of its tourism product. Predictably, the study uncovered results that were similar to those the exit surveys had been charting for years. Visitors rated the overall Bermuda vacation experience very highly, but there were some concerns about price. This sparked off an intense debate in Bermuda tourism circles concerning the whole price-value issue. Department of Tourism officials cautioned the industry to be more flexible and mindful of "value". Industry leaders countered that it was virtually impossible to lower prices in a high import-high operating cost environment, and that most of the major hotels had been operating in the red since 1987.

In a spirit of cooperation, the Government of Bermuda offered tax relief to those hotels wishing to refurbish their properties to bring them up to international standards. In addition, the Government joined together with the industry in a cooperative promotional programme (*Bermuda Breaks*) centring on value. Bermuda College also joined the effort to revitalize tourism by establishing a Centre for Tourism Research and Innovation in the Faculty of Hotel and Business Administration. One of the first activities of this new Centre was the hosting of the First Island Tourism International Forum (May 1992) centring on price-value issues in the 1990s.

The debate about price-value issues flies in the face of Bermuda's carefully cultivated image and its longstanding international identity as an upscale destination. The conventional wisdom holds that the kind of visitors Bermuda has attracted, and seeks to continue to attract, were/are price inelastic. In 1989, 70 percent of these visitors were college graduates, 74 percent of the household heads were in white collar occupations, and 61 percent of the visitor households had incomes over US$50,000, a visitor profile that would be the envy of any small island destination.

The Department of Tourism remains confident that Bermuda has a superb product and that tourism will turn up in a year's time. Rather than turning to deep discounting to promote more visitation volume, Bermuda is stressing value through more creative packaging (such as, shorter stay packages, a few all-inclusives, discounts for families with children) and has embarked on an aggressive marketing programme stressing the affordability of a Bermuda vacation and the unique quality of experience. The short-term goal is to get stayovers back to the 450,000 level and to try for a modest increase in the length of stay, while maintaining the island's bed capacity at 8,500, 9 percent lower than it was in 1980 [Brown & Riley 1992].

## St Maarten/St Martin

In 1991, St Maarten/St Martin experienced the first decline in both air and cruise arrivals since 1981. Stayovers fell 3 percent, including a 10 percent drop in winter arrivals, while cruise ship visitors fell 2.5 percent. While this may be a temporary aberration in response to the recession in the North American economy, there are obvious and abundant signs that the island's tourism economy is less healthy than the rosy picture painted in promotional brochures and investment literature. Together they suggest that the territory may be on the threshold of a new stage in the destination life cycle.

Between 1980 and 1988 the economy of St Maarten/St Martin grew at an unprecedented rate of 12 percent per annum (authors' estimate) and this boom was accompanied by routine annual budget and trade surpluses. By the end of the decade the economy had slowed considerably. Government (St Maarten) tax and non-tax revenues declined in 1989 and 1990. In 1991 and 1992, the Government of St Maarten desperately tried to improve its revenue collection by hiring more auditors and auditing a large number of hotels, restaurants, duty-free shops and other tourist related enterprises. In 1989, the St Maarten budget deficit was estimated at US$16.6 million and it has continued to grow. The balance of payments also deteriorated from a surplus of US$24.7 million in 1988 to a deficit of US$42.7 million in 1989 [*St Maarten Investor's Guide* 1990].

The contraction in the economy is partly explained by the all too familiar changes being experienced in St Maarten/St Martin's tourism industry. Both the private and public sector invested heavily in the industry in the 1980s. Predictably, growth in visitor accommodation far outstripped projected annual visitor arrivals resulting in a lot of excess capacity. As a direct result, average hotel occupancy (and profitability) plummeted. Between 1981 and 1988 the occupancy rate dropped from 77 percent to 55 percent [Caribbean Tourism Organization 1987; 1990]. To address this problem hotels began to severely discount rooms to tour operators. As a result most of the rooms were pre-sold in the major origin markets. To recover lost revenue the industry was forced to attract greater numbers of low-spending tourists on package tours. This "rate" strategy has not been successful. Deep discounting has led to the closure of a number of hotels, most significantly St Maarten Beach Club and the 650 room Maho Beach Hotel and Casino.

The number of hotel and business closures and the recycling of hotel properties that has occurred since 1987 has had a depressive effect on the investment climate and does not augur well for an early upturn in visitors and construction activity. The closure of the St Maarten landmark restaurant, the West Indian Tavern, and the opening of a "Subway" sandwich shop may also represent harbingers of things to come. Short-staying, low spending tourists have exerted, and are continuing to exert, a downward pressure on prices in all tourist related enterprises from car rentals to restaurants. The ubiquitous North American fast food chains are now competing for the tourist dollar alongside expensive French restaurants. There is a rush to advertise the lowest "happy hour" and T-shirt prices, and handbills/flyers litter the island. Philipsburg now has its complement of touts advertising low duty free prices and cheap food, and coaxing visitors into establishments. Parts of the island are taking on the appearance of the "veritable tourist slum" in Butler's predicted decline stage.

Current growth in hotel rooms is far off the projected growth of 7 percent per annum until 1995, when it was anticipated that the Dutch side alone would have 5,400 rooms [St Maarten Investor's Guide 1990]. In fact, with the closure of two major hotels, the number of rooms on the Dutch side has declined from an estimated 3,600 in 1989 to an estimated 3,000 in 1992. The French side, which experienced a somewhat later boom in hotel construction, is also seeing a considerable slowdown in activity. The precarious financial position of many hotels has led to a general decline in accommodation standards and in the condition of buildings and grounds, with many properties sorely in need of refurbishing and proper maintenance.

This decapitalization in the private sector has its public parallel. Government investment in the infrastructure has not kept up with visitor and resident demand for services. Parking is a major problem in both Philipsburg and Marigot, and on heavy cruise ship days traffic comes to a virtual standstill in Philipsburg. With close to 30,000 automobiles on the island, one for every two persons, the normal 15-minute trip from Philipsburg to Juliana Airport can extend to an hour during periods of heavy traffic, and the 25-minute trip from Philipsburg to Marigot to an hour and a half. Despite recent heavy investment in desalinization plants, water and electricity are both in short supply. Power outages are a normal occurrence (during a 4-month period in 1992 there were almost daily outages) and the public water system has experienced frequent shutdowns, low pressure and excessive turbidity. The visitor to Juliana International Airport, the second busiest in the region after San Juan, is often greeted by toilets that do not flush and badly discoloured water flowing through the taps.

The explosive growth fuelled by tourism has produced other damaging socio-economic and environmental costs familiar to other small, rapidly developing and overrun tropical island destinations. Crime has become endemic in an island which was virtually crime free in the 1960s and early 1970s. Burglar bars and iron gates are everywhere visible. The security guard business has mushroomed and many commercial and residential properties are posted with guard dog signs. St Maarten's more expensive residential areas for the rich and famous have become virtual enclaves with gates and private security forces patrolling 24 hours. Almost all rental cars have signs prominently displayed in their windows warning renters not to lock their valuables in the car (to prevent the costly replacement of broken car windows).

As a regional growth pole in the 1980s, St Maarten/St Martin attracted a lot of migrant labourers. Initially the demand for labour was met by Antilleans from the Dutch Leeward Islands (Curaçao and Aruba) who could enter St Maarten freely, and by Guadeloupians and Martiniquians who similarly had no restrictions entering French St Martin. However, as burgeoning hotel and other tourist related construction took off, large numbers of temporary workers from Haiti and the Dominican Republic were permitted to enter the island in a movement very reminiscent of the 1960s migration of Haitians to The Bahamas and Kittitians and Antiguans to the US Virgin Islands [de Albuquerque & McElroy 1982; McElroy & de Albuquerque 1988]. Most often without legal status and still considered to be temporary workers, Haitians and Dominicans live on the margins of the island economy and society. Relegated to poorly paid service jobs in the tourist industry (for example, maids, gardeners, janitors), and unable to afford the tourism related high rental prices, or to send their children to the various private schools, they have created mini-ghettos in places like Cole Bay, Over the Pond, and Marigot. These dilapidated urban fringe settlements look, smell, and sound remarkably like parts of Port au Prince or Santo Domingo.

Most of the small bars, clubs and shanty restaurants that have sprung up all over the island, have Dominican women, euphemistically referred to as "hostesses" in the region, in their employ. These structures, along with derelict cars, litter, uncleared brush, and the generally haphazard sprawl of development, give the island a run-down look that is quite at odds with the image portrayed in the promotional literature. Signs of the absence of any kind of controls or semblance of planning in the 1980s are apparent. These include improperly sited buildings, extensive clear cutting of vegetation, hillside and beach erosion, developments encroaching on beaches and lagoons, poor quality materials and inadequate construction, poorly designed and constructed access roads, improper sewage discharge, extensive marine and other pollution in Simpson's Bay, Great Bay and Marigot.

In a pattern very reminiscent of other mature small island destinations (such as, New Providence and St Thomas) the degradation of the natural environment has been accompanied by an increasing emphasis on the built-up environment with its standard visitor amusements — casinos, duty-free shopping, marinas, cabarets, ice capades, discotheques, falconry demonstrations, and a tiny zoo and botanical garden featuring mostly imported animals and plants and hardly any of the rapidly disappearing local fauna and flora. As a result, even to the most casual observer, St Maarten/ St Martin appears to be fast approaching the point where its "imported artificial facilities" have resulted in its resort image being increasingly "divorced from its geographic environment" [Butler 1980: 8].

## The Resort-Destination Life Cycle and the Future Prospects for Bermuda and St Maarten/St Martin

### Bermuda

As indicated earlier, Bermuda's Tourism Department officials and industry leaders are confident that the island will rebound from the current North American recession and return by the mid 1990s to sustainable levels of roughly 450,000 stayovers and 130,000 cruise arrivals annually. Although there is recognition that increased flexibility will be required to sell the Bermuda tourism product in a market where upscale visitors are more adventurous and have considerably more choices, there is general consensus that the destination enjoys its traditional international visibility and that the Bermudian vacation experience still retains its distinction of high quality among its competitors. Indeed, it is institutionally understood that the charm of Bermuda lies not in reflexively copying some preordained international standard of visitor comfort, but in maintaining some of its quaint style (for example, jackets and ties with Bermuda shorts) and in actively determining the kind of tourism experience visitors to the island should receive.

The soundness and projected sustainability of Bermuda's tourism is not fortuitous, but the result of careful planning and a high degree of local awareness of the costs/benefits of tourism. During the 1970s and early 1980s when the effects of visitor and resident crowding began to be felt, efforts were launched to promote more sustainable development by controlling visitor densities, limiting the number of vehicles on the island, and enacting and strictly ´enforcing ordinances designed to protect the fragile insular environment. In tourism terminology, Bermuda embarked upon a "soft tourism policy", emphasizing visual quality, the maintenance of natural and cultural amenities, quiet and safety, and encouraged widespread community awareness and support to facilitate these goals.

Specific ordinances were enacted preventing development that would disturb special natural vistas, open spaces and delicate areas rich in species diversity and historical memory. In addition, there are detailed and enforced regulations concerning the design and construction (for example, use of natural local materials) of tourist and residential facilities to preserve the old world ambience/colonial architectural flavour. There are also specific guidelines for residential landscaping and retaining endemic vegetation.

Most importantly, the impetus and direction for change came from strong citizen environmental awareness and widespread popular support for tough planning regulations. A 1988 survey concerning resident attitudes towards the growth environment trade-off, conducted during the Department of Planning's highly successful exhibition (*Bermuda 2000: The Changing Face of an Island*) revealed the depth of this support. Ninety-four percent of the respondents were "concerned" or "very concerned" that growth had resulted in a loss in the island's "environmental quality and attractiveness" [Bermuda Department of Planning 1990]. Nearly 90 percent felt Bermuda's physical appearance was "extremely important" not only for sustainable tourism but also for their own quality of life. Over four-fifths felt Bermuda was suffering from visitor saturation and respondents showed very little support for new hotels, cottage colonies or more cruise ships. Remarkably, almost 50 percent were prepared to accept some reduction in their standard of living to preserve the natural physical quality and pace of traditional Bermudian life.

## St Maarten/St Martin

The long-term prospects for St Maarten/St Martin appear much less promising than Bermuda. Although not quite fully in the decline stage of Butler's model, there are some very visible indications that the current stagnation is pushing the island in this direction. Both length of stay and per capita visitor expenditure have declined. Low-spending daytrippers (mostly cruise passengers) are becoming an increasingly more important element in the island's tourism. The number of hotel rooms has declined and hotel construction has come to a virtual standstill. In addition, property turnover is high as tourist facilities are constantly being recycled, with some being converted to non-tourist use, a shift that Butler [1980:9] noted would characterize the decline stage. To accelerate property recycling, the Dutch side is actively recruiting retirees (North American and European), another of Butler's indicators presaging the decline stage, by offering tax concessions in exchange for a minimum real estate investment of US$135,000 and the employment of one Antillean for a minimum of 30 hours a week.

While presently it is uncertain whether tourism's current stagnation will draw St Maarten/St Martin inevitably into the decline stage, the authors believe that a problematic long-term process has begun, of gradually intensifying financial, social, and ecological difficulties that sharply differentiate the industry's malaise today from its past growth trajectory. Further, it is believed that this process will be progressive and subtle and not necessarily signalled by a decline in visitor volumes. In fact, given the remarkable growth (10 percent per annum) in cruise ship traffic in the region, the authors expect cruise ship arrivals to increase, especially given the impending completion of the new cruise terminal in St Maarten. However, St Maarten will experience growing competition from other Caribbean destinations as they embark on port upgrading and build up their duty-free complexes. For example, the entry of The Bahamas into duty-free shopping on a select category of luxury items, as of January 1992, should also have some negative impacts on St Maarten/St Martin's cruise ship trade. Stayover arrivals may actually increase over the near term because of aggressive marketing of the island by tour operators and heavy discounting of airline seats and hotel rooms. The recent entry of Key Airlines, a charter airline, into the St Maarten/St Martin market and plans for the opening of an all-inclusive Jack Tar Resort, signal the continuation of the discount strategy and the entrenchment of pre-paid package tourism. However, this kind of tourism is often a lagged response to the declining lustre of a destination, with these tourists much more likely to be quickly lured on to the next "hot" destination with the best "bargain basement" prices.

In the absence of any belated attempts to introduce some measure of long-range planning on both sides of the island, there is little hope that the environmental degradation that has accompanied much of the growth can be arrested. All that both island governments can hope to do is mitigate some of the more serious effects of unplanned growth. Attempts at improving traffic flow in Marigot are steps in the right direction, but they must be accompanied by serious discussions about limiting the number of vehicles on the island. However, policy makers on the local island councils are not particularly forward-looking. Being the prime beneficiaries of the recent growth, they are locked into a trajectory of trying to maximize short-run tourism receipts by increasing visitor volumes while, unfortunately, social dysfunctions mount and ecological thresholds are violated.

# Conclusion

Given the fragile nature of the ecology, economy and society of small tropical islands and their propensity to promote large-scale mass tourism with its seeming inevitable life cycle dynamic towards environmental decline, Bermuda's comprehensive planning to control visitor densities and preserve its natural and cultural heritage, and target upscale visitors assures the island some measure of sustainable tourism development. In addition, Bermuda provides an example of a mature, long-standing tourism industry wholly integrated into the island society and an exception to Butler's prognosis of inevitable decline. In this same sense, Bermuda thus represents a model for other small island tourist destinations threatened with overrun.

In contrast, recent developments in St Maarten/St Martin seem more consistent with the contours of the "stagnation" and incipient "decline" phases of the life cycle. Unless local tourism policy is significantly redirected away from the traditional short-run focus on promoting annually higher visitor counts, towards the longer term goals of maximizing asset quality, visitor stay, and net visitor expenditure, future prospects seem bleak. Violating insular carrying capacities cannot continue ad infinitum without visibly damaging the destination's appeal and leaving behind resort relics of the past. Whatever the outcome, it is hoped that as the growth-versus-environment debate is played out across the Caribbean — as both increasing regional awareness and the dynamics of the life cycle predict — the experiences of both Bermuda and St Maarten/St Martin will be instructive.

# Postscript

In early 1993, because of continuing problems of mismanagement and widespread corruption in St Maarten, the Dutch side was put under "Higher Supervision" (an Effective Management Group was installed) from Curaçao. On 8 March 1993, a group of community activists calling themselves "United St Maarten Organizations and Concerned Citizens" began a popular strike action and put up road blocks throughout the Dutch side. This led to the cancellation of cruise ship calls and numerous scheduled flights, and the closure of most businesses in Philipsburg. The leaders of the action demanded the resignation of the Island and Executive Councils, the firing of GEBE (electricity and water company) management and board, the calling of new elections, and the lifting of "Higher Supervision". Troops were called in from Curaçao and the action ended peacefully on March 9 after the release of four community activists who had been detained earlier. St Maarten returned to normal on March 10. Since then the Effective Management Group has been quietly working to uncover the widespread bribery and pay-offs, much of it related to tourism development, and to remove incompetent public officials. It has been aided in its efforts by a citizen's watchdog group called "People Committed to Inform".

The strike action and the continued exposé of corruption in St Maarten has further tarnished the island's image. Cruise ship visitor figures, down by 32,000 in 1992 over 1991, continued to decline in the first quarter of 1993 [St Maarten Tourist Bureau 1993, pers. comm.]. In addition, the loss of Key Airlines (due to bankruptcy) in January 1993 had a significant impact on the winter season. The island will certainly weather these setbacks, but the long-term prospects look dim, unless it can muster the political will and community consensus to control and reverse some of the more adverse impacts of uncontrolled tourism development.

## References

Bermuda Department of Planning. 1990. "Visual quality in Bermuda". Discussion Paper No. 6. Hamilton.

Bermuda Department of Statistics. 1992a. *Quarterly Bulletin of Statistics.* 1st Quarter 1992. Hamilton.

Bermuda Department of Statistics. 1992b. *The 1991 Census of Population and Housing: An Executive Report.* Census Office. Hamilton.

Bermuda Department of Statistics. 1993. *Quarterly Bulletin of Statistics.* 4th Quarter (1992). Hamilton.

Bermuda Department of Tourism. 1991. *A Statistical Review of the Years 1980-1989.* Hamilton.

Brown, C., Walton Riley, & Cordell W. Riley. 1992. "The determinants of value in a Bermuda vacation: the good, the bad and the possibilities". Paper presented at the First Island Tourism International Forum, Bermuda College, May 17-20.

Butler, R.W. 1980. "The concept of the tourist area cycle of evolution: implications for management of resources". *Canadian Geographer* 24: 5-12.

Caribbean Tourism Organization. 1987. *Caribbean Tourism Statistical Report, 1986.* ChristChurch, Barbados.

Caribbean Tourism Organization. 1990. *Caribbean Tourism Statistical Report, 1989.* ChristChurch, Barbados.

Caribbean Tourism Organization. 1992. *Caribbean Tourism Statistical Report, 1991.* ChristChurch, Barbados.

Cohen, E. 1972. "Towards a sociology of international tourism". *Social Research* 39: 164-82.

Dann, G. 1988 "Tourism research in the Caribbean: an evaluation". *Leisure Studies* 10: 261-80.

Dann, G., & E. Cohen. 1991. "Sociology and tourism". *Annals of Tourism Research* 18: 155-69.

de Albuquerque, K., & J. McElroy. 1982. "West Indian migration to the United States Virgin Islands: demographic impacts and socio-economic consequences". *International Migration Review* 16: 61-101.

de Albuquerque, K., & J. McElroy. 1992. "Caribbean small island tourism styles and sustainable strategies". *Environmental Management* 16: 619-32.

Doxey, G.V. 1976. "When enough's enough: the natives are restless in old Niagara". *Heritage Canada* 2: 26-27.

*INSEE.* 1992. "Recensement de la population 1990". Pointe-à-Pitre, Guadeloupe.

Holder, J. 1988. "Pattern and impact of tourism in the environment of the Caribbean". *Tourism Management* 9: 119-27.

Manning, F. 1979. "Tourism and Bermuda's black clubs: a case of cultural revitalization". In *Tourism: Passport to Development*, edited by E. deKadt, pp 157-76. New York: Oxford University Press.

McElroy, J. 1975. "Tourist economy and island environment: an overview of structural disequilibrium". *Caribbean Educational Bulletin* 2: 40-58.

McElroy, J., & K. de Albuquerque. 1988. "The migration transition in small northern and eastern Caribbean States". *International Migration Review* 22: 30-58.

McElroy, J., & K. de Albuquerque. 1991. "Tourism Styles and Policy Responses in the Open Economy-Closed Environment Context". In *Caribbean Ecology and Economics,* edited by N. Girvan & D. Simmons, pp 143-64. Barbados: Caribbean Conservation Association.

McElroy, J., & K. de Albuquerque. 1992. "An integrated sustainable ecotourism for small Caribbean islands". Bloomington, Indiana: Indiana Center on Global Change and World Peace. Occasional Paper No. 8.

Netherlands Antilles Central Bureau of Statistics. 1993. "Preliminary results of the 1992 population census of Netherlands Antilles". Willemstad, Curaçao.

Samson, M.L. 1989. "The Netherlands Antilles". In *Urbanization, Planning and Development in the Caribbean,* edited by R.B. Potter, pp161-80. London: Mansell.

*St Maarten Investor's Guide.* 1990. Philipsburg, St Maarten: Beacon Capital Ventures.

Stough, R., & M. Feldman. 1982. "Tourist attraction development modeling: public sector policy and management". *Review of Regional Studies* 12: 22-39.

Wall, G. 1982. "Cycles and capacity: incipient theory or conceptual contradiction?". *Tourism Management* 3: 188-92.

Chapter 7

# The Cost of Housing in a Tourist Economy: The US Virgin Islands

Frank L. Mills

## Introduction

The devastating hurricane which swept through the Virgin Islands of the United States in September 1989 had a marked effect on this popular tourist destination. First, about 90 percent of the improved property in the island of St Croix was damaged, and about 50 percent in both the islands of St Thomas and St John suffered varying degrees of damage. Second, the destruction of hotels forced a reduction in the tourist trade, particularly in St Croix. The trade also suffered from the negative media reports circulated on the United States mainland in relation to the arrival of National Guard troops which were sent in to restore calm after initial rioting over food supplies. Third, economic growth slowed in response to the reduced tourist traffic. Further, many American residents immediately returned to the mainland, while others migrated to the Virgin Islands in search of jobs related to the reconstruction of the housing industry and to the islands in general.

Immediately after Hurricane Hugo in 1989, there was considerable activity in the construction industry as property owners in all three islands rushed to rebuild or repair homes that were destroyed or damaged. The short supply of labour and building materials had the effect of drastically increasing costs in a market in which they were already relatively high. These conditions in the housing market in the post-Hugo months served to focus attention once again on the relative shortage of affordable housing in the Virgin Islands. Residents in the lowest income brackets were worse off because many public housing units were destroyed or damaged and the local government could not readily find alternative shelter. Middle income families occupying rental housing units continued to strain at the relatively high cost of rent, as most could not afford to purchase a home. Despite the apparent shortage of housing that exists, about 20 percent of the housing stock was still listed as vacant.

This study presents the root causes of the housing shortage, attempts to explain the high property values and rent, and explores efforts to establish a rational housing policy to meet the needs of residents. It does so by describing the conditions which led to the demand for more housing units, then presents views on the characteristics of owner occupancy and renter occupancy. It also focuses attention on the anomaly of the relatively high proportion of vacant units that exist in the midst of a shortage of affordable housing. Associated with these conditions are the high cost of rent and the high value of homes. An explanation for this situation is sought through regression analysis. Finally, the latest attempts by the government to provide low and moderate income housing for more residents through an affordable housing policy, in response to the latest crisis in the housing industry, are considered.

## Background

The United States Virgin Islands was discovered as a tourist mecca after the Cuban Revolution of the 1950s, and as American tourists began to seek alternative Caribbean destinations. American tourists began to visit the islands in a steady stream which continues to the present day. Year round sunshine, sparkling blue waters, coral reefs and magnificent white sand beaches attracted hordes of holiday seekers arriving by air to these unspoiled islands. St Croix, the largest of the three main islands, covers 84 square miles (218km$^2$), and is mostly flat. St Thomas is 28 square miles (73km$^2$) in size, and offers dramatic rugged mountains that rise sharply from the coast up to elevations of about 1,500 feet (457m). These steep hills and mountains provide spectacular views of azure waters surrounding numerous islands and cays. St John, 20 square miles (52km$^2$) in extent offers similar landscapes and seascapes to St Thomas. Compared to other Caribbean islands, the total area of 132 square miles (342km$^2$) is small. However, steep slopes ranging from 10° to 60° and the extensive metamorphic rocks which underlie the subsoil on St Thomas and St John have significant implications for housing.

The demand for overnight accommodation by tourists generated a need for the construction of hotel rooms and related facilities. The building boom which naturally followed this spurt in tourism quickly exhausted local supplies of construction labour and the islands turned to immigrants from the Eastern

Table 7.1    Selected Indicators of Economic Growth

| Indicators | 1960 | 1970 | 1980 | 1990 |
|---|---|---|---|---|
| Cruise ship passengers ('000) | 56 | 251 | 692 | 1,120 |
| Air arrivals ('000) | 124 | 573 | 526 | 695 |
| Number of hotel rooms | 1,397 | 3,424 | 3,457 | 3,575 |
| Tourist expenditures (US$M) | 24.8 | 104.5 | 222.0 | 516.0 |
| Number of telephones | 3,905 | 22,506 | 36,973 | na |
| Per capita income (US$) | 625 | 2,584 | 6,230 | 11,052 |

na - not available

Source :
Miller (1979) and the Bureau of Economic Research, Virgin Islands (1992)

Notes:
(1) the number of telephones entry given for 1980 is for 1978;
(2) per capital income given for 1990 is for 1989.

Caribbean to fill the immediate needs. As tourism expanded, more foreign immigrants were allowed in to fill available jobs, and many entered the islands illegally.

All economic indicators pointed to dramatic growth (Table 7.1). The number of cruise ship passengers increased from 56,000 in 1960 to 1.1 million by 1990. Total visitor arrivals rose from 185,000 to 1.3 million over the same time period, and their expenditure multiplied almost 10 times from US$24.8 million in 1960 to US$240 million in 1978. These growth figures are also reflected in the number of tourist hotel rooms that were built to accommodate the increasing size of the tourist trade. At the same time, per capita income improved considerably from US$625 in 1960 to US$11,052 in 1990.

Figure 7.1 shows that the total number of housing units followed the same upward path as the increase in population. The number of units increased from 20,814 in 1970 to 32,650 in 1980 to 39,290 in 1990. Further evidence of the recent growth in the housing stock is provided by the 1970 Census of Population and Housing. The census showed that 67 percent of the housing units in the Virgin Islands had been built after 1960, and 44 percent were built since 1965. Most of the building activity was the result of privately financed construction in response to economic gains, even though the public sector contributed some units between 1967 and 1970 [Virgin Islands Planning Office 1977: 3-17].

What the data in Figure 7.1 do not reveal, however, is that while in the early years of the decade of the 1970s the building boom of the 1960s continued, there was a decline in building from 1973 to 1977. The decline in construction was "attributed to several high cost components including land scarcity,

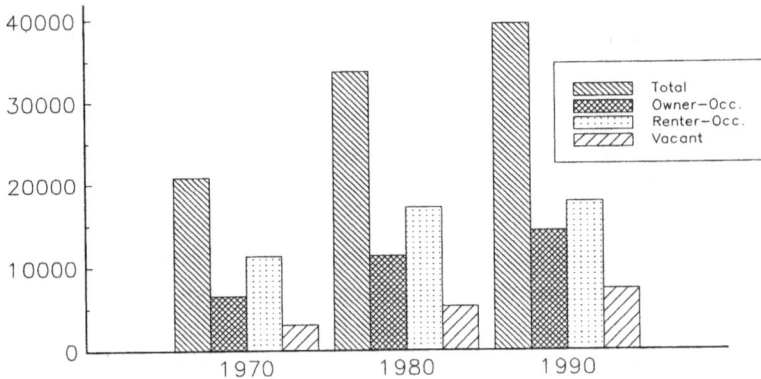

Figure 7.1  Tenure and vacancy of households

increased land costs, excessive rates of interest nation-wide, and rising costs of construction" [Virgin Islands Planning Office 1977:17]. Moreover, the Residential Construction Cost Index rose by 48 percent between 1970 and 1974. The mortgage market, restrained by the local statutory ceiling on interest rates, together with the storage of certain building materials, particularly structured steel, continued to affect the housing market in the 1980s. Even though about 20 percent of the housing stock was public low cost units, there was still a list of more than 1,000 applicants for entry to low cost public housing. Between 1970 and 1980, the total housing stock grew by 57 percent, whereas between 1980 and 1990 the growth rate dropped to 20 percent. Vacant units increased from 15.5 percent in 1980 to 18.5 percent in 1990.

Hurricane Hugo exacerbated the situation of scarcity by destroying some homes (which were not rebuilt), and it forced labour and construction costs up to a degree from which they have not been lowered. By 1990, statistics relating to both monthly rent and the resale value of homes had risen from their levels just prior to the hurricane. During this period, the average rent rose by more than 20 percent of pre-Hugo days, and the average resale value of owner occupied housing was US$161,000.

## Characteristics of the Housing Stock

### Limitations of the Data

The primary source of much of the data used below is the 1990 Virgin Islands Census of Population and Housing. The data were published in electronic form in Summary Tape File 1A (1991), and were issued in the following geographic hierarchical form: by territory, island, block numbering area (BNA) and finally by block group (BG). The BNA is the primary geographic unit of analysis in this study. Each BNA was designed to contain approximately 1,400 housing units. There were 16 BNAs on St Croix, 15 on St Thomas, and 2 on St John.

The data are subject to the common errors of most censuses. These include: not enumerating every household, not obtaining all required information, obtaining incorrect or inconsistent information, and recording information incorrectly. Further, errors could have occurred during review of enumerators' work by crew leaders or clerks, or during electronic processing. Information on vacant households or condominiums often came from neighbours and resident managers, and it may not always have been accurate.

Additional data were derived from a scientific telephone survey of households in the Virgin Islands [Mills 1991]. Housing units were contacted using the Waksberg [1978] procedure for random-digit dialling. It is estimated by the telephone company that about 89 percent of the households in the Virgin Islands have telephones. The margin of error for this survey was less than 5 percent. Additionally, the data from this survey are also subject to similar types of non-sampling errors mentioned above.

## Owner Occupied Housing

Of the total 39,290 housing units in the Virgin Islands in 1990, 36.3 percent were owner occupied; 45.2 percent were renter occupied; 12.9 percent were classified as seasonal/not occupied; 5.2 percent were vacant; and 0.5 percent were vacant for sale. The owner occupancy rate in the Virgin Islands in 1980 was 39.9 percent, and by 1990 that rate had grown to 44.6 percent (Table 7.2). However, this rate was much lower than the United States average of 64.2 percent. In the population at large, the percentages of black, white (mostly from the United States), and "other" residents are 77 percent, 14 percent, and 9 percent respectively. The table shows that in all racial groups in the Virgin Islands overall, the percentage of owner occupancy is less than 50 percent. Comparatively, however, a higher percentage of whites own homes than for any other single racial group. This is similar to the pattern in the United States where the ownership rate among whites is 67 percent [Devaney 1992].

The median value of owner occupied housing in 1990 was US$112,700. The lower and upper quartiles were US$76,500 and US$185,400 respectively. Value, as defined by the Census Bureau, is the owner's estimate of what their house and lot would sell for if they were up for sale. Comparatively, the Virgin Islands' median home value is noticeably higher than the equivalent national figure for the United States at US$79,100 [USBC 1992]. The Virgin Islands, however, is significantly below the 1990 median home value for Hawaii and

*Table 7.2*   Tenure of Housing Units, 1990

| Location | Total | Black | White | Other |
|---|---|---|---|---|
| **Total** | **14,272** | **9,967** | **2,897** | **1,408** |
| Virgin Islands (%) | | | | |
| Owner occupied | 44.6 | 43.3 | 47.3 | 49.1 |
| Renter occupied | 55.4 | 56.7 | 52.7 | 50.9 |
| St Croix (%) | | | | |
| Owner occupied | 48.3 | 47.4 | 49.1 | 51.7 |
| Renter occupied | 51.7 | 52.6 | 50.9 | 48.3 |
| St John (%) | | | | |
| Owner occupied | 45.4 | 47.1 | 43.9 | 12.5 |
| Renter occupied | 54.6 | 52.9 | 56.1 | 87.5 |
| St Thomas (%) | | | | |
| Owner occupied | 40.9 | 39.4 | 46.7 | 37.9 |
| Renter occupied | 59.1 | 60.6 | 53.3 | 62.1 |

California at US$245,300 and US$195,500 respectively. On the national scale, the Virgin Islands would rank below Maryland, ranked 10th with a median value of US$116,500 and above Delaware ranked 11th at US$100,100. If actual sales values of property were used, a different picture emerges. Table 7.3 shows prices over a 20-year period, which suggests that the manner in which the census data are presented obscures certain realities in the housing market in the Virgin Islands. It demonstrates, for example, that there are remarkable differences between the cost of homes in St Thomas and St John compared to St Croix. In St Thomas and St John, the average sale price of a home increased almost eightfold between 1970 and 1989, but in contrast did not quite quadruple in St Croix over the same time period. In 1989, the difference between average sale for a home in St Thomas and St John (US$226,062) and in St Croix (US$164,081) is about US$62,000. These sale prices appear to be much closer to reality than the census data suggest. While the number of homes sold over the period declined in St Thomas and St John and increased in St Croix, the number of condominium units sold more than doubled, and prices reflect the same remarkable increases within the 20-year period. It is significant to note that from 1980, the number of condominium units sold exceeded the number of homes sold in both St Thomas and St John and in St Croix.

It is argued below that the relatively high home value structure in the Virgin Islands places severe limitations on meeting the demand for home ownership

*Table 7.3*   Real Estate Sales, 1970–1989

| | 1970 | 1980 | 1989 |
|---|---|---|---|
| Homes Sold | | | |
| St Thomas/St John | 296 | 128 | 128 |
| St Croix | 182 | 189 | 129 |
| Average home sale price (US$) | | | |
| St Thomas/St. John | 30,259 | 115,547 | 226,062 |
| St Croix | 42,635 | 83,079 | 164,081 |
| Condominiums sold | | | |
| St Thomas/St John | 88 | 264 | 204 |
| St Croix | 236 | 111 | 182 |
| Average condominium price | | | |
| St Thomas/St John | 46,574 | 103,056 | 194,002 |
| St Croix | 46,985 | 65,725 | 182,481 |

Source: *Bureau of Economic Research, Virgin Islands [1992]*

of a large section of the population. This explains in part the slow upward pace of owner occupancy similar in proportion to that on the mainland United States.

**Renter Occupied Housing**

Among the three categories in the housing inventory of owner occupancy, renter occupancy and vacancy, renter occupancy showed the smallest numerical changes from 1980 to 1990; a mere 711 units (Figure 7.1). While the national renter occupancy rate for the United States was 35.8 percent in 1990, it was 55.4 percent in the Virgin Islands. Among blacks and whites in the Virgin Islands at large in 1990, proportionately more blacks were occupying rental units than were whites. The highest rental occupancy rate of 59.1 percent occurs on St Thomas and the lowest of 51.7 percent on St Croix (Table 7.2). In both islands, more blacks occupy rental units than do whites.

The median value of contract rent in the Virgin Islands in 1990 was US$323 [USBC 1991]. Contract rent is defined by the Census Bureau as the rent agreed to, or contracted for, regardless of any utilities or services that may be included. Lower and upper quartiles were US$176 and US$508 respectively in the Virgin Islands. By comparison, the US national figure for mainland rent was US$374 with Hawaii having the highest value at US$599 and US$561 for California.

The relatively low median rent of US$323 in the midst of well known high local market values for homes and monthly rent requires explanation. There was some suspicion at first concerning the accuracy of the monthly rent data that was reported by the Bureau of the Census. However, this figure was independently validated by a scientific telephone survey of households [Mills 1991]. An explanation lies partly in the large number of publicly subsidized housing units throughout the Virgin Islands and the great variability in the distribution of rent across the islands.

The first category of subsidized housing is Section 8 Leased Housing. This is a federally funded programme that is administered through the Department of Housing and Urban Development in Washington, DC. A total of 590 households in the islands benefit from this programme.

The other category is much larger and includes about 4,550 publicly supported low income family units and units for the elderly. However, Hurricane Hugo destroyed or damaged several hundred of these units in 1989. Occupants of these are classified into families which pay rent, families which pay no rent at all, and negative renters or families which received a stipend from the Virgin Islands Housing Authority. Of the total number of families in public housing in 1992, 2 percent were negative renters, 18 percent were paying zero rent, and 80 percent of the families paid up to a maximum of US$600 monthly. The median rent for paying families was US$193, and the lower and upper quartiles were US$92 and US$297 respectively.

However, when the data were disaggregated by block groups (BGs), another picture emerges. In BGs where there are public housing units for low income families, the median rent tends to be strongly influenced by the prevailing individual family rent. The lowest median rent recorded in one BG was US$79. In BGs where owner occupancy rate is high, rent determined by current market values tends to be very much higher. The highest median rent in a BG is US$1,001.

## Vacant Housing

One persistent question among potential home buyers and those in search of rental apartments is: why is it so difficult to find an affordable home that one can buy, or an affordable apartment to rent, when the number of vacant homes and apartments seems to be so high? An answer to this question will be attempted following the quantitative analysis below.

Figure 7.1 shows that the number of vacant units in the US Virgin Islands in 1990 was 7,270, or 14.7 percent of the housing stock. Figure 7.2, however, illustrates the classifications of vacant housing. Twenty-eight percent of the total vacant inventory was available for rent, 3 percent for sale, 16 percent already rented out or sold, and 11 percent was held for seasonal, recreational or occasional use. Almost half of the total (42 percent) fell into the category that includes units that were held for occupancy by caretakers or by owners for

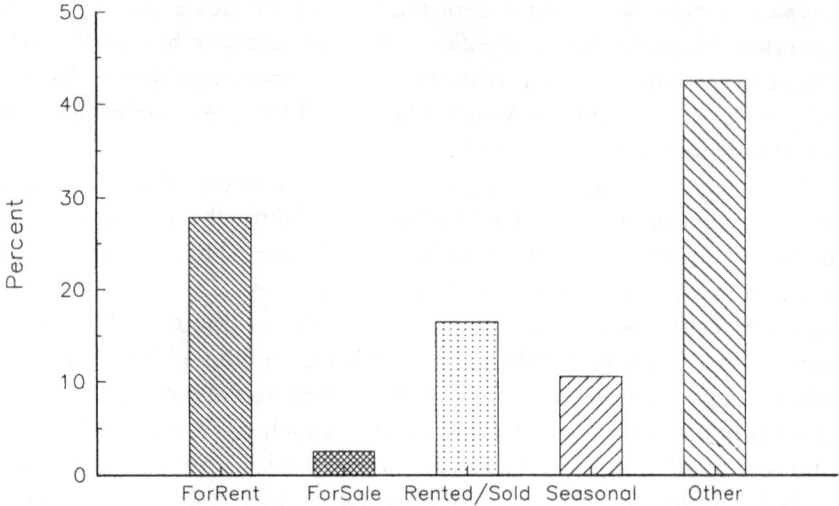

*Figure 7.2* Vacant housing inventory, 1990

personal reasons. It is quite likely that many of these other units could not be more appropriately classified because no one was available to provide the correct information to the enumerator.

Vacant housing units accounted for 11 percent of the housing inventory in the United States in 1990. National vacancy rates in 1989 were 7.1 percent in rental housing and 1.6 percent in home owner housing [Devaney 1992]. While the home owner vacancy rate of 1.6 percent in the United States was virtually unchanged between 1981 and 1989, it decreased from 1.8 percent in 1980 to 1.3 percent in the Virgin Islands in 1990. On the other hand, while the rental vacancy rate in the United States increased from 5 percent in 1980 to 7.1 percent in 1990, it decreased from 11.6 percent to 10.2 percent in 1990.

## The High Cost of Housing: Explanatory Models

One of the primary interests in this study is to explain the relatively high cost of rent to residents in this tourist economy. It was stated previously that the renter occupancy rate is considered high in the Virgin Islands, given that it is about 20 percentage points higher (55.4 percent) than it is for the United States generally (35.8 percent). The high rents which exist in the presence of a continuing shortage of affordable rental units would at first seem to be an anomaly because of the unusually large proportion of vacant housing units on the market. Economic theory would suggest that the relatively large supply of vacant units would act to keep rents low, but this is not the case.

A linear regression was utilized as an explanatory model in an effort to understand which variables substantively explain the structure of rents of occupied housing. The variable *median rent* is analysed first because it affects more than half of the householders. High *home value* is the other primary interest of focus in this paper and is analysed in a second regression model. An effort is also made to account for the situation wherein so many Virgin Islanders yearn to own their homes, yet even with a relatively high per capita income, it is not possible for a large segment of residents to do so. The regression model is also utilized in search of an explanation of high home values.

The variables selected for inclusion in the first model are *median rent* as the dependent variable and *owner occupancy rate, percent vacant-for-sale-only units,* and *percent of units used for seasonal or recreational use* as explanatory independent variables. The unit of observation is the census defined block numbering area (BNA) of about 1,400 households.

The rationale for including owner occupancy rate as an explanatory variable is that it is likely that in areas where owner occupancy is high, there is a greater effort to protect house values. Landlords might consider that high rent is an appropriate way of excluding tenants of low income who would be likely to create situations to make the neighbourhoods less attractive. In locations where owner occupancy is low, it is expected that land values will be low and rent will reflect this low income neighbourhood.

Vacant-for-sale-only units are likely to occur in residential neighbourhoods where land values are high, and thus rent will be high. The units here can be kept on the market indefinitely as they can be held for speculation with the knowledge that, ultimately, a well-to-do tourist will eventually purchase them. In a similar way, units held vacant for absentee owners who use them for seasonal and recreational purposes will occur in choice locations, and units will also probably be expensive. Rent will also reflect the quality of the neighbourhoods.

An obvious variable that is excluded from the regression model is household income, but these data are not yet available from the Bureau of the Census. However, the two variables which are related to vacancy capture, to some degree, this economic variable.

The second model regresses *median home values* on *median rent* and the percentage of whites who live in a BNA. The unit of observation is the median home value of owner occupied units in a BNA. The value is the respondent's estimate of how much the property (that is, the house and lot, the mobile home and lot, or the condominium unit) would sell if it were for sale [USBC 1991: B-150]. *Median rent* was defined above. The *percentage of whites* refers to that percentage of persons who identified themselves as white during the census.

The rationale for including *median rent* in this model is that in locations where rent in general is high, home values will also tend to be high. Similarly, we would expect to find low home values in areas where rent is low. The variable *percent whites* is included because whites tend to have higher household incomes and can thus afford more expensive homes. We expect that the higher the percentage of whites in a BNA, the higher the home values would tend to be.

## The Cost of Rent

The parameter estimates of the regression of *median rent* on *owner occupancy rate, vacant-for-sale units*, and *vacant for seasonal/recreational use* are shown in Table 7.4.

The estimate of the F-value confirms that the three variables do bear some relation to rent, and they explain a significant portion of the variation. The positive signs of the partial regression coefficients are as expected. That is, it is expected that BNAs with high *median rent* will also have relatively high *owner occupancy rates*, a high *percent of vacant-for-sale-only* units, and a high *percentage of units used for seasonal or recreational use*. The $R^2$ value of 71 percent indicates also that the 3 variables account for nearly three-quarters of the variation in rent. The *t* ratios and probability values support the claim that the explanatory variables all contribute substantively to the model. The standardized estimates of the regression coefficients impart relative importance to the influence of each of the variables on rents. Thus, they indicate that vacant units for sale exert more influence on the cost of rents in an area than do vacant units for seasonal use. They are almost of the same importance, and both much more influential than is the level of owner occupancy rate in the area.

Table 7.4   Regression Analysis of Median Rent on Owner Occupancy Rate, Vacant-for-Sale-Only Units and Seasonal-Recreational Units

| Median Rent | = 129.7 | +2.4 Owner-Occupier Rate | +26.6 Vacant Sale | +6.0 Seasonal/Recreational |
|---|---|---|---|---|
| Standard error | 43.0 | 0.9 | 5.1 | 1.2 |
| *t* ratio | 3.0 | 2.6 | 5.1 | 4.8 |
| Probability value | 0.0005 | 0.014 | 0.000 | 0.000 |
| Standardized estimate | | 0.272 | 0.536 | 0.492 |
| F – value | 23.4 | | | |
| Probability > F | 0.0001 | | | |
| $R^2$ | 0.708 | | | |

Substantively, for a one percent increase in the *vacant-for-sale* units in a BNA, the *median rent* will, on average, increase by about US$27. A one percent increase in the *vacant-for-seasonal-use* units will raise *median rent* on average by US$6, while a similar increase in owner occupancy rate will increase *median rent* by about US$2.

## The Value of Homes

The estimates for the second model of the regression of *home values* on *median rent* and *percent whites in the BNA* are presented in Table 7.5. The positive signs of the particular regression coefficients confirm that a BNA with a relatively high *median rent* and a high *percentage* of *whites* will most likely have a high *median home value*. The F and *t* ratio values indicate that the explanatory variables have meaning in the relationship, and the $R^2$ value suggest that two variables explain more than three-quarters of the variation in median home values. In addition, the standardized regression coefficients suggest that *median rent* is relatively more important in explaining *home values* than is the *percentage of whites* in the BNA.

The model indicates further that, on average, for each US$10 increase in *median rent* in an area, the *median home value* will increase by almost US$2,000. Further, for every 10 percent change in the *percentage of whites* in a BNA, *home value* will change by about US$8,500.

Table 7.5   Regression Analysis of Median Home Value on Median Rent and Percent White

**Median Home Value = 45,971 + 184 Median Rent + 846 Percent White**

| | | | |
|---|---|---|---|
| Standard error | 11,446.0 | 38.0 | 271.0 |
| t ratio | 4.0 | 4.8 | 3.1 |
| Probability value | 0.000 | 0.000 | 0.004 |
| Standardized estimate | | 0.581 | 0.374 |
| F – value | 54.4 | | |
| Probability > F | 0.0001 | | |
| $R^2$ | 0.784 | | |

# Explanation of the High Cost of Housing

In order to obtain a reasonable explanation of the high cost of housing in relation to the current high cost of rent and homes in the US Virgin Islands, it is necessary to put this condition in proper perspective. First, the economy of the territory in many ways reflects the effects of economic activities in the United States. Second, local government is limited by what it can do because of its political status with the federal government. Third, the relationship with the US Government sometimes allows it to participate in programmes that are beneficial to the territory.

Some of the conditions for the current crisis were precipitated at the federal level. While the housing industry in the Virgin Islands benefited from legislation passed by the Congress of the United States in 1974 "to provide a decent home and a suitable living environment for every American family" [Virgin Islands Planning Office 1977: 3-69], it is clear that the islands will receive less and less federal financial assistance in the foreseeable future. Between 1981 and 1986, direct expenditures of the Department of Housing and Urban Development decreased from US$32.2 billion to US$1.39 billion. The Tax Reform Act of 1986 has reduced the attractiveness of indirect expenditure programmes which have traditionally encouraged private sector investment through tax-exempt bond financing, tax write-offs, and the like. In the presence of this federal disengagement and in the absence of a sustained local effort to provide affordable housing, the demands of residents for decent homes have served to focus attention on the scarcity of homes in this market.

### The Rental Market

For families with moderate incomes (usually defined as a household whose income is between 80 percent and 120 percent of the median household income of the territory) or low incomes, (between 50 percent and 80 percent) the rental market in the US Virgin Islands is currently very tight. With the exception of federally subsidized housing projects prior to 1970, there is relatively little rental housing that has been provided for low and moderate income families. Data above showed that renter occupied housing increased by only 711 units between 1980 and 1990. While the total number of housing units grew by 17 percent between 1980 and 1990, the growth of rental units was a mere 4 percent over the same period. However, most of these units were constructed with the higher-income migrants from the mainland in mind. For the most part, the existing rental inventory consists of older residences that are converted to rental use, or small detached houses of marginal quality. Many of the families in these publicly subsidized projects have become trapped for years. It was estimated in 1985 that about 10 percent of the families had annual incomes of US$13,000, while many had incomes beyond US$25,000. While some of these families could afford to purchase low priced homes, it was virtually impossible for them to find affordable housing in the private market.

The real dilemma created for low and moderate income families is that while many would prefer to move out of public housing to rent or purchase higher quality homes, they are prevented from doing so because the rental market does not permit them. Simultaneously, very low income and elderly residents whose only option is to live in publicly subsidized housing are prevented from doing so by current tenants who cannot afford the few units that are available in the private housing market.

Much of the high cost of rental units is ascribed to the joint action of developers and real estate agents who have vested interests in maintaining high rents. Our regression model of median rent pointed to vacant units as big contributors to an explanation of the rental structure. Vacant units for sale are built, and exist in, choice residential seaside or hillside locations that would appeal to tourists. This phenomenon reflects the deliberate action of developers to build and cater to well-to-do tenants who can afford to pay the premium rates demanded in a market where there are few choices.

In a recent telephone survey of households [Mills 1991], 47 percent of the respondents said they rent or share rent. When asked what was the primary reason for renting rather than owning a home, 74 percent related their reason to not being able to afford it; 55 percent said their income was not high enough; 13 percent said they could not afford the down payment; 6 percent said they could not afford the mortgage payments. Further, only 2 percent said they liked living in the houses they were in; and 3 percent indicated they did not want the responsibility of owning a home.

Thus, the need to escape the condition of renting is evident, and the demand for affordable homes is also equally manifest. The following section on the housing market provides additional answers to the question of the high cost of housing.

**The Housing Market**

It was indicated in an earlier section that the physical geography of the Virgin Islands greatly enhances its attractiveness to tourists. That same environment imposes some very real costs on the residents who have to live there and who try to build homes. The hilly terrain, particularly on St Thomas and St John, which presents astonishing views, exacts steep prices both in raw land and in construction costs [Virgin Islands Planning Office 1974].

Construction materials, including sand, all have to be imported. The exception is building stone, which is produced by quarries from the copious metamorphic rocks on the islands. This rock type also increases the cost of building cisterns which by law are required for each residential structure. Cisterns are necessary to catch rainfall for potable water use. It is estimated that the construction of a cistern constitutes about one-third the cost of a home. Construction costs now exceed US$100 per square foot.

The data in Table 7.3 showed that condominium sales exceed those of homes sold. These units are above the purchasing capacity of most middle income residents, and they are generally not the preferred type of dwelling. Most condominiums are sold to seasonal residents and do not therefore enter into the stock of owner occupied units of residents. Most of the new single-family and multi-family units are built and marketed as second homes, and are not within the price range that many residents can afford.

It was noted in another study that *tract* building of unsubsidized single-family homes imposes a further limitation on home building because of the difficulty in assembling tracts of land of sufficient size for large-scale development [Department of Housing and Urban Development 1971: 8] and there are not many areas of 10 acres (4ha) or more where sites for multi-family units can be built. Privately owned raw land costs are, at a minimum, about US$55,000 per acre (US$136,000 per ha).

The construction industry on the islands is relatively small. This prohibits many local companies from building large subdivisions. Their size limits the volume of new housing units that they can construct, and they are unable to take advantage of economies of scale [Buckhurst Fish Hutton Katz Inc. 1991: 5].

There is a strong cultural attachment to the single-family, detached home, but this luxury cannot endure in the face of a finite landscape and the burgeoning cost of home building. Information from the housing survey [Mills 1991] indicates that about six out of ten (62 percent) households occupy single-family detached houses.

It is recalled that about three out of four householders indicated in the housing survey of 1991 that not being able to afford the purchase price of a home was a major deterrent. Private sector financial institutions contribute significantly to this condition in a number of ways. First, home buyers in the Virgin Islands are required to make down payments of 20 percent to 30 percent when purchasing a home or condominium with a conventional loan. This compares with about 5 percent to 10 percent in the United States. Second, mortgage lending rates are 1.0 to 1.5 points above those on the mainland with a term-to-maturity of 20 rather than 30 years. Third, there are perhaps no adjustable rate loans available. Fourth, mortgages backed by government are negligible. Fifth, the recent (1991) increase of the Federal Housing Administration's (FHA) guaranteed home loan ceiling of US$187,300, with a down payment of 5 percent or less, will make no substantive difference in home ownership since only three financial institutions or banks have so far been writing FHA guaranteed loans.

The attempts by the local government to meet the emergency in housing in 1970 did not resolve the problem entirely. By 1991, it was evident that low and moderate income families were being squeezed out of the housing market, and intervention was mandatory.

## An Affordable Housing Policy

One of the major effects of tourism as the dominant force in the economy of the Virgin Islands is that local residents must compete with vacationers and part-time residents for the available housing supply. Full-time residents have fared increasingly worse in this competition for adequate housing, and concerns about this disadvantage led to the Low and Moderate Income Affordable Housing Act in 1990. Objectives of the Act included [Buckhurst Fish Hutton Katz Inc. 1991: 1-2]:

1. the provision of decent, safe, sanitary, aesthetically acceptable, high quality affordable housing for persons and families of low and moderate income;
2. the provision of government-owned land and site improvements to reduce the cost of housing sites;
3. encouragement of investment in, and the development of, factory-built housing to reduce housing construction costs;
4. the provision of financing for owner occupied and retail housing developments on in-fill lots and as part of larger-scale residential subdivisions;
5. the offer of incentives, including tax exemptions, to encourage the construction of affordable housing; and
6. the provision of a mechanism for establishing and maintaining a Housing Trust Fund to facilitate the construction of new owner occupied and rental housing developments, and provide assistance to home buyers and renters.

Over the years, government's policy toward high rent and home ownership is reflected in the work of several agencies. In 1981, legislative action created the Virgin Islands Finance Housing Authority (VIFHA) with the responsibility for financing owner occupied housing developments and providing low interest mortgage loans to qualified low and moderate income homeowners. The Public Finance Authority provides funds for rental and owner occupied housing developments, and the Department of Housing, Parks and Recreation finances the acquisition and development of rental housing schemes.

The projected market demand by Buckhurst Fish Hutton Katz Inc. [1991] is programme. Some of these programmes have begun, but progress is retarded by the lack of government-owned land in areas that are conducive to the construction of affordable units at a price of no more than US$70,000. This goal appears ambitious, given the size of the construction industry. Moreover, the US$70,000 limit appears somewhat unrealistic in the face of the current level of labour and construction costs. The potential home buyer would certainly need assistance to enhance his or her capability to purchase. Possible avenues of assistance include increased availability of VIFHA insurance, primary mortgage insurance from private banks and other lending institutions, lower commercial mortgage rates, construction insurance and mortgage down payment assistance [Buckhurst Fish Hutton Katz Inc. 1991: 6].

It appears evident from the presentation above that despite the good intentions of the Affordable Housing Act, the housing crisis will not be resolved for quite some time. There are factors that are beyond the direct control of local government, not the least important of which include the negligible assistance of the federal government, the limited physical size of the islands, the difficult terrain, the competition from more well-to-do vacationers, and restrictive financial firms. Thus, it will be several years before the rent structure improves substantially and the housing market becomes more affordable to the majority of those who want to own their own homes.

## Acknowledgements

The author acknowledges the assistance of Martin Livingstone and De Anne Cummings-Scott, Research Analysts in the Eastern Caribbean Center, University of the Virgin Islands, in the collection and production of graphic charts.

## References

Buckhurst Fish Hutton Katz Inc. 1991. *US Virgin Islands Housing Demand Study.* Prepared by Buckhurst Fish Hutton Katz Inc., in association with Urbanomics and the Caribbean Research Institute, New York.

Department of Housing and Urban Development. 1972. *Analysis of the Virgin Islands, USA, Housing Market.* Washington, DC: Federal Housing Administration.

Devaney, J.F. 1992. *Housing in America: 1989/90.* Washington, DC: US Bureau of the Census, Department of Commerce.

Miller, R.W. 1979. *The Economy of the Virgin Islands,* Washington, DC: Office of Territorial Affairs. Department of the Interior.

Mills, F.L. 1991. *A Housing Needs Survey of Households in the US Virgin Islands.* US Virgin Islands: Caribbean Research Institute, University of the Virgin Islands.

US Bureau of the Census. 1991. *Census of Population and Housing, 1990: Summary Tape File 1 (Virgin Islands of the United States).* Washington, DC: Technical Documentation, Department of Commerce.

US Bureau of the Census. 1992. *1990 Housing Highlights: Financial Facts (CH-S-2)*. Washington, DC: Department of Commerce.

Waksberg, J. 1978. "Sampling methods for random digit dialing". *Journal of the American Statistical Association* 73: 40-46.

Virgin Islands Bureau of Economic Research. 1992. *US Virgin Islands Annual Tourism Indicators*. Charlotte Amalie, St Thomas, VI. Department of Economic Development and Agriculture. Government of the Virgin Islands.

Virgin Islands Planning Office. 1974. "The feasibility of medium-rise residential buildings on selected sites". Charlotte Amalie, St Thomas, VI.

Virgin Islands Planning Office. 1977. "Land use and housing elements: US Virgin Islands". Charlotte Amalie, St Thomas VI.

# Part 3

# Natural Hazards and Disaster Management

# Chapter 8

# Disaster Mitigation and Cost-Benefit Analysis: Conceptual Perspectives

Jeremy McA. Collymore

## Introduction

The frequent and consistently high levels of damage occurring to the economies of developing countries associated with natural disasters has heralded many calls for mitigation activity. However, at the same time, it is recognized that these countries are preoccupied with addressing more current and conspicuous problems such as unemployment, poor and inadequate housing, and inadequate health services.

Of immediate concern to proponents of disaster planning is how to impress on policy makers the significance of a long-term activity like disaster mitigation and the benefits which may accrue from it. This paper explores the extent to which cost-benefit analysis (CBA) may assist proponents of disaster mitigation in the Caribbean in addressing this immediate concern.

The issue of disaster mitigation is especially critical to developing countries since natural disasters can debilitate any progress made towards modernization. In many instances the cost of reconstruction and rehabilitation, and the loss of property associated with natural disasters in the developing countries can be as high as 2 percent of a country's gross national product [Burton et al. 1978].

**The Pan Caribbean Disaster Preparedness and Prevention Project**

The first sustained regional programme aimed at promoting institutionalized disaster management in the Caribbean was centred around the Pan Caribbean Disaster Preparedness and Prevention Project (PCDPPP) which started its activities in mid-1981. As a result of several devastating disasters in 1979 and 1980, Caribbean states initiated action to change their traditional approach to disaster management which largely concentrated on the provision of relief. The consensus in various fora around the region and internationally, to examine ways and means to set up specific machinery to cope more effectively with the natural disasters which periodically affect the region, led to the establishment of the PCDPPP.

The primary objectives of the PCDPPP included the following:

1. to support the development of comprehensive national and regional policies and legislation for the implementation of disaster preparedness, prevention, response and recovery action, and to strengthen the disaster management capacity of the relevant national bodies;

2. to raise the level of contingency planning in the region by assisting in the development and testing of emergency procedures at the local, national, subregional and regional levels;

3. to enhance the capacity of the region for timely dissemination of warnings and reliable communications in the case of a disaster;

4. to promote the use of loss reduction techniques such as hazard mapping, land use controls, and building regulations, and their application in the development process, and also to facilitate the exchange of research results and expertise in this area; and

5. to strengthen the capacity of the region for collection, exchange and dissemination of disaster related information and to sensitize the Caribbean public to disasters and the potential of preventive action.

Whilst evaluations of the PCDPPP have highlighted its central role in promoting disaster awareness and national programmes in disaster management, there is also consensus that its establishment structure created inherent problems for the project. For example, normally a project or programme is established on the basis of a memorandum of agreement between the sponsoring agencies and the government of a particular country. In the case of the PCDPPP, it was necessary to induce the individual governments to accept responsibility for their own disaster preparedness and response programmes in order to get the programme going in each country. Thus, the programme was only able to make significant progress in those countries that gave the project the cooperation and support it needed in order to be effective.

A second problem arose out of the need for a comprehensive understanding and management of the financial aspects of the programme. There was uncertainty as to the magnitude of the financing required for a successful outcome, and an absence of a long-term view of how the whole problem of disaster reduction was to be solved. Willingness of national governments to shoulder their part of the cost, and to fully employ the resources available internally, was not evident. The need for commitment from all parties to follow such a programme through to a successful conclusion, indicates that much work has to be done to establish a firm foundation for financial support; donors cannot be expected to provide money indefinitely under such conditions.

It is important to note these constraints as they have implications for ongoing regional initiatives to promote the development of a regional focal point for a comprehensive disaster management programme.

## Defining Disaster Mitigation

A disaster is a situation which involves the loss of life, injury to person or the destruction of property on a scale which overcomes the capacity of society to cope, without dramatic changes in its normal operation [Foster 1980; Williams 1984]. Natural events, such as hurricanes, floods, earthquakes and storms may induce disaster, and are therefore classed as natural hazards. Thus, in the present context, natural hazards are natural events, often of extreme magnitude, which when interfacing with social systems, produce negative or damaging effects.

Disaster mitigation is therefore concerned with modifying or reducing the impacts of natural hazards on human use systems. It seeks to accelerate the evolutionary process of adaptation and protection based on an understanding of known natural hazards, impacts and effects [Schramm 1984]. As such, disaster mitigation is a long incremental process aiming to alter the social, economic and political factors which contribute to the vulnerability of the community [Davis 1984].

In essence, disaster mitigation is considered to be part of the development planning process requiring long-term allocation of resources [UNDRO 1991; Organization of American States 1990; Kreimer & Munasingh 1990]. Consequently, it is enshrined in political and economic questions about who are the beneficiaries of mitigation activity, the extent of mitigation possible, desirable and affordable, and who are to bear the costs. Assessing the losses, the range of effects, and the nature and seriousness of the phenomena are indispensable initial steps in formulating mitigation programmes.

## Issues in Disaster Mitigation

The issues related to disaster mitigation can be categorized as:

1. political;

2. economic; *and*

3. methods and approaches.

This categorization is not designed or expected to be mutually exclusive since all categories are critical to the iterative process of policy formation.

### Political

Recent literature on disaster mitigation in developing countries has suggested that the development process as presently pursued has given rise not only to poverty and inequality but also to human vulnerability. Inevitably, large numbers of poor exploited people are forced to live in geographically vulnerable, marginal areas. Hence, in the context of developing countries, effective mitigation planning is seen to be conditional upon or associated with the process of social transformation within a society [Mumtaz 1984; Maskrey 1984; UNDP/UNDRO 1991]. Societal shift from non-industrialized to industrialized economies is often disruptive and uneven, leaving large gaps in social coping mechanisms and technology. As a result, the impact of disasters as a by-product of such change must be constantly evaluated as part of the development planning process.

Since the controllers of power and authority are seldom those who live in the vulnerable marginal areas there is often conflict in making authoritative decisions. Controversy exists about the extent to which the social and political mechanisms in the society should be modified to accommodate the needs and opinions of this large vulnerable population [Davis 1984]. Such concerns call for political decisions that will determine how the costs and benefits of any mitigation strategies are to be shared.

### Economic

Natural disasters can inflict extensive damage to an economy at a given point in time. In addition, their impacts can demobilize the economic engine of the country, thus inducing debilitating effects which can be cumulative. There are numerous Caribbean examples which illustrate this. For example, between 1979 and 1981 the island of St Vincent suffered the onslaught of five major hazards [Jones 1984]. There was a negative growth in the national economy and a 40 percent decline in agricultural output in 1979 following the eruption of the Soufrière volcano. Hurricane Allen swept across St Lucia in 1980 causing not only US$69 million in crop losses but at the same time destroying 90 percent of the banana crop which generally accounts for 80 percent of the island's annual agricultural output [OFDA 1988]. On the western rim of the Caribbean Basin, on 23 December 1972, a series of earthquakes hit the capital of Nicaragua, Managua, making inoperable 10 percent of the country's industrial capacity, 50 percent of commercial property and 70 percent of the government facilities [Funaro-Curtis 1982].

The above data on costs are based on visual estimation of damage or loss with the focus being assessment of the time period needed for recovery or a return to full production. In the case of agricultural damage, estimates are usually made on a crop-by-crop basis [Hammerton et al. 1983]. However, in a farming environment such as the Caribbean, where intercropping and mixed cropping are common amongst small farmers, there is definitely a need for reconsidering crop-by-crop estimation of losses.

Another example of the costs involved in a natural disaster relates to the impact of Hurricane David on Dominica. It struck Dominica on 29 August 1979, seriously damaging 50 percent of the island's housing stock of 16,000 houses; 2,000 of which were completely destroyed. Approximately two-thirds of the island's 80,000 population was left homeless. Nearly all the school buildings were badly damaged, requiring an estimated EC$6 million (US$2.2 million) to rebuild or repair 64 schools. The Princess Margaret Hospital in the capital Roseau lost roof sheets from almost all of its buildings. The main port in Woodbridge Bay was badly damaged and required a major reconstruction effort, estimated to have cost EC$10.8 million (US$4 million). A comparison of selected indicators in Table 8.1 shows that the impact of Hurricane David was felt in the island's economy for many years after the event. Up to 1983, agriculture and fishing had not regained the share of gross domestic product they held in 1978. Exports declined drastically in 1979, whilst GDP per capita in 1979 fell to approximately 20 percent below the 1978 level.

Given the diversity and intensity of social problems and the scarcity of capital in the Third World, there must be some rationale for public investment in mitigation. The question arises whether this rationale should be economic or social? Further, is the summation of losses associated with the impact of a disaster sufficient to justify investment of public funds in mitigation? Should public investment in disaster mitigation have an economic basis other than addressing market failures? In the final analysis, it has to be determined whether the existence of losses from disaster is evidence that there is too little mitigation; and what priority, if any, should be given to mitigation activities in the allocation of scarce resources?

*Table 8.1*   Comparison of Selected Economic Indicators, Dominica, Fiscal Years
1978-1983

| Selected Indicator | 1978 | 1979 | 1980 | 1981 | 1982 | 1983 |
|---|---|---|---|---|---|---|
| Gross Domestic Product | 102.0 | 81.0 | 88.0 | 100.0 | 103.0 | 107.0 |
| Agriculture/Fishing | 41.0 | 26.0 | 24.5 | 38.3 | 31.4 | 33.3 |
| Mining/Construction | 6.4 | 7.2 | 11.7 | 12.7 | 10.4 | 10.3 |
| Manufacturing | 5.5 | 4.5 | 5.0 | 5.4 | 8.0 | 8.2 |
| Wholesale/Retail trade | 10.8 | 7.1 | 9.4 | 10.6 | 12.0 | 11.0 |
| Hotels/Restaurant | 1.3 | 1.0 | 0.9 | 1.0 | 1.1 | 1.2 |
| Total exports | 42.9 | 25.4 | 26.3 | 50.9 | 66.0 | 74.2 |
| Total imports | 76.8 | 59.9 | 128.7 | 136.8 | 128.2 | 121.7 |
| GDP per capita (EC$) | 1243.0 | 975.0 | 1047.0 | 1190.0 | 1212.0 | 1230.0 |
| Change in consumer price index | +9.3 | +34.1 | +21.4 | +8.1 | +4.1 | +2.7 |

Source:
*Annual Reports of UN Economic Commission for Latin America and the Caribbean (UNECLAC)*

## Mitigation Methods and Approaches

The traditional economic approaches to hazard mitigation have generally
viewed mitigation in terms of minimizing the average annual damage
associated with natural hazards [see Deaton 1984; Florey 1986]. In this context
mitigation strategies are classified under two broad headings: structural; and
non-structural [Organization of American States 1990; Florey 1986; Foster
1980; Olson 1984].

Structural approaches can involve measures that focus on the strengthening
of buildings exposed to hazards or those which focus on site-level systems for
protecting structures, for example, levées. Caribbean examples include gabion
boxes to combat soil erosion in the Scotland District of Barbados [Patel, this
volume], and culverts and bridges constructed in Speightstown, Barbados, to
deal with flooding [Collymore & Griffith 1988]. These activities usually seek to
modify other hazards or the built environment.

The non-structural approach seeks to influence the institutional framework of
the community at risk through safety codes, tax incentives, land use
management, public education and disaster insurance. The islands of the
Caribbean Community have for a number of years been discussing a Uniform
Building Code but it is yet to be adopted by any of the member states of the
Community. Tax incentives and land use management are yet to be explicit
policy instruments of disaster management in the subregion, though the
ongoing debate on the availability of insurance and reinsurance in the region

will certainly bring these to the fore. Disaster insurance has been the primary mitigation strategy practised in the Caribbean. With uniform premiums based primarily on value of insured risk and indifferent to geographical location and to performance standards, it may be regarded to have been ineffective in encouraging reduction in regional vulnerability.

Recently there has emerged a growing opposition to this conceptualization of mitigation planning. There is a call for a different approach which stresses mitigation designed to enhance the economic output and environmental quality of the hazard area. Central to this new approach is areal productivity. It must be noted that even this strategy is fraught with measurement difficulties.

## Cost-Benefit Analysis (CBA) And Disaster Mitigation

Thus far the discussion has centred on the general issues and concerns which influence disaster policy. The question is whether CBA as an evaluation method can be applied to assist decision makers in shaping mitigation policy in the Caribbean.

Cost-benefit analysis is based on the social welfare function of well-being as measured from preferences, as expressed in the market by way of the proxy of willingness to pay. Central to the concept of cost-benefit analysis is the "potential Pareto criterion", which holds that if an action generates sufficient benefits for the gainers to compensate the losers and still be themselves better off, then social welfare is judged to have improved, even if the compensation is not paid.

The method of cost-benefit analysis is therefore concerned with identifying the effects of an activity on the individual welfare of all members of the society. These are monetized using scaled valued weights derived principally from market information on the expressed demand for goods and services. Benefits (positive impacts) and costs (negative impacts) are aggregated and discounted to present value, to reflect the observation that people tend to value effects differently depending on when they occur. A "net present value" is then used as the "grand index" of the action [Conn 1986; McAllister 1980; Sugden & Williams 1980; Westman & Conn 1976].

With respect to disaster mitigation, cost-benefit analysis calls for a comparison of mitigation costs with the losses expected to be averted, in order to identify an economically efficient level of hazard mitigation. This is represented schematically in Figure 8.1. The relative level of adjustment (A) to a given hazard is on the horizontal axis. The vertical axis represents annual dollar amounts (shown in present value terms). The C curve is the total annual cost of achieving various levels of adjustment. Unusually, the costs of

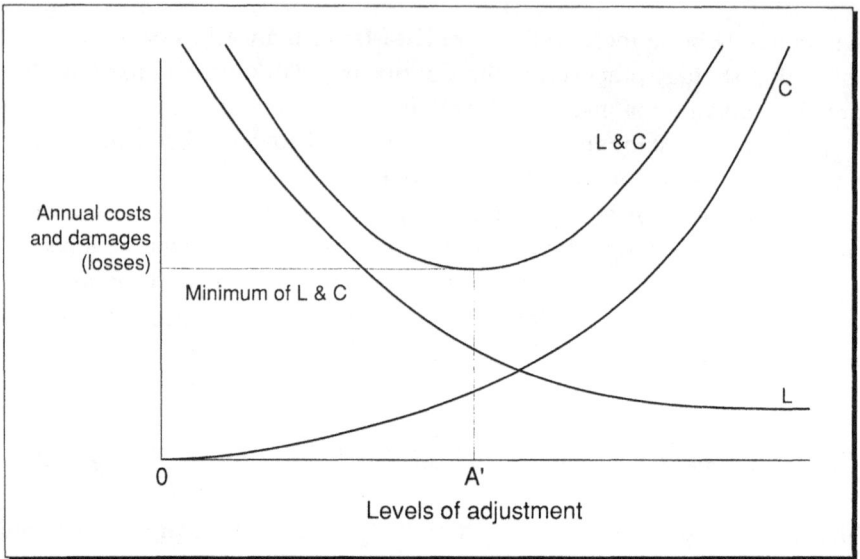

*Figure 8.1* The optimal level of hazard mitigation
Source: *Miliman [1983]*

adjustments climb rather rapidly as the level of adjustment is increased. The L curve represents the expected total losses, which often decline rapidly at first for initial levels of adjustment. The most efficient level of adjustment is the one which minimizes the sum of L and C. This minimum point is shown at A* on Figure 8.1. To the left of A* the extra losses avoided are greater than the extra costs of adjustment. To the right of A*, the extra costs of adjustment exceed the extra losses averted.

Determination of what is an acceptable level of risk is bound to be controversial. However, the idea of an optimal level of hazard mitigation need not be unacceptable if it is realized that all potential risks cannot be eliminated no matter the size of capital inputs. The estimation of the L and C curves is that they are expected to be imprecise for the foreseeable future. Two sets of probabilities are involved. The first is the probability of the hazardous event occurring, and the second is the probability of loss given that the hazardous event has occurred. Neither of these probabilities is easily defined or measured at this time.

This approach of minimizing the sum costs of adjustment and damages averted, "the efficiency level approach", provides a framework for accommodating both the loss reduction and net productivity of hazard zone area approaches to disaster mitigation. The costs of adjustment, properly defined, should include all relevant activities by the users of the hazard-prone area. Minimizing total social costs is another way of expressing maximization of the net productivity of the hazard-prone area [Miliman 1983].

Other costs which may stem from particular kinds of hazard mitigative measures, for example opportunities foregone for use of hazard areas as a result of development controls, are often neglected. Lind [1967] posits that risk bearing can be considered a cost of a disaster when risk-averse individuals are willing to pay a premium to change the distribution of losses.

The appropriate measures of losses and benefits, and hence the optimal level of mitigation, will therefore depend upon individual preferences, technology, subjective probabilities of disasters and the existence of markets for risk bearing.

Whilst the idea of an economic efficient level of disaster mitigation is appealing, there are many technical limitations in trying to define it. Problems arise in trying to estimate the L and C curves. Among the losses associated with natural disasters are deaths, social dislocation, disruption of economic activity, psychological trauma and property damage. Whilst losses due to property damage and economic disruption may lend themselves to monetization, the other losses have proved difficult to quantify.

The problem of technical limitations in estimating losses can be a serious handicap to a cost-benefit analysis of disaster mitigation programmes. To begin with, there is an absence of a reliable, comprehensive database on the character and extent of economic losses associated with disasters, a situation which is especially pronounced in developing countries in general as well as in the Caribbean. White and Haas [1975] indicate that estimates of economic loss can be inaccurate by a factor of two or three. This certainly could pose serious constraints on the reliability of any predicted efficient level of mitigation.

Providing estimates of expected damage to property, even for a single region and a single hazard, can be problematic. There are spatial variations in the structural characteristics of buildings in the Caribbean and hence their resistance to a given hazard [UNDP 1989; IMERU 1989; Collymore 1989]. Where there is a mixing and juxtaposition of different quality housing stock, as is particularly pronounced in Caribbean urban areas, the problems of estimating property damage are exacerbated. This is further confounded by the fact that even within a single island the impact of a disaster varies. For example, the eye of a hurricane (maximum damage is generally closest to the eye wall) may only cross part of even a fairly small island. The eye of Hurricane Gilbert was unusual in traversing the whole length of Jamaica's east-west axis, but even in this case, there was considerable spatial variability in damage [Barker & Miller 1990].

Similar problems also exist in estimating crop losses in the developing countries. Since peasant farmers tend to grow a variety of crops, which are planted at different times, estimating expected losses from a natural disaster is very difficult. This is especially so since different crops and combinations of crops have varying levels of resistance to any given event.

In this context, Miliman [1983] has suggested that adding together property damage and income losses results in some double counting. Property damage should represent the present value of losses in net incomes or expected losses of value added in production. He further suggests that it is incorrect to estimate losses as some fraction of property damage, or to use conventional property damage estimates as a surrogate for expected income losses. Damage estimates, rather than being based on book values or replacement costs, should reflect present worth (capitalized values) of expected income losses.

Another set of factors that limit the application of CBA in informing disaster mitigation policy formulation relate to the "willingness to pay criterion". By using market situations to determine costs and benefits, CBA implicitly accepts prevailing patterns of income distribution. In developing countries (where there is a skewed distribution of income), this has inherent disadvantages for the majority of the population. Thus, when mitigation planning is being pursued as part of the process of social transformation of society, as advocated by Mumtaz [1984] and Davis [1984], cost-benefit analysis becomes a questionable tool for informing decision making.

Kunreuther [1973], in his work in the United States, suggests that willingness to pay may be inadequate in measuring individual preferences. His research suggests that households fail to adopt a mitigation activity (the purchase of insurance), even though the expected utility model predicts that it was in their best interest to do so. This suggests that there are factors other than wealth on which preferences are based and, where risk is involved, these may be more difficult to estimate anyway.

Furthermore, since individuals do not always have the same attitudes in a collective situation as they do in an individual situation, it becomes difficult to infer public attitudes from individual market behaviour [Abselon 1979]. Sen [1973] argues that choices are not always "connected". This being so, then a choice of one good does not always mean it is preferred to another. On top of this, some types of disaster impacts almost entirely elude attempts to estimate their monetary value. Among these impacts are social and psychological trauma. These unmonetized and intangible impacts are difficult to estimate and are therefore given uneven treatment, if any, in CBA reports. Consequently, they tend to receive insufficient attention in the formation of opinion.

## Going Beyond Cost-Benefit Analysis

This discussion has suggested that the idea of an efficient level of disaster mitigation is appealing in that it facilitates and accommodates the two approaches to disaster mitigation in a single analytical framework, the economic efficient level of hazard adjustment. However, serious technical problems related to estimating expected costs and benefits, in association with controversial willingness to pay criterion, considerably limit the usefulness of cost-benefit analysis in informing disaster mitigation policy in developing regions such as the Caribbean. Further, it could be argued that CBA studies will systematically exaggerate benefits and underestimate costs.

Resulting methodologies need to address the question of practicality. What is the value of the correct but complex measures of losses when the disaster events are small? In these cases informed estimates may be more appropriate. However, in an environment in which events are small and frequent, a more complex methodology may be appropriate.

It is necessary also to consider the role of the public sector in disaster relief. If equity is as important a consideration as efficiency, then we need to ask ourselves whether disaster victims should receive special treatment above and beyond that accorded by national welfare policies for dealing with the poor or unfortunate. In other words, the desirability of separating disaster relief must be established.

The fundamental truth is that disaster relief generally deals with the cause and not the condition. The continual high damage to property in the Caribbean suggests some market failure in how individuals process information on hazards, and corrodes the heart of the CBA.

In light of the difficulties which may be encountered in executing a CBA, sometimes it may be more realistic to set a target first, then to analyse the costs of the different means of achieving the given target. Alternatively, based on prior cost analysis, the decision maker can look at how the maximum level of available funds can be used most effectively in a number of disaster mitigation activities.

The demonstration of the benefits of investing in mitigation policies and programmes is essential if the perceived political barriers to allocating scarce resources to this area are to be shaken. It is imperative that the multi-disciplinary academic research needed to refine the evaluation methodologies be pursued with great vigour.

Unfortunately, none of the Commonwealth Caribbean territories can be said to be engaged in comprehensive hazard management planning. In part, this can be attributed to the high tolerance levels for risk held by most individuals and businesses, which historically has made political indifference to disaster issues feasible. Consequently, there is a heavy reliance on information based mitigation strategies such as hurricane forecasting, warnings and preparedness information. Since the costs of exposure to hazards are not borne solely by those who knowingly subject themselves to the risk, the political feasibility of this strategy must be called into question because of the costs of rescue, clean up, health care, and rehabilitation are shifted to the society as a whole [Collymore 1989: 22].

The need in the Caribbean for an urgent re-examination of how national resources are utilized in the disaster management agendas cannot be over emphasized. CBA may not be the conceptually appropriate tool but it does provide a benchmark from which this evaluation may depart.

## References

Abelson, P. 1979. *Cost-Benefit Analysis and Environmental Problems*. Saxon House.
Barker, D., & D.J. Miller. 1990. "Hurricane Gilbert: anthropomorphising a natural disaster". *Area* 22: 107-16.
Burton, I., R.W. Kates, & G.F. White. 1978. *The Environment as Hazard*. New York: Oxford University Press.
Collymore, J. 1989. "Planning hazard mitigation for the Caribbean". *Journal of the Association of Professional Engineers of Trinidad and Tobago* 23: 19-25.
Collymore, J., & M. Griffith. 1988. "The Speightstown flood study". Report to Canadian High Commission, Barbados.
Conn, D. 1986. "Review of the techniques for weighing or valuing the benefits associated with environmental quality improvements". Report to International Joint Commission, Great Lakes Science Advisory Board, Social and Economic Considerations Committee.
Davis, I. 1984. "Disaster mitigation: prevention is better than cure". *Reading Rural Development Communications Bulletin* 18 (October). Reading: University of Reading.
Deaton, B. 1984. "The economics of disaster mitigation". Paper presented at International Conference on Disaster Mitigation Implementation. Jamaica.
Florey, 1986. "Incorporating national disaster risk information into economic analysis of agricultural projects". MSc thesis, Virginia Polytechnic & State University, Blacksburg, Virginia.
Foster, H.D. 1980. *Disaster Planning*. New York: Springer-Verlag.
Funaro-Curtis, R. 1982. "Natural disasters and the development process". *Water Resources Research* 5: 555-62.
Hammerton G., C. George, & R. Pilgrim. 1983. "Hurricanes and agriculture: losses and remedial action". *Disaster* 8, no. 4: 279-86.
IMERU. 1989. Draft Preliminary Report on the Technical Assessment and Impact Evaluation of Hurricane Gilbert, September 12, 1988. Kingston, Jamaica.
Jones. E. 1984. "Perspectives on natural hazards in the Caribbean: case studies of St Vincent, Dominica and St Lucia". Report of a Baseline Survey. Trinidad: Caribbean Agricultural Research and Development Institute.
Kunreuther, H. 1973. *Recovery from Natural Disasters: Insurance or Federal Aid?* Washington, DC: American Enterprise Institute.
Kreimer, A., & M. Munasingh (eds). 1990. *Managing Natural Disasters and the Environment*. Washington DC: World Bank.
Lind, R.C. 1967. "Flood control alternatives and the economics of flood protection". *Water Resources Research* 2.

Maskrey, A. 1984. "Community-based hazard mitigation". Paper presented at International Conference on Disaster Mitigation Implementation. Jamaica.

McAllister, D. 1980. *Evacuation in Environmental Planning*. Cambridge, Mass.: MIT Press.

Miliman, J. 1983. "An agenda for economic research on flood hazard mitigation". In *A Plan for Research on Floods and their Mitigation in the USA*, edited by S.A. Chagnon, R.J. Schicht, & R. Semonin. Champaign, Illinois: Illinois State Water Survey.

Mumtaz, B. 1984. "Mitigation in the context of development". Paper presented at International Conference on Disaster Mitigation Implementation. Jamaica.

Organization of American States. 1990. *Primer on Natural Hazard Management in Integrated Regional Development*. Washington, DC: DRA.

OFDA. 1988. *Disaster Relief Assistance and Related Data*. Washington, DC.

Olson, S. 1984. *Institutionalising Mitigation: Putting Hazard Reduction Policies and Practices "Inside" the Development Process*. Blacksburg: Virginia Tech.

Scramm, D. 1984. "Learning disaster mitigation". Paper presented at International Conference on Disaster Mitigation Implementation. Jamaica.

Sen, A. 1973. "Behaviour and the concept of preference". *Economics* 40: 241-59.

Sugden, R., & W. Williams. 1980. The Principles of Cost-Benefit Analysis. Oxford: Oxford University Press.

UNDP. 1989. *Hurricane Hugo in the Eastern Caribbean: Status of Damage Assessment and Rehabilitation Requirements*. Bridgetown, Barbados.

UNDP/UNDRO. 1991. *Disaster Management Manual*. Geneva: United Nations.

UNDRO. 1991. *Mitigation, Natural Disasters: Phenomena, Effects and Options*. Geneva: United Nations.

Westman, W., & D. Conn. 1976. *Quantifying Benefits of Pollution Control*. Sacramento, California: California Energy Resources Conservation and Development Commission.

White, G., & J. Haas. 1975. *Assessment of Research on Natural Hazards*. Cambridge, Mass. & London: MIT Press.

Williams, M. 1984. "Natural disaster and land use planning: some thoughts on the St Lucia experience". Paper presented at International Conference on Disaster Mitigation Implementation. Jamaica.

Chapter 9

# Tropical Cyclone Activity within the Caribbean Basin since 1500

Alison J. Reading and Rory P. D. Walsh

## Introduction

In ecological and geomorphological terms, tropical cyclones, in common with other high magnitude physical events such as landslides, earthquakes, and volcanic eruptions, cause periodic disturbance of the natural environment. These events are, however, an important element in the long-term development of the environment.

In human terms, because of the emphasis placed upon individual well-being and short-term conditions, tropical cyclones and other high magnitude physical events are often considered as hazards. Human sensitivity to these hazards is complex, and especially acute in island locations. It represents a combination of physical exposure, reflecting the magnitude and timing of events; and human vulnerability, reflecting the breadth of social and economic tolerance available at the same site [Smith 1992].

This paper examines the former, highlighting changes in cyclone tracks, frequencies and intensities for subregions within the Caribbean Basin. It then attempts tentatively to relate some of the identified changes over the past four centuries to changes in the atmospheric and oceanic circulation.

## Data Sources

The spatial distribution and historical geography of the numerous islands and ports within the West Indies, and particularly within the Caribbean, is such that there exists a relatively comprehensive record of cyclones stretching back to Colombian times. Such comprehensive historical data are not available for any other cyclone region.

The numerous parliamentary, state, religious, estate and seafarers' records have been utilized by climatologists and historians from the late eighteenth century onwards to create regional and local chronologies. Since 1871, the US Weather Bureau has published annual charts and summaries of cyclone activity across the region. (See, for example, Pielke [1990].) Unfortunately, the comprehensiveness, detail and spatial reliability of data decreases as one goes back in time and this has to be taken into account in any time series analysis. All data used to construct the cyclone chronologies in this study were critically assessed and rationalized before inclusion, as discussed in Walsh and Reading [1991]. The outcome of the evaluation is a list of known "definite" and "probable" cyclones. Further archival research would undoubtedly reveal more cyclone occurrences.

The data series can only be regarded as 100 percent accurate from about 1960, when remote sensing techniques began to be routinely employed for tracking weather systems in the region.

## Data Series Methodology

Because of the inconsistencies and incompatible nature of the written "historical" data and the "modern" charted data, two separate data series were constructed [Reading 1990]. The written records available for the period prior to 1871 are subjective and depend upon the observer's perception and interpretation of weather conditions. These data relate to areas affected, and to their impact on islands and coasts. Ten areas were defined for this period, each enclosing discrete land areas or associated groups of islands within the Caribbean (Figure 9.1). For the period 1871 onwards, the charted tracks of cyclones were used to extend the essentially "cyclone impact" series into the modern era. Cyclones were counted as "affecting" an area if they crossed, or tracked within 1° of latitude or longitude of land. Figure 9.2 is a summary of the data, showing the decadal frequency (number of cyclones per decade) in each of the 10 subregions.

For the "modern" charted period a 5° latitude/longitude grid was used to divide the Caribbean and adjacent Atlantic. The grid approximates to the West

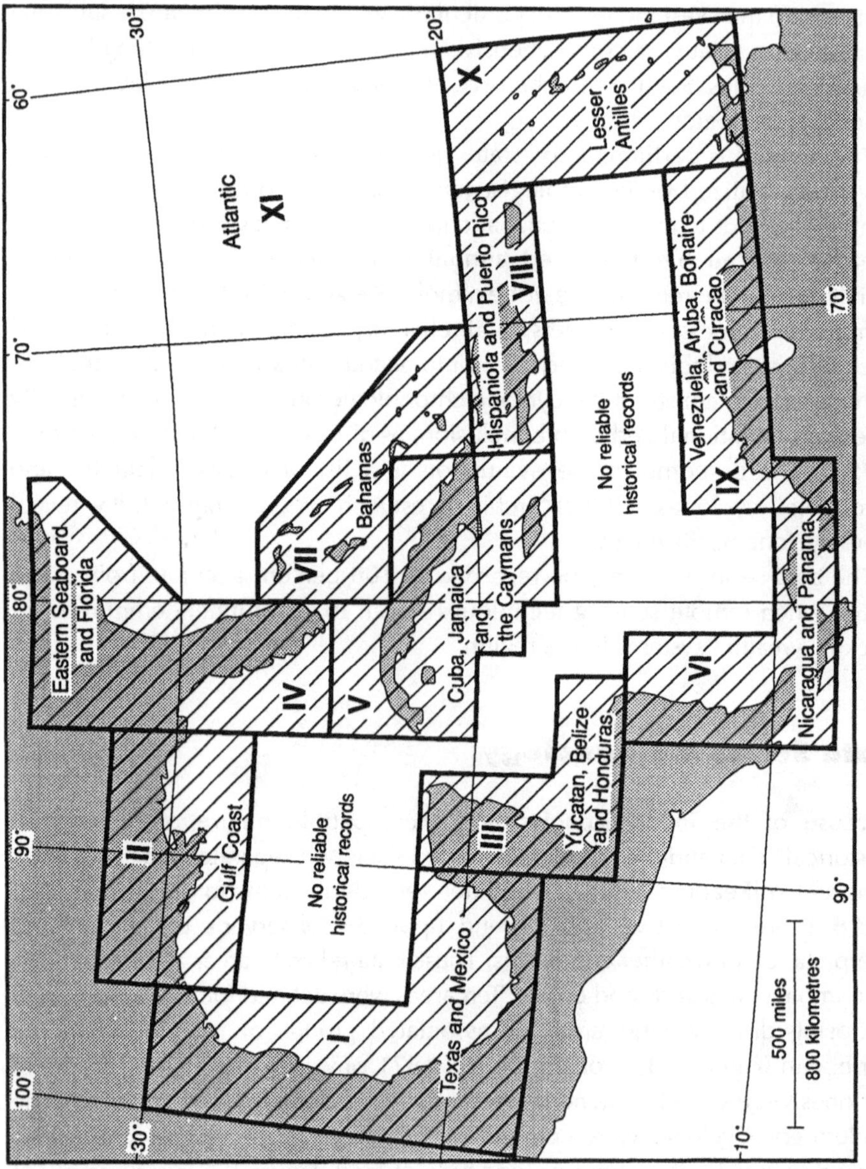

*Figure 9.1* Subregions of the Caribbbean used for historical data

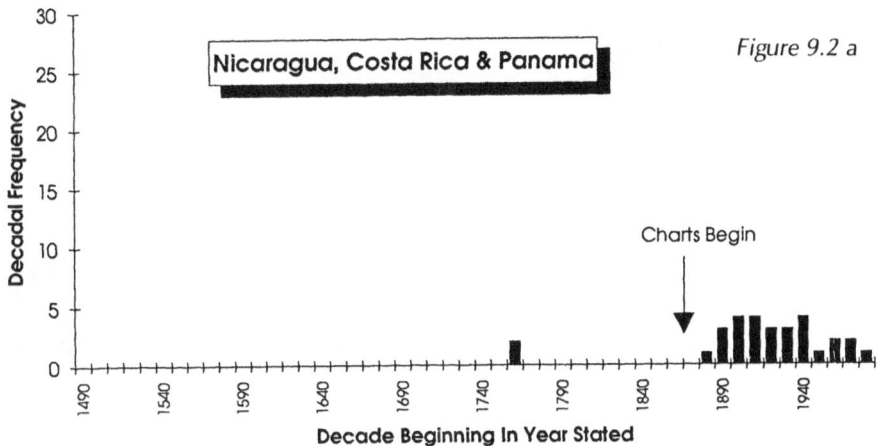

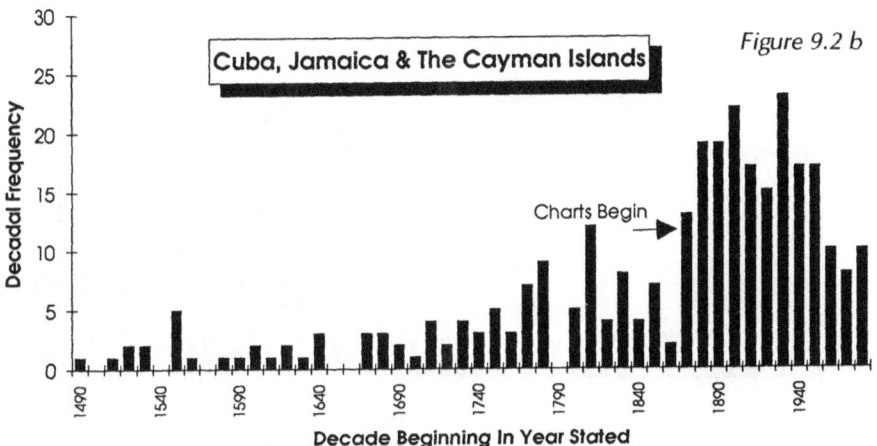

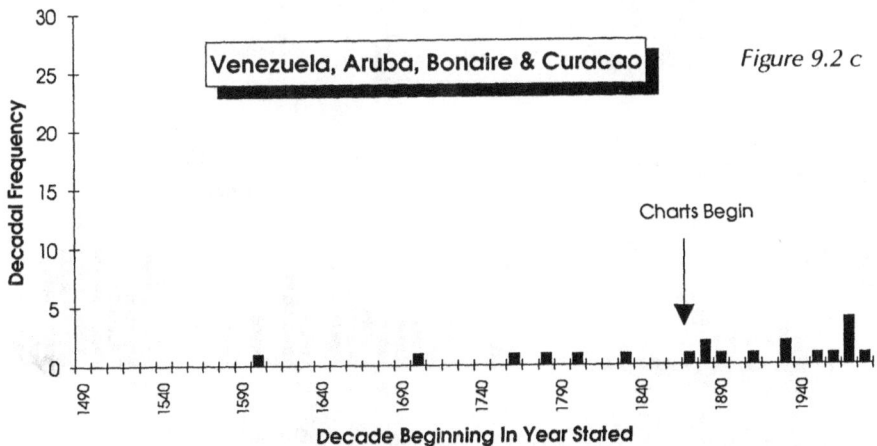

*Figure 9.2(a – j)* Decadal frequency of cyclones in ten subregions of the Caribbean

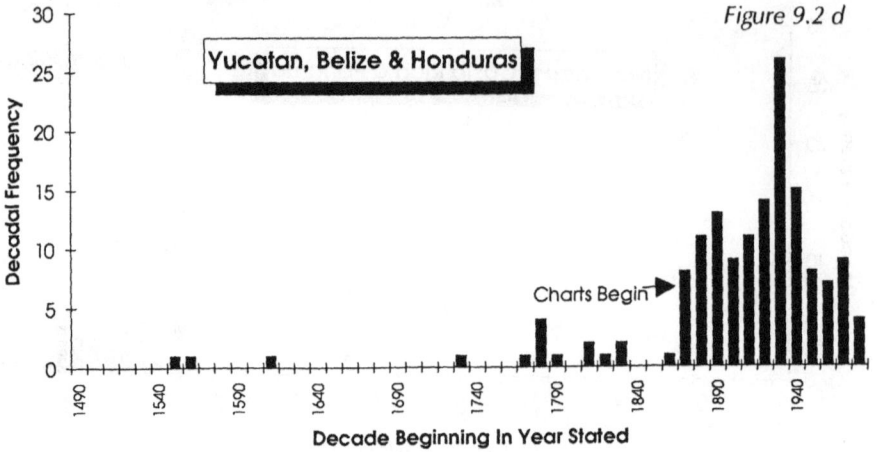

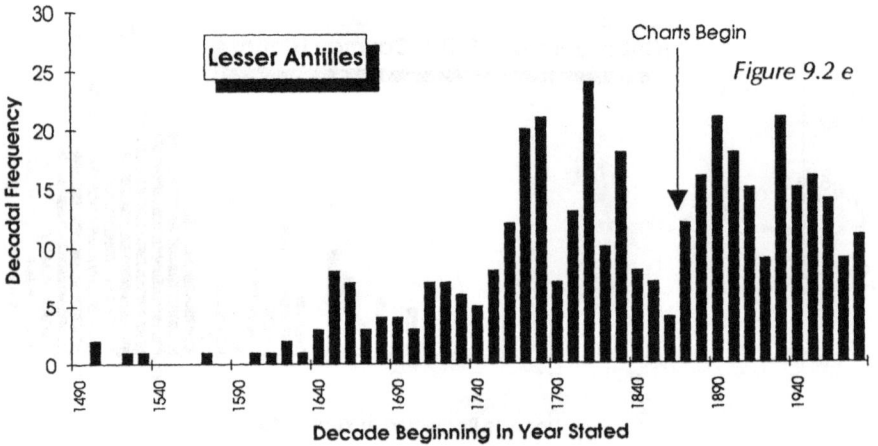

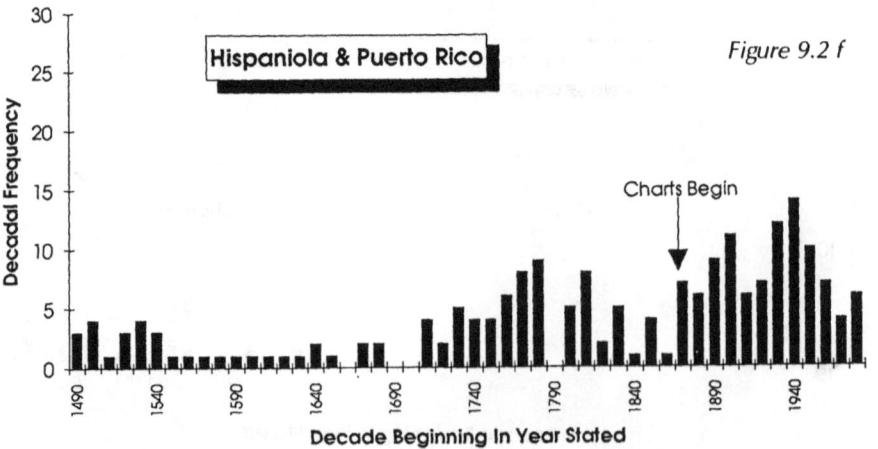

*Figure 9.2(a – j)* Decadal frequency of cyclones in ten subregions of the Caribbean

Figure 9.2 g

Texas & Mexico

Figure 9.2 h

U.S. Gulf Coast States

Figure 9.2 i

Florida & Eastern Seaboard

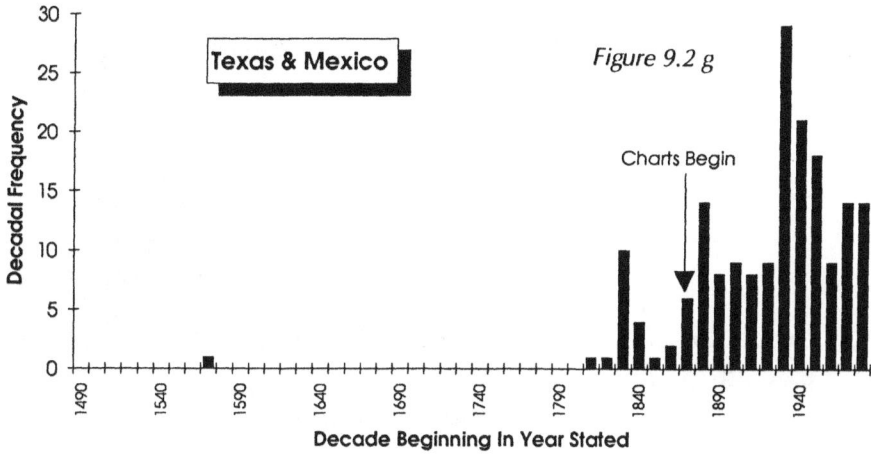

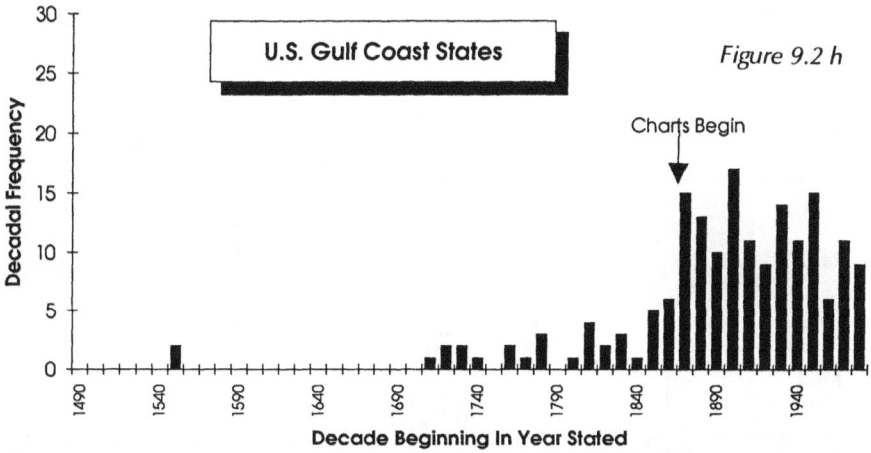

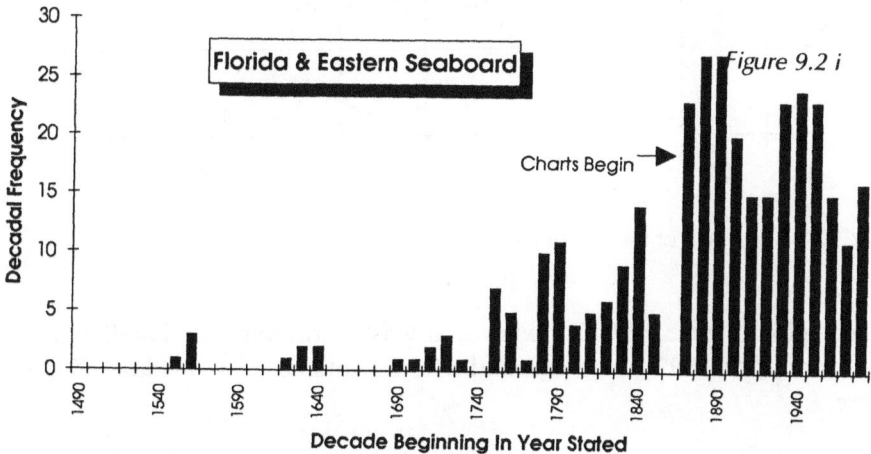

Figure 9.2(a – j)   Decadal frequency of cyclones in ten subregions of the Caribbean

**129**

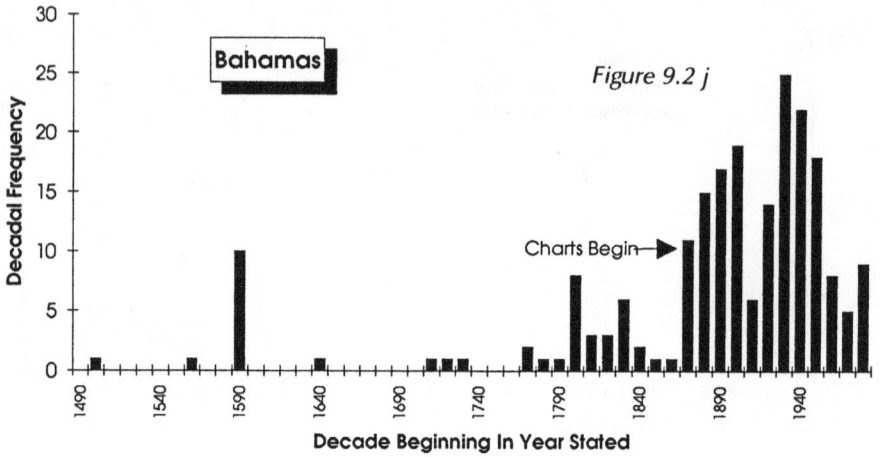

*Figure 9.2 (a – j)* Decadal frequency of cyclones in ten subregions of the Caribbean

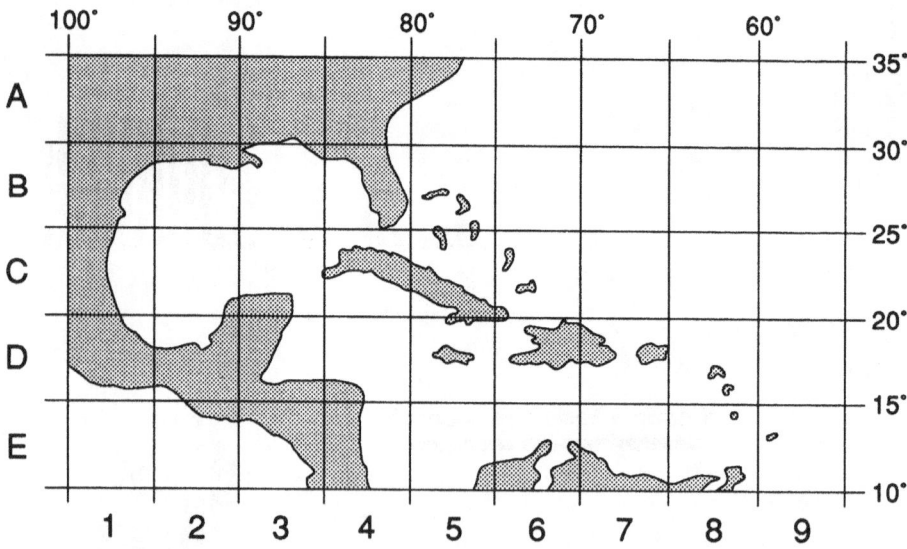

*Figure 9.3* Grid map of the Caribbean, charted data

Indies region (Figure 9.3). Cyclones of at least storm force (and additionally hurricanes after 1899) were counted as they entered an individual 5° grid square.

# The Historical Data Series

The length of accuracy and comprehensiveness of each cyclone series generated varies greatly with subregion, in relation to the date and continuity of European settlement, the extent to which documents survived wars, fires, cyclones and other misfortunes and the adequacy and degree of study of archival material. Four subregions, namely The Bahamas, Yucatan/Belize/Honduras, Nicaragua/Costa Rica/Panama and the Gulf Coast States have very incomplete records prior to the charted period, probably a reflection of a lack of archival research rather than a lack of records (Figure 9.2). Cyclones are known to be rare as far south as the Venezuelan/Aruba-Bonaire-Curaçao region and although the graph (Figure 9.2) shows few cyclones, it is thought to be reasonably representative from around the 18th century. The Florida/Eastern Seaboard and the Texas/Mexico series may have some validity back to the mid 18th and early 19th centuries respectively. There is an even longer record of cyclones for the Cuba/Jamaica/Cayman Islands region, due largely to the research effort of Millas [1968]. However, they are still considered incomplete prior to 1871. Millas [1968] has also been largely responsible for the quality and longevity of the Hispaniola/Puerto Rico series. The Lesser Antilles record is slightly shorter but more comprehensive from around 1650 onwards.

## Regional Variations in Cyclone Activity

All the data series show a long-term increase in cyclone activity which is entirely a function of the improving quality of data. For example, most subregions show an apparent increase in cyclone frequency corresponding to the introduction of charts in the 1870s. Notwithstanding this complication, the data series show peaks and troughs which are consistent between regions suggesting real changes in frequencies rather than deficiencies in the data.

The data indicate that, on a regional scale, cyclone activity has been high between 1765-92, 1804-37, 1876-1901 and 1928-1958. Cyclone activity has been low pre-1765, from 1793-1803 and from 1838-1874 and relatively low between 1902-1927 and since 1959.

## Cyclone Activity across the Lesser Antilles

This region is geographically very significant since the islands of the Lesser Antilles lie at the eastern entrance to the Caribbean along an approximate line at 61° W between 10° N and 19° N. Since the islands are rarely more than 50km apart there is little chance of a cyclone slipping through them unnoticed. Although Columbus arrived in the islands in the 1490s, and they were nominally Spanish until the 17th century, they remained effectively under the control of Amerindian Caribs until the arrival of the French, British and other northern European settlers and trading companies. Most islands were colonized by Europeans by the mid 17th century.

The data show some remarkable fluctuations in cyclone frequencies with activity low between 1650-1764, 1794-1805, 1838-1875 and high between 1765-1793, 1806-1837, 1876-1901, and 1928-1958. Of particular interest is the magnitude of the first two peaks (1765-1793 and 1806-1837). Given that there are possibly cyclones not recorded within these early peaks, we can assume that levels of activity at these times were at least on par with levels during the mid 20th century high.

### Cyclone Activity across Hispaniola and Puerto Rico

Data for the Hispaniola/Puerto Rico subregion, despite at times being incomplete, are also of considerable interest. They extend further back than the Lesser Antilles records, a function of the very early conquest of Hispaniola by the Spanish and archival research by Millas [1968]. Records from 1550 to 1710, however, probably considerably underestimate true cyclone frequencies. During this period Spanish interest in the islands waned and Hispaniola's original Arawak population was decimated, then virtually wiped out by disease. Records improve after 1710 when the French take over control; however, the complete lack of records in the 1790s may be spurious, reflecting political and social chaos which ensued during the French Revolution, and the subsequent revolution in Haiti.

The general pattern of cyclone activity is broadly similar to that in the Lesser Antilles. Peaks are again evident in the late 18th, early and late 19th and mid 20th centuries. Despite the incompleteness of data from 1550-1710 the more reliable records of the Spanish (1500-1550) and French (post-1710) periods indicate that frequencies were low up to the 1760s. Frequencies also appear to have been low in the mid 19th and early 20th centuries and in the last three decades of this century.

The mid 20th century peak and recent decline of activity has been more pronounced in Hispaniola/Puerto Rico than over the Lesser Antilles.

## The Modern (Charted) Period 1871-1989

Figure 9.4 indicates significant fluctuations in the frequency and spatial distribution of cyclones in the last twelve decades. At a regional scale, frequencies were low in the 1870s, in the 1910s and 1920s and relatively low in the past three decades, but peaked in the 1880s and 1890s and more

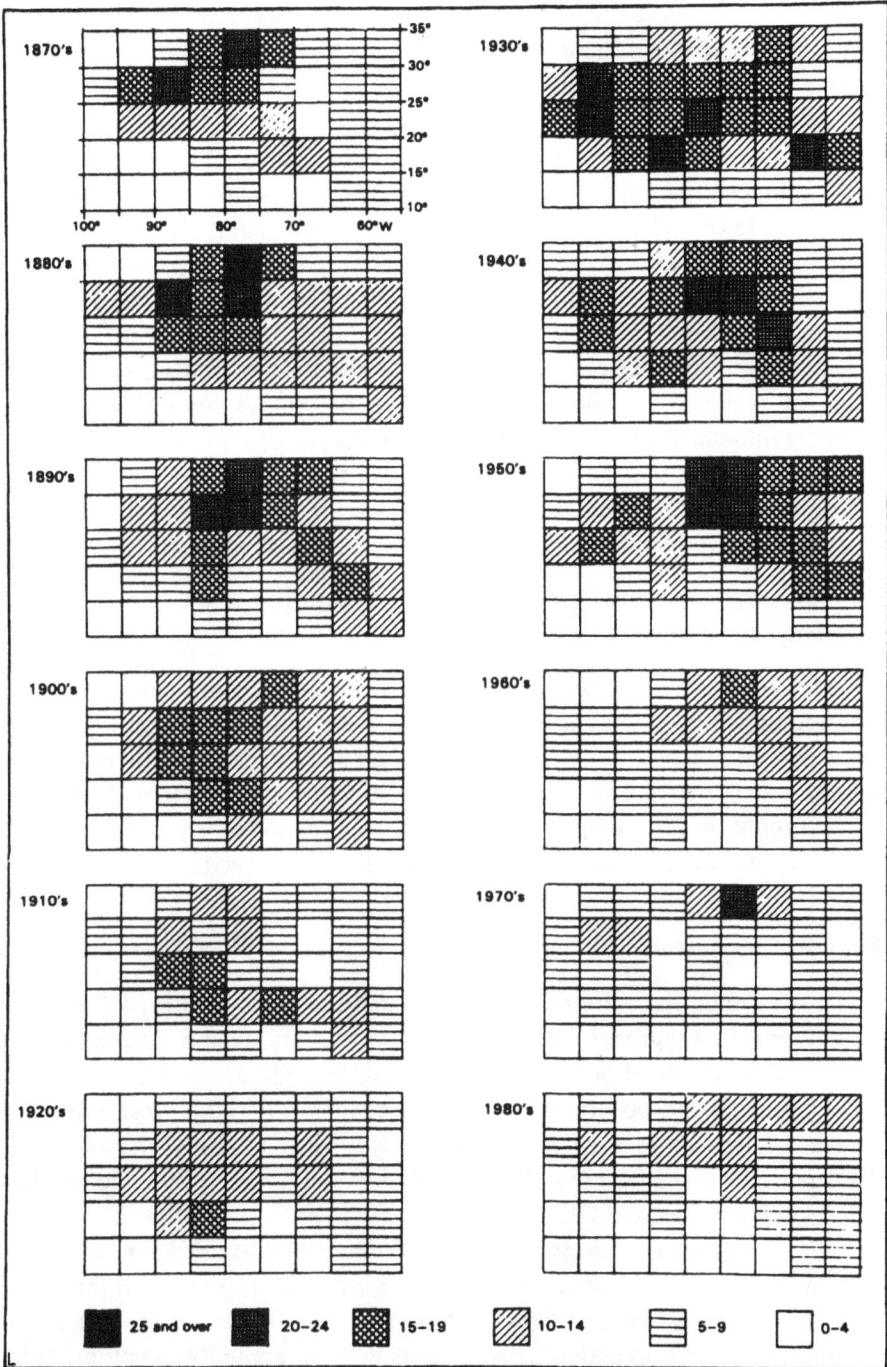

Figure 9.4    Decadal frequency of cyclones, 1870s – 1980s, per 5° grid square

strikingly in the 1930s, 1940s and 1950s. Superimposed upon these regional peaks and troughs are significant spatial shifts. During the charted periods the focus of activity has drifted first westwards and southwards, then strongly eastwards. Frequencies therefore tended to be higher in the west of the region in the 1880s and 1890s peak and early 20th century trough, and higher in the east of the region in the 1930s to 1950s peak and recent trough.

These shifts in tracks are seen clearly at an individual grid square level. In the 1880s and 1890s cyclone peak, frequencies were highest in the mid-Gulf and along the Atlantic seaboard (squares B3, A5 and B5). In the 1930s, the foci of activity lay further west in the Gulf of Mexico (B2/C2), further south over Cuba (C5) and over the northern Lesser Antilles (D8). By the 1940s and 1950s the focus of activity had moved eastwards over the northern Bahamas and adjacent Atlantic (B5/B6). Patterns in the troughs are also different. In the 1910s and 1920s activity was distinctly further south and west in the Caribbean, while during the past three decades cyclone activity has been maintained to a greater extent in the northeast of the region.

## Intensity Variations

Since 1886, the US Weather Bureau has differentiated between cyclones of storm force (sustained surface winds of between 34-63 knots) and hurricane force (sustained surface winds of 64 knots and above). Since 1899, changes in the intensity of cyclones have been displayed on the annual charts. This allows an examination of changes in the intensity characteristics of cyclones, obviously an important consideration in any studies of cyclone impact.

## Regional Variations

Figure 9.5 shows that patterns of hurricane frequency only loosely follow those of cyclones. At a regional scale, the mid 20th century peak is evident but it is the 1950s which stand out as having particularly high numbers of hurricanes. In the past two decades the number of hurricanes within the West Indies grid area has fallen dramatically, despite the very high intensity and degree of damage caused by a number of them (for example, David 1979, Gilbert 1988, Hugo 1989 and Andrew 1992).

The percentage of cyclones which have intensified to hurricane status has also varied markedly, from a low of 43 percent and 46 percent in the 1900s and 1930s respectively, to a high of 69 percent and 71 percent respectively in the intervening two decades. This suggests that the early 20th century trough was, to a considerable extent, associated with the failure of low pressure systems to develop to storm force. Of those that did, a high proportion

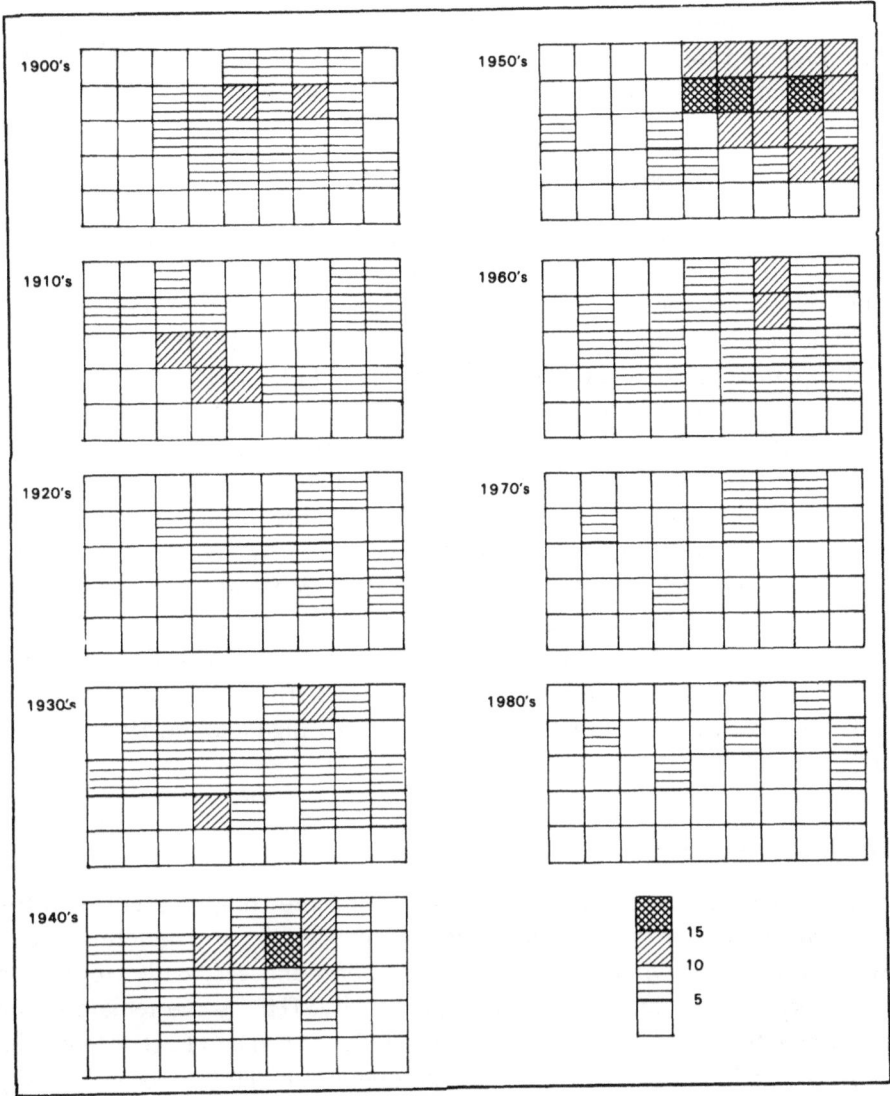

*Figure 9.5* Decadal frequency of hurricanes 1900s – 1980s, per 5° grid square

intensified further to become hurricanes. Thus, the low frequency of cyclones in the early part of this century may not correlate with low levels of cyclone damage. During the mid 20th century, changes in hurricane frequency lagged behind changes in cyclone frequency. The overall number and proportion of hurricanes progressively increased during the 1940s and 1950s and remained relatively high as cyclone numbers fell in the 1960s.

Patterns in the entire North Atlantic macro-region (the West Indies plus

Atlantic) are very similar except that the number and proportion of hurricanes has remained high over the Atlantic during the last three decades, further highlighting the shift east in cyclone activity mentioned above.

## Grid Square Variations

To investigate spatial variations in these regional patterns five grid squares were selected to provide a representative cross-section of the West Indies grid area. The grid squares approximate to the following land areas; (B2) Texas coast, (B6) Atlantic east of northern Bahamas, (C4) western Cuba, (D6) Haiti and western Dominican Republic and (E8) southern Windward Islands (Figure 9.6).

The greatest proportion of hurricanes occurs over the Atlantic (B6). In this square the mid 20th century peak was clearly characterized by an increase in hurricanes. Further south, over the Windward Islands (E8), the situation is somewhat different. Here, the mid 20th century peak was much less pronounced and was almost entirely the result of increases in storm activity. Very few of the cyclones which crossed the southern Windward Islands during the 1920s, 1930s or 1940s were hurricanes.

Since 1960, all areas show a fall in levels of cyclone activity although this is least pronounced in the most southerly area, E8. The proportion of systems which intensify to hurricanes remained relatively high into the 1960s (Figure 9.6).

## Origin of Cyclones

The tropical cyclones which affect the West Indies originate either in the western Atlantic or in the warm waters of the Caribbean. The former move west in the trade winds, before recurving north and eastwards around the periphery of the subtropical high pressure cell (STHP), some remain in the open Atlantic, while others enter the Eastern Caribbean and track through the West Indian islands. The cyclones which originate in the Caribbean intensify quickly and almost immediately become affected by the westerly mid-latitude circulation. Hence, they tend to track steeply north and east towards higher latitudes via the Gulf of Mexico and the coast of the USA.

To investigate the extent to which the different types of cyclones have been responsible for the peaks and troughs described above, all charted North Atlantic cyclones were differentiated into one of four categories (Table 9.1). The results are summarized in Figure 9.7.

The general increase in Atlantic storms and hurricanes shown in Figure 9.7 may, to some extent, reflect the improvement of data from the 1960s. However, the pattern is consistent with the shift east in cyclone activity mentioned above

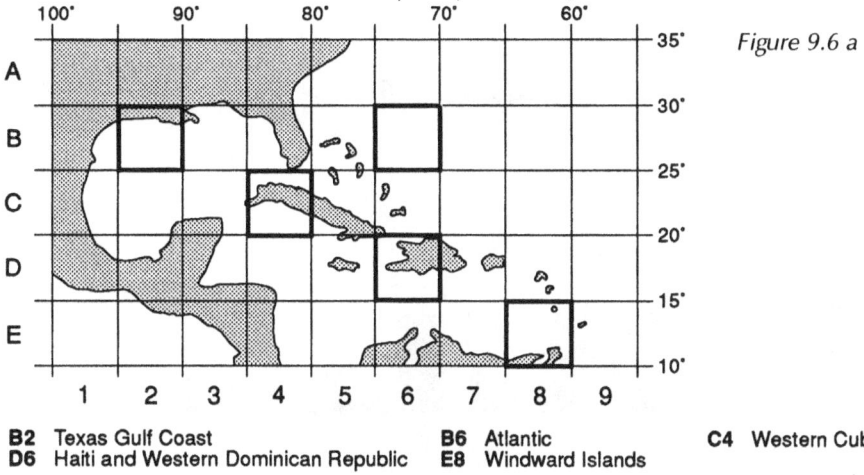

*Figure 9.6 a*

**B2** Texas Gulf Coast
**D6** Haiti and Western Dominican Republic
**B6** Atlantic
**E8** Windward Islands
**C4** Western Cuba

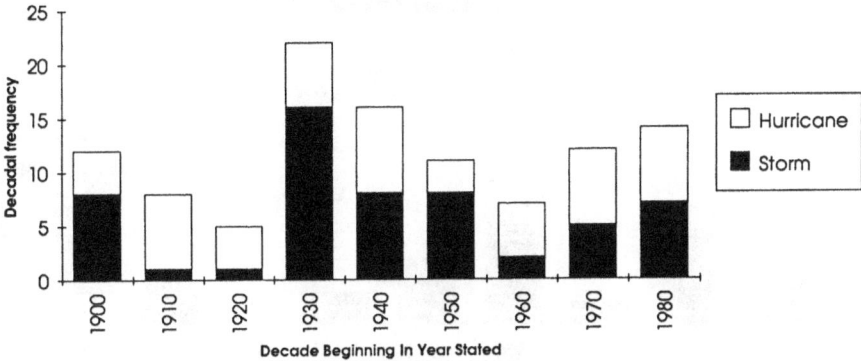

*Figure 9.6 b*

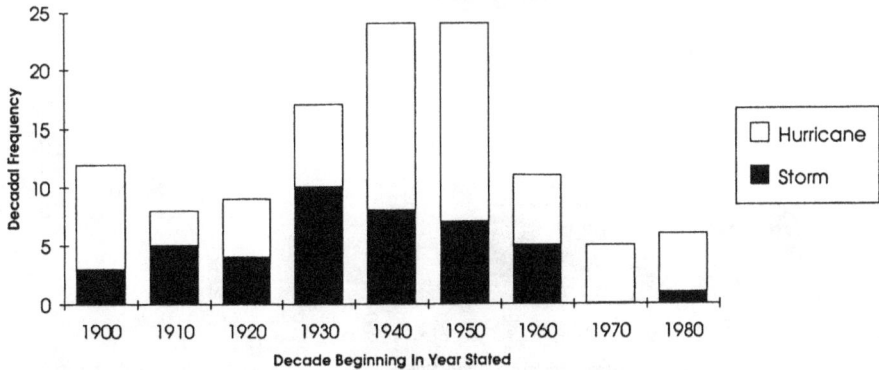

*Figure 9.6 c*

*Figure 9.6(a – f)* Spatial variations in intensity patterns for five selected grid squares

**C4  Western Cuba**

*Figure 9.6 d*

*Figure 9.6 e*

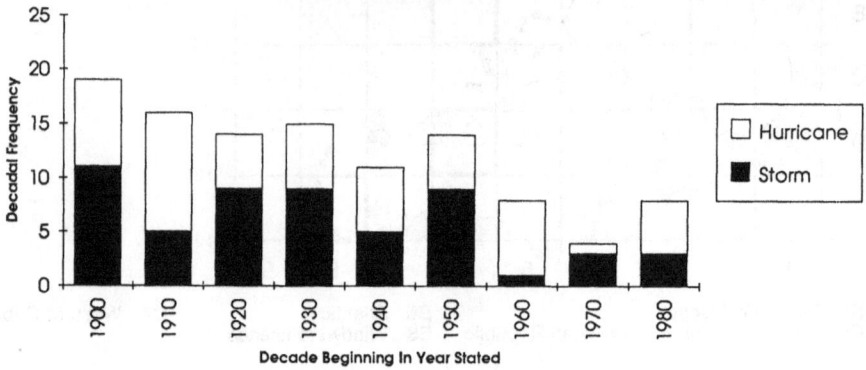

**D6  Haiti & W. Dominican Rep.**

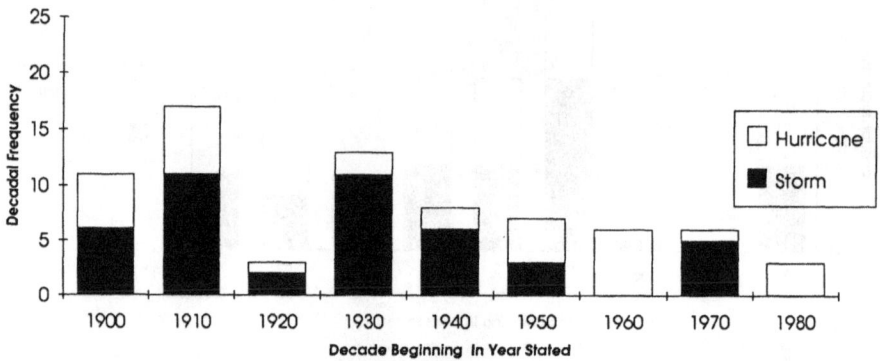

**E8  S. Windward Islands**

*Figure 9.6 f*

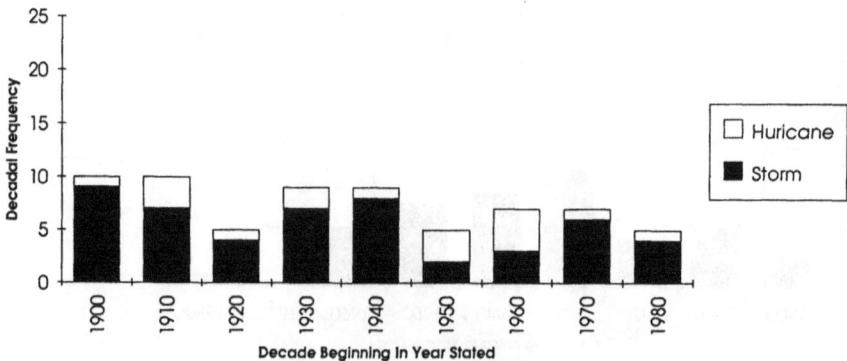

*Figure 9.6(a – f)*   Spatial variations in intensity patterns for five selected grid squares

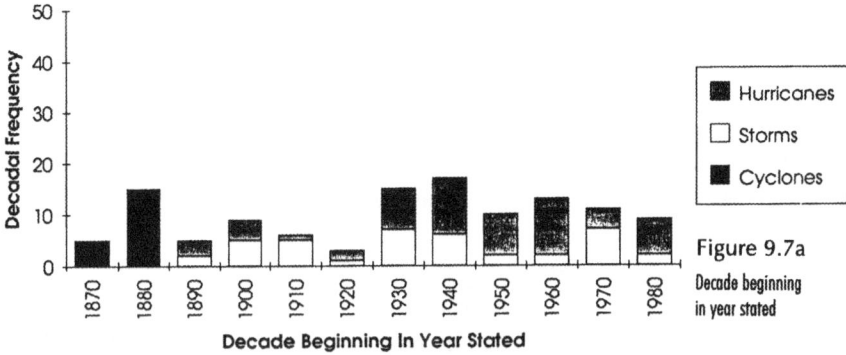

Figure 9.7a

Decade beginning in year stated

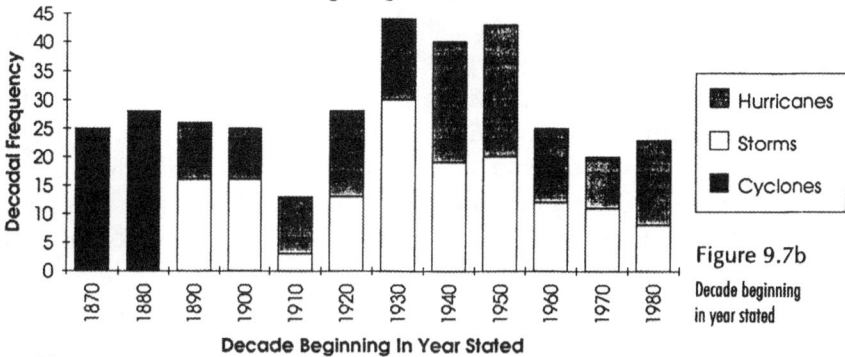

Figure 9.7b

Decade beginning in year stated

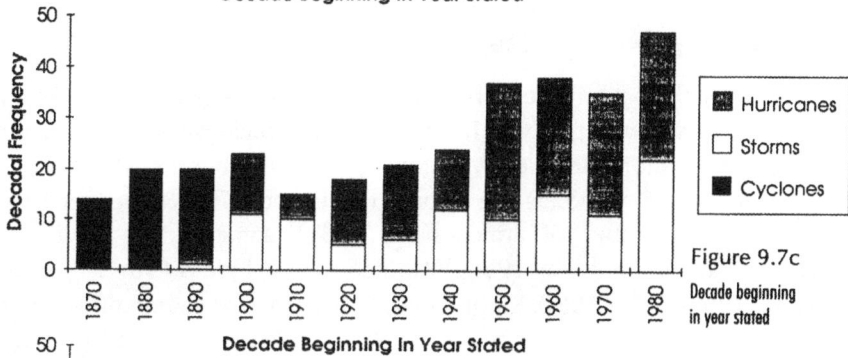

Figure 9.7c

Decade beginning in year stated

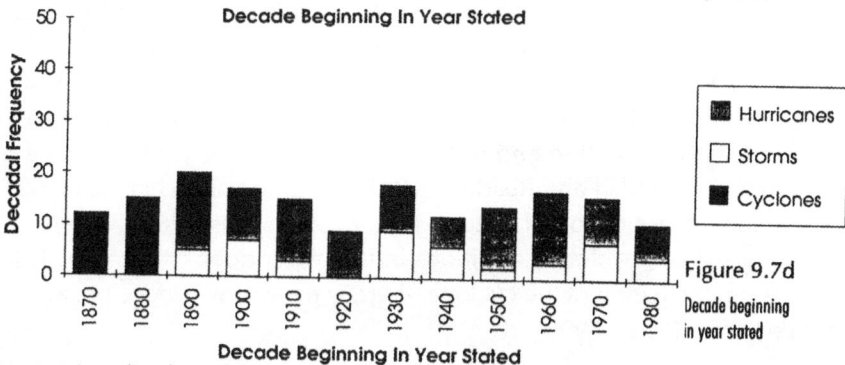

Figure 9.7d

Decade beginning in year stated

*Figure 9.7 (a – d)* The origins of cyclones in the North Atlantic

*Table 9.1*    Categories of Cyclones in the North Atlantic Region

| Type Name | Track |
|---|---|
| 1 Cape Verde | eastern Atlantic to eastern Caribbean |
| 2 Atlantic | eastern Atlantic to central/western Atlantic |
| 3 North Caribbean/ Western Atlantic | north of Greater Antilles to central Atlantic |
| 4 Western Caribbean | western Caribbean to Gulf of Mexico/USA/Atlantic |

and suggests that, while levels of activity have declined during the past three decades over the Caribbean, they have remained high over the Atlantic.

Figure 9.6 indicates that the mid 20th century peak was caused largely by an increase in Caribbean cyclones (type 3 and 4). The fact that the peak was most marked in the north and east of the region indicates that these systems did not track far westwards but recurved sharply over the Caribbean and Gulf of Mexico and then moved out into the Atlantic. In contrast, the number of Cape Verde type cyclones did not increase during the mid 20th century. This pattern is consistent with the general drift north and east of cyclone tracks during this century.

## Atmospheric and Oceanic Conditions likely to Influence Cyclone Activity

Explanations of the patterns described above and any attempts to predict future fluctuations in cyclone activity or hazard require knowledge of the circulatory influences on cyclone frequency, intensity and distribution. The linkages, however, are complex and, as yet, poorly understood [Gray & Sheaffer 1991]; nevertheless, a number of atmospheric and oceanic factors have been suggested as influential [Gray 1968; Wendland 1977; Eyre & Gray 1990; Gray & Sheaffer 1991; Pielke 1990; Riehl 1954]. The major circulatory influences on North Atlantic cyclone frequency and tracks include the summertime latitude of the Intertropical Convergence Zone (ITCZ), the summer position and strength of the subtropical high pressure cell (STHP), sea surface temperature (SST) and winter position of the STHP, the strength of the Atlantic trade winds, and the strength of El Niño and the Southern Oscillation (ENSO). These are discussed fully in Walsh and Reading [1991] and summarized in Table 9.2. In addition, the intensification of a storm to hurricane status is known to require the presence of anticyclone conditions in the upper troposphere to evacuate mass far from the region of the cyclone, thereby permitting surface pressures to continue to fall [Pielke 1990].

Table 9.2   Circulatory Factors Which May Influence Cyclonic Activity in the North Atlantic

| | | |
|---|---|---|
| **Latitude of Intertropical Convergence Zone (ITCZ)** | Favoured position for development is just poleward of the trough where wind shear is minimal. | Northerly/southerly positioned ITCZ pushes development and tracks northwards/southwards respectively. |
| **Summer position of Subtropical High Pressure (STHP)** | Associated with low level inversion and stability. Therefore the stronger it is and the closer it lies to the cyclone belt the less favourable are conditions for development. | An equatorwards shift (from mean $35°N$) or increase in intensity may lead to fewer and more southerly cyclones. |
| **Strength of trade winds** | Strong trades promote ocean evaporation convection, precipitation and latent heat release. May also aid advection of cold water westward. | If STHP lies westwards, cyclones track west into Caribbean and Gulf of Mexico. If STHP lies easterly, cyclones recurve at lower longitudes and may remain in Atlantic. |
| **Sea surface temperature and winter position of STHP** | Large expanse and depth of warm water ($26°$ C min.) required to provide heat energy for development. Controlled by solar radiation, flanks, reducing SST and cyclonic cloudiness, greenhouse gases and position of STHP. | If winter STHP is westerly, cold water allowed equatorwards around southern flanks, reducing SST and cyclone development. |
| **El Niño and the Southern Oscillation (ENSO)** | During strong ENSO, upper westerlies are increased, enhancing wind shear and impeding development. | Linkages between ENSO and cyclones complex. No direct relationships. |
| **Presence of upper troposphere high pressure** | High pressure over surface low pressure allows efficient evacuation of mass, permitting continued fall of surface pressure. | Upper troposphere high essential for intensification to hurricane. |

## Tentative Explanations of Patterns of Cyclone Activity in terms of Atmospheric and Oceanic Circulation

By using available historical information on atmospheric circulation, sea surface temperature and El Niño, it is possible to examine linkages between the above variables and cyclone activity in the various periods identified. Unfortunately, data on upper tropospheric conditions which would allow consideration of intensity changes are largely unavailable. Lamb and Johnson

[1959; 1961; 1966] provide information back to the late 18th century on the January and July latitude of the STHP; an east-west index of pressure difference; pressure indices of the strength of the trade winds in July at 60° W and 20° W; and the mean position of the ITCZ in the tropical Atlantic in July. Information on Atlantic sea surface temperatures is available from, for example, Rennell [1832], Barnett [1984], Folland et al. [1984], Folland and Parker [1990], Folland et al. [1990] and Quinn et al. [1987] also provide a historical time series of El Niño events stretching back to 1500.

### 1650-1764

This period of very low cyclone activity coincides with the height of the Little Ice Age of the temperate northern hemisphere. During this time the main elements of a weak circulation were displaced 3° to 5° south of their present positions and SSTs were perhaps 1.5°C below early 20th century levels. El Niños were also rather more common than in the 20th century. All these factors might be expected to lead to low levels of cyclone activity.

### 1765-1792

A 1°C rise in Atlantic SSTs from the low of the Little Ice Age [Rennell 1832; Lamb & Johnson 1959] is the only evidence to suggest why cyclone frequencies increased during this period.

### 1793-1803

An anomalously westerly position of the STHP [Lamb & Johnson 1959] may be linked to the low levels of cyclone activity during this period. Unfortunately, SST data, which could identify an associated equatorwards flux of cold water in the eastern Atlantic, are unavailable.

### 1804-1837

The return of high levels of cyclone activity during this period may be linked to the shift eastwards in the January position of the STHP. SST data for the period are again lacking.

### 1838-1875

This period of low cyclone frequencies corresponds with a decline in the strength of the July trade winds and a poleward migration of the ITCZ. The latter may help explain the more northerly track of the cyclones which did occur. Low SSTs are indicated by relatively low air temperatures in Trinidad and relatively low amounts of rainfall in the Eastern Caribbean [Walsh 1980]. The STHP was further south than usual, which may also have allowed cold water into the tropical Atlantic around its eastern flank.

## 1876-1898

A number of interrelated factors may be linked to the high cyclone frequencies of this period. For example, SSTs rose significantly, to 0.5°C above levels in the early 20th century, possibly associated with a northwards shift in the January position of the STHP. The strength of the trade winds also increased during this period.

The fact that this peak was strongest in the central and western parts of the region may be linked to the summer position of the STHP, which extended westwards across the southern United States. The frequency with which cyclones displayed a southerly track through the region may be linked with a sharp southward shift in the July position of the ITCZ.

## 1902-1927

Reasons for the marked fall in cyclone activity during this period are somewhat difficult to explain. By the middle of this period SSTs had fallen by 1°C from their 1880s peak, possibly because the further increase in trade winds led to upwelling of water in the eastern Atlantic and more effective advection of the cold water across the Tropical Atlantic. A similar phenomenon is seen in the North Indian Ocean when a stronger than normal southwest monsoon shifts cold water from the coast of Somalia and produces a midsummer decline in rainfall along the west coast of India [Saha 1974]. The reasoning, however, runs counter to Kraus's [1955] argument that strong trades should result in the intensification of the evaporation precipitation cycle.

The maintenance of a ridge of high pressure over the USA in July may explain the continued central and western focus in cyclone activity, while the shift northwards in the ITCZ may be associated with the more northerly tracks of cyclones during this period. While atmospheric conditions for the development of cyclones to storm force were clearly marginal during this period the proportion which developed further to hurricanes was relatively high. Whether or not the high pressure ridge over the USA was sufficiently deep and extensive to aid high level outflow of air from surface lows is unknown. The ENSO record shows that there were three strong and six moderate El Niño events during this period, a level of activity which is unexceptional.

## 1927-1958

This peak was very different to the late 19th century peak, being characterized by more northerly tracks and a more easterly focus to cyclone activity. A rise in SSTs, a migration eastwards of the STHP and the continued northerly position of the ITCZ may help explain these patterns. A northerly ITCZ and easterly STHP would also be consistent with there being a proportionally greater increase in the number of cyclones originating within the Caribbean compared with the number tracking west from the Cape Verde islands.

## 1959-1989

Once again the reasons for the decline in cyclone activity over the Caribbean but not over the Atlantic are equivocal. There has been a slight decline ($0.4^0C$) in SSTs from the mid 20th century and a number of strong ENSO events in the 1980s, although over the period as a whole the frequency of strong ENSOs was less than half that in the 1876-1901 cyclone peak.

An extension of the STHP south and eastwards may help explain the easterly migration of cyclone and hurricane tracks out into the Atlantic.

# Conclusions

This study suggests that there have been major changes in cyclone frequency, distribution and intensity within the Caribbean, West Indies and North Atlantic macro-region since Colombian times. It therefore follows that there have also been major changes in the levels of physical exposure to the cyclone hazard. Historical data, in particular from the Lesser Antilles and Hispaniola/Puerto Rico subregions, indicate major peaks in cyclone activity from 1765-92, 1804-37, 1876-1901 and 1928-58. Cyclones appear to have been very frequent before 1765, from 1793-1803 and between 1838-74. Cyclones were relatively infrequent from 1902-1927 and from 1959 onwards.

Analysis of the course of tropical cyclones over the past 120 years has revealed important spatial shifts in favoured tracks, namely a shift west and south followed by a distinct shift eastwards. The main focus of cyclone and hurricane activity now lies east of the West Indies in the open Atlantic.

Changes in patterns of hurricanes have only loosely followed changes in cyclone activity. Across the West Indies region the mid 20th century peak in activity was distinguished by a marked increase in the number of tropical storms. Much of this increase reflected a rise in the number of systems developing within the Caribbean and sharply recurving north and east towards the Atlantic. Increases in the proportion and number of storms intensifying to hurricanes lagged behind the increase in storms but remained relatively high as cyclone frequencies fell during the 1960s.

The early 20th century trough was characterized by a failure of low pressure systems to intensify to storm force, rather than a failure of some to develop further. During the past three decades, and despite fears over the effects of global warming, the number of cyclones occurring over the West Indies region has fallen markedly. However, and notwithstanding an improvement in data since 1960s, it appears that cyclone and hurricane numbers have at least been maintained over the Atlantic.

Reasons for the above patterns are poorly understood as linkages with the tropical and global oceanic and atmospheric circulation are complex, and historical information on the latter fragmentary. The spatial contrasts in changes in cyclone frequency within the North Atlantic, West Indies and Caribbean demonstrate the need for analysis at subregional scales. The very different spatial and intensity characteristics of the two most recent peaks suggest that similar regional levels of cyclone activity may have very different meteorological origins.

There is great scope for the improvement of many of the subregional chronologies through investigations of archival source material. Improvements in our understanding of the causes of changes in patterns of cyclone activity must await a more comprehensive knowledge of global circulatory processes.

## References

Barnett, T.P. 1984. "Long-term trends in surface temperature over the oceans". *Monthly Weather Review* 112: 303-12.

Eyre, L.A., & C. Gray. 1990. "Utilization of satellite imagery in the assessment of the effects of global warming on the frequency and distribution of tropical cyclones in the Caribbean, East Pacific and Australian regions", pp 365-75. *Proceedings 23rd International Symposium on Remote Sensing of Environment*. Thailand.

Folland, C.K., & D.E. Parker. 1990. "Observed variations of sea surface temperature". In *Climate-Ocean Interaction*, edited by M.E. Schlesinger, pp 21-52. Dordrecht: Kluwer Academic Press.

Folland, C.K., T.R. Karl, & K.Y. Vinnikov. 1990. "Observed climate variations and change". In *Climate Change: The IPCC Scientific Assessment*, edited by J.T. Houghton, G.J. Jenkins, & J.J. Ephrums, pp 195-238. WMO/UNEP Intergovernment Panel on Climate Change, Cambridge: Cambridge University Press.

Folland, C.K., D.E. Parker, & F.E. Kates .1984. "Worldwide marine temperature fluctuations 1856-1981". *Nature* 310: 670-73.

Gray, W.M. 1968. "Global view of the origin of tropical disturbances and storms". *Monthly Weather Review* 96: 55-73.

Gray, W.M., & J.D. Sheaffer. 1991. "El Niño and QBO influences on tropical activity". In *Teleconnections Linking Worldwide Climate Anomalies: Scientific Basis and Social Impact*, edited by M.H. Glantz & N. Nicholls, pp 257-84. Cambridge: Cambridge University Press.

Kraus, E.B. 1955. "Secular changes in tropical rainfall regimes". *Quarterly Journal of Royal Meteorological Society* 81: 198-210.

Lamb, H.H., & A.T. Johnson. 1959. "Climate variation and observed changes in the general circulation, Parts I and II". *Geografiska Annaler* 41A: 94-134.

Lamb, H.H., & A.T. Johnson. 1961. "Climate variation and observed changes in the general circulation, Part III". *Geografiska Annaler*, 43A: 363-400.

Lamb, H.H., & A.T. Johnson. 1966. "Secular variations of the atmospheric circulation since 1750". *Meteorological Office Geophysical Mem.* 110. London: HMSO.

Millas, J.C. 1968. *Hurricanes of the Caribbean and Adjacent Regions 1492-1800*. Miami: Academy Arts & Sciences, Americas.

Pielke, R.A. 1990. *The Hurricane*. London: Routledge.

Quinn, W.H., V.T. Neal. & S.E.A. de Mayalo. 1987. "El Niño occurrences over the past four and a half centuries". *Journal Geophysical Research 92, c13: 14, 449-61*.

Reading, A.J. 1990. "Caribbean tropical storm activity over the past four centuries". International Journal of Climatology 10: 365-376.

Rennell, J. 1832. *An Investigation of the Currents of the Atlantic Ocean and of Those which Prevail between the Indian and Atlantic Ocean*. London: Rivington.

Riehl, H. 1954. *Tropical Meteorology*, New York: McGraw-Hill.

Saha, K. 1974. "Some aspects of the Arabian Sea summer monsoon". *Tellus* 26: 464-76.

Smith, K. 1992. *Environmental Hazards*. London: Routledge.

Walsh, R.P.D. 1980. "Drainage density and hydrological process in a humid tropical environment: the Windward Islands". PhD thesis, University of Cambridge.

Walsh, R.P.D., & A.J. Reading. 1991. "Historical changes in tropical cyclone frequency within the Caribbean since 1500". *Wurzburger Geographische Arbeiten* 80: 199-240.

Wendland, W.M. 1977. "Tropical storm frequencies related to sea surface temperature". *Journal of Climatology* 2: 1329-351.

**Chapter 10**

# Landslides in Jamaica: Extent, Significance and Geological Zonation

Rafi Ahmad

## Introduction

Hazards related to slope instability are a major societal and environmental concern to Jamaica. Landslides are an important geomorphic process on the island being significantly controlled by the geological and tectonic framework [Ahmad 1989a;1989b; DeGraff et al. 1989; Manning et al. 1992; Ahmad et. al.1993a]. However, the landslide hazard in Jamaica is to a large extent a consequence of changing land use.

The high incidence of landslides in Jamaica is due to a combination of several geological, geophysical and geographical factors. The island is located within a 200km wide, seismically active plate boundary zone of Neogene deformation [Mann et al. 1985; 1990]. This is an area of geologically young landforms, steep hillsides, high annual precipitation and periodic short duration and high magnitude rainfall from various types of tropical storms which often reach hurricane force [Ahmad et al. 1993a].

This paper reviews the extent and significance of landslides in Jamaica and presents an analysis of landslide phenomena. A geological zonation of landslides is proposed for the purposes of landslide loss reduction.

## Land Use

Jamaica has a population density of 255 persons/km$^2$; 18,197km of roads with a density of 1.6km of road/km$^2$ , about 10 vehicles/km of road; and 293km of railway [*National Atlas of Jamaica* 1971; *World Resources* 1990-91]. Agriculture is a major economic activity on the island, utilizing some 47 percent of the land while about 18 percent is under forest and woodland. The remaining 35 percent may be classified as ruinate land. Anthropogenic activities have extensively interfered with the natural slopes during the last 400 years and the trend continues with new development encroaching on potentially unstable areas. Landsliding amplifies mass wasting in all of its watersheds. In general, active erosion of the young upland lithosols is aided by a steep topography, tropical climate, torrential rainfall, and changes in vegetation cover.

## Landslide Triggering Mechanisms

Slope movement processes observed in Jamaica are both a natural geodynamic phenomenon through which hillslopes evolve, as well as a consequence of changing land use following unsustainable development activities during the last 400 years. Tables 10.1 and 10.2 suggest that recurrent economic losses occur in the physical environment modified for human use.

The most effective mechanism for triggering widespread landslide activity on the island is provided by the seasonal pattern of rainfall punctuated with intense storm events. In general, landslides follow sustained rainfall which recharges the soils and deeply weathered bedrock present on steep slopes. This condition favours the development of excessive pore-water pressures which tend to reduce the shear resistance in slope materials leading to widespread slope failures. For example, in one recorded instance, approximately 300mm of rainfall in 48 hours initiated shallow landslides that were quickly transformed into rapidly moving debris flows that caused extensive damage [Earle 1991].

Earthquake events of Modified Mercalli Intensity VIII – X (greater than Richter Magnitude 6.5) have been responsible for liquefaction and large-scale landslides, whereas events below VIII have generally resulted in rock falls and debris slides [Ahmad 1989c]. The earthquake of 13 January 1993 (Duration Magnitude 5.4) triggered more than 40 landslides of different types in the parishes of Kingston and St Andrew [Ahmad 1993].

# Landslides: Extent and Significance

Tables 10.1 and 10.2 summarize the extent, human impact, and economic losses from major landslide events in Jamaica and are based on the compilation of the currently available data. In Jamaica, landslides have caused death and injury and have damaged or destroyed rural settlements, public and private property, roads, bridges and culverts, retaining walls, schools, agricultural lands and crops, water pipelines, telecommunication lines and cables, and electricity transmission lines. The causes of accelerated soil erosion on the island are intimately linked to the landslide related mass wasting [Gupta 1975; Manning et al. 1992].

Landslides severely disrupt the overland transport as the island's major road network transects high-risk areas (Figure 10.1, p154). Manning et al. [1992] mapped 478 landslides along 108km of roads in the Above Rocks area following Hurricane Gilbert in 1988. Hubbard and Fermor [1972] and Naughton [1984] noted the extent of rainfall-induced landslides and pointed out that the cost of repairing damage is a significant burden on the country's budget. A small landslide in the Bog Walk Gorge following a rainstorm event, 21-22 May 1991, blocked the main road connecting Kingston with the north coast for over six months [Ahmad 1991]. Vehicular traffic had to use longer alternative routes resulting in loss of time for commuters and wastage of very costly imported fuel. Movements on this landslide are currently reactivated after every spell of heavy rainfall leading to dislodgment of rocks and boulders which threaten the safety of road users. This type of hazard is serious and is common to many of the roads on the island. Blockage of the roads also affects the movement of tourists on the island [Ahmad 1993].

The impact of landslides on the island's water supplies is significant. In the wake of Hurricane Gilbert, a landslide near Bromley Hill damaged the Boar River water pipeline [Ahmad et al. 1993b]. This pipeline contributes approximately 4.5 million litres of water daily to the Constant Spring Filter Plant which supplies drinking water to the parishes of Kingston and St Andrew. The Yallahs Pipeline also is similarly affected. The problem of excessive siltation in the Hermitage reservoir in Upper St Andrew is related to rainfall-induced debris flows in the watershed of the Wagwater River. Very fine suspended sediment load in the surface waters following debris flows in 1991 resulted in very high turbidity levels in the domestic water supply of central Jamaica [Ahmad 1991]. Rainfall-induced debris flows significantly contribute to accelerated soil erosion throughout the island [McGregor 1988; McGregor & Barker 1991]. The volume of the landslide related sediment generated by hurricane rainfall in 1988 along roads in the Above Rocks area is estimated at 20,000m$^3$ [Manning et al. 1992]. This sediment has affected the channel flow

*Table 10.1* Some Major Slope Movements in Jamaica Including Fatalities, Injuries, and Economic Costs

| Event | Slope Movement Type |
|---|---|
| 1. Great Earthquake of June 7, 1692 | Widespread liquefaction, rock falls and avalanches, and other types of landslides; landslides dammed rivers |
| 2. Judgment Cliff landslide induced by rainfall of October 1692 (93?) | Complex rockslide-slump; volume $6.6 \times 10^6 m^3$; dammed Yallahs River, causing flooding |
| 3. Kingston earthquake of January 14, 1907 | Liquefaction, widespread landslide activity in eastern Jamaica |
| 4. Whitfield Hall landslide, Blue Mountains; torrential rains of 1909 | Complex landslide |
| 5. Millbank landslide, Portland, November 27, 1937; torrential rains | Complex rockslide slump; volume $2 \times 10^6 m^3$; dammed Rio Grande river for 6 months, causing flooding |
| 6. Chelsea landslide, Portland, November 1940 | Complex rockslide slump; volume $2 \times 10^6 m^3$; Swift River dammed, causing flooding |
| 7. Montego Bay earthquake of March 1, 1957 | Rock falls, rock slides, debris slides |
| 8. Hurricane Flora, October 8, 1963 | Extensive debris flows islandwide; Mahogany Vale footbridge landslide (volume $40,000 m^3$) dammed Yallahs River |
| 9. Heavy rainfall, June 10, 1969 | Extensive debris flows islandwide |
| 10. Hurricane Frederick, September 11-13, 1979 | Extensive debris flow activity in eastern Jamaica |
| 11. Flood rains, May–June 1986 | Extensive debris flow activity in eastern and central parishes |
| 12. Preston (St Mary) slope movements, March 1986 | Lateral spread, area 100 ha, volume $11.9 \times 10^6 m^3$ |
| 13. Hurricane Gilbert, September 12, 1988 | Extensive debris flows in the interior mountain ranges of eastern and central Jamaica |
| 14. Flood rains, May 21-22, 1991 | Extensive debris flows in eastern and central parishes |
| 15. Earthquake January 13, 1993, Kingston and St Andrew | Rock falls, rock slides, complex slides |

Note: 'X' indicates no data

| No. of persons killed/injured/ missing | Economic Cost | Reference/Comments |
|---|---|---|
| Very high; 3,000 killed; Catastrophic event | Port Royal destroyed; extensive damage islandwide | Tomblin and Robson [1977]; data on landslide not available |
| At least 19 killed | Homes and plantations destroyed | Zans [1959] |
| Very high, about 1000 killed, catastrophic event | 90,000 people homeless; submarine cables damaged; property damage in excess of 2m pounds sterling | Tomblin and Robson [1977], Isaacs [1985]; columns 3 and 4 represent total damage |
| X | Hundreds of hectares of cultivated land and coffee estates destroyed | Described by Eyre [1969] and reported in Maharaj [1992] |
| 5 killed, missing and injured not known | Extensive damage to agricultural lands, livestock, housing; road blocked; 2 bridges destroyed | Harris and Rammelaere [1986] |
| 10 killed | Extensive damage to agricultural property, roads and bridges | Harris and Rammelaere [1986] |
| 2 killed, 7 injured | Railway line blocked; damage statistics not available | Robinson et al. [1960] |
| X | Agriculture, houses, and roads damaged islandwide; damage statistics not available | Gupta [1975] |
| X | Extensive damage to public and private property; damage statistics not available | Newspaper reports |
| X | Extensive damage; data not available | Newspaper reports |
| None | Roads and bridges damaged and destroyed; cost of repairs US$16m | Wason [1986], Earle [1991] |
| None | Village of Preston destroyed; 17 families displaced; replacement cost in 1986 = US$273,000; Total economic cost = 264 person/years | Ahmad et al. [1993c] |
| None | Extensive damage; 478 landslides along 108km of roads in Above Rocks area; landslide damage approx. US$25m | Manning et al. [1992] |
| 1 killed, 1 injured | Extensive damage to agriculture, roads, bridges, private and public property; Bog Walk Gorge road blocked for 6 months; cost of repairs approx. US$30m | Ahmad [1991] |
| 1 killed | X | Ahmad [1993] |

*Table 10.2*  Prehistoric/Undated Landslide Events with Volumes in Excess of 1mm³

| EVENT | TYPE | COMMENTS/REFERENCE |
|---|---|---|
| 1. Kingston landslides originating in Hope River watershed near Papine, St Andrew | Rock avalanches, flow slides | Very large rock blocks and boulders spread over Liguanea Plain are remnants of these events. *Ahmad [1993, research in progress]* |
| 2. Liguanea Ridge and Stony Hill landslips, St Andrew | Complex slides | Large slides along the Wagwater Fault Zone. *Geological Sheet 22 [1974]* |
| 3. Williamsfield landslide, St Catherine | Debris-rock slide | In grandiorite. *Geological Sheet 22 [1971]* |
| 4. Rio Nuevo Valley landslides, St Mary, Guys Hill-Pembroke Hall-Lambkin Hill area | Lateral spreads and rock slump flow | Limestones and sandstones slipped over mudrocks. *Geological Sheet 21 [1970]* |
| 5. Landslides west of Ewarton, St Catherine, Mount Diablo | Complex slides | Tertiary limestones have slipped over Cretaceous basement. *Geological Sheet 19 [1968]* |
| 6. Spur Tree Fault Zone landslides, Manchester | Complex rock-debris slides | Tertiary limestones have slipped. *Geological Map, Jamaica [1984]* |

characteristics of the Rio Pedro and the Rio Cobre. The response of the offshore ecosystems (such as coral reefs) to the excessive sediment supplied via accelerated soil erosion and rapid mass movements during extreme rainfall events remains to be assessed.

The landslide damage described above has occurred and continues to occur in a physical environment that has been modified for human use.

The cumulative direct and indirect economic cost and social impact of Jamaican landslides cannot easily be quantified due to a lack of information, and much of the damage remains undocumented. Since landslides and floods occur simultaneously, damage due to landslides is often misleadingly ascribed to damage caused by floods. Costs, however, are undoubtedly high. For example, it has been estimated that throughout the Caribbean some US$15 million are spent annually to repair the landslide damage to roads [DeGraff et al. 1989].

## Perception of the Hazard and Response

A developing country like Jamaica cannot sustain recurrent economic losses, disruptions and attendant human miseries due to landslides. It has been suggested that " . . . of all natural hazards, slope failures are perhaps the most amenable to measures directed towards avoidance, prevention or corrections",

[Varnes 1984]. In Jamaica, however, there is no mechanism for responding to the landslide hazard. There are no loss reduction programmes and mitigation strategies do not exist. Although landslides continue to cause significant economic losses on a recurrent basis, a significant landslide event is not perceived as a disaster [Ahmad et al. 1993c]. This perception must change. There is an urgent need for a National Landslide Management Programme with emphasis on loss reduction. The preparation of landslide hazard zonation maps for all the major watersheds on the island should be the first step in this direction.

# Distribution of Landslides in Relation to Geology and Geomorphology

Figure 10.1 shows the geographic distribution of major landslides in Jamaica, and is based on the events listed in Tables 10.1 and 10.2. Although this inventory is biased towards the built environment, it nevertheless portrays a reasonably accurate picture of the spatial distribution of landslides, as it incorporates all those areas where recurrent landslide activity has been observed since the turn of the century. It includes landslides in both natural and man-made environments. The landslide distribution in Jamaica defines distinct zones of landslide concentration.

A comparison of this zonal distribution pattern with the underlying geology suggests that landslides occur preferentially in specific geological belts (Figure 10.2). In this section, landslides are examined in relation to the processes responsible for the geological evolution of landforms in Jamaica.

## Regional Geological Framework

The land area along the northern margin of the Caribbean Plate is made up of accreted Cretaceous-Palaeogene island arc terranes manifested by the islands of the Greater Antilles whose present-day tectonic configuration and geographic position were probably established in the Miocene [Mann et al. 1990; Pindell & Barrett 1990]. The northern Caribbean Plate boundary zone is marked by a set of two parallel Neogene, left-lateral, strike-slip fault zones which accommodate the eastward movement of the Caribbean Plate relative to the Americas [Mann et al. 1990]. The southern fault in this system, the Enriquillo-Plantain Garden Fault Zone, constitutes a local compressional or "restraining bend" on Jamaica where block convergence has resulted in topographic uplift and compression in the Blue Mountains and the Wagwater Belt [Mann et al. 1985]. The landforms on the island of Jamaica are strongly

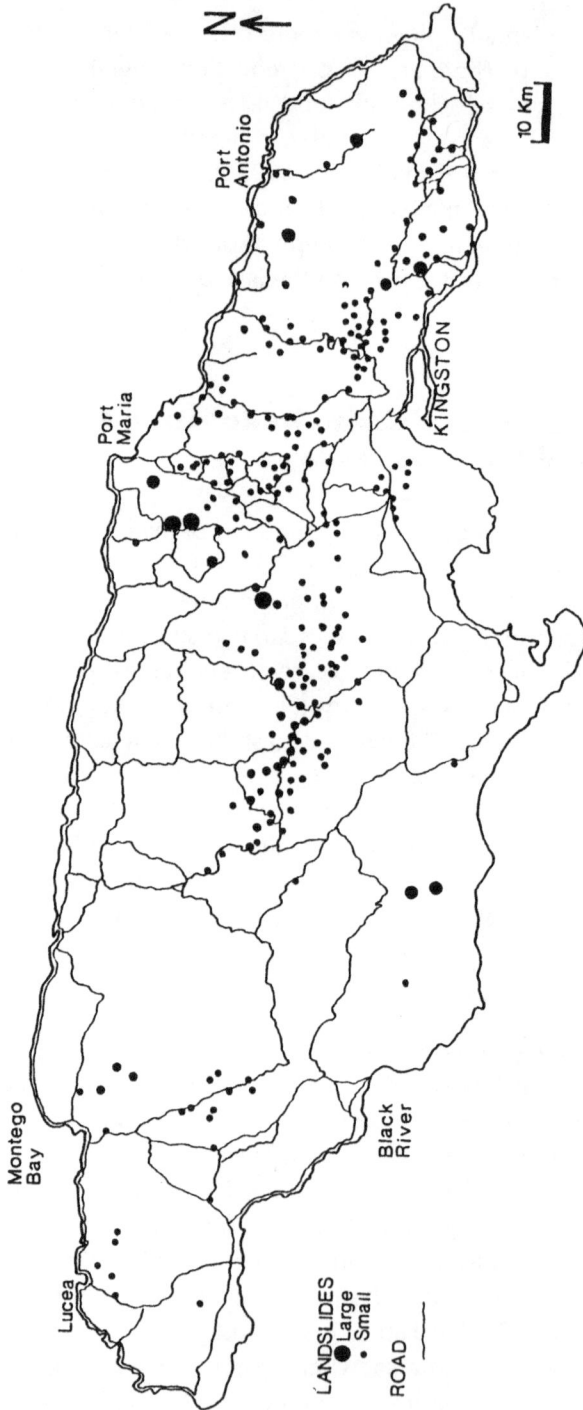

*Figure 10.1* Geographical distribution of major landslides in Jamaica based on the events listed in Tables 10.1 and 10.2

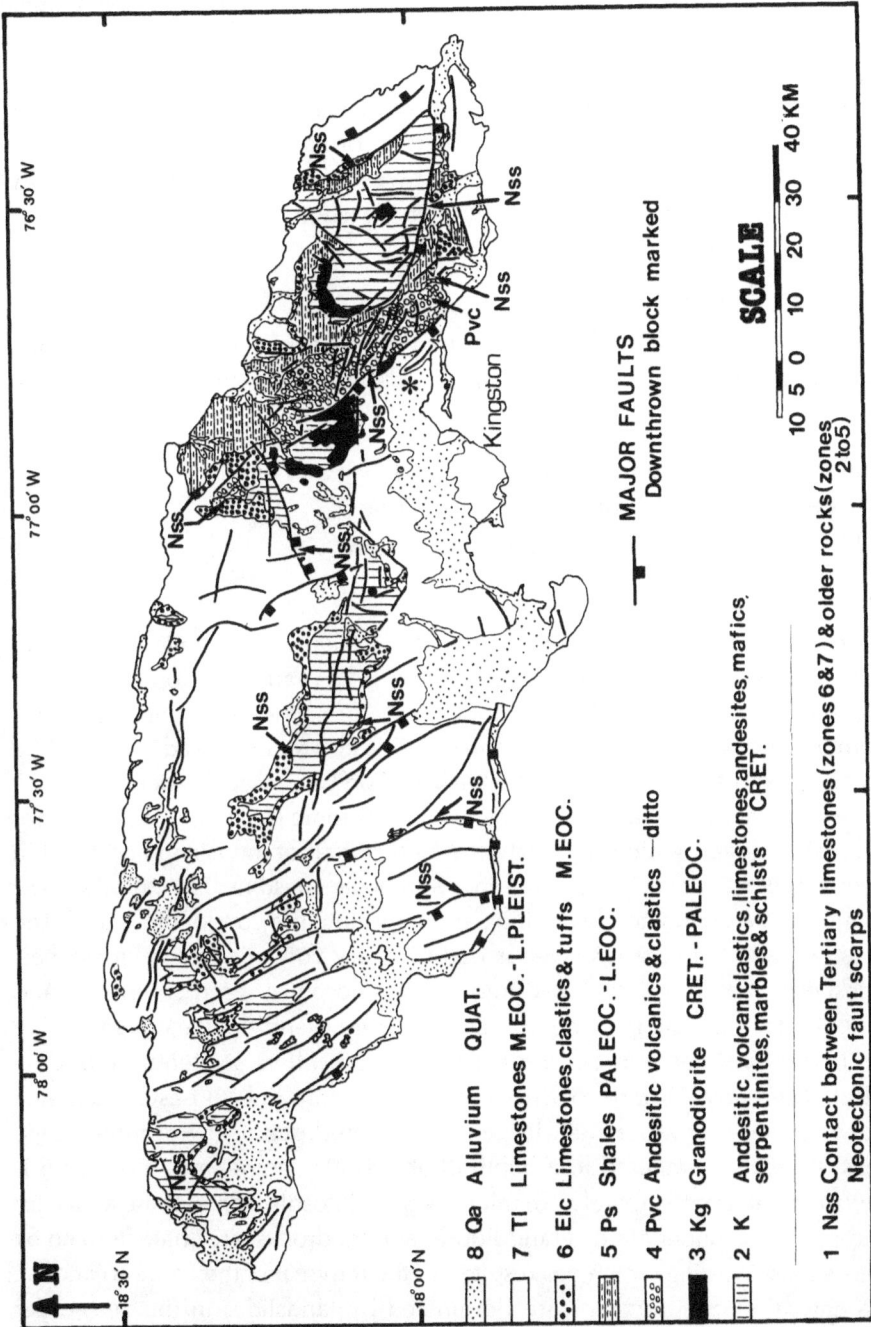

*Figure 10.2* Geology of Jamaica with 8 landslide zones

SCALE

10  5  0  10  20  30  40 KM

**MAJOR FAULTS**
▬ Downthrown block marked

8  Qa  Alluvium  QUAT.

7  Tl  Limestones M.EOC.- L.PLEIST.

6  Elc  Limestones,clastics & tuffs  M.EOC.

5  Ps  Shales PALEOC.- L.EOC.

4  Pvc  Andesitic volcanics & clastics —ditto

3  Kg  Granodiorite  CRET. - PALEOC.

2  K  Andesitic volcaniclastics,limestones,andesites,mafics,
      serpentinites,marbles& schists  CRET.

1  Nss  Contact between Tertiary limestones(zones 6&7 )&older rocks(zones
        2 to5)
        Neotectonic fault scarps

influenced by this neotectonic setting, characterized by steep dip-slip faults and a complex pattern of block faulting. As a result, the mountainous terrains are dominated by deeply incised, fault controlled valleys with steep slopes which are prone to slope movements.

The underlying geology and tectonic movements in the last 15 million years have profoundly influenced the evolution of landforms. The geological structure of Jamaica is controlled by northwest and west trending seismically active faults which define a "block and belt" structure (Figure 10.2).

## Landslide Habitats

The neotectonic landforms in Jamaica may be described with respect to three major morphotectonic units which are characterized by similar climatic conditions. These units are:

(a) the Interior Mountain Ranges which define a WNW-ESE orographic trend that controls the rainfall on the island;

(b) a highly dissected Limestone Plateau; and

(c) Alluvial Plains.

More than half of island's surface area (11,264km$^2$), lies above 300m, with approximately 3,570km$^2$ under slopes above 35°. A variety of slope movement types related to specific combinations of lithology, structure and geomorphology have been recognized. These are discussed below. The geological and structural information is based on Lewis and Draper [1990].

The ideal landslide habitats are the morphotectonic landforms of the Interior Mountain Ranges, which dominate the eastern half of the island and reach a maximum elevation of 2,256m within 20km of the coastline. Structurally, these mountains are dominated by faulting and constitute the core of the island. The rocks exposed here are Cretaceous early Tertiary volcaniclastics, limestones, andesites, mafic rocks, low-grade metamorphics, serpentinites, and granodiorites occupying some 30 percent of the island's surface area (Figure 10.2). The Cretaceous rocks are exposed in 28 inliers scattered across the island. The early Tertiary rocks occur in a tectonic belt in eastern Jamaica known as the Wagwater Belt. In general, the bedrock in the non-limestone areas is deeply weathered to a depth of about 30m, sometimes more, and is overlain by an approximately 1m thick layer of lithosols. Some of the areas, for example, those underlain by granodiorites and mudrocks, are characterized by intense mass wasting which has resulted in the removal of the entire soil cover. The natural slope processes are dominated by landslides in the zero-order drainage basins characteristic of these neotectonic landforms.

The steep slopes here are specially prone to slope movements after the disturbance of vegetation. The common types of failures are debris flows, debris avalanches, debris earth slides, slump earth flows, and rotational and translational slides (Table 10.3).

Much of the central and western part of the island is a highly dissected and faulted plateau of Tertiary limestones which fringe the Interior Mountain Ranges. It lies between 700m and 1,000m in elevation, and occupies some 60 percent to 65 percent of the island's surface area (Figure 10.2). The common failure types are rock slides, rock falls, rock avalanches, rock topples, debris flows and slides, and lateral spreads (Table 10.3). Some of the most spectacular and damaging landslides in Jamaica have their origin in the faulted contact between the plateau-forming Tertiary limestones and the underlying, less competent, older mudrocks, volcaniclastic sediments, and volcanic rocks (Table 10.3). Slope movements in this environment are often related to the deep-seated gravitational phenomenon of lateral spreading.

The incidence of landslides is comparatively less pronounced in the Quaternary alluvial deposits which mainly occur either as narrow Alluvial Plains fringing the upland landforms, chiefly along the south coast, or in interior valleys (Figure 10.2). The Quaternary deposits are, however, prone to liquefaction as was evident during the 1692 and 1907 earthquakes (Tables 10.1 to 10.3).

Geomorphological evidence indicates that gigantic prehistoric landslides have occurred in the Wagwater Belt, close to the city of Kingston. These landslides were responsible for the very large rock blocks and boulders (largest dimensions 0.5m to 3m) which the author has found stranded all over the Liguanea Plain and Hope River valley. That these boulders owe their present distribution to major flowslides that originated in the Hope River is supported by the fact that only two lithologies, conglomerates and andesites, make up the boulders, and that very large, exotic conglomerate and andesite boulders are found on top of Long Mountain at Beverley Hills (an elevation of 200m), which is underlain by Tertiary limestones. Andesites and conglomerates are exposed in the catchment of the Hope River.

## Geological Zonation of Landslides

The spatial distribution of landslides and landslide landforms in relation to the geological and geomorphical framework of Jamaica is described in the preceding section. It appears that the occurrence of landslides on the island is not a random phenomenon, being promoted by specific combinations of lithology, structure and geomorphology. The neotectonic landforms favour widespread landslide related mass movements which are triggered by

Table 10.3 Geological, Structural, Geomorphological, and Landslide Characteristics of the 8 Landslide Zones in Jamaica Identified on Figure 10.2

| Geological Landslide Zones | Lithology | Structure | Slope Features |
|---|---|---|---|
| 1. Zone Number/Map Symbol<br>2. Zone Name<br>3. Geological Province | 1. Bedrock<br>2. Weathering/Alteration<br>3. Slope Deposits | Joints/<br>Faults/<br>Shear Zones | E - Elevation in m<br>RI - Relief Intensity in m<br>SG - Slope Gradient in % |
| 1. 8–Qa<br><br>2. Quaternary clastics, alluvium and other superficial deposits<br><br>3. Qa1: Coastal plains, river valley dep., terrace dep., sand dunes; Liguanea Fm. 100m thick; Palisadoes tombolo; Qa2: Interior basins (poljes) | 1. Qa1: Unconsol. to poorly consol. clay, silt, sand, gravel and boulder; Qa2: Consol. to poorly consol. clay, silt and sand, terra rossa<br><br>2. Qa1: Generally rare, incohesive; Qa2: Locally pronounced, iron concretions, incohesive in near surface conditions<br><br>3. Qa1: Usually thin, local alluvial fans and cones, artificial fill; Qa2: Debris, colluvium as thick blankets | N/A | Qa1:<br>E<60<br>RI<5<br>SG generally >5<br><br>Qa2:<br>E Average 150<br>RI<10<br>SG – 5 to 16 |
| 1. 7–Tl<br><br>2. M. Eocene to L. Pleistocene limestones<br><br>3. White Limestone Group and Coastal Fm., dissected limestone plateaus and carbonate belts, covers about 70% of the surface area on the island, about 2,000m thick | 1. Limestones with subordinate marls and clastic rocks.<br><br>2. Generally rare<br><br>3. Usually thin debris and colluvium, sheared bedrock along fault scarps | Intense jointing and faulting, fault scarps typical | Highly dissected landforms, karst topography common<br>E – 60 to 1,000<br>RI – up to 200<br>SG – 16 to 50 |
| 1. 6–Elc<br><br>2. M. Eocene limestones and clastics<br><br>3. Yellow Limestone Group, basement of 7–Tl | 1. Limestones, mudstones, sandstones, conglomerates, tuffaceous beds, marly limestone, gypsum<br><br>2. Weathered; oxidation and hydration<br><br>3. Variable thickness, debris, colluvium, boulders | Joints and faults common, many slopes are fault scarps | Landslide landforms characteristic<br>E – 40 to 900<br>RI – up to 150<br>SG – 15 to 60 |
| 1. 5–Ps<br><br>2. Palaeocene to L. Eocene mudrocks<br><br>3. Richmond Fm., Wagwater Belt and fringes of Blue Mountain Inlier; >1,000m thick | 1. Interbedded sequence of shales, mudstones, siltstones, sandstones<br><br>2. Very highly weathered<br><br>3. Usually thick blanket of clay, silt and colluvium | Intense jointing and faulting, localized folding, bedrock is highly fractured | High drainage density, landslide landforms characteristic<br>E – highly variable up to 1,800<br>RI – highly variable, average 300<br>SG – highly variable up to 40, more along fault scarps |

| Major Slope Movements and Disasters | Damage | Qualitative Prediction | Recommended Control Works | Remarks |
|---|---|---|---|---|
| Type/Scale Example/ Triggering Mechanism (r - Rainfall, e - Earthquake) | 1. Casualties 2. Economic | 1. In Site and Scale 2. In Time | | |
| Liquefaction; extensive to localized. Port Royal, Kingston; earthquakes of 1692 and 1907. Surficial slides, creep, subsidence, failure of fills, localized, several events islandwide; rainfall; Qa2 surficial slides, localized; moderate to heavy rainfall | 1. Qa1: High   Qa2: X  2. Qa1: High   Qa2: X | 1. Probable from lithological and engineering properties; seismic/ liquefaction zonation  2. Strain monitoring in selected areas, rainfall monitoring | Drainage improvement; slope protection; piling and anchoring for fills; appropriate design criteria | Heavily populated; subject to multiple hazards; subject to creep and subsidence; critical facilities map may be used to select areas for detailed studies |
| Rock falls, rock topples, debris slides and avalanches, rock slides; generally localized, Bog Walk Gorge 1991; r and e | 1. X  2. Low to high | 1. Probable from lithological, structural and engineering characteristics of limestones  2. Monitoring of fault zones, monitoring of intensity and duration of rainfall | Usual rock slope engineering measures | Major roads and railway are prone to landslides, subject to multiple hazard, mitigation to be based on critical facilities maps |
| Lateral spreads, complex slides, rock slides, debris flows, rockfalls, rock topples; extensive, usually at fairly large scale, involves slippage of limestone blocks over soft rocks; Judgment Cliff, Guys Hill, Preston, Ivy Store, Ritchies; r and e | 1. High  2. High | 1. Probable from structural and lithological studies  2. Probable from rainfall monitoring | Topographical considerations make control works expensive and difficult; avoidance is the best strategy | Active zone; subject to multiple hazards; avoid new development |
| Complex slides, earthflows, creep, subsidence; extensive, often large-scale; St Mary, Portland, St Thomas, St Andrew, r | 1. X  2. Very high | 1. Probable from monitoring of landslide landforms  2. Monitoring of movement and strain, monitoring of rainfall | Improvement of surface and sub-surface drainage, requires a detailed study for counter-measures | Active zone; heavily populated, agricultural lands located in this zone, subject to multiple hazards, critical facilities mapping and landuse policy must be a top priority |

*Table 10.3 continued* Geological, structural, geomorphological, and landslide characteristics of the 8 landslide zones in Jamaica identified on Figure 10.2

| Geological Landslide Zones | Lithology | Structure | Slope Features |
|---|---|---|---|
| **1.** *Zone Number/map Symbol* <br> **2.** *Zone Name* <br> **3.** *Geological Province* | **1.** *Bedrock* <br> **2.** *Weathering/Alteration* <br> **3.** *Slope Deposits* | *Joints/* <br> *Faults/* <br> *Shear Zones* | *E – Elevation in m* <br> *RI – Relief Intensity in m* <br> *SG – Slope Gradient in %* |
| **1. 4–Pvc** <br><br> **2.** Palaeocene to L.Eocene coarse clastic rocks and andesitic volcanics <br><br> **3.** Wagwater Fm. and Newcastle Volcanic Fm., Wagwater Belt | **1.** Volcaniclastic conglomerates, sandstones, and shales; 1,200m to 1,600m thick; andesitic volcanics, >600m thick <br><br> **2.** Deeply weathered, pervasive hydro-thermal alteration <br><br> **3.** Usually thick blanket of debris, clay and broken rock fragments | Intensive development of joints, faults; shear zones common, fault scarps common | Landslide landforms common <br> E – highly variable 50 to 1,500 <br> RI – varible locally >300m <br> SG – variable 10 to 60, or more |
| **1. 3–Kg** <br><br> **2.** Cretaceous to Palaeocene grandiorite <br><br> **3.** Intrusive grandiorites in Cretaceous inliers, eg. Above Rocks, Flint River, Claverty Cottage | **1.** Grandiorite, locally with clay lenses <br><br> **2.** Deeply weathered, hydrothermally altered <br><br> **3.** Usually thick debris and colluvium, landslide deposits common | Intense development of joints, faults and shear zones | Generally hills of low relief, horst structures in Blue Mountains, very high drainage density <br> E – variable 60 to 1,000 <br> RI – variable up to 200 <br> SG – variable 16 to 50 |
| **1. 2–K** <br><br> **2.** Cretaceous rocks, undifferentiated <br><br> **3.** Exposed in 28 Cretaceous inliers; Blue Mountain Inlier, Central Inlier, Above Rocks Inlier, Lucea Inlier etc. | **1.** Volcaniclastic sediments, coarse and fine; tuffs; andesitic volcanics; subordinate limestones, marbles, schists, mafic volcanics, serpentinites, gabbros <br><br> **2.** Deeply weathered, extensive hydro-thermal alteration <br><br> **3.** Usually thick debris, rubble, alluvial cones, colluvium, frequent landslide deposits | Some sections highly deformed; intense development of joints, faults, shear zones, localized folding; most of the lithological contacts faulted, fault scarps common | Constitute interior mountain ranges and hills, landforms profoundly influenced by bedrock and structure, high drainage density <br> E – highly variable 60 to 2,256 <br> RI – in mountainous areas >300 <br> SG – highly variable 16 to 50 |
| **1. 1–Nss** <br><br> **2.** Neotectonic zones defined by faults and fault scarps <br><br> **3.** Stratigraphic /lithological /neotectonic zones; contact between zones 7–Tl and 6–Elc, and zones 2–K and 5–Ps | **1.** As in zones 2–K, 5–ps, 6–Elc and 7–Tl, fragmental rocks produced by faulting <br><br> **2.** Deeply weathered, hydro-thermal alteration <br><br> **3.** Coarse and fine debris and crushed rocks | Dominated by faulting | Fault scarps, fault controlled valleys |

Note: X =No Data

| Major Slope Movements and Disasters | Damage | Qualitative Prediction | Recommended Control Works | Remarks |
|---|---|---|---|---|
| Type/scale example/ Triggering Mechanism (r - Rainfall,e - Earthquake) | 1. Casualties 2. Economic | 1. In Site And Scale 2. In Time | | |
| Complex slides, rock slides, debris flows, debris avalanches extensive, several landslides in St Andrew, St Thomas and Portland; e and r | 1. X 2. Very high | 1. Probable from structure, lithology and engineering properties of materials 2. Probable from monitoring of active fault-zones and rainfall | Usual rock slope engineering methods | Active zone, subject to multiple hazards, roads affected, critical facilities mapping required |
| Debris flows in highly weathered and altered bedrock; extensive, especially in Above Rocks and Flint River; r | 1. Low 2. Very high | 1. Probable from lithology, structure and geomorphology 2. Probable from monitoring of intensity and duration of rainfall | Improve drainage; retaining walls, slope cribworks, anchoring; avoid new development | Severe landslide and erosion problem, very heavily populated, landuse policy needed, avoid new development |
| Rotational and translational slides, rock slides, rockfalls, slump-earth flows, debris flows, debris avalanches, debris slides; debris flows and slides extensively developed throughout the island; r and e, mostly rainfall induced | 1. X 2. Very high | 1. Probable from a systematic study of lithology, structure and geomorphology, engineering properties of materials 2. Probable from monitoring of ground conditions and rainfall, instrumentation | Avoid new development in high risk areas, improve drainage, vegetation of slopes, usual landslides control works | Active zone, rainfall-induced landslides and erosion are a major problem in all watersheds; road network severely affected; subject to multiple natural hazards; heavily populated; critical facilities mapping and landuse policy needed |
| All spectacular slope failures on the island occur in this zone, eg. at Judgment Cliff, Spur Tree Fault Zone, Liguanea Ridge, Millbank, Ewarton, etc.; both r and e | 1. High 2. Very high | 1. Probable, as suggested in zones 2 to 7 2. Probable, as suggested in zones 2 to 7 | Avoidance | Active zone; avoidance and relocation is the best countermeasure; reactivation as a result of seismic vibrations likely, multiple hazards |

excessive precipitation and/or earthquakes. The landslide hazard appears to be a function of changing land use. On a regional scale, a synthesis of these factors permits a grouping of landslides and associated landforms into eight distinct geological zones which also define the zones of landslide susceptibility (see Table 10.3 and Figure 10.2). This approach follows the methodology widely used in Japan [Oyagi 1989]. However, modifications have been made to accommodate the local geological environment.

## Methodology

The first step in the geological zonation of landslides is to establish whether the landslide related landforms have a preferential distribution with respect to the major lithologies and structures. This was achieved by superimposing the landslide inventory map on the geological and structural maps. It turned out that the landslide related landforms define 8 major zones which coincide with known stratigraphic and structural provinces on the island. These are shown on Figure 10.2, where each of these 8 zones has been assigned a specific map number and symbol, and a geological zone name based on the combined stratigraphic, lithological and tectonic characteristics of the geological province. The criteria used to define the various zones are:

(a) major bedrock lithology, weathering and alteration products and slope deposits;

(b) structural features including faults, fault scarps, shear zones, joints and folds;

(c) major geomorphical features highlighting average elevation, relief intensity and slope gradients; and

(d) examples of major slope movements and disasters including triggering mechanisms and damage statistics pertaining to casualties and economic losses where known.

As suggested by Oyagi [1989], this approach highlights those regional landslide criteria which are required in prediction, development of countermeasures, and land use planning. In Table 10.3, suggestions for a qualitative prediction of landslides in each zone have been made in site and scale, and in time on the basis of regional landslide criteria. Since geotechnical data on Jamaican rocks are not available, the countermeasures proposed are also qualitative in nature. However, they may be used as a basis for further studies. O'Hara and Bryce [1983] have proposed a qualitative geotechnical classification of Jamaican rocks and their inferences generally support the suggestions made here. The nature and significance of natural hazards in relation to land use has also been suggested for each zone (Table 10.3).

# Discussion

Based on the incidence of landsliding in relation to lithological characters, geological age, structure,and geomorphology, the island of Jamaica can be divided into 8 zones (Figure 10.2). These are:

1. Neotectonic (stratigraphic/structural) zones (Nss);
2. Cretaceous rocks, undifferentiated (K);
3. Cretaceous to Paleocene granodiorites (Kg);
4. Paleocene to Lower Eocene coarse clastic rocks and andesitic volcanics (Ps);
5. Paleocene to Lower Eocene mudrocks (Ps);
6. Middle Eocene limestones and clastics (Elc);
7. Middle Eocene to Lower Pleistocene limestones (Tl); and
8. Quaternary clastics, alluvium and other superficial deposits (Qa).

A summary description for each of these zones is included in Table 10.3. The characteristic features of each zone in relation to the landslide hazard are discussed below. The geology and geomorphology of the landslide habitats was described in the previous section and the major landslide events are listed in Tables 10.1 and 10.2.

## Zone 1

Zone 1 has been defined on the basis of neotectonic faults and fault scarps and stratigraphic/lithological features. This zone forms a widespread, landslide forming environment on the island and hosts some of the most spectacular and damaging landslides (Tables 10.1 to 10.3). In all recorded landslides in this zone, the Tertiary limestones, generally exposed along fault scarps, have slipped over a basement of older and less competent mudrocks (zone 5) and volcaniclastic sediments and igneous rocks (zone 2). Some of the typical examples are Judgment Cliff [Zans 1959]; Millbank [Harris & Rammelaere 1986]; Rio Nuevo Valley [*Geological Sheet 21* 1978]; Ewarton [*Geological Sheet 19* nd.]; and Spur Tree [*Geological Map of Jamaica* 1984]. The landslide at Preston Lands [Ahmad et al. 1993c] destroyed the village of Preston in the parish of St Mary in 1986. In some cases, like Judgment Cliff, the rupture surface lies within the lithological horizons containing gypsum. This condition provides an ideal environment for the overlying limestone slabs to slip over the less competent and weak basement rocks. The triggering mechanisms are both heavy rainfall and seismic vibrations.

This zone defines an active geological environment and is subject to multiple hazards. Therefore, from the point of view of loss reduction, avoidance and relocation are the best strategies (Table 10.3).

## Zone 2

Zone 2 includes the Cretaceous rocks that are exposed in 28 inliers across the island and constitute the Interior Mountain Ranges which receive the highest annual precipitation (Table 10.3). Historically, the areas included in Zone 2 have experienced the most severe and damaging rainfall-induced debris flows on the island (Tables 10.1 and 10.2). These debris flows have resulted in widespread blockage of roads, damage to agriculture, damage to infra-structure, and general degradation of watersheds, all of which were particularly evident during the 1986 flood rains [Wason 1986], Hurricane Gilbert in 1988 [Manning et al. 1992], and the May 1991 flood rains [Ahmad 1991]. One of the most serious consequences of rainfall-induced landslides in Zone 2 is accelerated soil erosion which, to a large extent, is a function of improper land use.

Since the areas included in Zone 2 are heavily populated, detailed landslide hazard zonation studies and critical facilities mapping must be employed in order to reduce loss reduction from frequent natural hazards that affect the watersheds in question (Table 10.3).

## Zone 3

Zone 3 includes all the areas where intrusive Cretaceous to Paleocene granodiorites are exposed, the largest being the Above Rocks Inlier of east-central Jamaica which has an area of $118km^2$ and a population density of 130 persons/$km^2$ [Manning et al. 1992]. The granodiorite terrain of Jamaica is characterized by an extensively faulted, deeply weathered, and hydrother-mally altered bedrock where landslide related soil erosion is seen at its most extreme. The hillslopes are generally deforested. The landslides in these areas are induced by heavy and sustained rainfall and cause a great deal of damage [Manning et al. 1992]. Following Hurricane Gilbert, a total of 478 landslides, with tracks ranging in size between 53m and 214m, were mapped along 108km of accessible roadway in the Above Rocks area [Manning et al. 1992].

It is recommended that all new development be avoided in Zone 3 as this terrain is subjected to a serious landslide and soil erosion problem (Table 10.3).

## Zone 4

Zone 4 is composed of coarse, clastic rocks and andesitic volcanics that are exposed in the Wagwater Belt of eastern Jamaica. Slope movements in this zone are mainly rock slides, rock avalanches, debris flows and complex slides which are triggered by both earthquakes and by heavy rainfall.

The Wagwater Belt is bounded by two major faults to the east and west. The eastern boundary is the Yallahs Plantain Garden Fault and the western boundary is defined by the Wagwater Fault. Geological and seismic evidence and records of past earthquakes [Tomblin & Robson 1977; Isaacs 1985] indicate that both these faults are seismically active and have a potential for generating destructive earthquakes. The earthquakes which have occurred in the Wagwater Belt in the 20th century triggered widespread landslides in the eastern parishes of St Andrew, St Mary, St Thomas and Portland [Ahmad 1993]. The author is presently investigating the hypothesis that gigantic flowslides originated in the southern part of the Wagwater Belt in the past, and were capable of travelling to the Liguanea Plain.

The Wagwater Belt is subject to multiple hazards and, therefore, critical facilities mapping, seismic hazard zonation, and landslide hazard zonation should form the basis for loss reduction strategies.

## Zone 5

Zone 5 constitutes a significant zone for landslides. The boundaries of this zone are generally defined by the neotectonic fault scarps in Zone 1 and Zone 6. Geologically, it is a part of the Wagwater Belt and is underlain by the Richmond Formation comprising an interbedded sequence of shales, mudstones, siltstones and sandstones. The rock strata here are severely fractured and deeply weathered. Landslide landforms are a characteristic feature of the hilly terrain underlain by these rocks. The drainage density is very high. The deforested hillslopes are marked by concave slope profiles. Rainfall-induced debris flows and avalanches have historically caused severe erosional problems in all the watersheds. The best examples of the high incidence of landslides in this zone are the upper section of the Yallahs River valley and the Buff Bay valley [Gupta 1975]. Heavy rainfall associated with tropical storms usually triggers widespread landslide activity throughout Zone 5. Other types of failures commonly occurring here include earth flows, creep and subsidence.

Landslide related rapid mass wasting in this zone affects large areas in the parishes of St Mary, Portland, St Thomas and St Andrew. The landslide loss reduction in Zone 5 should focus on the preparation of hazard zonation maps, erosion control and slope stabilization (Table 10.3).

## Zone 6

Zone 6 is a narrow zone generally lying between Zones 2 and 7. In stratigraphic terms, it is referred to as the Yellow Limestone Group. Its boundaries are often defined by neotectonic fault scarps of Zone 1. The lithology of Zone 6 is variable (Table 10.3). However, as far as landslides are concerned, it is the limestone blocks whose slippage on a relatively less competent basement have resulted in spectacular landslides throughout the island (Tables 10.1 to 10.3). In central Jamaica, a majority of the exposures of the Yellow Limestone Group have been disturbed by slope movements.

This zone defines a discrete landslide-forming environment on the island. The landslides in this zone have been triggered by both earthquakes and heavy rainfall. It is an active zone subject to multiple hazards. Avoidance is the best strategy for landslide loss reduction.

## Zone 7

Zone 7 is lithologically composed of Tertiary limestones which occupy some 65 percent of the island's surface area. The incidence of damaging landslides in this zone is less pronounced when compared with all other zones. However, the presence of joints, faults, and fault scarps has made a majority of slopes susceptible to localized rock falls, topples and avalanches, rock slides, and debris slides. These may be triggered as a result of earthquakes [Robinson et al. 1960] or rainfall [Ahmad 1991]. The Bog Walk Gorge landslide of 1991, which resulted in significant economic losses (Table 10.3), is a good example of the sorts of landslides that may be expected in Zone 7. Landslide loss reduction in this zone may be achieved through the preparation of landslide hazard and risk maps.

## Zone 8

Zone 8 includes unconsolidated to consolidated Quaternary clastic deposits. Most significant failures in this zone are related to liquefaction, as was observed during the earthquakes of 1692 and 1907 (Table 10.2). The Coastal Plains are the hub of economic and social activities on the island and, therefore, land use planning in these areas must be based on seismic/liquefaction hazard zonation.

# Conclusion

Economic losses from landslides have continued to increase in Jamaica during the past four decades. Much of this damage has occurred in the physical environment that has been modified for human use. Accelerated soil erosion in Jamaica is also partly a consequence of landslides. Clearly, there is an urgent need for a landslide loss reduction programme.

Among the various factors which control the occurrence of landslides in Jamaica, lithology, structure, and geomorphology are the most important. A geological zonation of landslides is therefore considered to be the most effective and inexpensive tool for loss reduction. In this study, a geological zonation of landslides has been proposed (Table 10.3), dividing the island into eight zones which also reflect landslide susceptibility. It provides regional landslide criteria that have been used in making suggestions for landslide prediction, countermeasures, and land use planning in Jamaica (Table 10.3). This approach has been successfully used in Japan [Oyagi 1989].

A very simple strategy for decreasing the landslide risk in Jamaica is to avoid development in all those areas listed in Table 10.3 where the inherent geologic-geomorphic constraints impose serious limitations on land use.

## Acknowledgements

Careful review by Duncan McGregor has considerably improved the manuscript. I would like to thank Nasima and Ghazzali for their help in typing.

## References

Ahmad, R. 1989a. "Geohazards in Jamaica and the Caribbean : the landslide problem — Part I". Courier, Caribbean Supplement 3, no. 6: 1-4 (UNESCO).

Ahmad, R. 1989b. "Geohazards in Jamaica and the Caribbean: the landslide problem — Part II". *Courier,* Caribbean Supplement 3, no. 7: 1-4 (UNESCO).

Ahmad, R. 1989c. "Earthquake-induced landslides in Jamaica". *Caribbean Landslide Working Group Newsletter* 1, no. 2: 2-7.

Ahmad, R. 1991. "Landslides triggered by the rainstorm of May 21-22, 1991". *Jamaica Journal Science & Technology* 2: 1-13.

Ahmad, R. 1993. "Woodford earthquake January 13, 1993: preliminary postearthquake geotechnical investigations, human impact and lesson learned". *Newsletter, Faculty of Natural Sciences* 6, no. 3: 4-6 (Kingston: University of the West Indies, Mona Campus).

Ahmad, R., F.N. Scatena, & A. Gupta. 1993a. "Morphology and sedimentation in Caribbean montane streams: examples from Jamaica and Puerto Rico". *Sedimentary Geology* 85: 157-69.

Ahmad, R., et al. 1993b. "Landslide damage to the Boar River water supply pipeline, Bromley Hill, Jamaica: case study of a landslide caused by Hurricane Gilbert". Bulletin International Association of Engineering Geology 47, 59-70.

Ahmad, R., B.E. Carby, & P.H. Saunders. 1993c. "The impact of slope movements on a rural community: lessons from Jamaica". In *Natural Disasters: Protecting Vulnerable Communities*, edited by P.A. Merriman & C.W.A. Browitt, pp 447-60. London: Thomas Telford.

DeGraff, J.V., et al. 1989. "Landslides: their extent and significance in the Caribbean". In *Landslides: Extent and Economic Significance*, edited by E.E. Brabb & B.L. Harrod, pp 51-80. Rotterdam: Balkema.

Earle, A.H. 1991. "Landslides in the Rio Minho watershed in central Jamaica". M.Phil thesis, University of the West Indies, Mona Campus, Jamaica.

*Geological Map of Jamaica*. 1984. 1:250,000 Geological Map of Jamaica. Kingston: Mines and Geology Division, Government of Jamaica.

*Geological Sheet 22.* 1971. 1:50,000, Above Rocks Geological Sheet with marginal notes. Kingston: Geological Survey Department, Government of Jamaica.

*Geological Sheet 25.* 1974. 1:50,000, Kingston Geological Sheet with marginal notes. Kingston: Mines and Geology Division, Government of Jamaica.

*Geological Sheet 21.* 1978. 1:50,000, Port Maria Geological Sheet with marginal notes. Kingston: Mines and Geology Division, Government of Jamaica.

*Geological Sheet 19.* n.d. 1:50,000, Linstead Geological Sheet with marginal notes. Kingston: Mines and Geology Division, Government of Jamaica.

Gupta, A. 1975. "Stream characteristics in eastern Jamaica, an environment of seasonal flow and large floods". *American Journal of Science* 275: 825-47.

Harris, N., & M. Rammelaere. 1986. "The 1938 Millbank slide and 1940 Chelsea slide — Millbank, Portland". Internal Report, Geological Survey Division. Kingston: Government of Jamaica.

Hubbard, R., & J. Fermor. 1972. "Landslides on Jamaican roads: an appraisal of causes". *Research Notes No. 7.* Department of Geography, University of the West Indies.

Isaacs, M.C. 1985. "A brief account of significant twentieth century earthquakes in Jamaica". *Journal Geological Society of Jamaica* 23: 25-34.

Lewis, J.F., & G. Draper. 1990. "Geology and tectonic evolution of northern Caribbean margin". In *The Caribbean Region, Geology of North America*, edited by G. Dengo & J.E. Case. Vol. H, pp 77-140. Boulder: Geological Society of America.

Maharaj, R.J. 1992. "Geotechnics and zonation of 'landslides' in upper St Andrew, Jamaica, West Indies". M.Phil thesis, University of the West Indies, Mona.

Mann, P., G. Draper, & K. Burke. 1985. "Neotectonics of a strike-slip restraining bend system, Jamaica". In *Strike-slip Deformation, Basin Formation and Sedimentation*, edited by K.T. Biddle & N. Christie-Black, pp 211-26. Society of Economic Palaeontologists and Mineralogists, Special Publication 37.

Mann, P., C. Schubert, & K. Burke. 1990. "Review of Caribbean neotectonics". In *The Caribbean Region, Geology of North America*, edited by G. Dengo & J.E. Case. Vol. H, pp 307-38. Boulder: Geological Society of America.

Manning, P.A.S., T. McCain, & R. Ahmad. 1992. "Landslides triggered by 1988 Hurricane Gilbert along roads in the Above Rocks area, Jamaica". *Journal Geological Society of Jamaica, Special Issue* no. 12: 34-53.

McGregor, D.F.M. 1988. "An investigation of soil status and land use on a steeply sloping hillside, Blue Mountains, Jamaica". *Singapore Journal of Tropical Geography* 9: 60-71.

McGregor, D.F.M., & D. Barker. 1991. "Land degradation and hillside farming in the Fall River Basin, Jamaica". *Applied Geography* 11: 143-56.

*National Atlas of Jamaica.* 1971. Kingston: Town Planning Department, Ministry of Finance and Planning.

Naughton, P.W. 1984. "Flood and landslide damage repair cost correlations for Kingston, Jamaica". *Caribbean Geography* 1: 198-202.

O'Hara, M., & R. Bryce. 1983. "A geotechnical classification of Jamaican rocks". Kingston: Geological Survey Division, Bulletin 10, Ministry of Mining and Energy.

Oyagi, N. 1989. "Geological and economic extent of landslides in Japan and Korea". In *Landslides: Extent and Economic Significance*, edited by E.E. Brabb & B.L. Harrod, pp 289-302. Rotterdam: Balkema.

Pindell, J.L., & S.F. Barrett. 1990. "Geological evolution of the Caribbean region: a plate tectonic perspective". In *The Caribbean Region, Geology of North America*, edited by G. Dengo & J.E. Case, Vol. H, pp 405-32. Boulder: Geological Society of America.

Robinson, E., H.R. Versey, & J.B. Williams. 1960. "The Jamaica earthquake of March 1, 1957". In *Transactions 2nd Caribbean Geological Conference 1959*, pp 50-57. Puerto Rico.

Tomblin, J.M., & G.R. Robson. 1977. *A Catalogue of Felt Earthquakes for Jamaica, with References to other Islands in the Greater Antilles, 1564-1971*. Kingston: Mines and Geology Division, Government of Jamaica, Special Publication 2.

Varnes, D.J. 1984. *Landslide Hazard Zonation: A Review of Principles and Practice*. Paris: UNESCO.

Wason, A.T. 1986. "Assessment of flood damage Jamaica, May-June 1986". Main Report of Pan Caribbean Disaster Preparedness and Prevention Project, Antigua, to Office of Disaster Preparedness, Kingston.

*World Resources*. "A Report by the World Resources Institute 1990-91". Oxford: Oxford University Press .

Zans, V.A. 1959. "Judgment Cliff landslide in the Yallahs Valley". *Geonotes (Journal of Geological Society of Jamaica)* 2: 43-48.

Chapter 11

# Evaluating Landslide Hazard for Land Use Planning: Upper St Andrew, Jamaica

Russell J. Maharaj

## Introduction

Natural disasters such as landslides are an almost universal phenomenon and Jamaica, like the rest of the Caribbean islands, is no exception to the occurrence and prevalence of these exogenetic lithospheric processes.

Landslides associated with torrential rainfall are very common on the mountainous terrain within the interior of the island of Jamaica, especially in the upper part of the parish of St Andrew. During and following rainfall events, slope failures are particularly common, especially on artificially steepened road-cut segments, for example, along the Irish Town and Woodford roads. The severity of the landslide problem is such that 886 failures, ranging from a few metres to hundreds of metres long, were mapped in Upper St Andrew between January and August 1989. This number increased to 950 following the torrential rainfall of May 1991, with reactivation of 540 failures, most of which were in soils.

Although landslides in Upper St Andrew are probably inevitable, the disasters they accentuate can be reduced or sometimes prevented. However, to achieve this goal, there must be adequate evaluation of the hazard so that appropriate countermeasures can be implemented. One of the first steps in reducing landslide hazard is to assess the extent of landslide hazard in the area. This involves the identification of present, past and potential landslide sites and the mapping of the geomorphic and engineering geologic conditions associated with failures.

A geotechnical study was initiated in January 1989 to examine various aspects of this problem and quantify the landslide hazard in Upper St Andrew. The aim was to map past, present and potential landslide sites; evaluate the landslide susceptibility within the area and assess the geotechnical conditions under which slope failures are taking place.

The purpose here is to propose a systematic approach to landslide hazard zonation, using Upper St Andrew as a case study. It also presents a quantitative method for the preparation of first generation landslide hazard zonation maps, using multivariate statistical analysis of two-dimensional geological, geotechnical and geomorphological parameters. Subsequently, these derivative landslide hazard maps can be used by planners, engineers and land developers to determine optimum land use management practice and to reduce some of the deleterious impacts of landslides.

## Geomorphology and Geology of the Study Area

An area of approximately $15km^2$, on the southwestern flank of the Blue Mountains and located in Upper St Andrew was investigated (Figure 11.1). More than 80 percent of the area has elevations between 150m to 310m above sea level, forming generally northwest-southeast trending ridge and valley systems. Maximum elevations are found to the northeast, while the lowest elevations are to the southwest and south. Slopes range from $30°$ to $45°$, with the gentlest slopes (less than $20°$) on alluvial deposits to the southwest of the

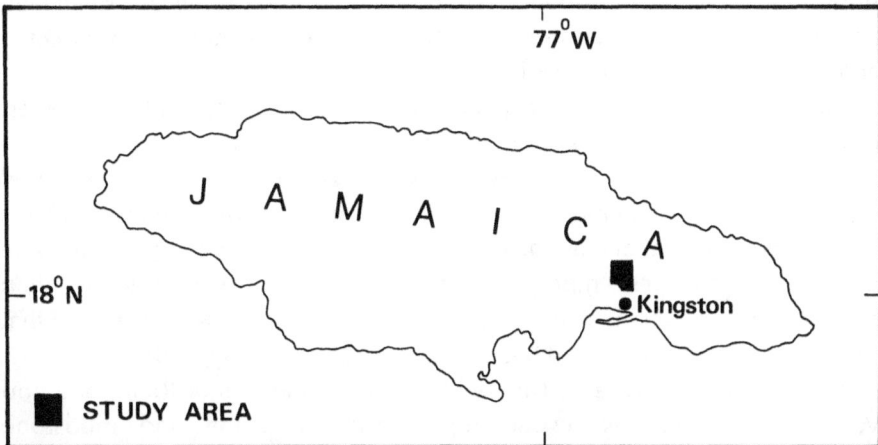

*Figure 11.1* Location map for Upper St Andrew

area. Slopes on clastic sediments are the steepest encountered, sometimes vertical in river valleys where they are usually faulted. Slopes on igneous lithologies are gentler and more dissected.

Karst topography and associated sub-surface drainage is found in the northwestern part of the study area. However, the drainage pattern is mainly dendritic, with most of the area drained by the Hope River which flows south, or the Wagwater River which flows northwest.

The study area forms part of a major northwest-southeast trending, up-faulted block of Tertiary clastics and volcanics which forms part of a suite of rocks referred to as the Wagwater Group. These lithologies are represented by the Wagwater, Richmond and Newcastle Volcanics Formation. The Wagwater Formation consists of terrestrial deposits of purple-red conglomerates, breccias, sandstones and mudstones. The Richmond Formation consists of a turbiditic sequence of yellow-brown (weathered) sandstones and mudstones, with lesser quantities of conglomerates and breccias, while Newcastle Volcanics consists of keratophyres and quartz keratophyres.

Intrusive lithologies of probable Cretaceous age, granodiorite and felsic acid intrusions (age unknown) are also present in the area. Other lithologies include altered tuffs (Purple Volcanics) of possible Upper to Lower Cretaceous age, middle Tertiary white limestones belonging to the White Limestone Group, and Quaternary deposits, including Recent alluvium and terrace deposits and several old landslips (Figure 11.2). The study area is partly bordered by Recent alluvium and terrace deposits to the southwest and south and the Wagwater fault, a major northwest trending lineament, with a 100m to 200m wide fracture zone [Geological Survey Division 1974; Green 1977]. Mesoscopic faults near parallel to the trend of the Wagwater fault are also present in the study area. However, east-southeast trending faults, such as the Jack's Hill fault and minor north-northwest trending fractures are common at the mesoscopic and macroscopic scale (Figure 11.2).

High angle faulting is very extensive within competent lithologies. Consequently, very steep and sometimes vertical slopes are common, especially in fault controlled river valleys. Cataclastic zones and associated mylonitic rocks are common within igneous lithologies, which have also been sites of hydrothermal alteration. This has resulted in the formation of unstable mineral assemblages, more susceptible to chemical weathering than original/primary mineral suites. In some cases, weathering is so extensive that some geological contacts and bedrock can hardly be recognized.

Bedding is well preserved in sedimentary sequences of Richmond and Wagwater Formations, especially in the sandstone and mudstone sequences. Beds vary from a few centimetres thick in mudstone to a metre thick in sandstones.

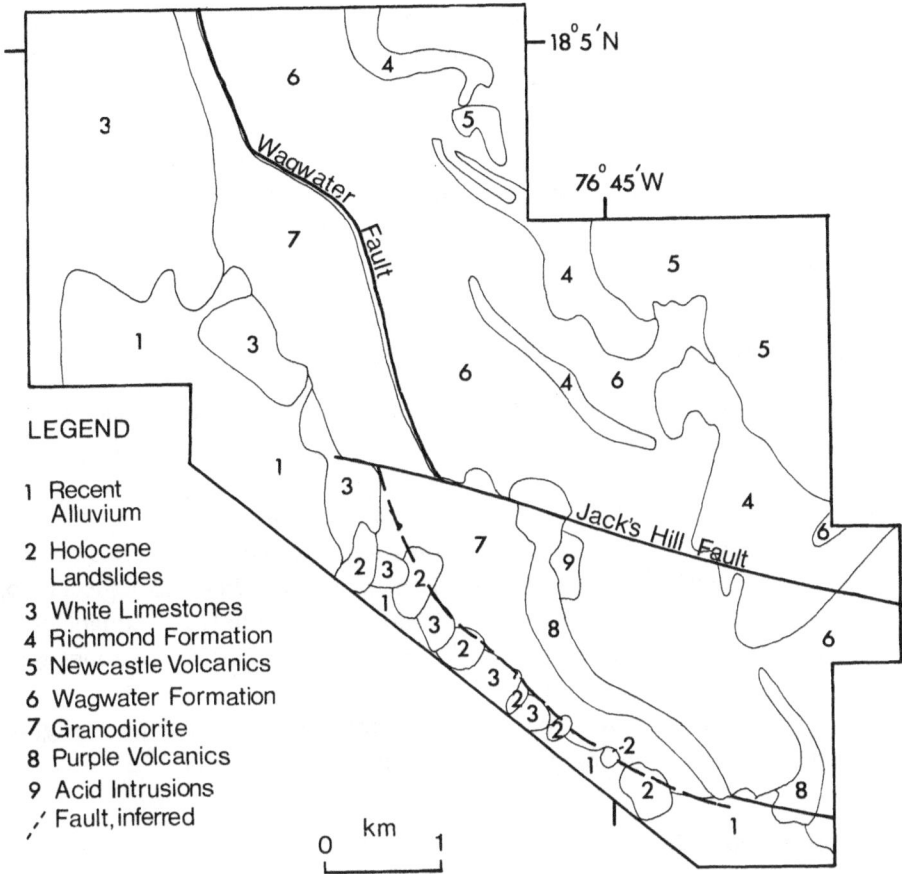

*Figure 11.2* Geological units in Upper St Andrew

Joints are prevalent within competent lithologies. These can be cooling joints associated with the Newcastle Volcanics or tectonic joints found in most competent bedrock types. These together with faults and bedding planes produce many potential failure surfaces within rock slopes.

The study area also lies within a seismically active zone, [Mann et al., 1985] and has experienced more than 15 major earthquakes between 1880 and 1960 [Shepherd & Aspinall 1980]. Therefore, it represents a neo-tectonically active area subject to seismic loading and associated ground motion.

Soils are generally sandy and vary from non-plastic to low plasticity silty to clayey sands. Gravelly soils are also present, but are more associated with highly fractured lithologies or coarse sedimentary sequences. These are some-times plastic. Fine soils are also present and are associated with mudstone sequences or highly weathered and altered igneous lithologies. These may be highly plastic and expansive silty to sandy clays. Most soils in the area can also be classified as lithosols.

Rainfall is mainly orographic, while the mean annual rainfall varies from less than 125cm to more than 250cm. Rainfall is generally bimodal, with peaks in July and October [Government of Jamaica and Ralph Field and Associates 1987], while torrential rainfall associated with hurricanes and tropical depressions is also common.

## Methodology

One of the simplest and most efficient methods of evaluating landslide risk, is by terrain evaluation procedures, especially multiple factor assessment [Lucini 1973; Drennon & Schleining 1975; Nielsen & Brabb 1977; Nielsen et al. 1979; DeGraff & Romesburg 1980; Brabb 1982; Varnes 1984; DeGraff 1987; 1989]. These workers used three main variables for multiple-factor assessment; a landslide inventory map, a slope category map, and a bedrock geological map. In the case of DeGraff and Romesburg [1980] and DeGraff [1989], quantitative statistical analyses were applied to the data, so as to determine zones with different degrees of susceptibility.

The method used here is based on DeGraff [1989] but has been slightly modified to incorporate engineering-geologic properties of soils.

### Landslide Mapping

The landslide inventory was compiled from review of topographic and geologic maps of the area, interpretation of black and white, panchromatic aerial photographs (1:10,000 and 1:50,000 scales, 1989 and 1986 editions, respectively) and field surveys following the interpretative procedures of Rib and Liang [1978]. However, since many landslides in the area were less than 20m in length, the use of small scale aerial photographs for mapping landslides was limited. Even at a scale of 1:10,000, few failures were capable of being mapped from aerial photographs. Consequently, many failures had to be mapped in the field, while at the same time failures tentatively identified on aerial photographs could be confirmed. Landslides were classified using Varnes' [1978] terminology.

At landslide sites, soils and bedrock properties were described based on Kezdi [1974] and American Society for Testing Materials [1982]. Soil properties included soil types, texture, plasticity, consistency, weathering, colour and water content. Bedrock characteristics described included textures, lithologies, weathering grades, colour, mineralogy, fracturing and degree of alteration. Soil samples were also collected for laboratory determination of their Atterberg limits and indices, natural water content, grain size distribution, specific gravity and shear strength. These data were subsequently used to prepare the geotechnical map of the area using the methodology suggested by Keaton [1984] and the International Association of Engineering Geology [1976] for engineering-geologic mapping. The eventual geotechnical map showed zones or areas with different soil and bedrock characteristics.

## Assessment of Landslide Hazard

The first step in landslide hazard assessment is the preparation of factor maps [DeGraff 1989]. These include a landslide inventory map showing all landslides mapped, a geotechnical map showing material types and a slope category map showing areas with different slope inclinations. The method for the preparation of the first two maps has been mentioned in the previous section, while simplified versions of these two maps are presented as Figures 11.3 and 11.4. The major characteristics of each geotechnical unit are presented in Table 11.1 and illustrated in Figure 11.4.

The slope category map was prepared from a published topographic map of the study area (which itself had been originally prepared by photogrammetric methods from aerial photographs). Five slope classes were selected for this study. Slope class A: more than 45°; class B: 30°-44°; class C: 20° -29°; class D: 10°-19° and class E: 0°-9°. The angle of slope was derived using the equation of Young [1972], where:

$$H = 1000 \ V. \cot \theta \ /S, \qquad (1)$$

and where

H = contour separation in millimetres

V = vertical contour interval in metres

S = map scale and

$\theta$ = slope angle

A template was prepared for each slope class, for use on a 1:10,000 topographic base map. Predetermined values of H were used to compute the corresponding values of with the same vertical interval and horizontal scale. Each template was placed on the map, and contour separations corresponding to the five slope classes were drawn. The final map produced was a slope category map or an isoclinal map (not presented here due to its complexity).

Factor analysis involved the overlaying of the geotechnical map with the slope map, to produce a map of geotechnical slope combinations. The geotechnical slope map was then overlain with the landslide inventory map. This showed geotechnical slope combinations associated and not associated

*Table 11.1*   Characteristics of Each Geotechnical Unit

| Geotechnical Units | Main Lithologic Types |
|---|---|
| A | Expansive, residual, gravelly to silty clays, overlying purple-red, moderately fractured to highly weathered shales, siltstones and sandstones. |
| B | Residual, clayey to gravelly sands, overlying purple-red, interbedded, slightly fractured and moderately to highly weathered sandstones, siltstones, conglomerates, and shales. |
| C | Expansive, residual, clayey to gravelly sands overlying purple-red, highly fractured and moderately to highly weathered sandstones, siltstones and shales. |
| D | Expansive, residual, gravelly to sandy silts overlying yellow-brown, highly fractured and highly weathered shales, siltstones and sandstones. |
| E | Residual, clayey to gravelly sands, overlying yellow-brown, moderately fractured and moderately to highly weathered breccias, conglomerates, sandstones, siltstones and shales. |
| F | Expansive, residual, gravelly to silty clays overlying yellow-brown, highly fractured and moderately weathered breccias, conglomerates, sandstones, siltstones and shales. |
| G | Expansive, gravelly to sandy silts, overlying highly fractured and moderately weathered breccias, tuffs and quartz keratophyres. |
| H | Residual, clayey to sandy gravels and clayey to gravelly sands, overlying highly fractured amd moderately weathered breccias, tuffs and quartz keratophyres. |
| I | Expansive, residual, clayey to gravelly silts overlying moderately fractured to highly weathered altered andestic and tuffaceous volcanics. |
| J | Slide and colluvial deposits consisting of low plasticity, clayey to sandy gravels. |
| K, L | Alluvial deposits consisting of clayey to silty gravels and constituting terrace deposits (K), together with alluvial terrace deposits of clayey to silty gravels, overlying sandy and silty clays (L). |
| M | Residual, gravelly to silty clays, overlying moderately fractured and moderately weathered white limestones. |
| N | Residual, clayey to silty gravels, overlying moderately fractured and moderately weathered white limestones. |
| O | Expansive, residual gravelly to clayey silts, overlying moderately fractured and moderately weathered white limestones. |
| P | Expansive, residual gravelly to silty clays, overlying highly fractured and highly weathered granodiorites. |
| Q | Residual, clayey to gravelly sands overlying highly fractured and highly weatherd granodiorites |
| R | Silty to sandy gravels, overlying highly fractured and highly weathered felsites (minor acid intrusions). |

Note: *Lithologic types within each geotechnical unit are listed starting with the most common and ending with the least common. See Figure 11.4 for their distribution.*

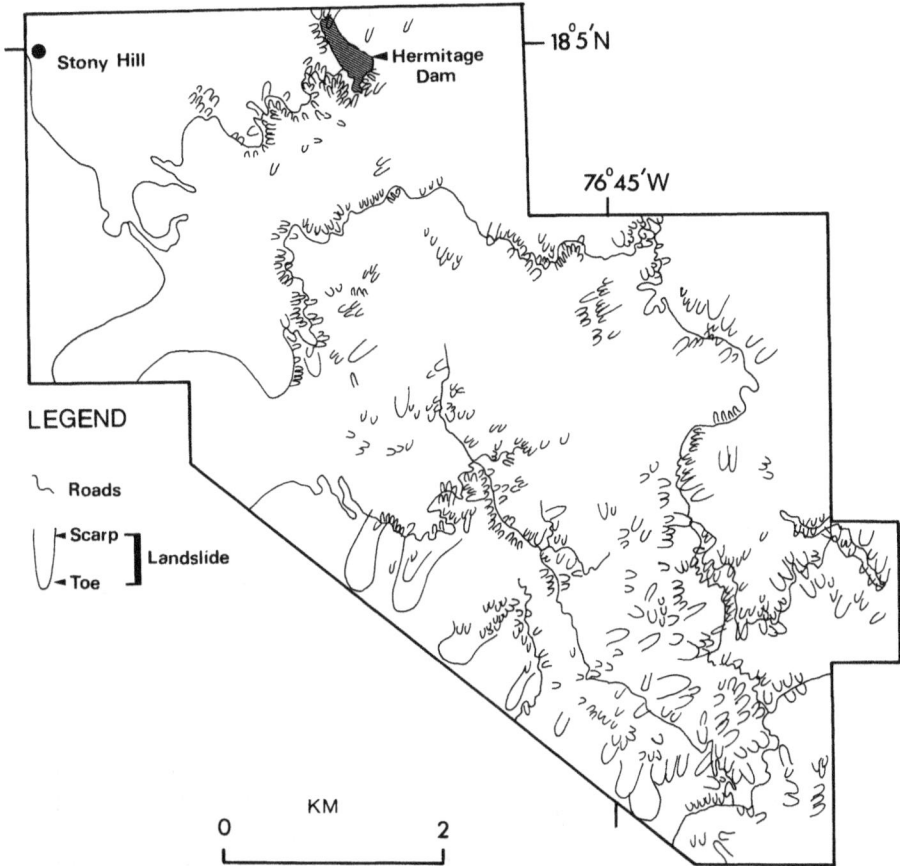

*Figure 11.3* Landslide inventory map of Upper St Andrew

with landslides. A table was then prepared showing the area of each geotechnical slope combination, together with a companion table showing the percentage of each combination associated with landslides.

The next step was to group the geotechnical slope combinations in a way that defines different levels of landslide hazard. The preparation of these above tables identifies a number of geotechnical slope combinations that have no association with landslides, which are defined as areas with very low landslide hazard. Factor analysis [DeGraff 1989] is then applied to the combinations represented in both tables. For each geotechnical slope combination, the area of existing landslides is divided by the total area of the combination. This showed the proportion of that combination associated with landslides which gives a better appreciation of the relative landslide hazard between combinations, since the combinations associated with the largest area under landslides may be the most hazardous, or alternatively, this may simply reflect the combinations most common in the area.

**177**

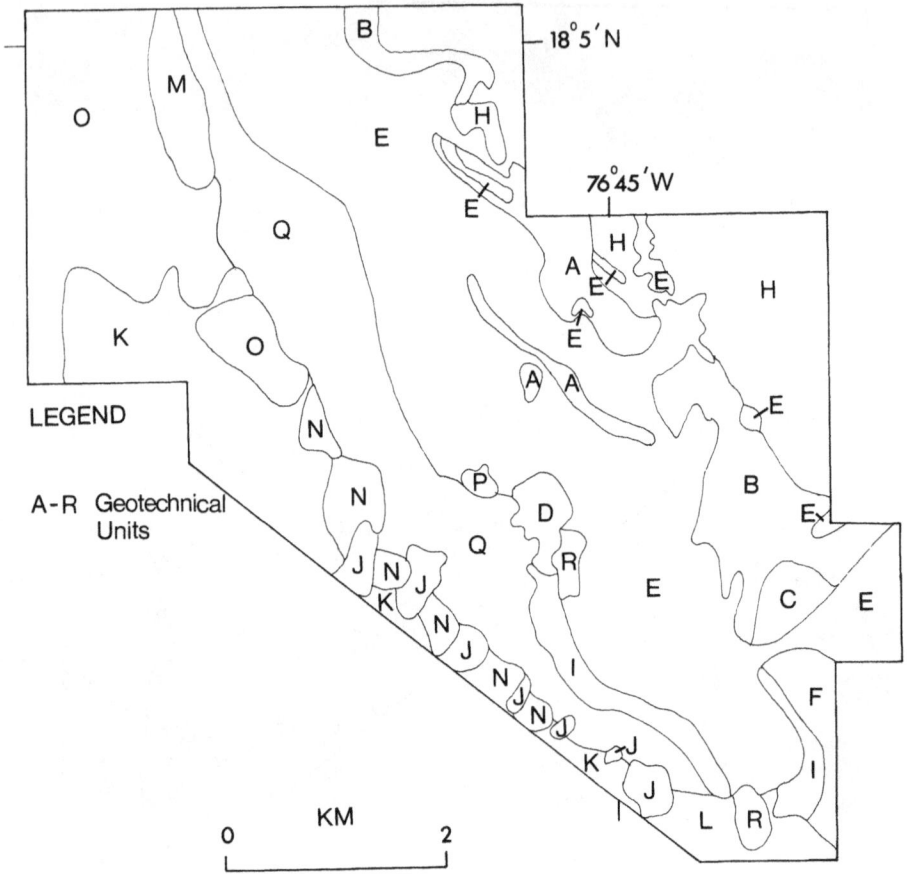

*Figure 11.4* Geotechnical map of the study area

The proportions calculated from the data in the above mentioned tables were then ranked in increasing order. This produced a range between 0.002 and 1.00. The range was then divided equally by four, to produce a total of five landslide hazard classes, including that designated above (of very low landslide hazard). To determine whether the partitioning of each class was optimal, a non-hierarchial cluster analysis was applied to the data. Cluster analysis in this case seeks to identify the class boundaries of the four desired classes that will give the minimum sum of the squared deviation about the four class mean values (that is, minimizes W in Equation 2, below). The upper and lower boundary of each class is subsequently adjusted or retained after cluster analysis, until the final class boundaries will produce the minimum sum of the squared deviations about the four class mean values. This involves calculation of the W-function [Anderberg 1973], where:

$$W = \sum_{i=1}^{j=4} \sum_{j=1}^{n_i} (X_{ij} - X_i)^2 = W_1 + W_2 + W_2 + W_4 \qquad (2)$$

The next step is the preparation of the landslide hazard map using the grouped proportions and final classes obtained by cluster analysis. The group of proportions with the largest values, towards the 1.00 end of the range, represents areas with extremely high landslide hazard. The group of proportions with the smallest values, towards the 0.002 end of the range, defines moderate hazard. The groups of proportions between these two values define areas with moderately high to high hazard and very high hazard. The geotechnical slope combinations identified from overlay of the slope and geotechnical maps are compared with their respective proportion of landslide area to assign the appropriate hazard designation. A final hazard zonation map is then produced based on the hazard designation of the range of proportions of landslides within each geotechnical slope combination.

## Results

### Landslide Processes and Distribution

A total of 886 landslides were mapped (Figure 11.3 and Table 11.2). Six failures were old landslide sites, while 880 were active failures. Based on Varnes' [1978] classification, 11 different types of landslides were mapped (Table 11.2). Analysis of landslides according to main type of slope movement shows that sliding failures are the most common (Table 11.2). Failures were also very common in debris (soil in which 20 percent to 80 percent of the materials have particles with a diameter greater than 2.00mm).

Table 11.2  Types and Frequencies of Mapped Landslides

| Types of landslides | Number of landslides | % of total number of landslides |
| --- | --- | --- |
| Rock falls | 16 | 1.9 |
| Debris falls | 1 | 0.1 |
| Debris slump | 7 | 0.8 |
| Earth slump | 4 | 0.5 |
| Debris block slides | 2 | 0.2 |
| Rock slides | 3 | 0.4 |
| Earth slides | 730 | 87.2 |
| Debris flows | 32 | 3.8 |
| Earth flows | 7 | 0.8 |
| Complex failures | 35 | 4.2 |

In lithological terms, landslides were most common in clastic sedimentary sequences, with 582 failures, and least common in Recent alluvium and terrace deposits and white limestones (Table 11.3). Intrusive igneous lithologies also had high incidences of landslide occurrence, with 209 failures, followed by altered volcanics with 67 failures (Table 11.3). Approximately 59 failures per square kilometre were recorded for the entire area, while the total failed area was $1.55km^2$. This represents 10 percent of the entire study area. Analysis of the total failed area under the various lithologies revealed that the old landslide deposits were the most susceptible to failures in the past, followed by altered volcanics (Table 11.3).

Table 11.3    Slope Failures Recorded for Different Lithologies

| Major Lithologies | Area $km^2$ | Number of Landslides | Number of Landslides per $km^2$ | Total Failed Area, $km^2$ | % of Total Area which has Failed |
|---|---|---|---|---|---|
| Conglomerates | | | | | |
| Sandstones, mud-stones & breccias | 7.19 | 582 | 81 | 0.69 | 9.60 |
| Altered volcanics | 1.14 | 67 | 59 | 0.19 | 16.67 |
| Landslide deposits | 0.33 | 20 | 67 | 0.33 | 100.00 |
| White limestones | 2.56 | 8 | 3 | 0.01 | 0.39 |
| Intrusive igneous lithologies | 3.15 | 209 | 66 | 0.32 | 10.16 |
| Alluvial deposits | 1.45 | 5 | 4 | 0.01 | 0.69 |
| TOTAL | 15.82 | 891 | 59 | 1.55 | 9.80 |

Table 11.4 shows the numbers of landslides mapped in each slope category. No failures were identified on slopes less than 10°, while most landslides were mapped on slopes between 20° to 44°, especially on slopes between 30° to 44°.

The geographical patterns displayed in Figure 11.3 reveal that many landslides are associated with roadways. Although most of these failures are relatively small, collectively, they account for a large area.

Table 11.4    Slope Failure Record for Each Slope Category

| Slope Classes | A. 45°+ | B. 30°-44° | C. 20°-29° | D. 10°-19° |
|---|---|---|---|---|
| Number of landslides | 34 | 445 | 344 | 63 |
| Percentage of total number of landslides | 3.84 | 50.23 | 38.83 | 7.11 |

## Assessment of Landslide Hazard

The landslide hazard map (Figure 11.5) shows five different categories of susceptibility to future landslides: very low (VL), moderate (M), moderately high to high (M-H), very high (H) and extremely high hazard (E). It depicts the order of relative landslide hazard or the varying degree of susceptibility to future landslide hazard in the study area. On the basis of this classification, it can be expected that, over time, higher hazard zones will experience more landslides than lower hazard areas. Table 11.5 shows the summary characteristics of each landslide susceptibility class.

Areas of very low susceptibility (VL) to landslides are underlain by white limestones and gravelly soils. These areas had no previous landslides (Table 11.5). Bedrock is moderately to highly fractured. Consequently, rock falls may occur occasionally. In such cases, small events are envisaged. Encroachment

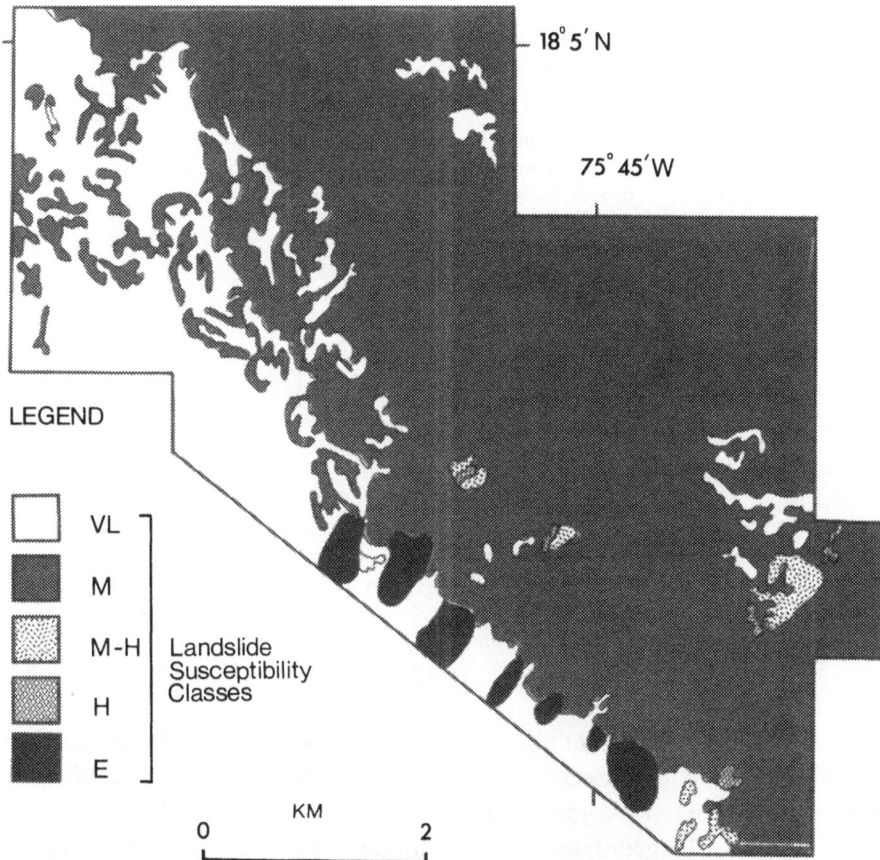

*Figure 11.5* Landslide susceptibility map for Upper St Andrew

*Table 11.5*　Engineering-Geologic Characteristics and Slope Failure Record for Each Landslide Susceptibility Class

| Relative Landslide Susceptibility | Range of Slope Angles at Landslide Sites | Major Types of Slope Materials | Total Failed Area, km$^2$ | Geotechnical Units Represented | % of the Total Failed Area | Proportional Range of Failed Area in Geotechnical–Slope Combination |
|---|---|---|---|---|---|---|
| VL | 0 - 45° | River alluvium, as well as white limestones and sandstones bedrock | 0.00 | G, K, M | 0.00 | 0.00 |
| M | 10° - 44° | Expansive clays to silty and gravelly sands with minor sandy gravels. Bedrock are clastic sediments, altered volcanics and intrusive igneous lithologies | 1.12 | A, D, E, F, H, I, Q | 72.26 | 0.002 - 0.12 |
| M-H | 10° - 44° | Expansive clays to clayey and gravelly sands and gravels. Bedrock are sandstones, mudrocks and intrusive igneous lithologies | 0.08 | L, B, C | 5.16 | 0.12 - 0.24 |
| H | 29° - 44° | Expansive clays to silty sands and gravels. Bedrock are sandstones, mudrocks and intrusive igneous lithologies | 0.02 | P, R | 1.29 | 0.24 - 0.36 |
| E | 0 to > 44° | Old landslide deposits, clayey to gravelly soils with low plasticity fines | 0.33 | J | 21.29 | 1.00 |

by landslides from adjacent higher terrain, or undercutting by landslides from lower elevations, may occur at geologic contacts with different lithologies. However, this may be a rare event. In most cases, soils are thin, with stony fragments and with generally very little non-plastic fines. In other cases, no soil may be present, especially on slopes greater than 45°.

*Areas of moderate susceptibility (M)* contained numerous failures. However, this reflects the fact that this particular susceptibility class covers the majority of the study area, and the proportion of failed area within this geotechnical slope combination is relatively low (less than 0.12 and greater than 0.002). The failed area was 1.12km², approximately 72 percent of the total failed area. Lithologies within this category vary considerably, ranging from coarse and fine grained clastic sediments to volcanic and intrusive igneous rocks, such as the Wagwater Formation, Newcastle Volcanic Formation and granodiorite, respectively. Soils are generally coarse, either of low plasticity or non-plastic. However, clays and silts were also present over highly weathered mudrocks. Slope angle seems to play an important role in controlling slope failure frequency. Although in this hazard category slopes range from 10° to more than 45°, slopes between 20° to 44° have higher incidence of failure. These slopes are steep enough for high shear stresses due to gravity to be created. They also allow percolation and collection of ground water, especially on concave slope elements. This can encourage high rates of weathering and the accumulation of a relatively deep, less stable regolith.

Most of the area comprises either very steep slopes of generally very massive and resistant bedrock, without soils, or slopes less than 10° with a thick soil mantle but with no previous failures.

*Areas of moderate to high susceptibility (M-H)* are generally small, but the proportions of failed area are greater than in the above categories. Proportions of failed area range from 0.12 to 0.24, with 0.08km² of failed area representing about 5 percent of the total (Table 11.5). Soils are variable, ranging from either stiff, expansive, highly plastic clays, to coarse, non-plastic to slightly plastic sands and gravels. Bedrock within this class is generally highly weathered, and the extent of weathering is much greater than in previous classes. Consequently, there are more potential failure sites. Failures, however, are most common on slopes ranging from 30° to more than 45°, although gentler slopes (between 10° to 19°) also fail.

*Areas of very high susceptibility (H)* occupy the smallest area affected by landslides, 0.02km², less than 2 percent of the total failed area. However, proportions of failed area within this geotechnical combination ranges from 0.24 to 0.36. Soils are either low plasticity clays, coarse gravels or gravelly sands. Failures are most common on slopes between 30° to 44°, although steeper slopes also fail.

*Areas of extreme susceptibility (E)* represent old landslide deposits, therefore the proportions of failed area is recorded as 1.00. This susceptibility class covers 0.33km², about 21 percent of the total failed area. All slope categories are represented in this class. Although slopes less than 10° are gentle, they may be meta-stable and, consequently, can still fail. Soils within this category are generally sandy and of are low plasticity to non-plastic. Clayey soils are found and are of moderate to high plasticity.

Additional slope instability problems may result due to encroachment by other failures on less susceptible areas and also by retrogressive landslide activity. In these cases, relatively stable or more stable areas may fail due to removal of basal and or lateral slope support. Thus, areas of a relatively low susceptibility adjacent to an area of relatively higher susceptibility can actually have a higher susceptibility than that determined by the factor analysis. Additional slope stability problems may also result from road construction and vegetation removal. The association of many landslides with cut-slopes suggests that poor road design may affect the long-term stability of slopes and induce failures.

## Use of the Susceptibility Map

The landslide susceptibility map is a special purpose map, showing zones with different degrees of susceptibility to future slope movements (Figure 11.5). Although it was compiled based on previous slope failure activity within the study area, the boundaries illustrated should not be regarded as rigid. Changes in natural and anthropogenic variables may alter the local soil and bedrock conditions and, therefore, the susceptibility of slope materials to failure. As a result, this map is intended primarily as a guide to slope instability for use by land owners, planners and developers interested in community level developments. Although this study was undertaken at a scale of 1:10,000 and incorporates some level of detail, it is by no means the final word on landslide susceptibility within the study area. The map therefore should not replace site specific, engineering studies for particular community developments, such as housing and road construction. Finally, this map can also be used as a database for planning site-specific studies within possible problem areas that should receive further attention.

### Acknowledgements

The author is grateful to the University of the West Indies, Mona Campus for supporting this research, Mr Rafi Ahmad for supervising this research and to Ms V. Sooknanan and Mrs C. Douglas for typing this manuscript. Comments by Dr D.F.M. McGregor, University of London, on an earlier version of this manuscript and by Mr Jerome V. DeGraff, United States Forest Service, California, during the early stages of this study are gratefully acknowledged.

# References

Anderberg, M. 1973. *Cluster Analysis for Applications.* New York: Academic Press.

American Society for Testing Materials. 1982. *Annual Book of ASTM Standards, Part 19, Natural Building Stones; Soil and Rock.* Philadelphia: ASTM.

Brabb, E.E. 1982. "Preparation and use of a landslide susceptibility map for a county near San Francisco, California, U.S.A." In *Proceedings, International Seminar on Landslide and Mud flows.* Alma-Ata, USSR: October 1981: 407-19.

DeGraff, J. V. 1987. "Landslide hazard on Dominica, West Indies: final report". Unpublished report to the Commonwealth of Dominica and the Department of Regional Development of the Organization of American States.

DeGraff, J. V. 1989. "Assessing landslide hazard for regional development planning in the eastern Caribbean". In *Proceedings of a Meeting of Experts on Hazard Mapping in the Caribbean,* Kingston , Jamaica, 30 November to 4 December, edited by D. Barker, pp 40-45. PCDPPP/ODP/Department of Geography, University of the West Indies.

DeGraff, J. V., & H. C. Romesburg. 1980. "Regional landslide susceptibility assessment for wildland management, a matrix approach". In *Thresholds in Geomorphology,* edited by D.R. Coates & J. Vitek, pp 401-14. Boston: Unwin and Allen.

Drennon, C. B., & W. G. Schleining. 1975. "Landslide hazard mapping on a shoe string". *American Society of Civil Engineers, Journal of Surveying & Mapping Division,* Su1: 107-14.

Geological Survey Division. 1974. *Kingston Geological Sheet 25 (Jamaica),* Scale 1:50,000.

Government of Jamaica, & Ralph Field and Associates. 1987. *Country Environmental Profile: Jamaica.* Kingston.

Green, G. W. 1977. "Structure and stratigraphy of Wagwater Belt, Kingston, Jamaica". *Overseas Geology and Mineral Resources* 48.

International Association of Engineering Geology. 1976. *Engineering Geological Maps. A Guide to their Preparation.* Paris: UNESCO.

Keaton, J. R. 1984. "Genesis-lithology-qualifier (GLQ) system of engineering geology mapping symbols". *Association Engineering Geologists' Bulletin* 21: 355-64.

Kezdi, A. 1974. *Handbook of Soil Mechanics,* Vol. 1, *Soil Physics.* Amsterdam: Elsevier.

Lucini, P. 1973. "The potential landslides forecasting of the Argille Varicolori Scagliose complex in IGM 174 IV SE Map, Savignano di Puglia (Compania)". *Geologia Applicata Idrogeologia* 8: 311-16.

Mann, P., G. Draper, & K. Burke. 1985. "Neo-tectonics of a strike-slip restraining bend system, Jamaica". In *Strike-slip Deformation, Basin Formation and Sedimentation,* edited by K.T. Biddle & N. Christie-Black, pp 211-26. Society of Economic Paleontologists and Mineralogists Special Publication 37.

Nielsen, T. H., & E. E. Brabb. 1977. "Slope-stability studies in the San Francisco Bay region, California". In *Landslides,* (Geological Society of America Reviews in Engineering Geology), edited by D.F. Coates. Vol. 3: 235-43.

Nielsen, T. H., R.H. Wright, T.C. Vlasic, & W. E. Spangle. 1979. "Relative slope stability and land use planning in the San Franciso Bay Region, California". *U.S. Geological Survey Professional Paper,* no. 944: 96.

Rib, H.T., & T. Liang. 1978. "Recognition and identification". In *Landslides: Analysis and Control,* edited by R.L. Schuster & R.J. Krizek, pp 34-80. Transportation Research Board Special Report 176. Washington DC: National Academy of Sciences, Washington.

Shepherd, J.B., & W.P. Aspinall. 1980. "Seismicity and seismic intensities in Jamaica, West Indies: a problem in risk assessment". *Earthquake Engineering and Structural Dynamics* 8: 315-35.

Varnes, D.J. 1978. "Slope movement types and processes". In *Landslides: Analysis and Control*, edited by R.L Schuster & R.J. Krizek, pp 11-23. Transportation Research Board Special Report 176. Washington, DC: National Academy of Sciences.

Varnes, D.J. 1984. *Landslide Hazard Zonation. A Review of Principles and Practice*. Paris: UNESCO.

Young, A. 1972. *Slopes*. Edinburgh: Oliver and Boyd.

# Part 4

# Land Resources and Development Planning

Chapter 12

# Soil Erosion, Environmental Change and Development in the Caribbean: A Deepening Crisis?

Duncan F. M. McGregor

## Introduction

The linkages between soil erosion and land degradation are well established, and the deteriorating situation on many Caribbean islands is widely recognized [Eyre 1992; McGregor 1986; 1988; McGregor & Barker 1991; Paskett & Philoctete 1990; Watts 1988]. A number of strategies have been proposed, and some have been implemented in the past [Sheng 1972; 1981]. Yet land degradation has rarely been halted, and in no substantive case permanently reversed. It is clear that in many areas throughout the Caribbean, farming steep and unstable hillslopes is becoming a progressively less productive pursuit. This decline in hillside farming systems has been ascribed to the interaction of physical and human variables, and is not new. Watts [1987], for example, documents Caribbean-wide abandonment of exhausted land in the heyday of plantation monoculture. The persistence of land degradation may be related to human, as much as physical, factors. However, the threat of global warming has recently focused concern for the environment. In the particular context of land degradation, the potential effects of projected climate change now require urgent consideration.

This paper illustrates the present-day context of soil erosion in the Caribbean through consideration of studies of soil erosion in Jamaica. The potential influences of climate change on the extent and importance of soil erosion, and hence on land degradation, are discussed, and possible scenarios outlined.

The Caribbean, as a region, exhibits high rates of geomorphological activity consequent on the combination of geology and climate. The relative northward movement of South America towards North America since Cretaceous times has thrown up igneous mountain ranges, has induced continuing volcanic activity, and has resulted in laying down of soluble calcareous or relatively unconsolidated sedimentary rock. Much of the region has been subjected to tectonic movement, with recurrent phases of faulting, folding and uplift. The climate is generally warm (and equable) and relatively humid, with northeasterly trade winds from the Atlantic ensuring annual precipitation totals exceeding 1,000mm throughout the majority of the region's islands [Watts 1987], and totals frequently exceeding 2,000mm where convective and orographic rainfall is concentrated against rising ground.

The geomorphological results of the combination of tectonic activity and subsequent weathering and erosion are steep slopes and highly dissected terrain. Chemical weathering rates are generally high, preparing the bedrock for downslope transport by mass movement. Slope failure is mostly triggered by the effects of seasonal heavy rainfall and by individual storm events such as hurricanes, but is often significantly affected, and indeed induced, by human activity. A further significant trigger is earthquake shock, particularly where the earthquake is preceded by heavy rainfall. Loss of life due to slope failure is not uncommon [DeGraff et al. 1989], and damage to crops, houses and communications is an ever present drain on resources. Losses may be much higher in the aftermath of an extreme event. For example, Barker and Miller [1990] quote provisional estimates of repair costs to roads amounting to US$19.3 million in the aftermath of Hurricane Gilbert in 1988, the bulk of which is attributed to rainfall induced slope failure and surface runoff.

While rapid mass movements tend to be localized and temporally irregular in occurrence, soil erosion is spatially and temporally continuous throughout the Caribbean. High natural soil erosion rates, a result of the combination of sloping terrain, thin and highly erodible soils, and the intense nature of many tropical rainstorms, are exacerbated by human activity. Deforestation, intensified land use (related to demographic pressures) and inappropriate land use are the principal factors in accelerating natural rates of erosion. Soil erosion is perhaps the most outwardly obvious manifestation of land degradation, being at once both a symptom and a cause of land degradation.

This paper will use soil erosion in Jamaica as a case study, but similar, or worse, cases of soil erosion are relatively widespread throughout the region. Perhaps the most dramatic case of extreme land degradation linked to soil erosion is that of Haiti, where it is reckoned that large areas of marginal land are effectively irreversibly degraded, and where each year about 6,000ha of land are abandoned to erosion [Paskett & Philoctete 1990]. Conditions in the Dominican Republic are scarcely better [Lugo et al. 1981]; 20th century cultivation of cotton has effectively stripped topsoil from lower slopes throughout Montserrat and Nevis [Watts 1973]; while the Scotland District of Barbados is in an advanced state of degradation [Carson & Tam 1977; Patel, this volume].

Deforestation has been, and remains, a key component in the land degradation equation, and also a starting point for human induced soil erosion. Lugo et al. [1981] indicate a patchy Caribbean-wide picture, with some islands showing marked deforestation in recent decades, while collated data indicate reversal of this trend on others. In Jamaica, however, Eyre [1987] indicates not only a gradual reduction in area of forest land up to the mid 1980s of around 3.3 percent per annum, but that much of the clearance was in small lots of between 20ha and 25ha. Over 50 percent of a sample of more than 500 lots had been cleared for "peasant agriculture" [Eyre 1987].

Further, it has been suggested [Eyre 1986] that surface climatology is changing in many parts of the Caribbean region, towards increasing aridity, and that this change is significantly influenced by high rates of deforestation. Deforestation and other resource pressures, as argued by Hulme [1989] and others, may lead to positive feedback effects through a cycle of increased albedo due to the increasing area of bare ground, associated radiation losses, consequent subsiding air, and reduced probability of rainfall.

## Soil Erosion in Jamaica

Soil erosion is ubiquitous on farmed land in Jamaica, but is at its most spectacular on the southern flanks of the Blue Mountains (see Figure 12.1 for location), where soils are generally highly weathered, thin (about 1m deep), acidic clay loams. Some chemical characteristics of a typical agricultural soil developed from massive lavas of the mid-Eocene Newcastle Formation are shown in Table 12.1. The relatively low organic carbon content gives an indication of relatively low fertility and relatively high erodibility. Organic carbon does not build up in these soils due to a combination of the relatively high rates of erosion and local agricultural practices. Clean weeding takes place, and the residues are not generally used as mulches but often added to

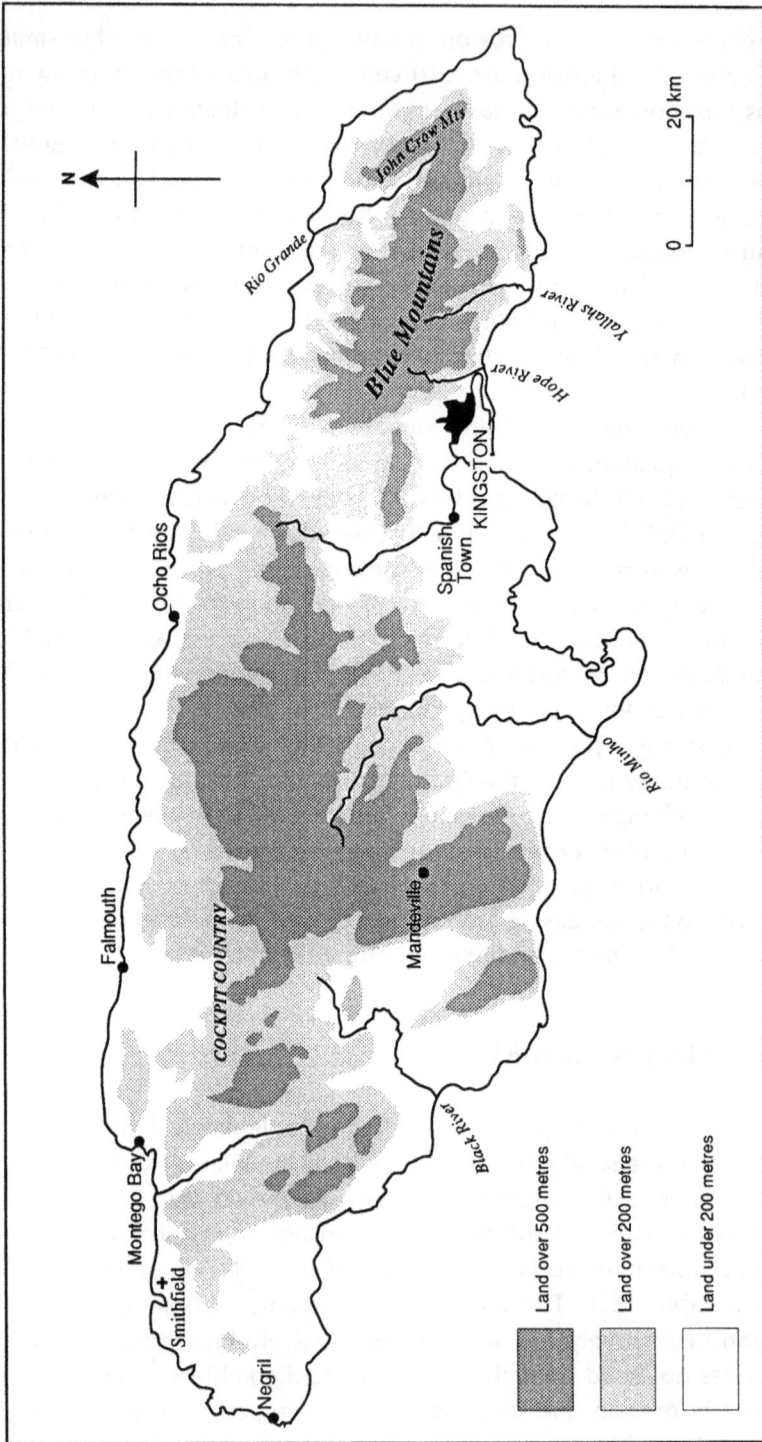

*Figure 12.1* Jamaica: Location map.

Table 12.1   Soil Profile Characteristics, Bellevue

| Depth (cm) | n | pH | % Organic C | CEC (me/100g) | Sum of Bases Exchangeable (me/100g) | BSP |
|---|---|---|---|---|---|---|
| 0-25 | 7 | 6.54 | 2.54 | 29.3 | 6.4 | 22 |
| 26-50 | 6 | 6.19 | 1.71 | 24.7 | 5.9 | 24 |
| 51-75 | 5 | 6.07 | 1.56 | 29.8 | 4.1 | 18 |
| 76-100 | 5 | 6.26 | 0.69 | 29.8 | 1.8 | 6 |

Source: McGregor [1988]

contour bunds. Cation exchange capacity (CEC) in these samples rates quite highly in comparison to many other tropical soils, but a more critical indicator of fertility is the base saturation percentage (BSP — the percentage of CEC accounted for by exchangeable bases). BSP levels are relatively low at the top of these profiles, and decline down profile to very low levels. The BSP is only a general indicator of chemical fertility and does not distinguish between individual bases, the imbalance between which may cause different, possibly severe, plant nutritional problems.

## Soil Erosion Data for Jamaica

The most comprehensive data on soil erosion available from Jamaica derive from the government-run experimental station at Smithfield (see Figure 12.1 for location), which has monitored permanent plots since 1969 under the Soil Conservation Division. In the Blue Mountains area, field-based measurements of erosion were obtained using soil troughs (sediment traps) by Richardson [1982] under forest, and by McGregor [1988] in a mixed crop plot. Other data relevant to soil erosion in Jamaica relate to estimates made without direct measurement of the erosion process itself.

A tabulation of published rates of soil erosion in Jamaica, converted to a common scale, is presented (Table 12.2). These data show a variable picture, but generally appear to indicate very high rates of erosion. It should be emphasized, however, that these figures have shortcomings. Critically, they subsume different methods of measurement, and they consider a variety of land uses and agricultural practices. The wide range of estimates, both within and between sources, indicates the need for caution in extrapolating these figures.

It is likely that estimates of erosion based on trap measurements will be accurate at the field scale, provided that the experimental monitoring period is of sufficient duration to cover "normal" seasonality. Only long-term, permanent

*Table 12.2*    Published Estimates of Soil Erosion, Jamaica

|  | Method | Land Use | Erosion (tonnes/ ha/annum) |
|---|---|---|---|
| Champion [1966] | USLE/guesstimate | overall | 97 |
| Richardson [1982] | traps | forest | 35-225 |
| UNDP/FAO [1982] | USLE | overall | 160-280 |
|  |  | agriculture | 24-99 |
|  |  | gully erosion | 54-93 |
| Government experimental station [1980-84] | traps | agriculture | 28-101 |
|  |  | yam | 17-133 |
| McGregor [1988] | traps | agriculture | 22-294 |
|  |  | (average) | (80) |
| Lal et al. [1989] | not stated | agriculture | 90 |

installations such as those of the Smithfield experimental station can encompass the effects of extreme meteorological events, which often have substantial direct impact on the soil resource over short periods. Shorter-term experiments, such as those of McGregor [1988] and Richardson [1982], are useful indicators of relative soil losses under different types of land use, but cannot in themselves be extrapolated to the general case. Within site variability of measured erosion rates may be high, though largely accounted for by variations in crop type and by associated agricultural practices (as indicated, for example, by data from McGregor [1988] (Figure 12.2).

Consideration must also be given to the problems of extrapolation from the plot scale to the catchment scale. This has not been examined in Jamaica, but may be illustrated briefly by reference to work elsewhere. Millington [1981] compared, for two small catchments in Sierra Leone, reservoir sedimentation rates (macro-scale), erosion plots (meso-scale) and erosion pins (micro-scale). His results show wide variation between techniques, even when similar land use is considered. This reflects the complexity of the transfer of eroded material through the catchment, and in particular the well established fact that estimates from field plots tend to *overestimate* catchment erosion rates. Bounded or small field plots take no account of the reality that much of the sediment moved in a particular storm event does not leave the catchment, but comes to rest in sediment sinks within the catchment, and indeed downslope from the field plot.

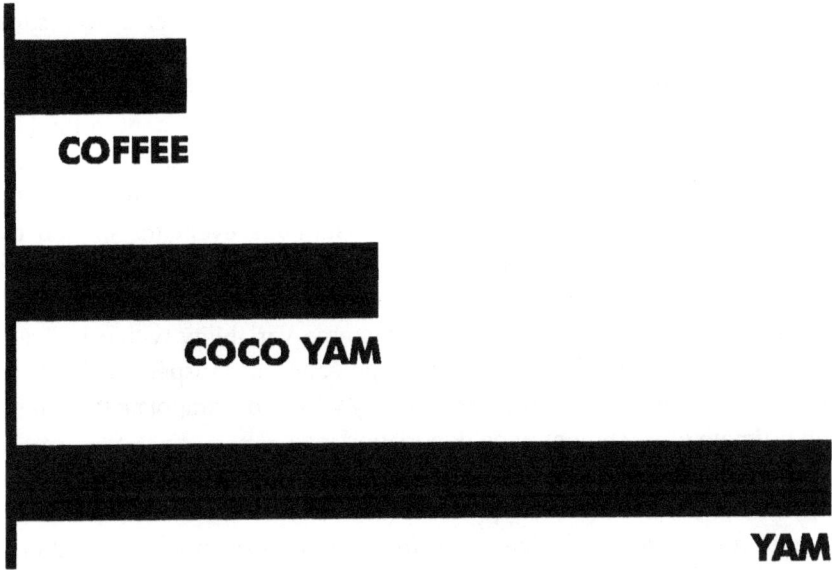

*Figure 12.2* Relative soil loss from different crop types, Bellevue
Source: *McGregor [1988]*.

Equally, measurement of sediment discharge from streams may provide general, corroborative evidence, but does not in itself indicate which parts of the catchment are most prone to erosion, or indeed which are the contributing areas for transfer of sediment into that particular stream. Accurate quantitative linkages of sediment transfer from hillslope to stream network have rarely been attempted worldwide, and not convincingly demonstrated in the literature.

At the regional scale, it can be noted that two of the estimates in Table 12.2 rely on blanket application of the Universal Soil Loss Equation, designed by the United States Department of Agriculture. (See, for example, Wischmeier & Smith [1978] for use in mainland USA, and of questionable application to the humid tropical situation.) More sophisticated models, developed for use in humid tropical situations [Morgan et al. 1984], have not as yet been applied in the Jamaican situation.

The data presented in Table 12.2 do, however, summarize the database presently available for soil erosion in Jamaica, and as such provide a baseline from which further work can proceed, and on which refinements may be established. The figures are based on estimates either at the plot scale or at the generalized regional scale. Linkage of these two extremes of scale would be achievable through catchment-scale estimates, usually by means of stream sediment discharge or reservoir sedimentation rates. In a rare example, Miller [1992] reports data for reduction in storage capacity of the Hermitage Reservoir (to the northwest of Kingston) for the period 1927 to 1963, but corroboration of the Table 12.2 figures at the catchment scale from stream sediment discharge is not found in the literature.

Wood [1977] illustrates the difficulties in achieving this linkage successfully in the Jamaican case. Wood, in a study of suspended sediment in the Hope River, on the eastern flank of the Kingston Metropolitan Area, emphasized the high, but highly variable, concentrations of suspended sediment in the Hope River. For example, one particular high magnitude event transported over 8,000 tonnes of suspended sediment in just over 30 hours, while four other measured events of lower discharge magnitude totalled less than 500 tonnes of suspended sediment in over 80 hours. Extreme variability within individual events is indicated, both of discharge and of suspended sediment concentrations, and no attempt was made by Wood to extrapolate these results to an estimate of catchment-wide denudation rates.

Bearing in mind the reservations expressed above, an overall impression may be drawn from the data presented in Table 12.2. Wide variations of estimate are present (not least within individual estimates), but there is some convergence on a figure somewhere between 80 and 100 tonnes/ hectare/annum for agricultural land. Adding in gully erosion, which probably, including land abandoned due to extensive gullying, runs at an average of about 50 percent of erosion from agricultural land in this terrain [Champion 1966], overall erosion rates of between 120 and 150 tonnes/ hectare/annum are indicated.

Common sense and experience suggest, however, that these reflect gross rates from individual plots, and do not truly reflect catchment-wide rates. Net rates must be lower, due to localized deposition into sediment sinks in individual fields and in the catchment as a whole, and taking into account the counterbalancing effect of soil conservation structures and practices. As has been noted earlier, there are no comparative figures for stream sediment output available, from which catchment-wide estimates may be derived.

These rates may be compared with likely rates of soil formation due to natural weathering. The author has found no published figures for natural rates of soil formation in Jamaica. In fact, there is relatively little literature on this subject, either general or specific, due no doubt to the difficulty in measuring or estimating, with any degree of certainty, a phenomenon as slow as soil formation. Morgan [1986] reviews some relevant literature, which suggests that rates of soil formation in a humid tropical area such as Jamaica will be relatively high in a global context, but unlikely to exceed rates of the order of 1mm/annum. This equates to a catchment-wide average of the order of 10 tonnes/hectare/annum, an estimate which must be regarded as the maximum likely in the Jamaican case.

## Jamaica: The Contemporary Situation

While re-emphasizing the likely overestimate of catchment-wide erosion rates indicated in Table 12.2, it is clear that net erosion is much higher than natural replenishment, particularly at the field scale. This simple deduction is borne out by field experience in the Yallahs catchment over the period since 1950, Clarke and Hodgkiss's 1974 map indicating the estimated extent of relative stripping of topsoil within the catchment up to that time (Figure 12.3).

The situation of net erosion, if allowed to continue unchecked, will eventually result in systems collapse. A simplified positive feedback is indicated: from topsoil loss and the gradual exposure of less fertile subsoil (see Table 12.1), through net losses of nutrients, to reductions in vegetative biomass and attendant reductions in agricultural output, to eventual systems collapse. The state of systems collapse has already been reached in parts of nearby Haiti [Paskett & Philoctete 1990], and locally elsewhere throughout the Caribbean. Systems collapse may be close in the Scotland District of Barbados, as indicated by Patel [this volume], in large areas of the Dominican Republic, and elsewhere.

In parts of Jamaica, a situation close to agricultural systems collapse arose through the period to 1950. This situation, documented elsewhere [Barker &

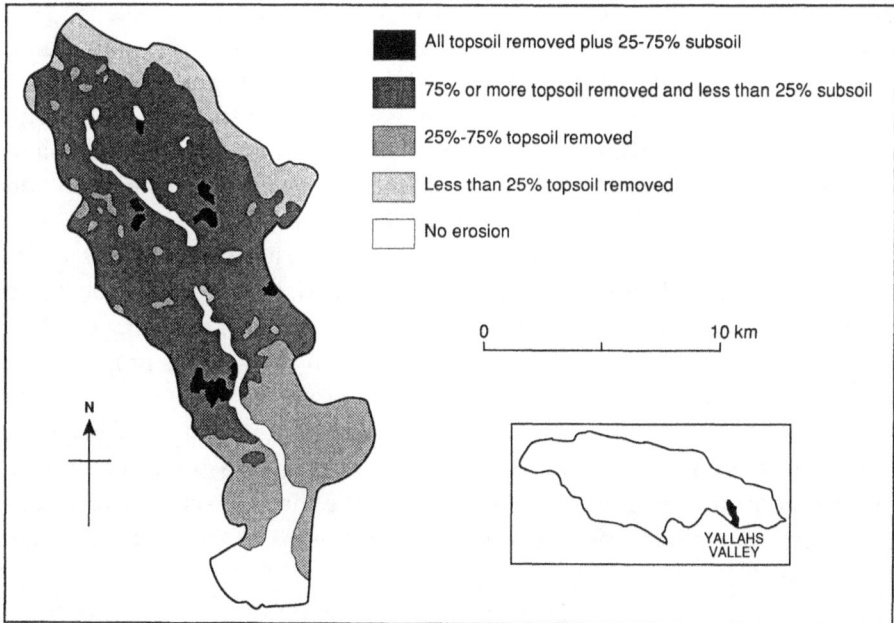

All topsoil removed plus 25-75% subsoil

75% or more topsoil removed and less than 25% subsoil

25%-75% topsoil removed

Less than 25% topsoil removed

No erosion

0          10 km

N

YALLAHS
VALLEY

*Figure 12.3*  Clarke and Hodgkiss 1974 estimate of topsoil erosion in Yallahs catchment

**197**

McGregor 1988], arose through a protracted period of intense and inappropriate land use of hillslopes. The important role of human activity, including progressive deforestation, in creating the advanced state of land degradation reached in rural Jamaica by 1950 cannot be overemphasized. The situation, however, was perceptibly worsened by the inability of the agricultural system to withstand extreme natural events, notably Hurricane Charlie in 1951. This point will be returned to below, in the context of potential climate change in the Caribbean region.

The work of Sheng [1972; 1981] has shown conclusively that much can be done to impede the progress of land degradation on steep slopes such as those of the Jamaican Blue Mountains, though sensible strategies exclude most agriculture on slopes above 25°. Much was achieved by the Land Authority schemes set up elsewhere in Jamaica (including the Yallahs Valley) in the 1950s to address the problems of watershed rehabilitation [Floyd 1970; Baxter 1975]. As detailed elsewhere [Barker & McGregor 1988; McGregor & Barker 1991], the success of these schemes was prejudiced by the cessation of direct funding around the end of the 1960s, and by the devolution of responsibilities for different aspects of land management to a number of separate planning agencies.

Since 1969, the situation has deteriorated perceptibly throughout the Yallahs Valley and elsewhere in rural Jamaica. In similar vein to the devastation wrought by Hurricane Charlie in 1951, Hurricane Allen (1980) and Hurricane Gilbert (1988) hit rural Jamaica hard. Despite being relatively dry over the land area for such an extreme event [Eyre 1989], a prolonged period of subsequent rainfall associated Hurricane Gilbert with widespread slope failure (particularly affecting the road network and agricultural land), accelerated soil erosion, and severe loss of natural and planted tree and shrub cover [Barker & Miller 1990].

The effects of individual extreme events, such as Hurricane Gilbert, on the farming economy have undoubtedly contributed to a recently observed marked increase in land degradation in rural farming areas [Eyre 1992; McGregor & Barker 1991], making recovery from such events progressively more difficult. This raises the wider question of the links between extreme natural events, soil erosion and land degradation in the Caribbean. In particular, the question is raised as to whether one, or a series, of extreme events can push a degraded landscape over the threshold of recovery. This question is particularly pertinent at present, in terms of the ongoing debate concerning global warming.

## Climate Change and the Caribbean

Recent reports by the Intergovernmental Panel on Climate Change (IPCC) [1990; 1992], based on the collation of the results of world-wide research into present and future climate change, indicate a general increase in global temperatures over the last 100 years or so (Figure 12.4). General circulation models (GCMs) being developed at present indicate a recent warming trend of about 0.3°C per decade, much of which is popularly ascribed to increases in the so-called greenhouse gases. This rate of warming is in fact no more than measured rates of temperature variation experienced in the past. These trends are, however, underpinned by observed increases in greenhouse gases which would certainly, at the very least, assist any natural trend towards temperature increase. Whether natural or human induced, this global temperature rise, if it continues into the next century, has significant potential implications for the Caribbean region.

The separate smoothed graphs of overall temperature anomalies (Figure 12.5a) and sea surface temperature (SST) anomalies (Figure 12.5b) produced by IPCC [1992] indicate that, although slightly lagging behind overall trends, SST data also show a recent positive trend. The GCM predictions, based on a

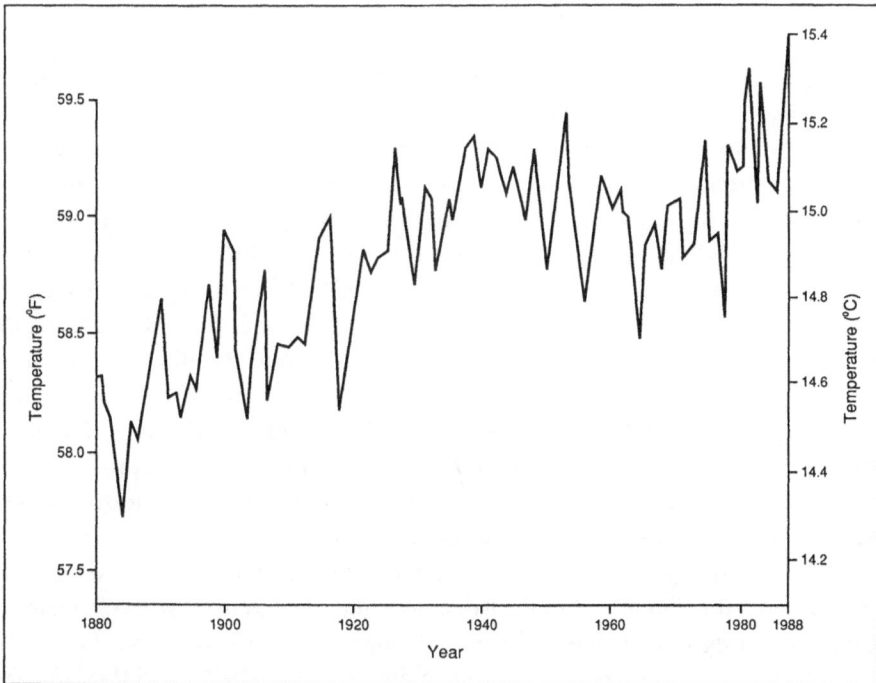

*Figure 12.4* Global temperature rise, averaged figures 1880–1988

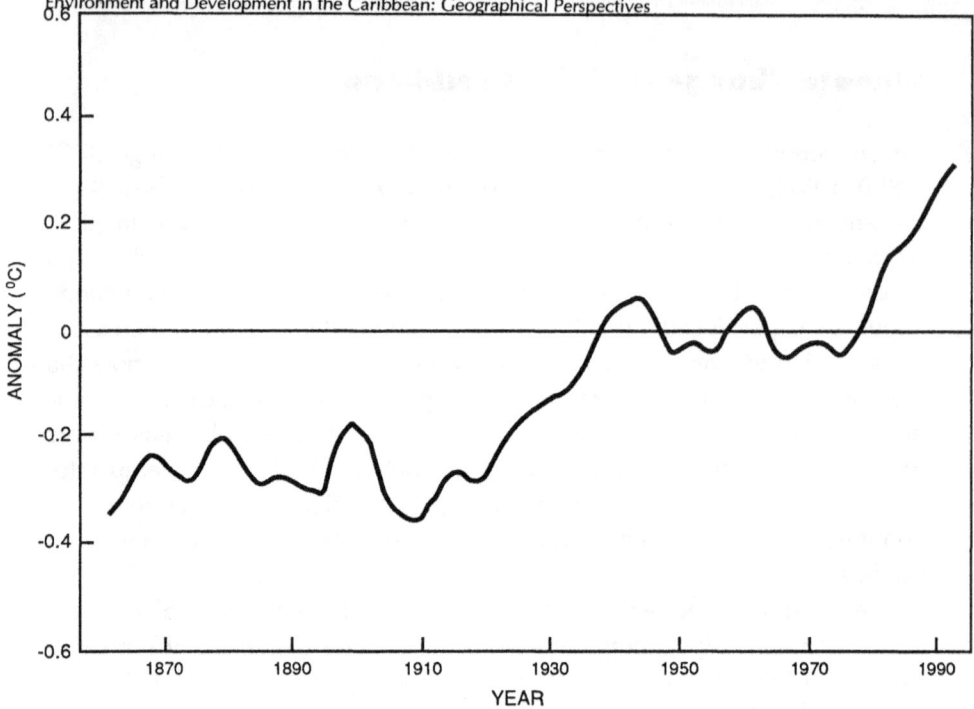

*Figure 12.5a* Combined surface temperature anomalies from long-term average

doubling of atmospheric $CO_2$ content over the next 70 years, indicate significant average rises in global SST.

With relatively uniform warming predicted over tropical oceans by IPCC [1992], increases in SST are probable, therefore, in the Caribbean region. A recent review suggests that air temperature warming will be of the order of 3°C in the region by the year 2060 [Wigley & Santer 1993]. This will inevitably lead to increases in SST. Critically, an increase of SST over the threshold of 26°C (necessary through a water depth of at least 60m) will significantly increase the probability of hurricane activity. Emanuel [1987] has calculated that estimates based on August mean conditions over the tropical oceans predicted by a GCM with twice the present $CO_2$ content, indicate a 40 percent to 50 percent increase in the destructive potential of hurricanes consequent on rises in SST of between 2°C and 5°C. Not only is an increase in storm intensity generally forecast by Emanuel, but changes in typical storm tracks may also occur, towards a greater frequency in higher latitudes (for example the Leeward Islands and the Greater Antilles) due to shifts in position of the equatorial pressure trough and the subtropical high pressure belt (as has been demonstrated through records by Walsh and Reading [1991] and Reading and Walsh [this volume]).

**200**

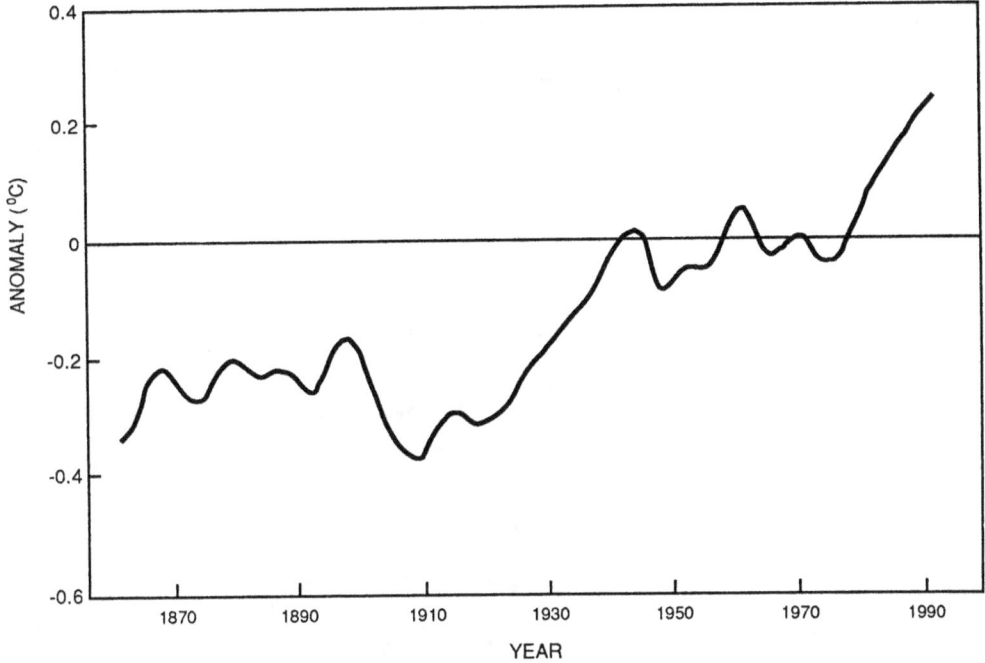

*Figure 12.5b* Sea surface temperature anomalies from long-term average

In the Caribbean region, however, recent surface temperatures have been marginally below the long-term average for the Americas. Figure 12.6 shows comparative averages, in °C, for the period 1981 to 1990, relative to 1951 to 1980. Again it must be considered that this variation may exhibit no more than the "normal" long-term climatic variability experienced over the period of records.

This recent pattern of below average surface temperatures may be reflected in a recent slight fall in the incidence of hurricanes and tropical cyclones indicated by Walsh and Reading [1991] (Figure 12.7). With reference to earlier discussion, it is worthy of comment that Walsh and Reading's data indicate a significant rise in frequency of hurricanes and tropical cyclones in the 20 years leading up to the near collapse of much of the Jamaican rural farming system in the early 1950s.

Whether the recent, violent Hurricanes Gilbert (1988), Hugo (1989) and Andrew (1992) are early indicators of changing conditions is speculative, but cannot be discounted. Prediction is still in its relative infancy. GCMs as yet cannot simulate hurricanes in detail, but do simulate "tropical disturbances". Conflicting results are presented. For example, Haarsma et al. [1992] found that the number of tropical disturbances modelled as consequent on a

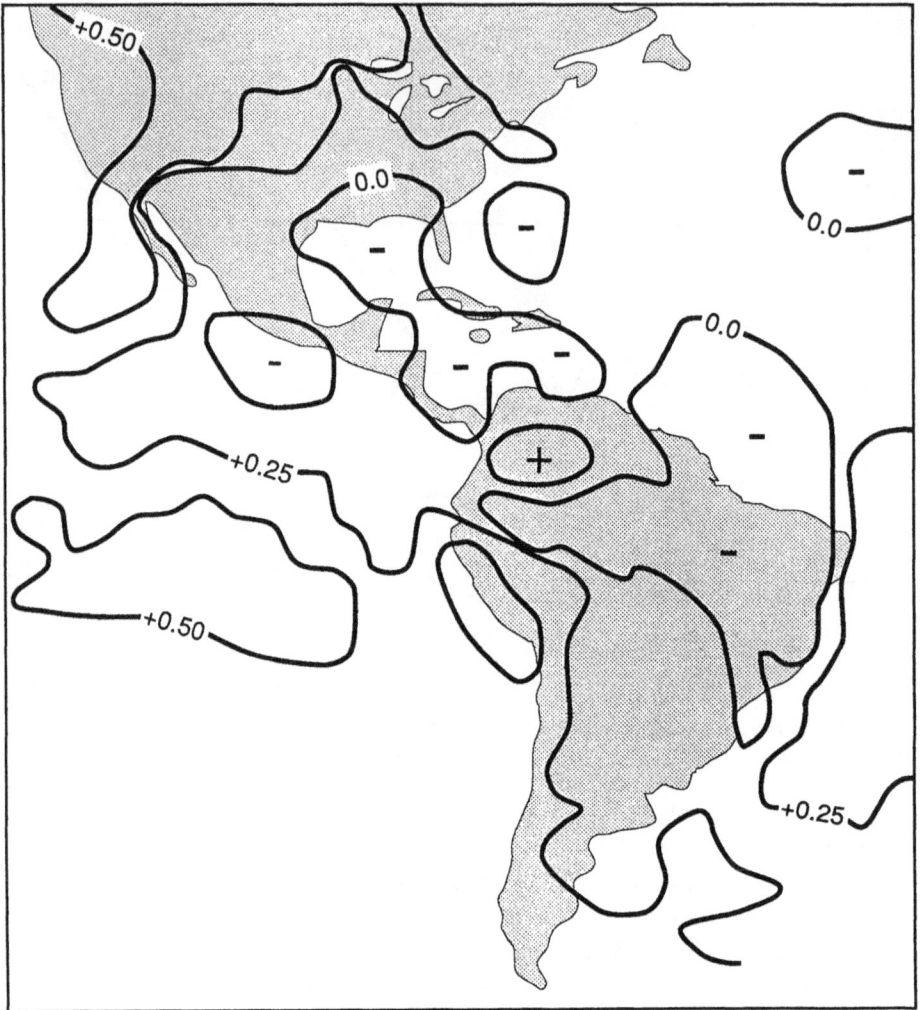

*Figure 12.6* Surface temperature anomalies for the Americas: 1981-1990 with respect to 1951-1980. Isolines in °C

doubling of $CO_2$ increased, but with little change in their structure and intensity. Emanuel [1987], on the other hand, modelled significant increases in maximum pressure drop (and hence maximum wind speed in the storm) at the centre of simulated tropical storms resulting from a SST drop of 3°C.

Gray [1993] has recently reviewed recent climatic data from the region, and has extrapolated the likely effects of temperature rise in the region as continued decreasing rainfall, increases in surface wind speeds, and increases in evaporation. He notes that these factors would increase levels of erosion generally, both directly and indirectly through decreases in overall vegetative

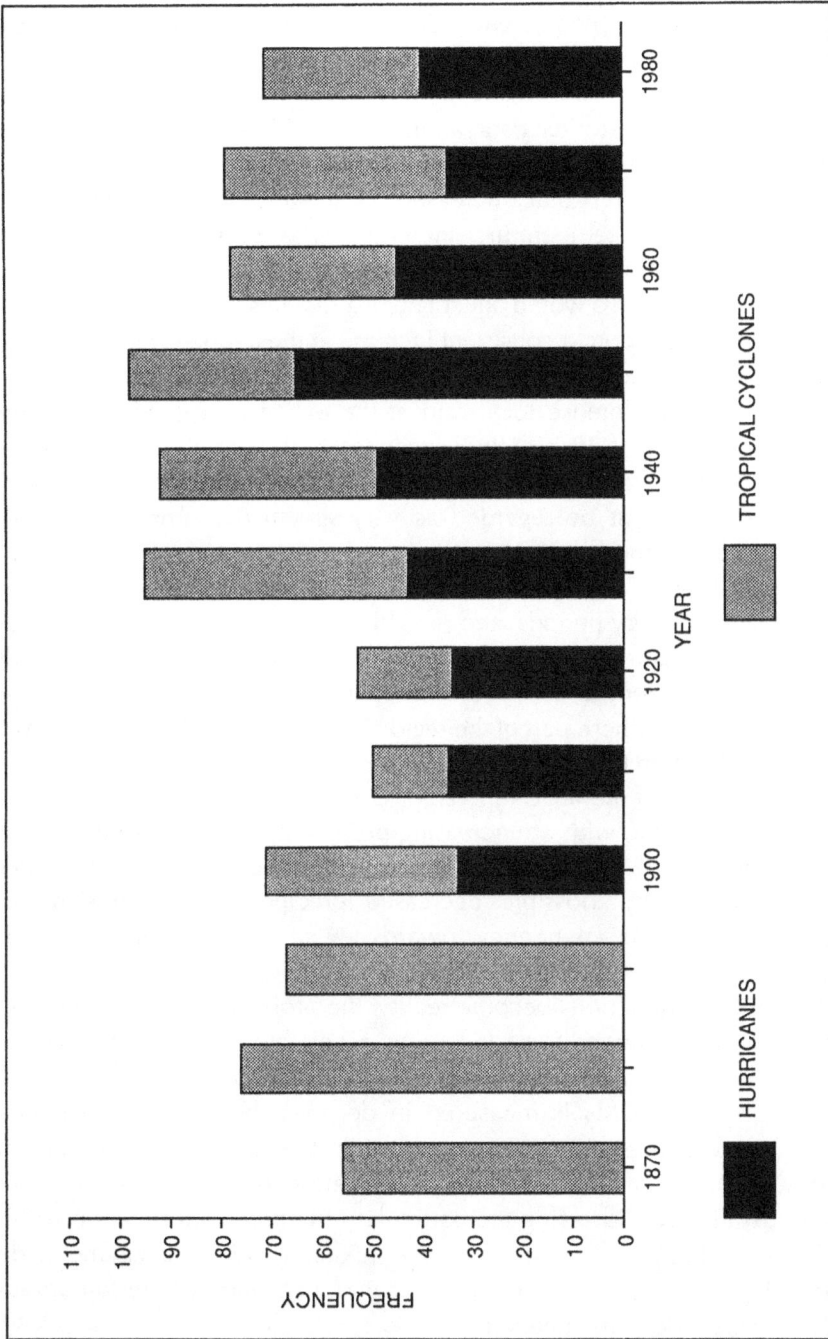

*Figure 12.7* Decadal Incidence of hurricanes and tropical cyclones

cover. He points out that the greater the SST, the more moisture is evaporated from the ocean and the more latent heat is available for release in convection. Other things being equal, more active convection will lead to more frequent intensification of tropical storms and to hurricane strength. Schapiro [1982] has noted that, based on historical data, an increase of SST of 1.5°C is found to be associated with an increase in hurricane frequency of 1.6 ± 1.2 per year. It seems likely, therefore, that increased frequency of hurricanes would accompany regional temperature increases. The possibility of favoured hurricane tracks shifting from those commonly experienced at present remains, if the extent to which this would affect Jamaica remains uncertain.

In the 1990 IPCC report, a consistent increase in the frequency of convective precipitation at the expense of large-scale precipitation was noted, with the implication of more intense local rain at the expense of gentler but more persistent rainfall events. IPCC [1992] suggests that the Caribbean would suffer a decrease in precipitation regionally under global warming of up to 350mm per decade. This must be regarded as very speculative, and needs to be considered against the likelihood of greater hurricane and tropical cyclone frequency. It would, however, imply increased seasonality, with reduced precipitation during dry periods, and possibly fewer but more high magnitude precipitation events in wet seasons. Wigley and Santer [1993] have recently refined this prediction, and hypothesize that increases in precipitation are more likely in the southern part of the region, with winter and spring decreases slightly more likely in the north of the Caribbean Basin.

The implications of the IPCC reports for Caribbean agriculture are therefore potentially significant, with an increasing probability indicated of more, and possibly more violent, storm activity. This scenario is combined with projected increased seasonality, possible decreased precipitation in parts of the Caribbean Basin, and a tendency towards fewer but more intense rainfall events.

If these GCM predictions become reality, the probability would inevitably increase of climatic conditions favouring accelerated soil erosion and an intensification of land degradation in upland farming areas. The time scale envisaged by the GCMs is measured in decades, but one of the critical thresholds, sea surface temperatures of above 26°C, is already exceeded in the region. Clearly, modelling is still at a relatively early stage, and improved models specifically addressing the particular environmental situation within the Caribbean Basin are required before confident predictions may be made. The warning, however, is real and is set against a situation where soil erosion and land degradation are continuing apace.

## Land Degradation: The Way Ahead?

Despite the variable quality of the database relating to rates of soil erosion and to predictions of climate change, it is clear that the present crisis of land degradation on erosion prone Caribbean farm lands will deepen inexorably unless concerted action is forthcoming. The crisis is real, now, for the farmer supporting a family from a declining natural resource base, and can only be exacerbated by the forecasted climate changes in the region. The time scale of degradation to the point of systems collapse may be short — perhaps a matter of as little as a decade or two in the worst affected areas of Jamaica — and can only be shortened further by adverse climate changes.

The crucial question is what can be done? Clearly, the "do nothing" option is a recipe for progressively deepening rural poverty. Also, little can be done by the individual small farmer, as present short-term planning horizons are necessitated by the declining natural resource base and wider economic circumstances.

Improved modelling of soil erosion rates under the present range of land uses would assist in understanding the magnitude of the problem, but this route requires a protracted period of field observation to be effective. Improved modelling of future climate change would also contribute, but would accurate prediction be sufficient to allow sufficient time to react? At the current rate of progress, for example, global warming driven by human action could become a reality before significant deviation from long-term natural trends can be identified.

The development and implementation of management options is urgently required. This requires a combination of thorough and appropriate research into the dynamics of existing agricultural systems within the Caribbean, and the exploration of the feasibility of applying farming techniques, potentially appropriate to the Caribbean situation, which have proved to be successful elsewhere. Paradoxically, excellent work of this nature has been carried out for many years in Jamaica, at the Smithfield experimental station, yet there has been little diffusion of perceived successes from the experimental plot to the Jamaican hillside. It would be both simplistic and unfair to lay the blame at the door of successive governments, which have had a complex of problems to wrestle with. But a mobilization of political will is a necessary prerequisite for the implementation and eventual success of a comprehensive rural development plan such as would be required to arrest the degradation caused by Jamaican hillside farming.

A necessity for further research, and for subsequent incorporation into a development strategy, is the development of a thorough understanding of farmers' knowledge of indigenous agronomic techniques, such as "food forests", and of their perception of erosion and erosion control strategies. The arguments have been rehearsed both in Jamaica [McGregor & Barker 1991] and elsewhere in the Caribbean [Brierley 1974; Hills 1988]. An adaptive form of shifting cultivation, incorporating lengthy fallow periods, might be a buffer against progressive land degradation, but seems unlikely to be economically sustainable under present population densities.

As Sheng [1972; 1981] suggests, the options for successful management of soil erosion on such steeply sloping terrains as have been considered here, are relatively few. Forms of agroforestry and forestry are suggested by Sheng as the only sensible options. These, however, offer little prospect of sufficient economic return to support the present densities of population. Short of physically moving significant numbers of people from the hillsides to other parts of Jamaica, technically possible but socially undesirable, the systematic development of off-farm income opportunities would be necessary to underpin extensive agroforestry or forestry options. This again demands political action, and a wider solution to Jamaica's economic problems, though some significant recent developments have been made in this respect in terms of local involvement in National Park activities (see Smith and Barker & Miller in this volume).

As Lal [1990] points out, the usefulness of agroforestry in controlling erosion on tropical steeplands has been demonstrated for only a few soils and environments. Agroforestry systems undoubtedly have the potential to provide a sustainable management alternative for food crop production in such terrain, but longer-term research needs to be carried out into the choice of appropriate tree species, into intercropping options, into rotational sequences, and into soil and water conserving properties of potentially beneficial options.

It is worth remembering that there are limits to the efficacy of technologies, that steep hillsides in the humid tropics are inherently a limiting situation, and that few options hold out the hope of economic returns for other than low population densities. In the Caribbean, the key to controlling soil erosion, to adapting to changing climatic circumstances, and to development of sustainable land use, lies in the types of research outlined above.

Time is not on the side of the Caribbean hillside farmer. The overriding problems are twofold. First, it is necessary to define, through appropriately focused research, a suitable strategy. Secondly, it is necessary to fund such a strategy swiftly and with proper regard for the longer-term prospect of maintaining hillside agriculture at a level which is sustainable both in economic terms and in terms of the conservation of soil resources.

# References

Barker, D., & D.F.M. McGregor. 1988. "Land degradation in the Yallahs Basin, Jamaica: historical notes and contemporary observations". *Geography* 73: 116-24.

Barker, D., & D.J. Miller. 1990. "Hurricane Gilbert: anthropomorphising a natural disaster". *Area* 22: 107-16.

Baxter, A.E. 1975. "The diffusion of innovations: soil conservation techniques, the Yallahs Valley, Jamaica". *Jamaica Journal* 9: 51-56.

Brierley, J.S. 1974. *Small Farming in Grenada, West Indies*. Winnipeg: Manitoba Geographical Series No.4.

Carson, M.A., & S.W. Tam. 1977. "The land conservation conundrum of eastern Barbados". *Annals of the Association of American Geographers* 67: 185-203.

Champion, H.G. 1966. *Report on Soil Erosion in the Mahogany Vale Catchment and its Control with Special Reference to Sedimentation in the Future Reservoir*. London: Howard Humphries and Sons.

Clarke, C.G., & A.G. Hodgkiss. 1974. *Jamaica in Maps*. London: University of London Press.

DeGraff, J.V., et al. 1989. "Landslides: their extent and significance in the Caribbean". In *Landslides: Extent and Economic Significance*, edited by E.E Brabb & B.L. Harrod, pp 51-80. Rotterdam: Balkema.

Emanuel, K.A. 1987. "The dependence of hurricane intensity on climate". *Nature* 326: 483-85.

Eyre, L.A. 1986. "Vegetation change and desertification in the Caribbean". *Proceedings ISLSCP Conference, Rome, December 1985*. European Science Association Special Publication 248: 509-14.

Eyre, L.A. 1987. "Jamaica: test case for tropical deforestation?" *Ambio* 16: 338-43.

Eyre, L.A. 1989. "Hurricane Gilbert: Caribbean record breaker". *Weather* 44: 160-64.

Eyre, L.A. 1992. "The effects of environmental degradation in the Cane River and Rio Minho Watersheds, Jamaica: a commentary". In *Natural Hazards in the Caribbean*, edited by R. Ahmad. *Journal of the Geological Society of Jamaica*, Special Issue No. 12:57-65.

Floyd, B. 1970. "Agricultural innovation in Jamaica: the Yallahs Valley Land Authority". *Economic Geography* 46: 63-77.

Gray, C.R. 1993. "Regional meteorology and hurricanes". In *Climatic Change in the Intra-Americas Sea*, edited by G.A. Maul, pp 87-99. London: Edward Arnold (for UNEP).

GOJ/UNDP/FAO. 1982. *Development Plan for the Upper Yallahs Valley*. Kingston: Government of Jamaica/UN Development Programme/Food and Agricultural Organisation. Project Working Paper WP/23.

Haarsma, R.J., J.F.B. Mitchell, & C.A. Senior. 1992. "Tropical disturbances in a GCM". *Climate Dynamics*. In press.

Hills, T.L. 1988. "The Caribbean peasant food forest: ecological artistry or random chaos". In *Small Farming and Peasant Resources in the Caribbean*, edited by J.S. Brierley & H. Rubenstein, pp 1-28. Winnipeg: University of Manitoba.

Hulme, M. 1989. "Is environmental degradation causing drought in the Sahel? An assessment from recent empirical research". *Geography* 74: 38-46.

Intergovernmental Panel on Climate Change. 1990. *Climate Change: The IPCC Scientific Assessment*, edited by J.T. Houghton, G.J. Jenkins, & J.J. Ephraums. Cambridge: Cambridge University Press.

Intergovernmental Panel on Climate Change. 1992. *Climate Change 1992: The Supplementary Report to the IPCC Scientific Assessment*, edited by J.T. Houghton, B.A. Callander, & S.K. Varney. Cambridge: Cambridge University Press.

Lal, R. 1990. "Agroforestry systems to control erosion on arable tropical steeplands". *IASH-AISH Publ.* No.192 (Proceedings of the Fiji Symposium on Research Needs and Applications to Reduce Erosion and Sedimentation in Tropical Steeplands): 338-46.

Lal, R., G.F. Hall, & F.P. Miller. 1989. "Soil degradation: I. basic processes". *Land Degradation and Rehabilitation* 1: 51-69.

Lugo, A.E., R. Schmidt, & S. Brown. 1981. "Tropical forests in the Caribbean". *Ambio* 10: 318-24.

McGregor, D.F.M. 1986. "Assessment of soil erosion hazard in the Upper Yallahs Valley, Jamaica". *Caribbean Geography* 2: 138-43.

McGregor, D.F.M. 1988. "An investigation of soil status and land use on a steeply sloping hillside, Blue Mountains, Jamaica". *Singapore Journal of Tropical Geography* 9: 60-71.

McGregor, D.F.M., & D. Barker. 1991. "Land degradation and hillside farming in the Fall River Basin, Jamaica". *Applied Geography* 11: 143-56.

Miller, L.A. 1992. "A preliminary assessment of the economic cost of land degradation: the Hermitage catchment, Jamaica". *Caribbean Geography* 3: 244-52.

Millington, A.C. 1981. "Relationship between three scales of erosion measurement on two small basins in Sierra Leone". *International Association for Scientific Hydrology Publications* 133: 485-92.

Morgan, R.P.C. 1986. *Soil Erosion and Conservation.* Harlow: Longman.

Morgan, R.P.C., D.D.V. Morgan, & H.J. Finney. 1984. "A predictive model for the assessment of soil erosion risk". *Journal of Agricultural Engineering Research* 30: 245-53.

Paskett, C.J., & C-E. Philoctete. 1990. "Soil conservation in Haiti". *Journal of Soil and Water Conservation* 45: 457-59.

Richardson, J.H. 1982. "Some implications of tropical forest replacement in Jamaica". *Zeitschrift fur Geomorphologie*, Suppl.-Bd. 44: 107-18.

Schapiro, L.J. 1982. "Hurricane climatic fluctuations. Part II: Relation to large-scale circulation". *Monthly Weather Review* 110: 1014-023.

Sheng, T.C. 1972. "A treatment oriented land capability classification scheme for hilly marginal lands in the humid tropics". *Journal of the Science Research Council of Jamaica* 3: 93-112.

Sheng, T.C. 1981. "The need for soil conservation structures for steep cultivated slopes in the humid tropics". In *Tropical Agricultural Hydrology*, edited by R. Lal & E.W. Russell, pp 357-72. Chichester: John Wiley.

Soil Conservation Department. N.d. "Interim results of yam multicropping — Smithfield runoff plots". Kingston: Soil Conservation Department.

Walsh, R.P.D., & A.J. Reading. 1991. "Historical changes in tropical cyclone frequency within the Caribbean since 1500". *Wurzburger Geographische Arbeiten* 80: 199-240.

Watts, D. 1973. "From sugar plantation to open range grazing: changes in the land use of Nevis, West Indies, 1950-1970". *Geography* 58: 65-68.

Watts, D. 1987. *The West Indies: Patterns of Development, Culture and Environmental Change Since 1492.* Cambridge: Cambridge University Press.

Watts, D. 1988. "Development and renewable resource depletion in the Caribbean". *Journal of Biogeography* 15: 119-26.

Wigley, T.M.L., & B.D. Santer. 1993. "Future climate of the Gulf/Caribbean Basin from the global circulation models". In *Climatic Change in the Intra-Americas Sea*, edited by G.A. Maul, pp 31-54. London: Edward Arnold (for UNEP).

Wischmeier, W.H., & D.D. Smith. 1978. "Predicting rainfall erosion losses". *United States Department of Agriculture, Agricultural Research Service Handbook* No. 537.

Wood, P.A. 1977. "Suspended sediment in a tropical environment of seasonal flow and large floods: Hope River, Jamaica". *Journal of Tropical Geography* 45: 65-69.

Chapter 13

# Coastal Development and Geomorphological Processes: Scotland District, Barbados

Fatima Patel

## Introduction

This study deals with the recognition and prediction of geomorphological changes and hazards on the East Coast of the Scotland District of Barbados, with the aim of assisting the physical planning process. The study area (Figure 13.1) extends along the East Coast Road from Cattlewash to Chalky Mount and has an area of approximately 4km$^2$ (Figure 13.2). Relative to much of the rest of Barbados, the study area (referred to as the East Coast) is underdeveloped. Housing density is low (50 houses per km$^2$) and land use is agricultural. It is, however, one of the few stretches of the eastern coastline along which a first class road runs, and is therefore a prime recreation area on this part of the island. Recently, there has been speculation that the area could be developed for tourism and sporting activities. A housing development has also recently been approved by Parliament on a large spur which is part of the scenic vista. This latter development has concerned environmentalists and other groups in the country who argue that these developments will have adverse effects on the natural and historical landscape [Barbados National Trust 1991].

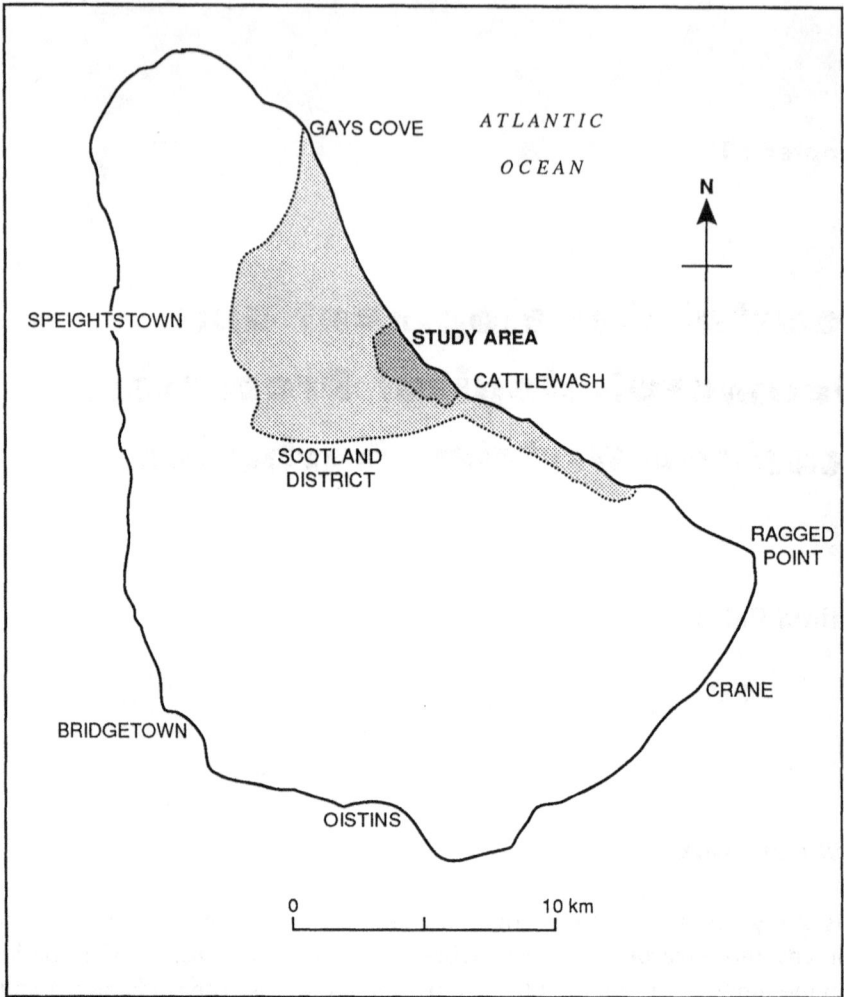

*Figure 13.1* The study area

## Methodology

This research investigates the impacts this development could have upon the physical landscape. First, it describes and explains the geomorphology and identifies existing geomorphic hazards. Linkages between geomorphic hazards and previous and present land use are sought. An attempt is then made to predict possible future geomorphic changes and hazards, especially with respect to potential future land use and infrastructural development.

The recognition of a hazard requires the understanding of the geomorphic system as a whole and in terms of its parts, as well as the variable processes that operate in and on the system which may produce landform change.

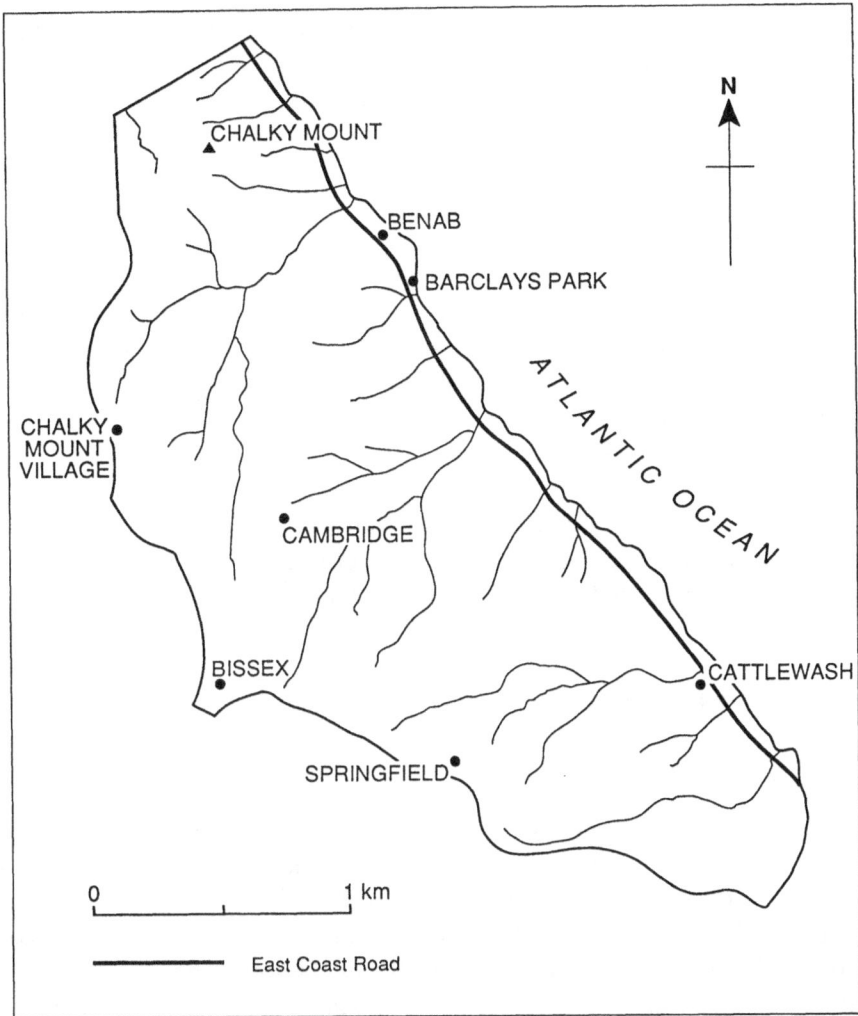

*Figure 13.2* Principal locations in the study area

Essential to the effort of prediction is the consideration of *complexity* and *singularity,* and the *sensitivity* of the landform to geomorphic change [Schumm 1988].

Evaluating geomorphic change involves the factor of time – time for monitoring changes in landform, in processes, and in energy inputs. As an appropriate time span was not available to the present study, alternative strategies for evaluating change were modified and adopted from Cooke and Doornkamp [1990]. These included extensive field surveys to establish the geomorphic character of the landscape, and also measuring and examining slope profiles together with erosion and other mass wasting features. Examination of soils in the field and in the laboratory provided an understanding of the characteristics and behaviour of slope materials which influence morphology and process. Evidence of geomorphic change, both direct and supporting, was gleaned from the historical record, including published works and aerial photographs. The latter were used extensively in morphological and geomorphological mapping, description and analysis.

After the geomorphic character of the landforms was described and features of instability mapped, stable and unstable landforms were compared, differences between them described, and critical threshold conditions identified. This strategy assists in establishing the sensitivity of the landscape to geomorphic change [Brunsden & Thornes 1979]. The Ergodic Hypothesis, a strategy described as *location for time substitution* [Schumm 1988], attempts to replace a sequence of events through time by a sequence of events described at different locations at the present. The complex response of a landform to a particular geomorphic change can thus be predicted by examining a similar landform that has already experienced that change.

## Slope Form, Materials and Processes

### Geology

The Scotland District provides an exposure of Barbados' inner core, a mixture of sedimentary rocks whose stratigraphy and history attracts much debate and interest [Director of Surveys 1982; Speed 1988].

The geology dates back to the Lower Eocene, to the formation of the basal complex, the Scotland Group. The Oceanic Group and the Bissex Hill Formation, accompanied by thrust faulting, isoclinal folding, and shearing on a NE-SW axis, were emplaced during the late Eocene to Miocene period; the date of diapiric intrusion by the Joe's River Beds is uncertain. After several periods of submergence and emergence, during which the Coral Cap of the rest of the island was formed, the area was finally uplifted and eroded to its present form [Director of Surveys 1982]. The result is a number of thrust faulted sedimentary blocks intruded by mudstone diapirs (Figure 13.3).

The Scotland Group consists essentially of alternating beds of weak sandstones and shales which have been highly folded and fractured, and which show a high degree of weathering. The Lower Scotland Formation, consisting of shaly mudstones with thin sandstone beds, underlies much of the surface geology. The Upper Scotland Formation, or the Scotland Sandstones, makes up an important lithological unit, outcropping over 42

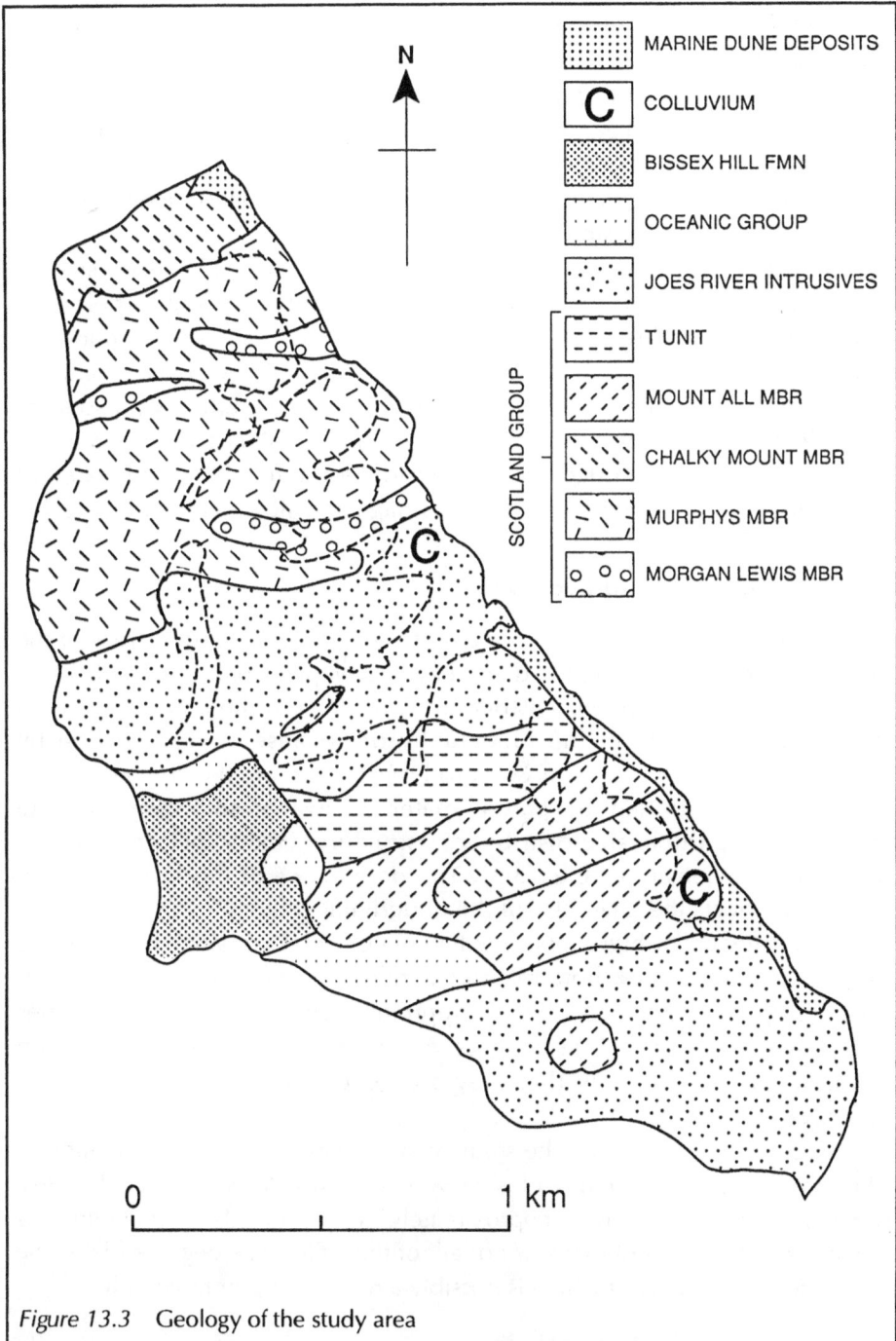

*Figure 13.3*   Geology of the study area

percent of the study area. It consists of well-bedded, medium to coarse grained sandstones with thin beds of silty and clayey shales. The Chalky Mount Member is the most resistant, and hence most outstanding member. The Mount All Member has thinner sandstone beds, while the weakest of these members, the Murphy's Member, is very thinly bedded and well sheared. The Scotland Sandstone soils are very thin, with poorly structured subsurface horizons, and they are fairly well drained, but exhibit extremely variable permeabilities. The T-unit, the youngest member of this group, is lithologically similar to the Scotland Shales.

The Oceanic and Bissex Hill Formations consist of microfossil-rich mudstones, marls and sandstones [Director of Surveys 1982]. Their soils are poorly structured, but are well drained and have moderate permeabilities [Vernon & Carroll 1965]. The Joe's River Beds, a diapiric intrusion, consists of a highly sheared, structureless, commonly oil-soaked, organic-rich sandy mudstone matrix containing blocks of sedimentary rocks. It can be regarded as a cohesionless soil with rapid external drainage, poor to imperfect internal drainage and slow permeabilities.

## Soils, Topography and Drainage

Drift deposits, the products of modern erosion, cover extensive areas of the lower slopes, and modern sand dunes have developed along the shorelines.

The soils of the Scotland District are considered to be immature due to the "unstable nature of the topography or because of rejuvenation by accelerated erosion" [Vernon & Carroll 1965], and are thus recognized to be strongly controlled by parent material. Twelve soil samples were analysed for particle size distribution, structure, colour, pH, free $CaCO_3$ content, and density (Table 13.1). The dominance of the sand and clay fractions reflects the character of the underlying geology.

Relief is generally high; there are few major breaks of slope between the divide and the valley bottom, and active incision, for the most part, extends up to the drainage divides. Approximately 25 percent of the slopes are above 30 percent (17°) steepness. An examination of the profiles along some of the slopes show that they are generally complex, and mainly concave or straight.

The drainage pattern over the study area is dendritic and the orientation of the major valleys coincides closely with the NE-SW fault and fold axes. Drainage density is high, approximately 40km/km$^2$, but streamflow is ephemeral. The sides of many, if not all, of the valleys are degraded by slope processes, the severity of which is possibly a result of recent rapid uplift.

## Geomorphological Processes

The geomorphological processes operating are largely fluvial and gravity-driven slope processes, the mapping of which was simplified by dividing them into groups based on the intensity of the process, and the type of change induced by it (Table 13.2, *p218*). Figure 13.4 (*p218*) shows the distribution of these process groups over the study area.

### Erodibility

Erosion by sheetwash and rilling is extensive, especially on devegetated slopes. Rills often grade downslope into gullies. Gullies are also formed from mass movements where extensional cracking produces trenches, and through soil piping. On convexo-concave slopes, initiation of gully erosion occurs just below the steepest segment, with deepest channel flow at the base, and surface wash on the convex portions. Soil erosion is so severe on these slopes that bedrock is commonly exposed.

Generally, the Scotland soils have moderately low permeabilities, imperfect drainage and blocky structure [Vernon & Carroll 1965], features indicative of weak soils. They are all classified as presenting moderate to high erosion hazards [Vernon & Carroll 1965]. Factors that lead to the development of soil pipes [Cooke & Doornkamp 1990], such as seasonal rainfall, soil cracking in dry periods, incomplete vegetation cover, relatively impermeable layers in the soil profile and steep hydraulic gradients, are present in the study area.

The steepness of the slopes implies the potential for high runoff velocities; while the long slopes may allow high volumes of overland flow to be generated. The sparse scrub that covers most of the eroded slopes does little to improve soil strength or restrict erosion. Isolated trees, shrubs and rock outcrops divert drainage around them and encourage channel development. Where soils have been completely eroded by surface wash on convex slopes, lineations in bedrock structures, such as outstanding sandstone beds, divert drainage and allow channel development downslope.

### Mass Wasting

The combination of inherent factors present in the study area – the lithological and structural characteristics, the morphology and the vegetation cover – indicates that the potential for instability and failure in the Scotland rocks is high.

Creep features including tension tracks, terracettes on convex slopes, and hummocky micro-relief on concave slopes are common, especially on the rocks of the Joe's River Beds. Slides and slumps are common on the more structured Scotland Group rocks. As available potential energies are greatest

*Table 13.1* Index Properties of Some East Coast Soils

| Sample Index No. | Mapping Unit | Site Description | Colour | Mottling | Structure |
|---|---|---|---|---|---|
| 1.1 | 120 | Small flow/slide behind house | 2.5Y 5/2 | None | Coarse angular blocky |
| 2.1 | 120 | Fissure marginal o landslide | 5Y 5/3 | None | Very coarse sub-angular locky |
| 4.1 | 122 | Shallow flow | 2.5Y 3/2 | Common 10YR 5/6 | Coarse angular blocky |
| 5.1 | 130 | Steep slope with terracetes and shallow flow | 5Y 5/3 | | Blocky angular |
| 5.2 | 130 | Eroded cutting well weathered 'A' horizon | 2.5Y 5/6 | None | Blocky angular |
| 3.3 | 144 | Gully wall | 2.5Y 5/2 | | Coarse to very coarse angular with shale fragments |
| 3.4 | 144 | Surface wash eroded top soil | 5Y 4/2 | | Coarse to very coarse angular to sub-angular blocky |
| 3.1 | 164 | Channel wall | 2.5/10R 5/4 | Up to 40% 10YR 5/1 7.5R 5/6 | Coarse angular blocky |
| 3.2 | 164 | Gullied footpath on channel side | 5Y 5/3 | None | Medium sub-angular blocky peds in loose sand |
| 6.1 | 164 | Eroded bluff 'A' horizon | 2.5Y 4/2 | Few 2.5Y 5/4 | Coarse angular blocky |
| 6.2 | 164 | Eroded bluff 'B' horizon | 2.5Y 5/4-5/6 | Few 10YR 5/8 | Very coarse angular blocky |
| 5.3 | 168 | Surface soil | 2.5Y 4/4 | None | Apedal-loose sandy |

*Data in last six columns all obtained from samples.*
*1 Mapping units from Vernon and Carroll (1965), Soil and Land Use Surveys, no. 18*
*2 Locations of samples sites are on Figure 2*
*3 Tested at Government Soil Laboratory, Barbados*

| Density (g/cm) | Free CaCo | pH %) | Sand (%) | Silt (%) | Clay %) |
|---|---|---|---|---|---|
| 2.48 | 10 | 6.7 | 44 | 20 | 36 |
| 2.58 | 10 | 6.8 | 20 | 30 | 50 |
| 2.45 | 10 | 6.6 | 36 | 20 | 44 |
| 2.58 | 1.0-2.0 | 6.9 | 16 | 28 | 56 |
| 2.58 | 0.5-1.0 | 6.6 | 66 | 14 | 20 |
| 2.50 | 10 | 7.2 | 39 | 26 | 35 |
| 2.65 | 10 | 6.8 | 52 | 19 | 29 |
| 2.50 | 10 | 6.9 | 53 | 13 | 34 |
| 2.48 | 10 | 6.5 | 66 | 13 | 21 |
| 2.45 | 1.0-2.0 | 6.6 | 47 | 22 | 31 |
| 2.69 | 0.5-1.0 | 6.6 | 60 | 13 | 27 |
| 2.63 | 10 | 6.7 | 89 | 3 | 8 |

Table 13.2   Geomorphical Process Types

| Process Intensity & Types | Processes |
|---|---|
| I | Surface wash erosion, creep |
| II | Rill erosion, progressive creep, shallow flows and slides |
| III | Severe and extensive rill erosion, gully erosion, flows and slides |
| IV | Severe and extensive gully erosion, severe and extensive flows and slides |

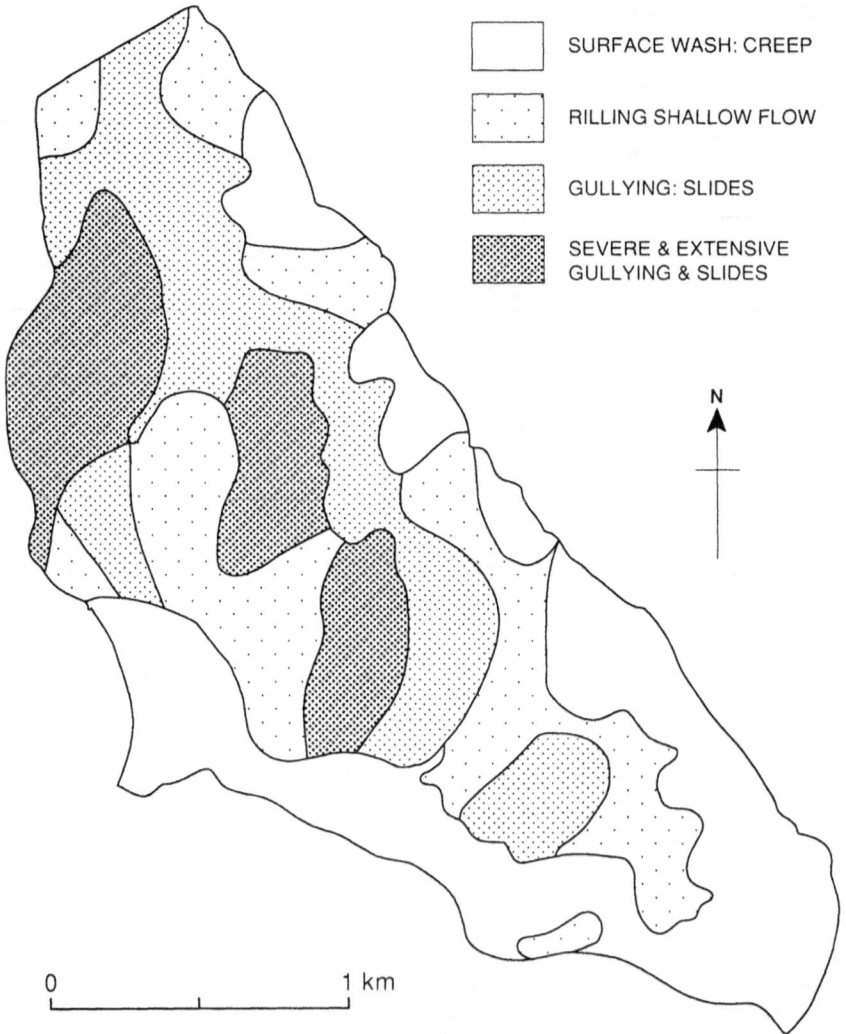

Legend:
- SURFACE WASH: CREEP
- RILLING SHALLOW FLOW
- GULLYING: SLIDES
- SEVERE & EXTENSIVE GULLYING & SLIDES

0 _____ 1 km

Figure 13.4   Intensity of geomorphic change

on steep and concave slopes, slides and slumps are most active on these segments, while creep and flow are more common on convex slopes.

The "soft, friable" [Vernon & Carroll 1965] nature of the rocks within the study area makes them susceptible to deep weathering. Almost every bedrock outcrop is easily indented or broken with a field hammer, indicating a high degree of weathering. Stability is further decreased by planes of failure provided by the high density of joints and bedding planes. The low and uneven permeabilities due to weathered sandstone-clay layers [Vernon & Carroll 1965] affect the rate and direction of subsurface flow and the development of perched water tables, hence reducing soil stability.

Of the twelve field samples analysed, the five collected from failed soils had the highest clay content (Table 13.1). Soil smectoid content and plasticity indices are high for the Scotland soils [Warkentin n.d.], thus they are easily deformed. Low shrinkage limits of these soils give them poor structure, aereation, and a high amount of cracking on drying [Warkentin n.d.], thus infiltrating water seeps through cracks, providing weak planar surfaces for failure.

The Scotland Soils generally have high cation exchange capacities, and this is indicative of potential instability [Kenney 1984]. A severe problem in soils on Joe's River Beds is caused by "hidden oil(s) seeps and underlying layers of soils containing chemical salts harmful to plants, such as sulphate and chloride of sodium" [Cumberbatch 1967]. Black, oily, sandy shales and salt accumulations were seen in Joe's River Bed outcrops and weathered Murphy's Member rocks. These hinder vegetation growth, and decrease shear strengths.

Joe's River Bed soils have shearing and residual angles of 24° and 21° to 22° respectively [Liang et al. 1979], indicating that a stable slope under normal saturation conditions should stand at 12.5°. Index properties of other rocks in the study area also indicate low shear strengths, yet most of the slopes over the study area are much steeper. A good vegetation cover such as forest, which reduces the risk of shallow slope failures [Selby 1982], is absent on almost every East Coast slope on which failure has occurred.

Material, morphological and climatic conditions over the study areas expose the inherent weaknesses in the geomorphic system and facilitate slope failure.

The seasonal moisture regime is especially conducive to creep movements and also triggers more discrete, higher-magnitude events. Major landslides in the study area have occurred during or after intense rainfall events [Cumberbatch n.d.], due to the creation of a sudden increase in load. The high incidence of gullying, stream incision and bank erosion in the study area remove base support, easily leading to failure induced by slope over-steepening; this is especially effective where shear strengths are low.

## Deposition

Depositional material (head, drift and colluvium) is shown to be distributed along some of the major valleys and lower slopes (Figure 13.3). The major fluvial depositional processes on the slopes result from surface wash. The deposits, derived from the underlying geology or the colluvium itself, are seen either issuing from the mouth of rills and gullies or along the gully course where the slope is flattened. The slope surface is smothered by a veneer of silt and clay, inhibiting further vegetation growth, and contributing to the build-up of colluvial material on the slopes.

The colluvium generally lies unconformably on an erosional bedrock surface. Anthropogenic material observed below the surface of some deposits is indicative of rapid deposition. Sections of colluvium with buried lines of pebbles and, in one instance, imbricated boulders up to 1.5m long, are also indicative of former periods of high energy (storm) events.

# Interrelationships Between Geomorphology and Land Use

The existing slope processes on the East Coast are largely a function of the morphological, material and climate characteristics of the area. Existing land use, how it affects geomorphological change and how geomorphological change has affected it, needs to be assessed before any predictions of future land use impacts are to be made.

Figures 13.5a and 13.5b show existing land use and land use changes since 1951, based on the analysis of 1951, 1982 and 1991 aerial photographs. There has been a rapid decline in arable land use. Apart from the woods and pasture, the rest of the land is now "rabland" and is covered with scrub, much of which is grazed, and interspersed with drought resistant plants. Except for locations at the coastline, housing and roads continue to be confined to the tops of ridges, with changes in intensities rather than location.

Much of the recreational use of the area is distributed along the East Coast Road, where the shoreline attracts surfing and picnicking, although the rugged topography inland does attract a few sightseers and hikers. Barclays Park is the only recreational facility in the area. The only industrial activity, although not new to the area, is quarrying. In the late 1980s excavation started on a sandstone hill east of Springfield Plantation (Figure 13.5b).

## The Effects of Land Use on Slope Processes

The first human impact on the geomorphic processes in the Scotland District began in the early 17th century with the advent of the Europeans, who cleared

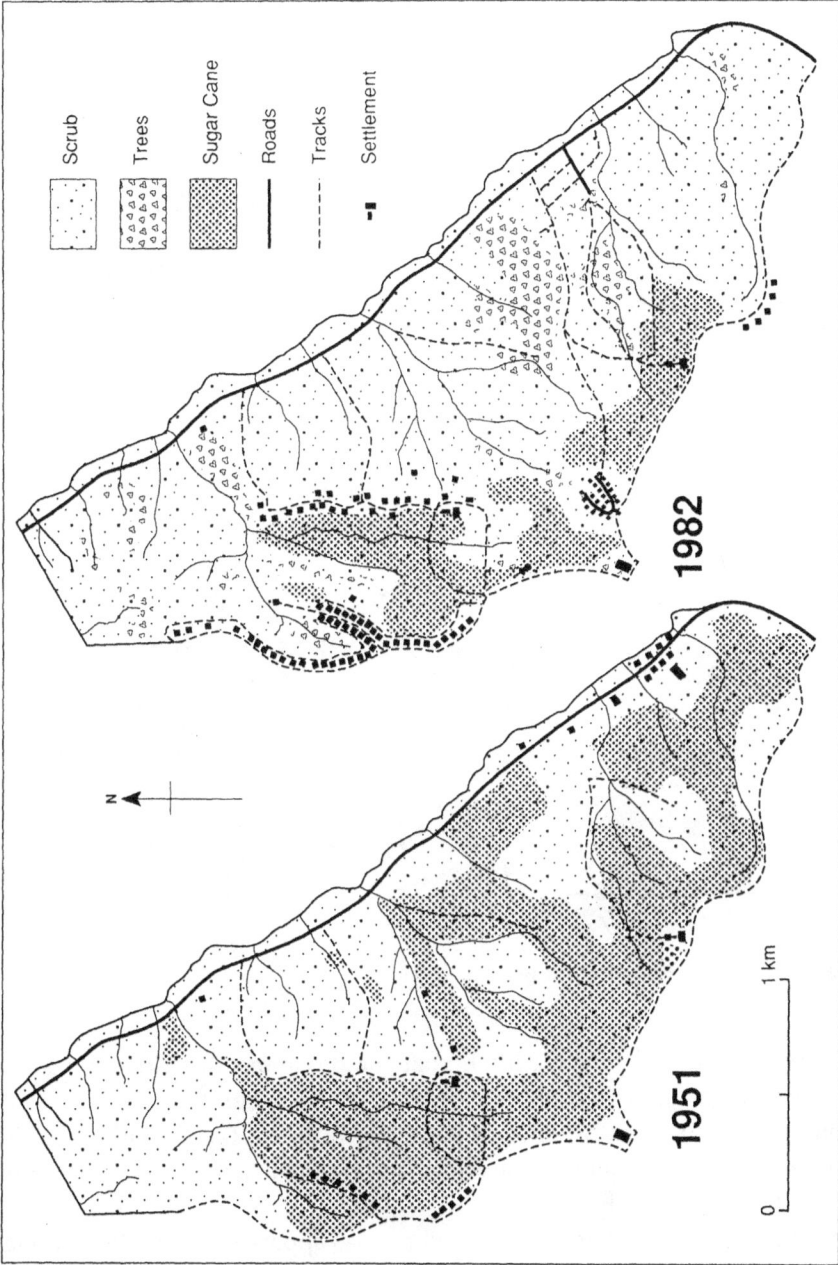

*Figure 13.5a* Land use in the study area, 1951 and 1982
Note: Land under scrub used for livestock grazing

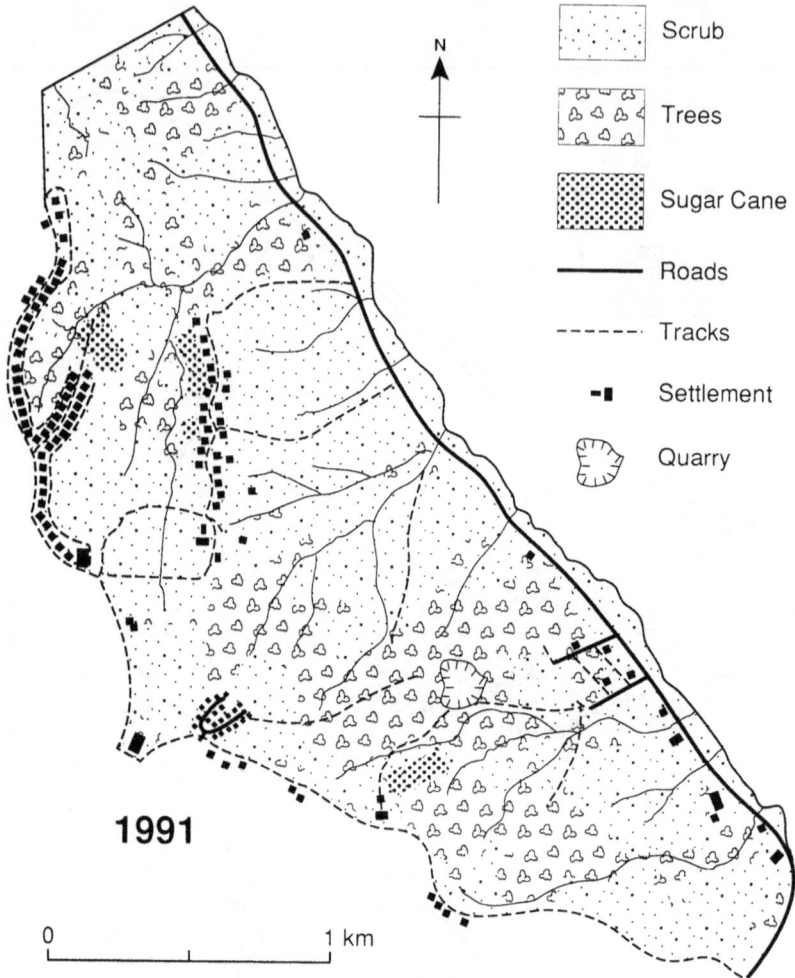

*Figure 13.5b* Land use in the study area, 1991

the virgin forest for cultivation [Cumberbatch n.d.], immediately removing this stabilizing factor and disturbing the natural balance. Soil erosion was recognized as a problem as early as 1661 and mass wasting as early as 1750 [Cumberbatch n.d.]. Inherent physical and human factors are both held responsible for these early problems.

Vertical ploughing (up and down the slope) has apparently been the norm as the clay-rich soil needed to be quickly drained [Vamos 1985]. This led to channelling of overland flow and to gullying [Cumberbatch n.d.]. However, contour ploughing was no better an alternative, as it led either to the ponding of water which resulted in mass movement due to increased subsurface porewater pressure, or to the bursting of furrows and gullying (Cumberbatch n.d.]. Both vertical and contour furrows are shown on 1951 photographs and the relict features can be seen in the field. The older system of cane holes, which is thought to check soil erosion, was also used, as relict cane holes were seen at Cambridge. Other poor agronomic practices included cultivating on steep slopes (up to 50 percent [26.5°]) which by nature tend to be unstable. Many of these now experience some degree of slope instability.

The land use and geomorphological maps (Figures 13.5b and 13.4, respectively) show a correlation between areas used intensively for grazing and severely eroded areas. The windward Cambridge slopes can be compared to the leeward slopes, where controlled grazing is practiced and a perennial grass cover is maintained, although it is true that desiccating salt winds may be partially responsible for the disparity. However, other windward slopes on similar rock types such as at Cattlewash, where some of the slopes are fenced off from roving livestock, do not experience such severe erosion.

During the dry season, when vegetation growth is slow, animals graze almost to the bare ground, rendering the soil vulnerable to wind erosion and, with the next rainfall event, to rainsplash and surface wash erosion. One Cambridge resident, observed tethering his cow on a poorly grassed sandstone/shale outcrop and asked of the possible erosion risk, replied that his practice was not a problem because "when the rains fall, the grass will grow back".

The continued trampling of the soil surface by animal hooves along trails and footpaths has led to gully development through soil compaction, the reduction in infiltration capacity and resultant increase in runoff. Cattle trails also aggravate terracette development on steep hillslopes. Trampling impacts on root penetration and seedling growth and, together with desiccating winds, restricts the regrowth of grasses and shrubs.

Drainage of both waste water and precipitation from roads and houses is responsible for much of the slope failure and erosion on the East Coast slopes. Domestic waste water drains away from houses on Cambridge Road through crude gutters, forming small gullies which lead into larger gullies downslope. Much of the failure occurring on the slopes does so directly behind houses where domestic waste water and sewage percolates, not only increasing hydrostatic and seepage pressures, but also altering the soil's chemical balance [Kenney 1984].

## The Effect of Geomorphic Hazards on Land Use

The geomorphological processes or changes taking place on the East Coast have restricted land use, and can therefore be termed hazards. How land users respond to these hazards is of importance in determining impacts of future development.

The generally low fertility, rapid exhaustion, high erosion and mass wasting of the soils have been largely responsible for the abandonment of extensive cultivation. These problems were considered so great that the Soil Conservation Scheme was set up in 1957 [Cumberbatch n.d.] with the primary purpose of saving agricultural land. The scheme's efforts at reshaping the land were not used in the study area except at Barclays Park, where the road cuts through the base of the slope and gabions were emplaced to help stabilize it. The main attempt at combating slope problems has been the general abandonment of cultivation, and reforestation of the slopes (Figure 13.5b).

The scheme also attempted to reclaim overgrazed lands by prohibiting grazing and impounding animals found on slopes declared "protected" [Cumberbatch n.d.]. However, residents of the area interviewed by the author, to "beat the system", allowed their animals to graze at night when the slopes were not monitored. Despite this, "spectacular results" [Cumberbatch n.d.] were achieved on the Cambridge and Chalky Mount slopes. However, the Soil Conservation Scheme is not as active today and, therefore, grazing continues indiscriminately.

The faulty siting of villages and roads is "contributing to their own ruin" [Cumberbatch n.d.]. Despite repeated slope failure, settlement has increased on Cambridge and Chalky Mount slopes, where mass wasting threatens property. Residents have had to plant dense shrubs behind their houses, restrict their water use and, in some cases, forego the installation of water toilets, in order to reduce the landsliding risk [Cumberbatch n.d.].

Almost every road other than the East Coast Road has been damaged as a direct result of slope processes. Cracking, buckling and slipping of paved roads due to creep and discrete movements is common, as well as the erosion of pavements on roads which cross drainage lines, such as Springfield Road. This results in constant costly maintenance.

## Potential Land Use and Possible Impacts

Following recent trends, arable land use is unlikely to increase. Overgrazing, however, is likely to continue until effective control is reintroduced. Forestry is the recommended land use for the area [Vernon & Carroll 1965] and should the trend towards reforestation continue, improvements in slope stability could result.

Following the trend of the last 40 years, the development of housing at existing sites can be expected to increase. With declines in agriculture, the "special environmental protection" [Government of Barbados 1986], provided in the 1986 Physical Development Plan. Structural development (including access roads and parks) for tourism and residential use can be expected.

During the construction process, machinery tracks can create routes susceptible to rilling and gullying; and during surface preparation, the removal of vegetation and excavation can have a similar effect to that of quarrying. Disturbed ground in the study area is considered potentially unstable [Vernon & Carroll 1965]. Loading and unloading of slopes at different levels for foundation surfaces will result in localized increases and decreases in shear stresses and strengths, leading to further instability [Toy & Hadley 1987]. The introduction of domestic water and sewage onto the slopes has already been shown to induce slope processes.

Paved surfaces will locally reduce infiltration, but will increase runoff, which is easily channelled into weaker, uncovered material alongside paved areas and under structures, resulting in erosion and undermining of structures. Existing gullies and proposed drainage lines will probably be straightened and concreted, increasing channel efficiency, and domestic and meteoric runoff will reach the main stream quickly [Toy & Hadley 1987]. Unless this main stream channel is also paved, increased downcutting may result and some base support of the slopes may be lost. This runoff will also have a serious impact on the coastal system.

The area has potential for increased hiking and camping and watersport activity. Hiking trails and camping grounds will have to be established and, unless carefully planned and controlled, could have an effect similar to that of grazing. Further, gully development could result from intense use of trails. Car parking and facilities similar to Barclays Park will have to be emplaced to accommodate increased visitors, and this will have an impact on shoreline processes.

## Geomorphological Sensitivity and Land Use Change

In order to evaluate geomorphological change, the innate complexity of the system must be understood. There are four major components of the East Coast system which determine its geomorphology and which interact together to produce a complex system – morphology, materials, climate and land use.

The concavity of the largely valley head catchments on the East Coast results in the concentration of runoff and subsurface flow; hence, a dense drainage network is developed. Additionally, the slopes are steep, imparting high energy to gravity-driven processes. The geomorphic response to the morphology, therefore, is in a high concentration of erosive forces (Figure 13.6a).

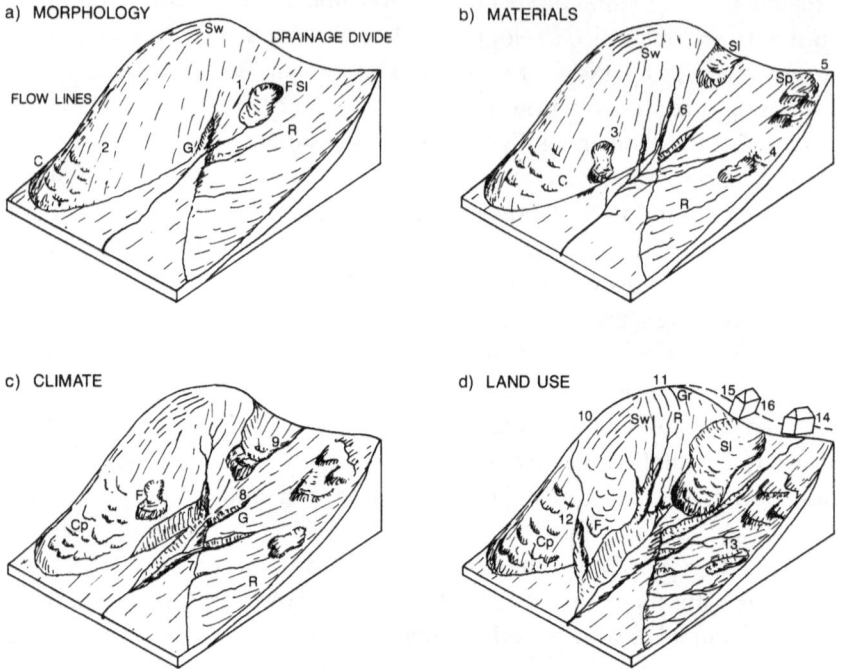

*Figure 13.6* The geomorphological response of the system to its various components

The highly weathered state and low strength of the East Coast materials renders them highly erodible and unstable. The geomorphic response to materials is thus an increase in the *extensification* of slope processes (Figure 13.6b).

Marked extremes in the moisture regime due to desiccating salt winds and intense seasonal rainfall aggravates already weak material properties and introduces sudden energy inputs into the system. The geomorphic response to the climate is thus an *intensification* of slope processes (Figure 13.6c).

The development of the land for human use has resulted in the deformation of surface form and materials, alterations in vegetation, and changes in soil moisture conditions and quality. The geomorphic response to land use on the East Coast is thus seen both in the *intensification and extensification* of slope processes (Figure 13.6d).

Identifying the "variability in condition and change" (singularity) [Schumm 1988] within the major components of the geomorphological system that make it complex "is the key to the difficulty of short-term prediction".

## Estimating the Relationship between Geomorphological Process and Land Use

The geomorphological processes related to different morphological features were determined by superimposing morphological and geomorphological maps and estimating the areal extent of the processes within each slope steepness class (Table 13.3).

Table 13.3   The Percentage Areal Extent of Process Types for Different Slope Steepness

| Slope Steepness % | Area km$^2$ | Process type (%) | | | |
|---|---|---|---|---|---|
| | | I | II | III | IV |
| 0-19 | 1.3 | 65 | 46 | 20 | 4 |
| 20-29 | 1.4 | 78 | 57 | 33 | 9 |
| 30-49 | 1.2 | 55 | 47 | 32 | 13 |
| 50+ | 0.1 | 100 | 100 | 100 | 94 |

Note: *Percentage areas affected by each process type are not mutually exclusive*

The geology and the soils of the East Coast were divided into several broad material groups (Figure 13.3), and the areal extent of each process type was estimated for each group (Table 13.4) by superimposing geological and geomorphological maps.

Table 13.4   The Percentage Areal Extent of Process Types Different Material Groups

| Material Group | Area km$^2$ | Process type (%) | | | |
|---|---|---|---|---|---|
| | | I | II | II | IV |
| Joe's River Bed | 12.0 | 71 | 57 | 30 | 6 |
| Murphy's Sandstone | 10.0 | 36 | 52 | 38 | 15 |
| Chalky Mount Member | 9.2 | 46 | 27 | 6 | 11 |
| Scotland Shales | 4.0 | 43 | 50 | 24 | 2 |
| Bissex Hill and Oceanics | 4.8 | 56 | 12 | - | - |

Note: *Percentage areas affected by each process type are not mutually exclusive*

Land use and geomorphological maps were superimposed and the percentage of the areal extent of each land use which could be correlated with geomorphic processes was tabulated (Table 13.5).

## Mapping Susceptibility: The Propensity to Change

In mapping its susceptibility towards geomorphic change, the singularity of the landform was first considered. The area was divided into units based on the

*Table 13.5* The Percentage Areal Extent of Process Types for Different Land Uses

| Land Use | Area km$^2$ | Process Type (%) | | | |
|---|---|---|---|---|---|
| | | I | II | III | IV |
| Settlement | 0.05 | - | 100 | 100 | 50 |
| Unpaved footpaths | - | - | 100 | 30 | - |
| Cultivation | 0.28 | 100 | 100 | 60 | 30 |
| Pasture (controlled grazing) | 0.52 | 90 | 20 | - | - |
| Scrub (uncontrolled grazing) | 0.80 | 100 | 100 | 90 | 20 |
| Scrub (other) | 1.60 | 100 | 60 | 60 | 50 |
| Forest (being stabilized) | 0.63 | 60 | 50 | 10 | - |

Note: *Percentage areas affected by each process type are not mutually exclusive.*

combination of morphology and materials. Boundaries of the mapped units are shown in Figure 13.7. Each unit was then assessed for susceptibility towards geomorphic change by means of a list of potential instability features (resisting and disturbing forces), using the checklist method, adapted from Cooke and Doornkamp [1990: 119-21]. Relief, drainage, materials and paleofeatures were used as major categories of instability features. Subcategories were selected; those under relief including valley depth, slope steepness, slope length; those under drainage including drainage density, stream gradient; and so on. Each subcategory was then assigned a range of values, normally from low (1) to high (4), following the method of Cooke and Doornkamp [1990], and appropriate values for each subcategory were assigned in the field for each mapping unit.

Each mapping unit was then classed according to the sum of tabulated susceptibility scores. The resulting susceptibility map (Figure 13.7) thus gives the propensity of each mapping unit, relative to other units, to experience geomorphic change.

## Prediction of Change: The Response of the East Coast Geomorphological System to Land Use Change

Convergence is an inherent factor of the East Coast geomorphic system, but did not pose a problem in the appreciation of its complexity, as the processes operating were understood. However, land use, and specifically the rate of land use changes (some areas have undergone four land use changes in four decades), introduces the problem of divergence, and therefore increases the complexity of the system and the difficulty of prediction.

In predicting the impact of potential development (land use change) on the geomorphological system, the complex response of the system to land use changes, and the resultant altered sensitivity must be assessed. This is achieved

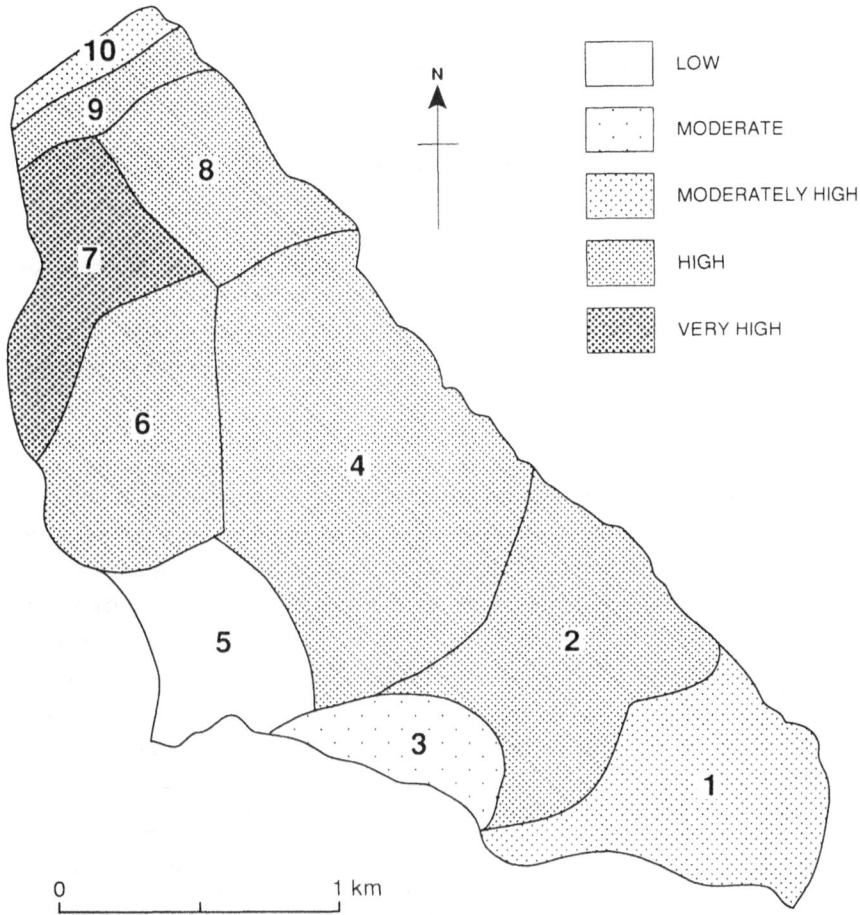

*Figure 13.7* Susceptibility to geomorphic change

through *location for time substitution* [Schumm 1988]. The intensity and susceptibility maps (Figures 13.4 and 13.7) are superimposed and where anomalies exist, the land use map (Figure 13.5b) is overlaid and any possible causal land use variables are considered. Where a particular land use is deemed responsible for the intensity at a certain location, it is assumed that if that land use were to take place in areas with similar susceptibility value, the same intensity of processes would result. Using these assumptions, an assessment of Table 13.5, and a knowledge of some patterns of change, the impact of land use change on geomorphic processes for each mapping unit is estimated, and the resulting hazard is predicted (Tables 13.6 and 13.7).

Table 13.6 shows the hazard class, the processes characterizing that hazard class, and actual hazard produced.

*Table 13.6* Hazard Classes

| Hazard Class | Induced Processes | Hazard |
|---|---|---|
| A | Surface wash erosion | Soil loss; can lead to more severe erosion if unchecked |
| B | Rilling leading to gullying | Extensive soil loss; can expose bedrock |
| C | Deep gullying | Intensive soil loss; can remove slope toe support leading to slope failure |
| D | Soil creep | Soil loss upslope; can progress to shallow flow. Increases slope instability |
| E | Flows and shallow slides | Unstable slope; structural damage |
| F | Deep-seated failures | Highly unstable slope; extensive structural damage |

Table 13.7 summarizes the predicted hazard types for each mapping unit, for three representative land use changes, namely settlement, cultivation, and grazing. One example will suffice to illustrate the predictive value of the Table. Mapping Unit 4 is underlain by Joe's River Beds and has a high susceptibility classification due mainly to the susceptible material type (a). Settlement would be likely to induce deep gullying (C) and flows and shallow slides (E), the disruptive impact of building within this particular unit being to alter the sensitivity to failure of the material (a). Hazards induced by cultivation would also be likely to include hazard types A (surface wash erosion), C and E;

*Table 13.7* Predicted Hazard Classes for Different Land Uses

| Mapping Unit | Susceptibility Class | Settlement | Cultivation | Grazing |
|---|---|---|---|---|
| (1) JRB/CW | Mod. High | C, E (a) | A, B, D (a) | A, B, D (a) |
| (2) MA/CM/CW | High | B, F (a) (b) | A | A |
| (3) OC | Moderate | B | A, B | A |
| (4) JRB | High | C, E (a) (b) | C, E (a) | A |
| (5) BHF | Low | B | | A |
| (6) JRB | High | C, E (a) (b) | C, E (a) | A |
| (7) Mu/CM | Very High | F, MC (b) (EH) | A, B (a) | A |
| (8) Mu | High | F, C | A, B (a) | A |
| (9) CM | High | B, C | A, B (a) | A |
| (10) Mu/Sh | Mod, High | E, C (a) | A, B, C (a) | A |

(a) – *Hazard due to susceptible material type*
(b) – *Hazard due to altered sensitivity*
(EH) – *Existing hazard*

whereas the less radical impact of grazing would only be likely to induce surface wash erosion (A).

Table 13.7 must be regarded as a "best estimate" of hazard response to land use change, and should not be expected to predict infallibly changes at specific locations for specific land uses. This is due to the "large number of combinations of values of interdependent variables" [Leopold & Langbein 1963] that determine change, and of which only some were actually assessed in this study. In addition, the assessment is based on average values across the mapping unit.

Further research would be needed to refine the classification, based on experience of its application to the field situation. However, the utility of the method as a predictive tool in determining hazard response demonstrably assists in effective land use planning in this highly sensitive environment.

## Conclusion

The landforms of the East Coast of the Scotland District have been shown to be in a state of change, as the intensity of the geomorphic processes is high (Figure 13.4). This level of intensity reflects the endemic instability characteristics of the area; by virtue of its geology, it is highly susceptible to geomorphological change (Figure 13.7). However, there has been an intensification and an extension of this inherent sensitivity through previous and existing land use. This altered sensitivity and increased intensity of change results in geomorphological processes that are hazardous to these same land uses.

Despite the difficulties of predicting geomorphic changes, an assessment of the geomorphic response to potential land use change (development) has been made. This assessment shows that potentially high risks of geomorphic hazards can be expected with certain land use changes.

## References

Barbados National Trust. 1991. "The Trust fights to preserve the east coast". *Our Heritage,*6, no. 7.

Brunsden, D., & J.B. Thornes. 1979. "Landscape sensitivity and change". *Transactions of the Institute of British Geographers* 4: 463-84.

Cooke, R.U., & J.C. Doornkamp. 1990. *Geomorphology in Environmental Management: A New Introduction.* 2nd ed. Oxford: Oxford University Press.

Cumberbatch, E.R. St J. 1967. "Conservation and reclamation in the Scotland District, Barbados". *Bulletin of the Ministry of Agriculture, Barbados* 49.

Cumberbatch, E.R. St J. n.d. *An Assessment of the Soil Conservation Scheme, Scotland District, Barbados 1957-1969.* Ministry of Agriculture, Barbados.

Director of Surveys. 1982. *Geology of the Scotland Area, Barbados 1:20,000.* Director of Surveys, Barbados.

Government of Barbados. 1986. Physical Development Plan, Barbados.

Kenney, C. 1984. "Problems and behaviour of soils relevant to slope instability". In *Slope Instability*, edited by D. Brunsden & D.B. Prior, pp 27-65. Chichester: John Wiley.

Leopold, L.B., & W.B. Langbein. 1963. "Association and indeterminacy in geomorphology". In *The Fabric of Geology*, edited by C.C. Albritton, pp 84-92. Reading: Addison-Wesley.

Liang, F.A., M. Newton, & R. Blesh. 1979. *Scotland District of Barbados: Evaluation of Problems and Treatment of Erosion and Unstable Ground.* Washington, DC: Organization of American States.

Schumm, S.A. 1988. "Geomorphic hazards – problems of prediction". *Zeitschrift für Geomophologie* suppl. bd. 67: 17-24.

Selby, M.J. 1982. *Hillslope Materials and Processes,* Oxford: Oxford University Press.

Speed, R. 1988. "Geologic history of Barbados: a preliminary synthesis". In *Transactions of 11th Caribbean Geological Conference, Dover Beach, Barbados, 20-26 July 1986,* edited by L.H. Barker, 1-29.

Toy, T.J., & R.F. Hadley. 1987. *Geomorphology and Reclamation of Disturbed Lands.* New York: Academic Press.

Vamos, I.P. 1985. *Coastal Protection of Barbados National Park.* Unpublished study for the Partners of America.

Vernon, K.C., & D.M. Carroll. 1965. *Soil and Land Use Surveys No.18 Barbados.* St. Augustine, Trinidad and Tobago: Soil and Land Use Section. Imperial College of Tropical Agriculture, University of the West Indies.

Warkentin, B.P. N.d. "Properties of some clay soils of Barbados with special reference to clays on the Scotland Formation".

Chapter 14

# Drainage and Irrigation Projects in Guyana: Environmental Considerations

Patrick E. Williams

## Introduction

According to a United Nations Report [UNEP 1986], by year 2000 AD the world's population will have grown from 5 billion to about 6 billion. Almost 90 percent of the additional people are expected to emerge in the developing world. It is evident, therefore, that alleviating poverty, maintaining food supply and improving the general welfare of people in developing countries will be a major challenge to decision makers over the next few decades. Consequently, increased involvement in development activities by various agencies to meet these needs can be seen as an ongoing strategy in developing countries.

Recently, however, there has been increasing concern over the conflicts that emerge between development strategies and environmental interests in both developed and developing countries. Many of these countries have, in principle, accepted the importance of environmental protection. Nevertheless, there is disagreement and confusion about how to incorporate environmental considerations into the economic development process and how to ascertain what proportion of the proceeds of development should be allocated towards preserving the environment.

In Guyana, most postwar development planning was preoccupied with economic growth. As such, large quantities of investment resources were concentrated on the major sectors of the economy, especially agriculture, construction and mining. In several areas on the coastal plain, large-scale drainage and irrigation schemes were introduced to increase agricultural production and productivity. Similarly, there was a rapid expansion in the bauxite, gold and diamond mining activities.

However, after over thirty years of experience in managing large-scale drainage and irrigation schemes, and an even more protracted period in large-scale mining, efforts were never really concentrated on the environmental consequences of these development activities. The main reasons for environmental problems in the agricultural and mining sectors include shortage of qualified personnel, insufficient financial resources and lack of public awareness of the intricate link between the environment and development activities.

The primary objective here is to highlight some of the environmental issues that have emerged in Guyana as a result of the implementation of large drainage and irrigation projects. It is stressed that a more integrated approach to planning is required if environmental issues are to be properly attended. The focus is a case study of the Mahaica-Mahaicony-Abary (MMA) drainage and irrigation project in Guyana. The paper deals specifically with the management of the project, and ways in which environmental concerns can be addressed. Some policy guidelines for the establishment of drainage and irrigation projects are included, and also lessons from which smaller Caribbean countries may learn from the Guyanese experience are outlined.

## Development Projects and the Environment

As observed by Szekely [1987], there are two different views pertaining to development activities and the environment. First, there is the opinion that the environment, like any other factor (for example, economic growth, employment, industrialization) should not be a dominant consideration in the development process. Rather, it should be seen really as one element of the development equation.

Second, there is the view that any development process inevitably requires some "sacrifices" of the environment where the development is taking place. This asserts, for example, that for the benefit of a drainage and irrigation scheme some flora and fauna would ultimately be lost through inundation. The major argument here is that all development requires some "trade-off" and this is translated into resource destruction. Essentially then, the notion is that development without destruction is only of theoretical value. In essence, it argues for development to occur now and for the costs of environmental deterioration to be borne by future generations.

These two views are not necessarily accepted in their entirety. According to Dixon and Carpenter [1988], while environmental and natural resource deterioration may result from existing conditions as well as development projects, it does not always have to be so. In their view, technical and managerial means are available to control, and in some circumstances even prevent, the unwanted consequences of development.

The realization that development activities are inextricably linked to the environment has fostered the emergence of a wide range of research techniques. As Turner [1990] observed, environmental economics as a new discipline focuses attention on the boundaries of economics and natural systems. It therefore advocates a pluralistic approach to environmental management. The consensus among environmental economists is that environmental protection policies and economic growth policies should be devised and implemented in such a way that they complement each other.

The need to incorporate the concerns of environmentalists into the development process has been widely recognized. Szekely [1987] noted that planners and decision makers need to integrate two aspects of the environment into their thinking. The first is that the environment is a fundamental component of the production function and is not an element external to the economy. Second, environmental protection is not only a regulatory activity but its concerns also include the enhancement of natural resources.

However, the views of environmentalists have never been readily accepted among development planners in developing countries. Among those who promote sectoral interests such as agricultural production and urban growth, there has been a polarization of views rather than cooperation. Environmental groups have made only a limited impact in terms of bridging the gap between physical and economic planners to help them address environmental concerns in development activities.

## Drainage and Irrigation Projects in Guyana

In developing countries, dam construction and other forms of physical development have had serious adverse environmental impacts on riverine wetlands (see, for example, Petts [1984]; Adams & Hughes [1986]). The severity of the impacts is compounded by the often limited knowledge of riverine ecology and hydrology in the local project areas, and by the pressures exacted upon resources by urgent socio-economic imperatives. Guyana is no exception to this general comment having embarked upon several major drainage and irrigation projects in its coastal wetlands during the last 40 years.

The first of these was the Boeraserie project, begun in 1959. It is located

**235**

between the Demerara and Essequibo rivers (Figure 14.1), and 49,000 acres (19,600ha) of the project area's 139,000 acres (55,600ha) is "new land", that is, reclaimed from wilderness wetlands. In 1961, the Black Bush Polder Project, located in the eastern part of the country between the Berbice and Corentyne Rivers, earmarked 23,645 acres (4,458ha) for rice production. The

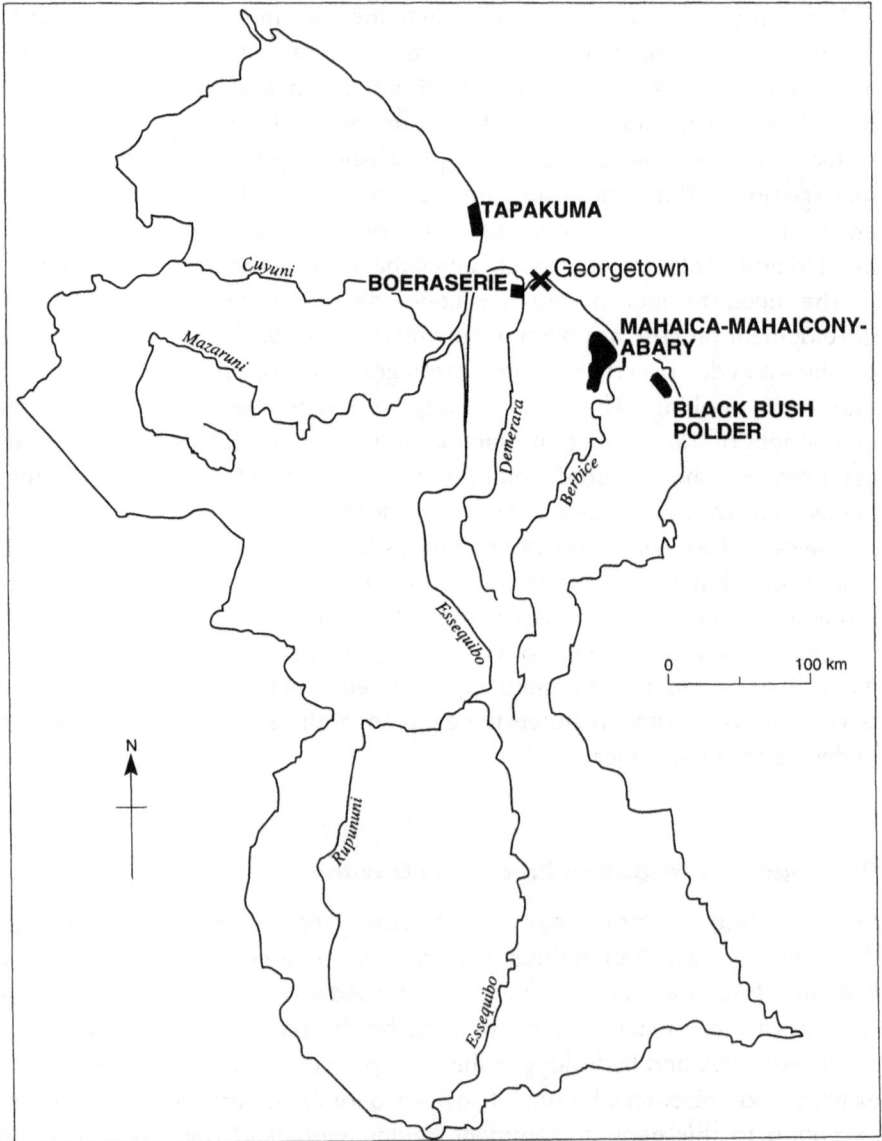

*Figure 14.1* Drainage and irrigation projects in Guyana

Tapakuma Irrigation Project, located on the Essequibo Coast, northwest of Georgetown was established in 1963. The area formerly specialized in sugar cane until prices collapsed in 1923. The project has identified some 35,600 acres (14,240ha) out of a total of 51,800 acres (20,720ha) as land suitable for annual double cropping with rice under irrigated conditions.

The area now defined as the MMA Drainage and Irrigation Project first came into prominence in the drought years of 1939 and 1940. A technical feasibility study was conducted in that period to determine the cost of empoldering the frontlands between the Mahaica and Berbice rivers. The project was considered feasible but the funds that were provided to embark upon it were diverted to other priority areas.

## The Mahaica-Mahaicony-Abary (MMA) Drainage and Irrigation Project

After a number of feasibility studies, the first phase of the MMA project was embarked upon in 1980 [Town & Country Planning Department 1979]. This phase covered the lands between the Abary and Berbice Rivers and was referred to as the MMA-ADA (Abary Development Authority). From an engineering point of view, the MMA project consists of the construction and supervision of secondary drainage and irrigation canals, hydraulic structures and all-weather roads. It also has a water control and irrigation system initiated by the construction of the conservancy and main channels.

Phase one of the project comprised a catchment area of the conservancy of 312 square miles (808km$^2$), of which just over 40 percent is the inundated area (see Figure 14.2). The catchment area is expected to provide irrigation water for approximately 46,400 acres (18,616ha) for rice production, 13,700 acres (5,544ha) for sugar cane and 146,140 acres (59,142ha) for flood protection. The estimated cost of implementing phase one of the MMA project was put at US$72.6m. In 1978 a sum of US$49.5m was made available by the Inter-American Development Bank for the project. This phase of the project was to be completed around 1982.

### Environmental Management of MMA

The environmental concerns of the MMA project are the responsibility of the Environmental Monitoring and Control Unit (EMCU) established in the latter part of 1985. In accordance with the loan agreement (OC-465/GY) between the Government of Guyana and the Inter-American Development Bank (IDB), quarterly reports on water quality and plant species were to be submitted. Since it was established, the EMCU has broadened its scope of operation. The

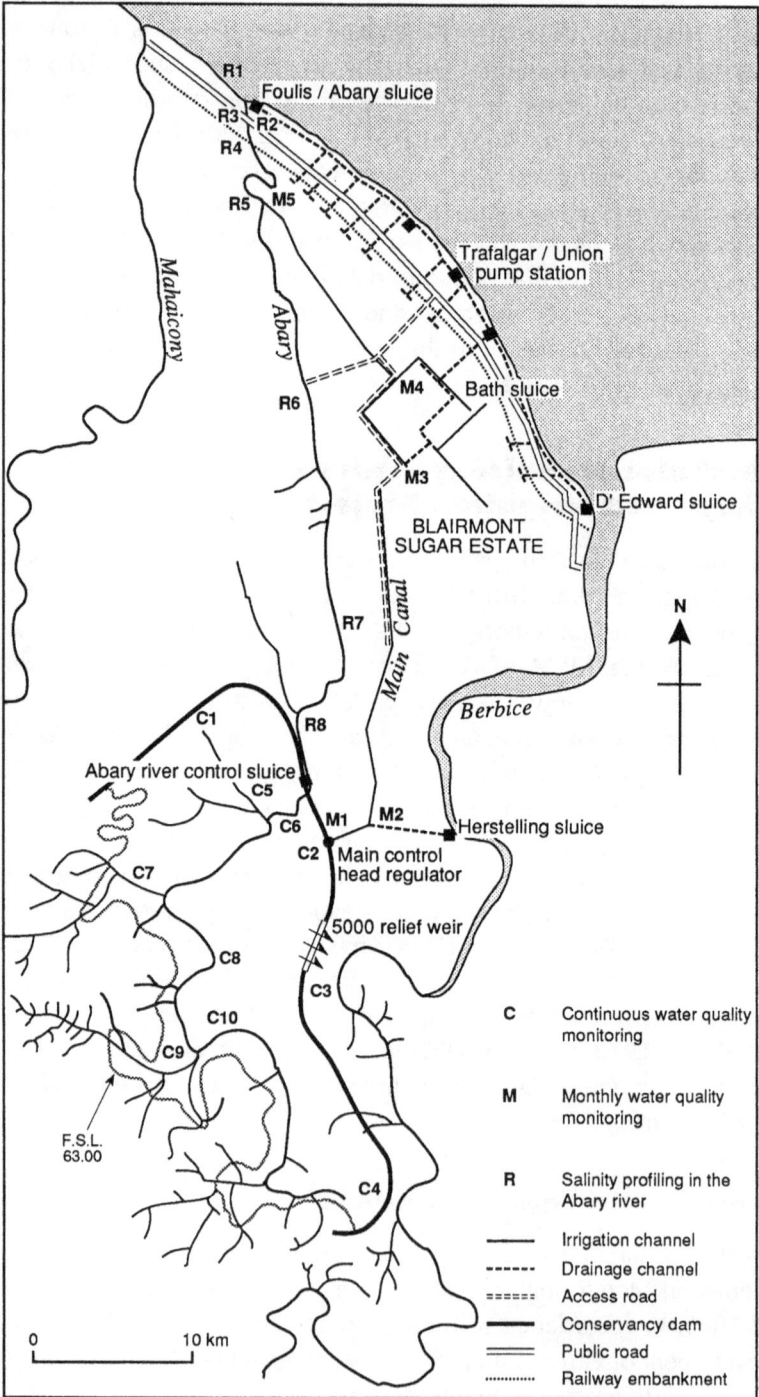

*Figure 14.2*    MMA Project catchment area

unit now has the task of carrying out environmental impact assessment studies, including monitoring and quantifying the environmental effects, both harmful and beneficial, and taking measures not only to reduce possible negative effects but also where possible to introduce measures which could result in increased production and productivity.

However, the work of the environmental unit of the project has been constrained by a number of problems. First, the unit has never been given the priority it deserves in the project's administrative structure. Although the project began in 1980, it was not until five years later that the EMCU was set up, and its initial work did not commence until 1986 when equipment was procured for carrying out scientific field research.

Secondly, funding for the environmental unit has always been low on the project's list of priorities. The unit has a number of subsections which undertake various types of studies, including water sampling, fisheries and ornithological work among others. However, shortage of funds prevents the EMCU from carrying out these studies on a regular basis.

Thirdly, there is the problem of staffing. The work of the unit is severely affected by the number as well as the quality of staff available. At present only the EMCU manager has been exposed to university level training. However, as pointed out by the MMA environmental consultant, Pastakia [1990], while the present level of performance of the EMCU is of a high quality, its standard of work could be much higher if the technicians were exposed to university level training.

**Environmental Concerns of the MMA Project**

Drainage and irrigation projects have become increasingly important in many developing countries of Asia, Africa, and Latin America where rapid population growth has dictated that more food be produced. In addition to negative environmental impacts, there is evidence of adverse health effects emerging as a result of associated environmental changes. Similar considerations arise in the context of Guyana's experience. Since implementation of the MMA project, a number of interrelated environmental concerns among academics, research scientists and policy makers have been raised. The environmental impacts of such projects, which have the potential to affect health and the long-term viability, have not been fully analysed.

**Pre-Project Evaluation**

There are no comprehensive records available of the flora and fauna in the project area prior to inundation. The absence of scientific data was compounded by the fact that the project feasibility studies prior to 1980 did not include in depth and comprehensive environmental studies. At the time, the government felt it was economically expedient to deal with the construction aspects of the scheme first, and it also lacked interest in environmental issues. Also, the funds from the IDB were quite slow in being disbursed, forcing the planners to focus primarily on completing the project. In fact, it was the loan agency itself that insisted on an environmental input into the project, but by that time the project was almost complete.

Thus, environmentalists fear that valuable biotic species might have disappeared or diminished in number during the period of flooding. Pre-flooding research could have identified endangered species for selective relocation, and provided a database against which the nature and scale of changes could be assessed.

## Aquatic Weeds

In the Abary Conservancy, approximately 31 species of weeds were identified. One of the major concerns is the rapid growth and spread of the water hyacinth (*Eichbornia crasspipes*), a plant native to the Amazon Basin [Barrett 1977]. Guyana's relative proximity to the Amazon basin has made hopes for successful biological control of the plant very remote [Harley 1992]. The profuse growth of these plants is partly attributed to agronomic practices, especially the use of chemical fertilizers in the agricultural areas of the project [Harley 1992]. The presence of water hyacinth has served not only to impede the flow of drainage and irrigation water, but also to increase the overall cost of clearing the drainage and irrigation channels. Available data indicate that the costs of weed clearance in the MMA drainage and irrigation system have been increasing rapidly. For example, in 1987 weed clearance costs were estimated at G$3.7m (1982 G$1: US$ 0.59). Such an increase is obviously inimical to the proper maintenance of the project, and also has implications for what could be spent on other environmental aspects. On the other hand, experiments to put the plant to economic use have not been very successful; for example, efforts to use water hyacinth as fodder for the livestock industry failed because of high water content and its low nutrient status.

Several major concerns arise from prolific weed growth. It has the potential, by reducing riverine flow through the extensive root system, to increase the risk of flooding in the project area. There is evidence in the Abary river system that when there is salt water incursion from the Atlantic, especially in the dry season, weeds are killed and this possibly has an impact on water quality. The decaying plants add small amounts of hydrogen sulphide to the water, the effects of which are not immediately known. Rambajan [1989] reports that algal blooms make the water of rivers unpleasant for bathing and other domestic use and reduce the oxygen content of the water making it difficult for other organisms like fishes to live there. Finally, aquatic weeds harbour vector diseases, and insects and snails spread diseases like malaria and schistosomiasis.

## Water Quality
While frequent water sampling tests have revealed that there is no immediate environmental threat to the project area, there are two aspects of water quality that present potential threat. These are the acidity and salinity levels of the water. At present, sampling tests have shown that in the upper catchment area of the conservancy the water is highly acidic with pH levels of 3.3 to 4.0 maximum. This is due mainly to the presence of a white sand belt through which the water flows. However, in the lower conservancy, the pH level averages about 5.0 to 6.5. The contributory factor for this lower acidity is the presence of clay soils through which the water flows before reaching the main canal. The presence of decaying vegetation in the conservancy has the potential of increasing the acidity level of the water and hence the need for constant monitoring. Since the MMA is an agricultural project, highly acidic conditions will have deleterious effects on farmlands, especially for the varieties of rice, the target crop of that area which thrives best in slightly acid soils.

Added to the potential threat of acidity in the project area is the potential incursion of salt water, especially in the dry season. Elsewhere in Guyana, for example in the Tapakuma project area, data for 1912, 1926, 1942 and 1959 for the Pomeroon River (that project's principal river), show evidence of high saline intrusion detrimental to plant species.

In the MMA project, the saline front is much further downstream in the Abary River than the Mahaica and Mahaicony rivers, especially in the dry season when there is a reduction in the number of rainfed streams flowing into these rivers as the swamps are affected by evaporation. At present, penetration of salt water far into the Abary River is restricted by releasing a flow of 50 cusecs of water from the conservancy in the dry season. However, should there be a problem with maintaining the constant flow of water into the river, either through malfunctioning of the drainage mechanism or a dramatic fall in the water level in the conservancy, salt water could penetrate the upper reaches of the Abary River. This would be detrimental to both flora and fauna and the existing ecosystem in the riverine areas.

## Predation
The opening up of the MMA project has prejudiced the survival of many animal species. In the conservancy itself, many animals became marooned on small islands and, with increased accessibility, fell easy prey to hunters as well as animal predators. While the actual numbers of the various animal species

are unknown, there is evidence, based on field sightings, that populations have definitely declined. For example, two surveys of the caiman populations revealed that, in 1986, 200 caiman were found in the main canal, while in 1987 only 138 were observed. This reptile is killed by many farmers because it is seen as a threat to livestock. The EMCU, in an attempt to reverse the trend, has had to initiate an "open" and "closed" season to protect some animal species. This project is being pursued with the Wild Life Division of the Ministry of Agriculture.

## Public Health and Vector Disease

The MMA project, through the creation of the conservancy and drainage canals, has significantly increased the area of surface water. The effect is that it has actually increased the size of the breeding grounds for mosquitoes and snails which are carriers of such diseases as malaria and schistosomiasis. The World Health Organization (WHO), for example, has estimated that over 2 billion people living in the developing world are at risk, and about 100 million clinical cases exist giving rise to approximately 2 million deaths annually from malaria. Globally, large-scale irrigation projects where health risks from the spread of water-borne vector diseases have emerged include the Gezira and Khashm-el-Girba in the Sudan, the High Aswan Dam in Egypt, and the Kariba reservoir of Zambia. Closer to Guyana, similar problems have arisen as a result of the Curua-una Dams in Brazil, and the Brokopendo in neighbouring Suriname.

These diseases are said to be on the rise in the Abary area, and if they are attributed to the conservancy, then some environmental considerations might have to come into effect. For example, it could necessitate spraying the conservancy area with chemicals which, in turn, would have deleterious effects on flora and fauna.

## Channelization

One observable consequence of the MMA project is that it has changed the wetlands along the coast into dryland areas. These wetlands were a haven for birds (egrets in particular) and fish (tilapia). This ecosystem has now been severely disrupted as a result of the disappearance of the salt marshes. The egrets have virtually disappeared through migration, and depletion of fish stocks has made it quite difficult for low income residents in the project area to acquire cheap and readily available fish supplies. Although the problem has been noted in technical reports, to date there has been no detailed research documenting its scale and magnitude.

# Policy Considerations for Drainage and Irrigation Projects

It is over a decade since the MMA drainage and irrigation project was implemented. It has induced environmental changes to an area of approximately 500 square miles (1,295km$^2$). As was noted above, the project is not the first of its kind in Guyana, but it is obvious that lessons of the past have not been learnt. There is an urgent need for new policy directions to be sought to deal with emerging areas of environmental concern arising from the MMA and similar projects.

## Administrative Structure

At present, the national body responsible for environmental matters in Guyana is the Guyana Agency for Health Sciences Education, Environment and Food Policy (GAHEF). There is, currently, little interaction between that agency and the EMCU primarily because the MMA is an autonomous body. It is proposed that institutional reorganization take place so that GAHEF should bear overall responsibility not only for the MMA, but for all drainage and irrigation schemes. In each scheme there should be an environmental monitoring unit to conduct research, and data derived from their work could be fed into the central unit at GAHEF. Also, their field stations could be used as training units for staff.

## Research and Development

In Guyana over the past three decades, tens of thousands of hectares of land have been converted into drainage and irrigation systems. However, over this period there has been little associated technological change. Many of the schemes have utilized concepts devised in the early parts of this century. It is therefore necessary to adopt a broad research and development programme that will use cost-effective technology. The suggestion is that the MMA and related projects should develop a close relationship with national and inter-national agencies that conduct research into irrigation projects. Three research areas could be focused on: bringing drainage and irrigation systems up to date; ensuring a sustainable environment; and investigating cost-effective and efficient technology for maintenance.

## Training

It is proposed that efforts be made to improve training opportunities not only for those currently operating in the field of environmental science, but for those who also have an interest in the field. In Guyana at present, trained specialists in the field are woefully short in supply, and there is a reliance on expatriates to carry out many of the functions. It is anticipated that as development activities increase the demand for specialists will also increase.

## Concluding Comments

Development activities in general and investment in drainage and irrigation schemes in particular have provoked a number of environmental concerns in Guyana. These range from the spread of infectious diseases, the disappearance of species of flora and fauna, to the decline of water quality. Further, some of these issues are quite pertinent to the smaller Caribbean territories and Guyana's experiences could be of benefit to them.

First, there is a need to ensure that proper environmental impact assessment studies are part of the overall feasibility study of major development projects. This aspect is even more crucial for these smaller territories since, generally, island ecosystems are far more fragile than those of the large continental countries. Development activities which have negative environmental effects may have a proportionately more severe impact in small island states than in geographically much larger countries like Guyana. Small Caribbean islands are highly dependent on tourism so that any large-scale development project with adverse environmental consequences is likely to have a negative effect on the tourist industry and, by extension, on their economies.

Secondly, it is necessary to put in place strong institutional mechanisms for environmental protection. Environmental concerns are best addressed by separate units acting in a coordinated way, and should not be simply tagged on to the responsibilities of different ministries. This particular aspect is evolving in Guyana with the creation of institutions such as GAHEF and EMCU as well as the recent formulation of policy guidelines for environmental protection. Another example is the Kaiteur National Park which comprises pristine tropical rain forests surrounding the Kaiteur Falls on the upper reaches of the Potaro River. It was established as early as the 1920s, but the new interest in the environment has prompted the extension of its boundaries. The National Park Commission now has responsibility for the Kaiteur National Park and the Rainforest Reserve, approximately 1 million acres (over 400,000ha), for biodiversity studies. The policy is to protect some areas, as to rehabilitate other areas that have already been degraded. The close proximity of Caribbean territories to the developed industrialized north, which is always on the look out for new markets and investment opportunities, makes them particularly vulnerable to resource exploitation and utilization, and underlines the need to enforce policies designed to protect their fragile environment.

Thirdly, there is a need to recognize that strong links exist between development and the environment. The responses to some environmental issues in Guyana are reactions to particular concerns and are, in the main, corrective measures. This situation need not arise, and other territories in the region could adopt a more positive approach by being cognizant of these linkages, and taking preventative measures to avert environmental degradation.

Fourthly, it is desirable to educate and inform people with regard to environmental issues. As illustrated in the case study, wildlife has been significantly affected in the project area, partly due to the absence of public concern about the environment and also because of a lack of basic knowledge about ecosystem functioning and conservation.

Fifthly, sound and effective methods of on-the-job (hands on) training for field personnel (technicians) which are appropriate to poor countries are required as an integral part of these kinds of development projects.

Development activities and environmental issues are intricately linked. The former are concerned essentially with investment in various sectors of the economy with a view to increasing production and productivity, and the general welfare of the beneficiaries. Environmental concerns include, in addition to regulatory activities, the enhancement of natural resources. In Guyana, huge investment has been made on development activities in the agricultural sector, primarily on drainage and irrigation schemes. The benefits from these schemes were expected to improve significantly living conditions for the poor. However, due consideration was not given to the environmental consequences of these schemes. The result is that a number of serious environmental problems are now associated with drainage and irrigation projects. These include health, flora and fauna destruction and even in some cases economic considerations.

To deal with the new environmental concerns caused by increasing development activities in Guyana, it is felt that new institutional arrangements, (training, management, legislation) and financial efforts need to be put in place. These have been quite slow in emerging, and with the passage of time this can make environmental problems even more acute. The experiences of Guyana are not singular to that country alone, and in many respects the smaller countries of the Caribbean can benefit by emphasizing the need to ensure that institutions are put in place to integrate development planning and the environment.

## References

Adams, W.M., & F.M.R. Hughes. 1986. "The environmental effects of dam construction in tropical Africa: impacts and planning procedures". *Geoforum* 17: 403-10.

Barrett, S.C.H. 1977. "*Eichhornia crasspipes (Mart) Solvas* (water hyacinth)". *Biotropika* 9: 230-38.

Dixon, J.A., & R.A. Carpenter. 1988. *Economic Analysis of the Environmental Impacts of Development Projects*. London: Earthscan, in association with Asian Development Bank.

Harley, K.L.S. 1992. "Survey of water hyacinth and other floating aquatic weeds in Guyana". Consultancy Report, Australia: CSIRO.

*Irrigation and Drainage Research.* 1990. The World Bank/UNDP Vol. 1.

McEvoy, J., & T. Dietz. 1977. *Handbook for Environmental Planning: The Social Consequences of Environmental Change.* New York: John Wiley.

Pastakia, C.M.R. 1990. "Evaluation of environmental management programme". Guyana: Environmental Monitoring and Control Unit, MMA, Final Report.

Petts, G.E. 1984. *Impounded Rivers: Perspectives for Ecological Management.* Chichester: John Wiley.

Rambajan, I. 1989. "Final report: health impact assessment studies (human disease potential vectors) in MMA/ADA". Georgetown, Guyana: Ministry of Health.

Szekely, F. 1987. *Strategies to Strengthen Environmental Quality in the IDB Development Project Cycle.* Washington, DC: International Development Bank.

Town & Country Planning Department. (January) 1979. "A sub-regional physical development plan, Mahaica - Mahaicony - Abary Vol. 1 and Part II, Urban and Regional Planning Project". Georgetown, Guyana.

Turner, R.K. 1990. *Sustainable Environmental Management.* Boulder: Westview Press.

United Nations Environment Programme. 1986. *The State of the Environment and Health.*

# Part 5

# National Parks in Jamaica: Problems and Prospects

Chapter 15

# Implementing a National Park System for Jamaica: The PARC Project

David C. Smith

## Introduction

Jamaica's first national park, the Montego Bay Marine Park, was officially opened in June 1992, and a second, the Blue and John Crow Mountains National Park, opened in February 1993. Two more national parks, based on the Cockpit Country and the lower morass wetland of the Black River will be established in the near future. Protection of Jamaican natural resources has been legislated from the 19th century through laws protecting forests, plants and animals. However, in the 1970s and 1980s active enforcement of environmental laws was allowed to lapse, with consequent degradation of forests and other natural areas under government ownership. Despite the fact that national parks and other types of protected areas have been sketched out as part of the country's national planning process for many years [see *A National Physical Plan for Jamaica, 1970-1990*, 1971; *The National Physical Plan 1978-1998, Jamaica*, 1978] and specific areas declared protected, little effort was made to monitor or enforce protection.

## The PARC Project

The initial formal step taken on the road to establishing the first national parks occurred in November 1989 when the Protected Areas Resource Conservation (PARC) project agreement was signed by the governments of Jamaica and the United States of America. The Planning Institute of Jamaica (PIOJ) was charged with overall responsibility for running the PARC project. The Jamaica Conservation Development Trust (JCDT), an NGO, will be charged with responsibility for running the first two national parks under a delegation agreement with the Natural Resources Conservation Authority (NRCA, formerly the NRCD). The NRCA oversees policy direction for the national parks.

*Table 15.1*   Responsibilities and Institutions within PARC

**Funding** — US Agency for International Development

**Coordination & Administration** — Planning Institute of Jamaica

**Montego Bay Marine Park** — Natural Resources Conservation Authority

**Blue & John Crow Mountains National Park** — Forestry & Soil Conservation Division

**Conservation Data Centre** — University of the West Indies

**Planning of National Parks system
& National Parks Trust Fund** — Jamaica Conservation Development Trust

**Technical Assistance** — The Nature Conservancy

The specific aim of the PARC project was to establish a viable national park system and to initiate protection in two areas of Jamaica [see also Lee 1992]. Table 15.1 lists the institutions and responsibilities of the various agencies involved in the initial stage of the PARC project. Table 15.2 lists the principal components of the project together with the main agencies with which they were to be associated.

*Table 15.2*   Components of the PARC Project and Associated Agencies

**The Montego Bay Marine Park** — Natural Resources Conservation Authority

**The Blue and John Crow Mountains National Park** — Forestry & Soil Conservation Division

**The Conservation Data Centre** — University of the West Indies, Jamaica Conservation Development Trust, The Nature Conservancy

**The National Parks Trust Fund** — Jamaica Conservation Development Trust

**A Plan for a System of National Parks** — Jamaica Conservation Development Trust

**Legislation** — Contracted by Planning Institute of Jamaica

Presently, the JCDT employs all national park personnel. In Montego Bay this consists of a complement of 4 rangers and 6 staff, and in the Blue and John Crow Mountains National Park 13 people are employed, 7 as full-time rangers. The JCDT has established a National Parks Trust Fund that is responsible for staff salaries.

The National Park Management Plan for the Montego Bay Park has been approved by the NRCA, whilst the National Park Management Plan for the Blue and John Crow National Mountains Park is in the final stages of review at the time of writing. Both have involved public review procedures: draft plans were deposited in local libraries for public scrutiny, various organizations were invited to comment, and formal public meetings were held to present the plans to interested parties and discuss their contents.

At some time in the future, it is anticipated that the management function of the national parks will be transferred to the private sector (to NGOs), as central government funds are unlikely to be forthcoming for running a national park system. A local group could take over responsibility for a national park in its entirety, or a section of a park. In either case, interested private organizations and NGOs would be required to submit management plans for approval before such concessions were granted. Several local groups in the existing parks are already anticipating such an eventuality, and have formed conservation trusts.

## Implementation

A Project Management Unit (PMU) was set up to account for funds and coordinate efforts, and is located at the Planning Institute Of Jamaica (PIOJ). Most of the project components got off to late starts due to a multiplicity of problems, many related to having several institutions involved in the project. In the early stages, for example, significant delays were experienced in hiring suitable staff, importing equipment, and major bottlenecks were identified at USAID in Jamaica and Washington and in clearing customs in Jamaica.

An early lesson learned was that financial resources are not the only limiting factors in natural resource protection. There is a significant shortage of human resources too. Individuals who are suitably qualified by virtue of their training at the University of the West Indies are often in jobs that do not accord with their qualifications, because opportunities in their fields are not available when they enter the job market. For example, both park managers have degrees in zoology and experience in natural resource management, but were working for a commercial brewery when they were recruited. This reflects a shortage of well-paid jobs in environmental management at the time. As the Park system develops it is expected that the number of employment opportunities for graduates and other professionals will increase. In the initial stages, however, training on the job will continue to be an extremely important factor in human resource development.

The Parks were based on a model that seeks to involve communities located within the boundaries of the parks in advising management on programmes and projects. To this end, local advisory committees (LACs) were established to meet with management regularly. An LAC is a flexible mechanism and, in practice, its form has varied with the degree of local organization within the area in which it is established. In Montego Bay for example, the local advisory committee is a formal entity, composed of organizations which send their representatives to committee meetings, and whose membership was originally named by the NRCA. The organizations involved are broad based, ranging from the Cha iber of Commerce and the Hotel and Tourist Association to fishing cooperatives. An organization wishing to join the LAC must apply and be formally admitted by the LAC. The group does fulfil its function and in its regular meetings the community acquaints the park management with their needs and concerns.

The Blue and John Crow Mountains National Park (Figure 15.1) covers a much larger geographical area (78,000ha) than the Montego Bay Marine Park (317ha) and has three local advisory committees, involving communities in places far from urban centres. The three LACs are located at the major entry points into the parks and within the administrative zones of the park. Membership is somewhat more informal than the LAC in Montego Bay, and numbers involved vary according to area.

Local Advisory Committee 1 meets in Minto All-Age School, and serves the communities of Hagley Gap, Minto, Epping Farm, and Penlyne Castle, a population of about 2,000. Membership is on an individual basis and anyone who lives in the area is welcome to attend and participate. The committee has an executive consisting of a chairman, secretary and other members whose responsibility is to follow up on actions decided by the LAC and liaise with Park management in between the regular meetings. The Committee has formed several groups to address local problems. The Land Committee is seeking suitable land for farmers who currently farm inside the Forest Reserve with a view to relocating them. The Water Committee is trying to find alternative sources of water for the district which experiences a chronic water shortage. Farmers have ad hoc meetings approximately once per month to discuss and address some of their problems.

Local Advisory Committee 2 meets in Hollywell Recreational Park and serves Hollywell Section, Woodford, and Newcastle, a rural population of between 2,000 and 3,000. Again, membership is on an individual basis rather than representative of particular organizations. This community has a mix of

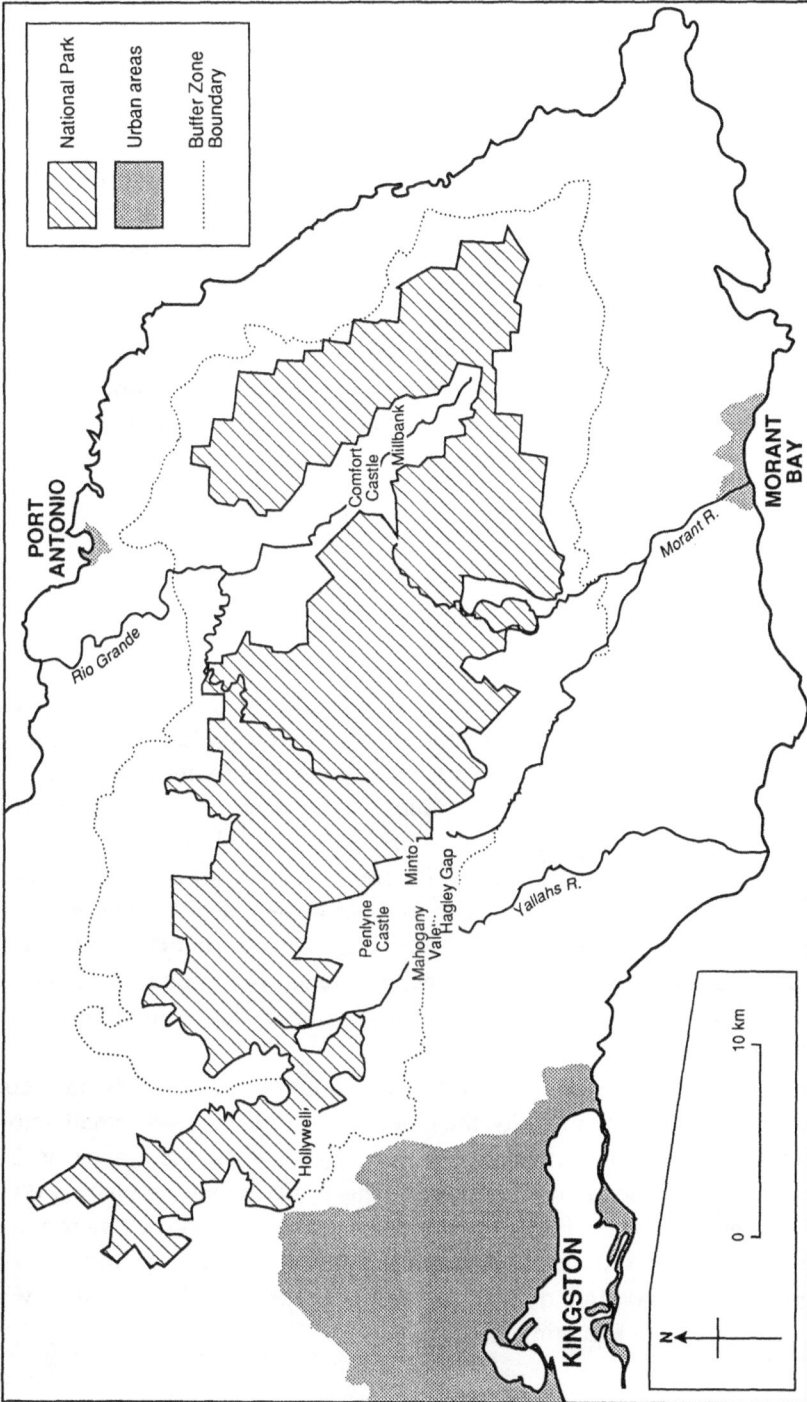

*Figure 15.1* Location of Blue and John Crow Mountains National Park in eastern Jamaica

farmers of widely divergent incomes and includes well-off people who work in Kingston but live in the area. The committee is not as active as LAC1 and was established six months afterward. The major emphasis in their work is to eventually manage the Hollywell recreational area.

Local Advisory Committee 3 meets in Millbank in the Rio Grande valley and serves Alligator Church, Seaman's Valley, Comfort Castle, Cornwall Barracks and several other communities; the rural population is approximately 6,000. This is the most recently established of the LACs and its meetings are incorporated into the monthly meetings of the Millbank Progressive Group, a community development organization. The major areas of concern here are development of income generating projects that use natural resources sustainably and the repair of the road to the community. Although the road climbs no hills, it takes an hour to traverse the 15 miles (24km) from Port Antonio in a four-wheel drive because the surface is so bad.

## Enforcement

Public education has taken place through the rangers and community outreach officers to the users of the park. In both parks, rangers have been using interpretive enforcement and confiscation. For example, in Montego Bay Marine Park, spear guns are taken from fishermen who are caught fishing in exclusion zones. Ships caught dumping in the park have been warned and made to clean up spills. In this context, no prosecution has taken place yet but it is the intention of the Port Authority and NRCA to prosecute in the future, although one problem is that NRCA does not have a lawyer on its staff. In the case of the Blue and John Crow Mountains, confiscation of illegally cut logs has taken place on several occasions, and recently prosecutions have been made; but there seems to be a lack of institutional support in enforcement of the Forestry Act.

All cases brought before the Court so far have been successfully prosecuted. However, although found guilty, the defendants were fined very small amounts (well within the maximum fines permitted by law, which themselves are fairly lenient) or admonished and discharged. This is a common problem at present with the enforcement of any environmental law in Jamaica. Environmental offences, ranging from illegal sand mining to poaching lobsters out of season, are not seen as important and an offender is not penalized to an extent which will deter him from repeating the offence.

# Community Involvement: Progress Reports

Attendance at local advisory committee meetings is one way to gauge interest in the parks' operation. If this criterion is used, it seems that interest has fallen off in Montego Bay but is being maintained in the rural areas of the Blue and John Crow Mountains. One reason for the fall off in Montego Bay is that, initially, many of the local advisory committee's efforts were directed at getting the park started. Now the park is a reality, the routine of daily operations and the present emphasis, on developing sustainable income streams, may not be appealing to the original committee members.

Another method of gauging interest is the degree of involvement by the local community in projects sponsored or organized by the parks. This has not yet been formally assessed, but there appears to be some interest that did not exist before. The main activities of the local advisory committees to date are summarized below.

## Local Advisory Committee 1

The residents in this area, through their own community resources, have built a bridge across the Yallahs river at Mahogany Vale, valued at approximately J$1 million. Virtually all the funds were raised themselves, a prominent local farmer designed the bridge, equipment was loaned and the community provided their own labour during its construction. They have also refurbished a school damaged in Hurricane Gilbert and completed a water supply project for coffee farmers. Currently, with the help of the National Water Commission (NWC), they are improving the water supply to the communities of Minto, Epping Forest and Penlyne Castle, which previously have been served by a single, one-inch diameter water pipe. A spring was identified, capped and a gravity feed pump acquired, and pipes donated by the NWC are being laid by local voluntary community labour.

Prior to the establishment of the national park, local people acted as informal trail guides in the area. One component of the park plan has been to formalize these arrangements through the formation of a business company, run by local people as an income generating enterprise. This involved setting up a limited liability company called Top of Jamaica Blue Mountain Tours. An eight-week tour guide training programme was mounted and attended by 18 people. Initially, the salaries of members of the Tour Group were paid out of central funds, but this was phased out in March 1993 so that they now must meet their own salary bill. The services offered by the Tour Group include trail guides, babysitting facilities in the Portland Gap trail cabins for parents wishing to hike to the peak, and a general 24-hour presence for hikers in the area. Another aspect of the park plan which is progressing slowly but surely is the attempt to relocate about 50 farmers currently cultivating in the Forest Reserve. A Forestry Department property of 600 acres (240ha) has been identified, 100 acres (40ha) of which is suitable for relocating the farmers. The farmers have consented to move provided suitable land is found, and a highly successful multiple agency meeting has drafted plans to assist the farmers with soil conservation training and agroforestry techniques, as well as to provide some security of tenure.

### Local Advisory Committee 2

Another tour company, Blue Mountain Adventure Tours, has been established in this area, and ten people attended the two-month tour guide training programme. Members of the tour company provide a tour service attached to The Gap Cafe located next to Hollywell and provide the cafe with a variety of local food products.

The principal concern of this LAC, however, has been the establishment of an NGO called the Hollywell Conservation Trust. Members of the Trust hope eventually to take over the management of Hollywell recreational area.

### Local Advisory Committee 3

This local advisory committee operates as an agenda item during meetings of a local community organization, the Millbank Progressive Group. The national park was included in a play put on by young people of the Millbank Youth Group in the emancipation day celebrations for 1992, a cultural event called "Ole Time Sin' Ting!"

However, the local advisory committee through the community group is preoccupied with attempts to improve road communications in their section of the Rio Grande valley, since it is their only link with Port Antonio and the rest of Jamaica. The record rainfall of the first half of 1993, and the accompanying floods, isolated the communities of Millbank, Comfort Castle and adjoining areas for over a month. It is likely that road improvement will be a priority for people in the area for some time to come.

### Montego Bay Local Advisory Committee

A volunteer ranger group has been formed that meets weekly; membership is 30 with some 15 regular attenders. Members are mainly young people, who go out with the full-time rangers on patrol, assist in public awareness programmes, engage in limited fund raising activities and are involved in regular clean up projects and field trips.

The Montego Bay Marine Park Trust has been formed by the LAC in order to raise funds to support the park financially and eventually hope to take over the management of it. So far, it is the large hotels in the area rather than the small hotels that have put money into the organization. Both this and the Hollywell Trust are not as active as their membership would wish.

A zoning scheme has been introduced within the national park to designate areas for water sports, fishing (with lines and pots only) and non-fishing areas. In early 1993 a moratorium on spear fishing was implemented in the national park. A feature of the park's activities has been to find alternative employment for the spear fishermen, mainly young people displaced from tourism jobs, who are prepared to do other things besides fishing to earn a living. They have been provided with snorkeling equipment and a training programme (including first aid) and have become licensed Jamaica Tourist Board operators.

## Sustainability

The cost of parks is high and while USAID is willing to fund establishment costs they will not fund recurrent costs. One of the newer solutions to the problem of financing the protection of natural areas is the use of debt. The sometimes controversial debt-for-nature swap is one method of using the sovereign debt of a country to pay the cost of conservation. One such debt-for-nature swap was undertaken by the Jamaica Conservation Development Trust and The Nature Conservancy. US$437,956 of Jamaican commercial debt was purchased, and converted into local currency, yielding J$12.3 million at the exchange rate which prevailed at the time. This will capitalize a trust fund that will pay the recurrent costs needed to run the national park system in Jamaica. The Jamaica National Park Trust Fund is now seeking funding from other sources.

## Summary

Enforcement of environmental laws and regulations has been taking place and individuals, companies and government have been the subject of enforcement activities. There seems to be less removal of timber from the north slopes of the Blue Mountains, and several independent sources have indicated that people are afraid to cut trees in the Park because the rangers might catch them. A problem is the slow development of regulations provided for by the Natural

Resources Conservation Authority Act, the reluctance of judges to impose realistic fines and lack of sufficient manpower to adequately patrol the park areas.

Community involvement has been facilitated, but the major problem will be to sustain levels of interest through all aspects of park operation and to assist efforts that communities make to manage some of the areas themselves. While much of the work of the community groups may not be seen as conservation in the strictest sense, the communities have a positive attitude towards the parks and many of their activities concerned with land, farming and water supply will indirectly benefit the protected areas, for example, by relocating people's farms outside the park.

Financial sustainability of the park is a long way from being achieved and will require the design of income generation capacity from park operations. None of the national parks will charge for admission but will need to charge for services offered and expect to generate income through licensing operations. It is expected that tourism will play a role here.

The original complex administrative arrangements have been simplified and there are now only two agencies, the Natural Resources Conservation Authority and the Jamaica Conservation Development Trust, that have prime responsibility for park management. All other agencies involved in activities that impinge on national parks liaise with the NRCA or JCDT.

## References

Lee, D. 1992. "The PARC project: new beginning". *Jamaica Naturalist*, 17-18, 20-21.

*A National Physical Plan for Jamaica, 1970-1990*. 1971. Kingston: Town Planning Department.

*The National Physical Plan 1978-1998, Jamaica*. 1978. Kingston: Town Planning Department.

CHAPTER 16

# The Cockpit Country:
# A World Heritage Site?

L. Alan Eyre

## Introduction

### Jamaica's Cockpit Country

The area known as the Cockpit Country, with a contiguous extent of 446km$^2$ of uninhabited, roadless rain forest, represents Jamaica's largest wilderness [Eyre 1992]. With its many endemic and endangered species of flora and fauna, it is a priceless, though dwindling, biological resource of global significance [Thompson et al. 1986].

An area of approximately 600km$^2$ , which includes the contiguous forest, has been under consideration as a potential national park for 22 years [Aiken et al. 1986; Cotterell 1979]. A small scale map was published in 1970 [Jamaica Ministry of Finance and Planning 1970] which had drawn on it only a vague boundary. In those 22 years the rain forest has been reduced in areal size by at least a quarter and has been degraded considerably. Indeed, a survey showed that there was a 16 percent reduction in the area of rain forest (Figure 16.1) over a period of less than six years, 1981-1987 [Eyre 1989]. Unplanned roads and trails have been driven into and through it, in one instance involving a massive blasting operation through tower karst. Despite the fact that the exceptional character of the

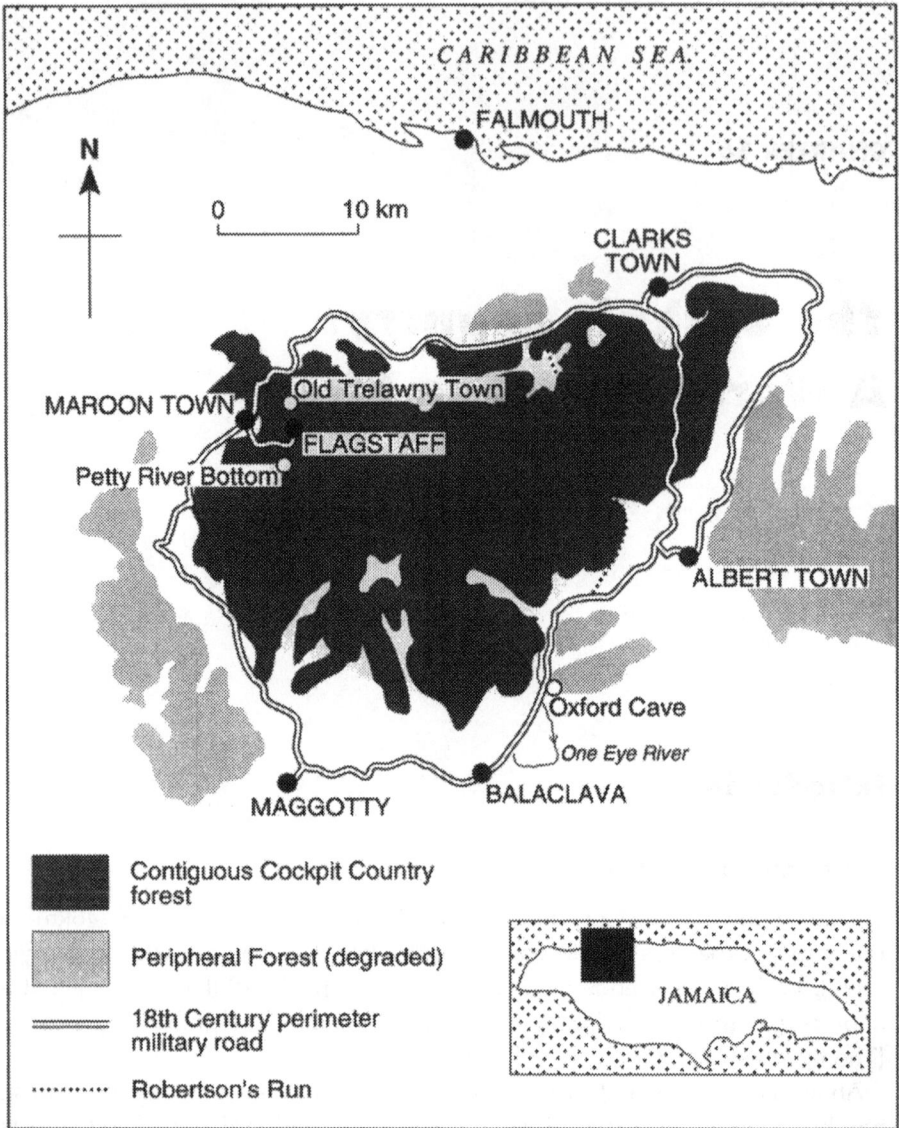

*Figure 16.1* The Cockpit Country and environs

Cockpit Country landscape is widely recognized by scientists, the Jamaican government, NGOs such as the Jamaica Conservation Development Trust (JCDT), and donor agencies such as USAID and the International Union for the Conservation of Nature (IUCN), remain vague and ambivalent towards its conservation and environmentally friendly development. In its publication *National Parks: Saving our Livelihood* [n.d.] the JCDT shows the Cockpit Country on the map as a "Proposed

National Park", but inexplicably fails to mention it in the text or even to include it in the list of those areas "which qualify in this category" [p2]. In a personal letter to the author [1991], Susan Anderson, the Parks and Protected Areas Officer of the JCDT, indicated that the Trust intended to include the Cockpit Country in a Proposed System of Protected Natural Areas (PNAs), but amazingly it was sixth in priority; eighth if the two national parks that subsequently have been established are included.*

In the author's view, such a low priority in relation to other areas betrays a dangerous ignorance of this superb ecosystem which is extremely hard to comprehend. It is now time to press that a real effort be made to obtain the World Heritage status that the Cockpit Country merits.

## The World Heritage Convention

UNESCO's World Heritage Convention of 1972 invites member states to submit proposed sites and national parks for inclusion on its listing of *"natural features consisting of physical and biological formations, or groups of such formations, which are of outstanding universal value from the aesthetic or scientific point of view"* [UNESCO 1972]. The World Heritage Committee has stated quite categorically that "the criterion of *outstanding universal value* is a very stringent one" [UNESCO 1989], pointing out that a property not accepted may, of course, still have great intrinsic value and merit preservation.

The World Heritage Convention is particularly anxious to assist states in the conservation of "areas which constitute the habitat of threatened species of animals and plants of *outstanding universal value* from the point of view of science or conservation" [UNESCO 1989]. Funding is available, under some tight conditions, for saving threatened biota and even entire landscapes.

## Criteria for World Heritage

Mosley, a world authority on the requirements for the designation of World Heritage status, and one of its referees, has emphasized that the features must be compared with "other sites of the same type both inside and outside the state's borders". Thus, one task of the referee is comparative. Does the proposed site have classic features that are prime quality examples of their type? Is there a range of features making this site a superlative one in its class? If the area is not protected will a loss of "universal value" occur? Is the loss already far advanced and is protection vital for what remains?

*Editors' Note: Smith, this volume, suggests that the present plans for a system of national parks envisage the Black River Morass and the Cockpit Country as the next two parks to be designated.

Of great importance in the case of Cockpit Country is the condition that the ecosystem be "self-perpetuating" and be of "sufficient size and contain necessary habitat requirements for the survival and continuity of endangered species" [Mosley 1989]. The 600km$^2$ originally proposed for the Cockpit Country National Park is perhaps adequate, but barely so. Every effort should be made to increase the area to be protected.

## The Cockpit Country: A World Class Environment

The Cockpit Country of Jamaica was recognized as a world class biological environment almost as soon as it was discovered by Europeans [Sinha 1972]. This is indicated by the fact that the museums, herbaria and botanic gardens of Europe and North America possess enormous stocks of flora and fauna of Cockpit Country provenance. Many of these specimens were collected and deposited from as early as the 17th century, and, in fact, contributed significantly to the development of modern biological science in the pre-Linnaean period [Senior 1983: item *Flora*].

With the rise of geomorphology as a sub-discipline bridging geography and geology, the Cockpit Country came to be acknowledged as a world class geomorphical as well as a biological environment. Tropical karst limestone terrain is developed over a large area, with a very wide range of features, many of spectacular dimensions and varied character [Morrissey 1983]. Sweeting carried out her pioneering studies of tropical karst in the Cockpit Country in the 1950s, and her famous traverse with Zans, another geomorphologist of international standing, is legendary – Zans emerged from the Troy to Windsor trail on a stretcher. Sweeting [1958] went on to make the region famous worldwide with her writings. Zans, for whom that traverse was his last journey, probably knew more about the Cockpit Country than anyone else except G. Proctor from Harvard. Sadly, his administrative duties as Director of the Geological Survey meant that much of that knowledge died with him, since only a fraction was ever published.

For number, accessibility, complexity and variety, though not for size, the underground karst features of the Cockpit Country are also world class, and have attracted speleologists and caving clubs from all over the world for more than a century [Fincham 1977; Sweeting 1957]. The number of surveyed caves in Jamaica per square kilometre is among the highest of any country in the world, and most of these caves, including the largest and best decorated, are within and around the margins of the Cockpit Country. In a brief review of his years of study, Zans reported data on 270 caves [Zans 1959] and, with others, published a synopsis of the state of knowledge of the entire region in 1962 [Zans et al. 1962].

## Threatened Endemic Species of World Significance

The author is confident that the Cockpit Country would merit World Heritage status on the criterion of the threat to endemic species of world significance alone, and even more so when linked with other endangered aspects of the total environment. Binney et al. [1991] in their volume *Jamaica's Heritage* have described the Cockpit Country as "an ecological wonder".

World Heritage gives special attention to areas where "the threat of disappearance caused by accelerated deterioration" is clearly evident. In this case, this point is embarrassingly manifest. It should be emphasized, however that UNESCO is not a saviour of last resort when a world class resource has almost disappeared, and where the national will to save the resource is absent.

In respect of biology, out of 423 endemic Jamaican macrospecies, Jamaica has recently lost 52, and a further 244 are categorized as rare, endangered or vulnerable [Eyre 1991a; Morgan & Woods 1986]. The Cockpit Country wilderness provides the only remaining refuge for most of these species.

The climax forest of the Cockpit Country has been designated Lowland Evergreen rain forest on limestone terrain [Asprey & Loveless 1985; Swabey 1949]. Species endemism in the Cockpit Country is the most striking characteristic of this ecosystem. "No two hills are exactly alike in their vegetation" [Binney et al. 1991]. This reservoir of endemism is recognized as of universal scientific interest: 101 plant species are endemic to the Cockpit Country, not found even in other limestone forests elsewhere in Jamaica [Proctor 1986].

Species diversity in respect of ferns, bromeliads, and other epiphytes, rain forest emergents, land snails and fireflies is internationally regarded as being exceptional. The fact that the six principal canopy emergents represent six different botanical *families* is remarkable. It has been established that the Cockpit Country contains, relative to its area, more species of ferns than any other rain forest in the tropics; most of Jamaica's 550 indigenous species of ferns are to be found in the Cockpit Country [Proctor 1972; Binney et al. 1991]. The prickly pole palm, once very abundant and providing valuable food for wild hogs as well as a flexible wood once used to make bows, was said as long ago as 1946 to be "very scarce" [Swabey 1946].

The Cockpit Country is one of the last places in the world where saplings of *Swietenia mahogani*, the world's premier cabinet timber made famous in Europe by Chippendale, Adam and Sheraton, can still be found, though mature specimens of this 40m emergent are now extremely rare. This fact alone is surely a prime reason for conservation of this rain forest ecosystem, with the hope that some of the saplings may eventually reach maturity and so save one of the world's most valuable and majestic trees.

In respect of fauna, of 80 endemic species of fireflies in Jamaica, many of the more spectacular ones occur in the Cockpit Country, but most of these are now vulnerable due to deterioration of habitat. Some species are confined to a single cockpit less than one square kilometre in area. Many species of fauna exhibit features of universal interest. One genus of crab completes its entire life cycle without leaving the canopy bromeliads which form its sole habitat. One rare bat species, *Noctilio leporinus*, occurs at Oxford Cave. Very few specimens of this large bat have ever been collected or studied, but it is particularly interesting because it is a fish eating species. It is also unusual among Chiroptera in that it has been occasionally observed to fly and feed in bright sunlight [Lynn 1949]. The Cockpit Country is almost the last refuge for Jamaica's 18 species of native frogs [Lynn 1940], one of only two remaining habitats for the western hemisphere's largest swallowtail butterfly *Papilio homerus* [Turner 1991], and almost the very last retreat for the beautifully marked Jamaica boa.

## Historical Value

The World Heritage Convention [UNESCO 1972] specifies as one major criterion the following: "sites: works of man or the combined works of nature and man which are of outstanding universal value from the historical point of view".

The Cockpit Country is rich in sites and associations with the Maroon Wars [Eyre 1980; Price 1971; Robinson 1969]. Among the many locations which should be conserved and which, if interpretive facilities were developed, would raise the consciousness of black people everywhere, are Petty River Bottom, Quao Pond, Accompong, Old Trelawny Town, Flagstaff, Robertson's Run, Hector's River, One Eye River and various major battle sites.

The Maroon Wars were not just of local or national significance. They were part of the universal struggle of blacks against dehumanization and slavery, and an early phase of the search for freedom and a democracy that included blacks in the New World [Hart 1985]. It could be argued that the Maroon chiefdoms were the first genuine independent black political entities in the New World, anticipating the Haitian Revolution by 140 years. Moreover, they were never vanquished in open war; the British were so worn down militarily that they made two treaties with the Maroons, the famous Peace Treaty with Cudjoe in 1739 and that with Montague in 1796. The fact that the British blatantly used the 1796 Treaty as a subterfuge for conquest and virtual enslavement only makes the associations more poignant.

It is only the colonial control of the literary and educational media which has prevented great Maroons such as Cudjoe and Shaw, who held the vaunted

British Army to a military stalemate in the Cockpit Country for more than half a century, from being acknowledged as the universally significant leaders that they really were.

## Archaeological Value

The World Heritage Convention exists to protect "elements of an archaeological nature . . . including sites which are of outstanding universal value from the ethnological or anthropological point of view" [UNESCO 1972].

The Cockpit Country does not contain any such elements of universal value *per se* but where elements of national or regional significance in one category are associated with universal values in other categories, such elements are considered to add merit to an area or location. Arawak sites on the fringes of the Cockpit Country qualify in this connection, such as the rock carvings at Pantrepant. However, proper inventory, documentation and site protection are required.

Scholarly archaeological work by the sub-Department of Archaeology at the University of the West Indies in the vicinity of the Cockpit Country, and its subsequent publication, would be a valuable support in the presentation of Jamaica's case of World Heritage listing. This work need not be necessarily Arawak oriented.

## Natural Beauty

A category "natural beauty" appears quite specifically in the World Heritage Convention. Such "beauty" has to meet the aesthetic tastes of all 21 committee members — all of whom are from different states and regions of the world — before it can be considered "universal".

Obviously, not every World Heritage park must rival the Grand Canyon or Kakadu National Park. The author has been nine times to Kakadu (and there can be no doubt of its spectacular character) and has also published research on many other national parks [Eyre 1990]. Based on personal knowledge and experience, therefore, the author considers that the Cockpit Country has a good case for being accepted by World Heritage on the grounds of "natural beauty", especially when considered in conjunction with the other categories already discussed.

# Problems with Meeting World Heritage Criteria

It is the view of the Jamaica Conservation Development Trust that "establishing other proposed National Parks [other, that is, than the two already partially funded] will not prove difficult" [JCDT 1992]. At this juncture, the author is not so sanguine, only mildly hopeful. Nevertheless, one is happy to acknowledge that there are a few zealous crusaders for the cause, and their ardour may perhaps in time warm a very tepid government establishment and spur it to action.

UNESCO is unlikely even to begin to consider World Heritage status for the Cockpit Country until Jamaica unequivocally establishes a National Park Service, even if it only takes the form of an Eve-like excision of a rib from the side of the Ministry of Agriculture. It would, of course, be much better if such a Service is established from the start as an autonomous and irreducible entity funded indirectly by the Prime Minister's Office or the Ministry of Finance. Talk of such a Service being gestated from the Ministry with the portfolio of Tourism is, in my opinion, irresponsible and fails to appreciate that the real issue is environment, not tourist dollars. The latter should be seen only as a useful source of income for development. World Heritage will not look with favour on any proposal which does not have environmental conservation as its focus.

In order to convince World Heritage that Jamaica is serious about a Cockpit Country National Park, government will have to fulfil several preconditions. It is "required" to draw up a very detailed inventory of the features of any cultural or natural heritage site it wishes World Heritage to consider for listing. Typical examples of these inventories are *Blue Mountains for World Heritage* [Mosley 1989] and *Kakadu: A World Heritage of Unsurpassed Beauty* [Ovington 1986]. These are authoritative studies carried out by scholars who are nationals of the countries about which they are writing, and who have long familiarity with the specific environments proposed for listing. It is a pity that no area bibliography has ever been compiled of the significant amount of scientific work carried out in the Cockpit Country over three centuries, and it is possible that UNESCO would request such before beginning the referee process.

On the basis of such documentation, and after careful scrutiny on site by its own scholars, World Heritage alone decides whether the proposal merits inclusion in its prestigious listing. However, documentation is not enough, notwithstanding its academic acceptability. There must be compelling evidence that "the duty of ensuring conservation" is being aggressively and competently undertaken by the government and/or private sector of the nation state presenting the proposal, in advance of expected listing.

In the case of the Cockpit Country, World Heritage will demand proof of serious efforts to carry out the following obligations: to arrest and reverse the deforestation that is devastating the area; to adequately protect endangered species; to control trespass and illegal use; to end the serious poaching of parrots, butterflies and other wildlife that presently occurs on a significant scale; and to educate the local population in environmentally friendly utilization of the forest and water resources. Sadly, within the Cockpit Country, none of these conditions are evident. It is easy to explain away the indifference, but surely none of the requirements are impossible or even difficult to implement.

From a scientific and international standpoint, the Blue and John Crow Mountains National Park, Jamaica's first major terrestrial park to be formally established and opened to the public, cannot compare with the Cockpit Country. The former may be a vital component of our park system, and protection for the watersheds within it is a national priority. But it is not a world class ecosystem like the Cockpit Country, and will never qualify for World Heritage. Local official interest and even international involvement in the Blue and John Crow Mountains National Park seems to derive more from its proximity to Kingston and ease of access from metropolitan population centres than from the intrinsic quality of the environment.

## Does World Heritage Listing Guarantee Conservation?

One may ask the question: does a World Heritage listing for an area guarantee conservation? In theory the answer is affirmative. In practice, experience so far with many World Heritage properties suggests that while it may reduce vulnerability and make sustainable conservation possible, even affluent countries have problems maintaining the conservation momentum which UNESCO listing offers. For example, the Grand Canyon, surely among the very prime of World Heritage properties, has seemingly intractable problems with air pollution and user-induced degradation. In many African and Latin American parks, listing has failed to stop poaching. Many world class parks such as Uluru (Ayers' Rock) in Australia and Popocatepetl in Mexico have daunting difficulties with waste disposal and littering.

World Heritage listing is a solemn and serious joint commitment, entered into between a sovereign government and a prestigious and relatively well funded international institution, and is not to be undertaken lightly. If a national government should subsequently renege on the commitment (which, to the author's knowledge, has never happened to date anywhere in the world), this state could be worse than the first. The disappointment could be bitter, and the collapse of the agreement could be disastrous to the very environment which it was hoped to save.

## Will the Cockpit Country be Saved?

There is a spirit of ideological rethinking evident in Jamaica and the wider Caribbean that envisages a fruitful marriage between ecology and economics [Girvan 1991; Mills 1991]. With the new paradigms which are emerging, reversing deforestation and conserving the rich resources of the Cockpit Country will be economically viable — and should be sustainable indefinitely [Eyre 1991b]. Binney et al. [1991] envisage profitable private sector involvement: "Interest from the tourist sector would help to provide impetus for active conservation and sustainable development of this valuable area where more than one hundred species of plants are rare and endangered". Boo [1990] strongly urges the further development of Caribbean ecotourism as a conservation strategy.

Establishment of a forest canopy research facility in the prime rain forests south of Windsor, similar to those maintained in several other countries in the tropics [Mitchell 1986], would help to convince UNESCO that Jamaica is serious about research and conservation in its premier ecosystem.

It may be appropriate to conclude with a word from the Rt Hon P. J. Patterson, Prime Minister of Jamaica [1989], who has promised an agenda for conservation: "There is an urgent need for us all to develop a higher degree of consciousness about the environment. The initiatives of voluntary groups will help to ensure that this generation succeeds in welding a coalition of forces, determined to preserve and bequeath a rich diverse natural heritage to successive generations."

As stated earlier, the criteria for World Heritage are stringent. Even if the goal is not achieved, the nation will bequeath a burden to future generations if it does not save the Cockpit Country, its only world class ecological wonderland.

## References

Aiken, K.E., E. Garraway, & R. Boothe. 1986. *A Case for Protected Forested Areas in Jamaica*. Kingston: Zoology Department, University of the West Indies, Mona.

Asprey, G.F., & A.R. Loveless. 1985. "The dry evergreen forests of Jamaica". *Journal of Ecology* 46: 547-70.

Binney, M., J. Harris, & K. Martin. 1991. *Jamaica's Heritage: An Untapped Resource*. Kingston: Mill Press.

Boo, E. 1990. *Ecotourism: The Potentials and Pitfalls.*2 Vols. Washington, DC: World Wildlife Fund.

Cotterell, C. 1979. *The Proposed Development of the Cockpit Country.* Kingston: Natural Resources Conservation Division.

Eyre, L.A. 1980. "The Maroon Wars in Jamaica – a geographical appraisal". *Jamaica Historical Review* 12: 80-102.

Eyre, L.A. 1989. "Slow death of a tropical rain forest: the Cockpit Country of Jamaica, West Indies". In *Environmental Quality and Ecosystem Stability,* edited by M. Luria, Y. Steinberger, & E. Spanier.Vol. IV-A: 599-606. Jerusalem, Israel:Environmental Quality, ISEQS Pub.

Eyre, L.A. 1990. "The tropical national parks of Latin America and the Caribbean: present problems and future potential". In *Conference of Latin Americanist Geographers Yearbook 1990,* edited by R.B. Kent, pp 15-33. Alabama: Auburn University.

Eyre, L.A. 1991a. "Jamaica's crisis in forestry and watershed management". *Jamaica Naturalist* 1: 27-44.

Eyre, L.A. 1991b. "Loss and degradation of the tropical forests. What has gone wrong? What can be done?". In *International Seminar on Regional Policies and Development in the Third World.* Varanasi, India: Hindu University of Benares.

Eyre, L.A. 1992. *Depletion of the Jamaican Rain Forest: The Social and Cultural Consequences.* Quito: Universidad San Francisco de Quito and the Association of Academic Programs in Latin America and the Caribbean.

Fincham, A.G. 1977. *Jamaica Underground.* Kingston: Geological Society of Jamaica.

Girvan, N.P. 1991. "Economics and environment in the Caribbean: an overview". In *Caribbean Ecology and Economics,* edited by N.P. Girvan & D. Simmons, pp xi-xxiv. St Michael, Barbados: Caribbean Conservation Association.

Hart, R. 1985. *Slaves Who Abolished Slavery.* Volume 2 , Blacks in Rebellion. Kingston: Institute of Social and Economic Research, University of the West Indies, Mona.

Jamaica Conservation Development Trust. 1992. "Jamaica's first debt-for-nature swap completed". *Tody News* 4, no. 1: 1-2.

Jamaica Conservation Development Trust. N.d. *National Parks: Saving our Livelihood.* Kingston.

Jamaica Ministry of Finance and Planning. 1970. *A National Physical Plan for Jamaica 1979-1990.* Kingston.

Lynn, W.G. 1940. *The Herpetology of Jamaica.* Kingston: Institute of Jamaica (Science Series No. 1).

Lynn, W.G. 1949. "The bats of Jamaica". In *Glimpses of Jamaican Natural History,* edited by C.B. Lewis. Vol. 1:18-21.Kingston: Institute of Jamaica.

Mills, C.W. 1991. "Marxism and Caribbean development: a contribution to rethinking". In *Rethinking Development,* edited by J. Wedderburn, pp 15-54. Kingston: Consortium Graduate School of Social Sciences, University of the West Indies, Mona.

Mitchell, A.W. 1986. *The Enchanted Canopy.* New York: Macmillan.

Morgan, G.S., & C.A. Woods. 1986. "Extinction and the zoogeography of West Indian land mammals". *Biological Journal of the Linnaean Society* 28: 167-203.

Morrissey, M. 1983. *Cockpit Country Field Guide.* Kingston: School of Education, University of the West Indies, Mona.

Mosley, G. 1989. *Blue Mountains for World Heritage.* Sydney: Colong Foundation for Wilderness.

Ovington, D. 1986. *Kakadu: A World Heritage of Unsurpassed Beauty.* Canberra: Australian Government Publishing Service.

Patterson, P.J. 1989. "National parks: a vehicle for sustainable development". *Tody News* 1, no. 2: 1-2.

Price, R. (ed). 1971. *Maroon Societies.* New York: Anchor Books.

Proctor, G. 1972. "Ferns". *Jamaica Journal* 6: 36-39.

Proctor, G. 1986. "Cockpit Country forests". In *The Forests of Jamaica*, edited by D.A. Thompson, P.K. Bretting, & M. Humphreys, pp 43-48. Kingston: Jamaican Society of Scientists and Technologists.

Robinson, C. 1969. *The Fighting Maroons of Jamaica*. Kingston: Collins and Sangster.

Senior, O. 1983. *A-Z of Jamaican Heritage*. Kingston: Heinemann Caribbean.

Sinha, S.C. 1972. "Plant collectors in Jamaica before 1900, with a biography of Sir Hans Sloane". *Jamaica Journal* 6: 29-35.

Swabey, C. 1946. "Some trees of Jamaica". In *Glimpses of Jamaican Natural History*, edited by C.B. Lewis. Vol. 2: 70-97. Kingston: Institute of Jamaica.

Swabey, C. 1949. "Classification of vegetation in Jamaica". In *Glimpses of Jamaican Natural History*, edited by C.B. Lewis. Vol. 1: 55-61. Kingston: Institute of Jamaica.

Sweeting, M.M. 1957. "Notes on the caves of Jamaica". *Transactions of the Caves Research Group of Great Britain* 5: 1-11.

Sweeting, M.M. 1958. "The karstlands of Jamaica". *Geographical Journal* 124: 184-99.

Thompson, D.A., P.K. Bretting, & M. Humphreys. 1986. *Forests of Jamaica*. Kingston: Jamaican Society of Scientists and Technologists.

Turner, T.W. 1991. "*Papilio homerus (Papilionidae)* in Jamaica, West Indies: field observations and description of immature stages". *Journal of the Lepidopterists' Society* 45: 259-71.

United Nations Educational, Scientific and Cultural Organization. 1972. *Convention Concerning the Protection of the World Cultural and Natural Heritage*. Paris.

United Nations Educational, Scientific and Cultural Organization. 1989. *A Legacy for All: The World's Major Natural, Cultural and Historic Sites*. Paris.

Zans, V.A. 1959. "Caves and cave exploration in Jamaica". *Geonotes (Journal of Geological Society of Jamaica)* 2, no. 2: 59-69.

Zans, V.A. et al. 1962. *Synopsis of the Geology of Jamaica*. Kingston: Geological Survey Department.

Chapter 17

# Farming on the Fringe: Small-Scale Agriculture on the Edge of the Cockpit Country

David Barker and David J. Miller

## Introduction

The Cockpit Country is a distinct natural region of northwest Jamaica (Figure 17.1), and is so named because of the landscape's similarity to cock-fighting arenas. It is one of the world's classic regions for the study of tropical karst geomorphology, thanks largely to the pioneering geographical work of Marjorie Sweeting [Sweeting 1958]. A wilderness area of enormous biological and geomorphological interest and an intriguing cultural history, the area was first proposed as a national park in 1970. However, designation of large tracts of the region as Forest Reserve from the early 1940s, attest to a long history of concern over resource conservation.

But fresh plans for Jamaica's national parks are being drafted at a time when the Cockpit Country's forests are apparently diminishing at unprecedented rates, through deforestation and clearance for agriculture, and charcoal production [Eyre 1989]. Much of the pressure on the primary wet limestone rain forest originates in the populated border areas located around the perimeter of the Cockpit Country. Thus, plans for a national park should be based not only on a scientific appraisal of its ecological resources and potential, but also on an understanding of the socio-economic pressures to use forest lands which emanate from the border zones.

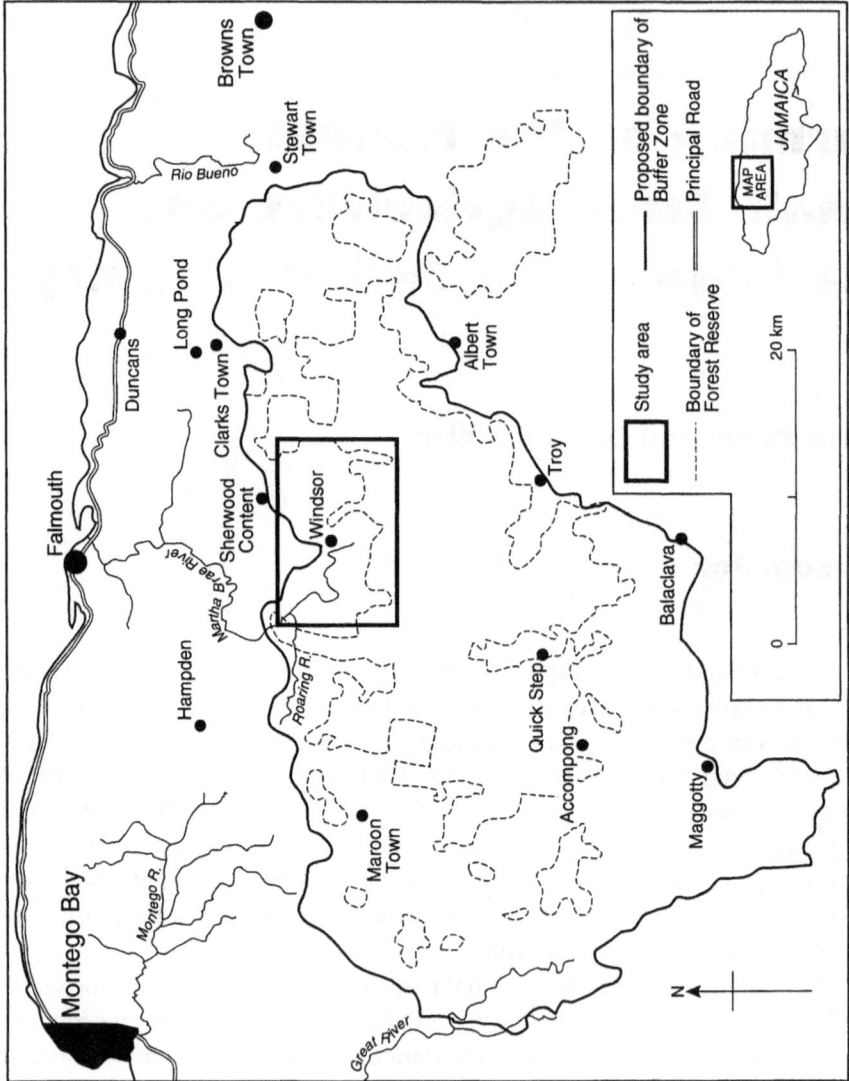

*Figure 17.1* Cockpit Country in its regional context

The Cockpit Country is used here in a regional context, to include both the wilderness of wet limestone rain forest and its immediate border zones. The core of the region is easily identified on maps and aerial photographs (1:25,000) by contiguous, uninhabited forest and an absence of surface drainage. In the border zones, the rivers re-emerge on the surface, the forest is more patchy, and there is settled agriculture. A broad regional interpretation is useful because it incorporates the critical border zones into the geographical definition of the Cockpit Country.

The study presented here is part of a larger research project to map and analyse the process of encroachment and invasion by pioneer small farmers into the glades and fertile cockpits of the proposed national park area. Two facets of the encroachment process are documented here. Firstly, the characteristics of small-scale farming systems in one section of the Cockpit Country's northern border area are discussed. Secondly, using a set of 1961 aerial photographs covering the same area, a number of linear tracks and glades were identified as old farming encroachments into primary forest. Field investigations determined their current land use status.

The activities of small farmers are a critical component in the process of deforestation. However, the integrity of the national park, especially if it is to be maintained as a wilderness area, will depend upon the acceptance of its status, and partial involvement in its operations by local communities located around its perimeter.


# The Physical and Human Geography of the Cockpit Country

## Geology and Geomorphology

Most of the Cockpit Country comprises the White Limestone Group of mid Eocene to lower Miocene age, and many of the lower-lying areas and flanks are floored by alluvial clay of Quaternary to recent age, derived from the weathering of the limestones. Post-Cretaceous movement has resulted in a northwards dip of the limestones. The Cockpit Country is marked by predominant north-south fault lines [Wadge & Draper 1977] which show up clearly as strong lineaments on aerial photographs. The northern margin is bounded by the structurally complex Duanvale Fault system. The main phase of the structural movement is thought to be late Miocene, though the strong geomorphological expression of many of the north-south trending faults could indicate that later movements have taken place along them.

About 60 percent of all karst in Jamaica is cockpit karst [Day 1979], the Cockpit Country being the classic area [Sweeting 1958; Versey 1972]. Cockpit karst comprises steep-sided, enclosed depressions with convex inwards side slopes, forming depressions which are star shaped or polygonal in plan. The depressions have a concave floor covered with a variable amount of rubble and soil, and intervening conical hills. The cockpits tend to be contiguous with an identifiable divide between each depression, whilst the lowest part of the depression has a joint controlled vertical shaft in solid limestone but at least in part choked with debris [Smith et al. 1972; Wadge & Draper 1977].

The slopes of the conical hills are highly irregular and display a number of facets, ranging from vertical cliffs to steps and to talus accumulations [Aub 1969]. The cockpits and conical hills are often arranged in lines [Sweeting 1958] following joint or fault patterns, though elsewhere no structural guide can be identified [Wadge & Draper 1977].

The cockpits originated by vertically directed solution processes with minor collapse [Sweeting 1958; Smith et al. 1972]. It seems possible that the solutional mechanisms which initiated the cockpits depended upon a link between the surface solution and an underground drainage system via the central shaft; this link being no longer operative due to increased secondary permeability within the limestone, reduction in rainfall or the general lowering of the water table [Day 1979].

On the borders of the Cockpit Country, degraded cockpits, glades and interior valleys (poljes) are present [Sweeting 1958; Smith et al. 1972]. For example, poljes are conspicuous to the north of the Duanvale Fault zone [Smith et al. 1972], where the structural and lithological nature of the limestones promotes lateral water movement and impedes vertical drainage. Here, a series of east-west trending poljes in the Windsor, Coxheath and Campbells area terminate to the west in the Queen of Spain's Valley, the best known and largest polje in Jamaica [Pfeffer 1986]. Tower karst also is found immediately to the north of the cockpit karst in the Duanvale Fault zone, and is associated with rapid spring-head recession especially when springs are cutting back along fault lines, as occurs in the Windsor area. Such recession gives rise to flat floored, steep-sided and steep-headed pocket-valleys which accompany the tower karst [Sweeting 1958].

## Hydrology, Soils, Flora and Fauna

The highest rainfall totals in the Cockpit Country occur in the central core, with typical annual values ranging between 2,500mm to 3,800mm, diminishing to about 1,750mm to 2,500mm on its borders. Given the general pattern of rainfall, and significant variations in elevation, there is variation in microclimate, which is likely to be more pronounced where there has been the removal of forest cover.

May is by far the wettest month in the Cockpit Country, accounting for about 19 percent of total annual rainfall. A second wet period occurs in September and October, accounting for another 27 percent of annual precipitation. During thunderstorms, rainfall is torrential, and hail is experienced from time to time. The driest months are January and March.

The hills of Jamaica's Central Inlier to the south of the Cockpit Country form the main watershed of the island. Therefore, in the Cockpit Country, there is a predominant water movement towards the north coast, which issues in springs (such as at Fontabelle) and blue holes (for example, Dornock Head) along the margins of the White Limestone areas, especially at fault lines. These form the sources of the Martha Brae and other northwards flowing rivers [Day 1985; Eyre 1990].

The bases of some cockpits contain ponds in the wet season forming small perched water tables [Sweeting 1958], though most of the cockpits are hydrologically relict. The only surface flow visible at present is within the soil infill of degraded cockpits [Day 1979] and the most significant water movement within the cockpits themselves is slow vertical percolation through the limestones.

The White Limestone of the Cockpit Country has an incomplete cover of red bauxitic soil. On cockpit sides, an easily erodible and very shallow brown or red-brown clay loam is also present and occurs in pockets between bare limestone. Many of the cockpit floors contain moderately deep yellowish-brown clay soils.

The natural limestone rain forest of the region is termed "mesic" and in the core of the Cockpit Country is still pristine and undisturbed. Biologically, it is an important habitat for Jamaica's flora and fauna, with a remarkable degree of endemism. There are at least 100 species of endemic plants [see Eyre, this volume], and endemic fauna include two species of frogs and two species of lizards. Ecologists stress that endemism may be highly localized, and confined to individual karst towers. In addition to endemic species, the Cockpit Country has become an important refuge for endangered Jamaican species such as the yellow snake, the Giant Swallowtail butterfly, black-billed and yellow-billed parrots and two species of pigeon.

## Settlement and Land Use

The Cockpit Country is a significant historical and cultural landscape in Jamaica. The Maroons fought the British army to a stalemate in a series of military campaigns [Eyre 1980; Robinson 1969]. The ensuing treaty recognized the rights of Maroons to live in and enjoy some degree of autonomy at Accompong on the southern margins, where they have retained their identity and distinctive land tenure [Spence 1989; Barker & Spence 1988].

The history of the human use of the Cockpit Country began with the Maroons. There is also a long history of settled plantation agriculture in the border zones, and the sugar belts to the north and southwest are still in production. From time to time the plantocracy owned small sugar estates well inside the area of cockpit karst [Eyre 1987]. During the 18th and 19th centuries, the British extracted timber (hardwood forest emergents such as mahogany) from the forests for export.

After early forest clearance for plantations, the mid 19th century was the next major period of forest removal in the border zones. There was rapid new settlement and associated peasant cultivation by freed slaves, and Baptist missionaries founded free villages, such as that of Martha Brae [Hall 1959]. The larger settlements of Balaclava and Albert Town also have distinctively 19th century place names.

Since the 19th century, the principal contiguous area of primary forest has progressively contracted and fragmented, as rural populations have increased and the cultivated area has expanded. Recent data [Eyre 1989] suggest an acceleration in the rate of deforestation of the Cockpit Country, and that only 446km$^2$ of main contiguous rain forest area remains intact. He estimated an alarming 15.9 percent reduction in the category "tropical deciduous forest" between 1981 and 1987, which represents an annual rate of deforestation of 2.8 percent.

## The Study Area

The study area is located astride the main contiguous forested area of the Cockpit Country and the southern margin of a sugar belt focused on factories located at Long Pond, near Clark's Town, and at Hampden (see Figure 17.1), and includes the rural communities of Sherwood, Content and Windsor.

Within the study area, there is a striking physical boundary which separates the contiguous forested area from settled agricultural areas. In part at least, this is a function of the local geology (Figure 17.2), and the boundary, coincidentally, also demarcates cockpit karst (to the south) from tower karst and poljes (to the north) (Figure 17.3). Thus the study area has two distinctive landscapes: uninhabited wet limestone rain forest of the cockpit karst, and a patchwork of agriculture and woodland in the tower

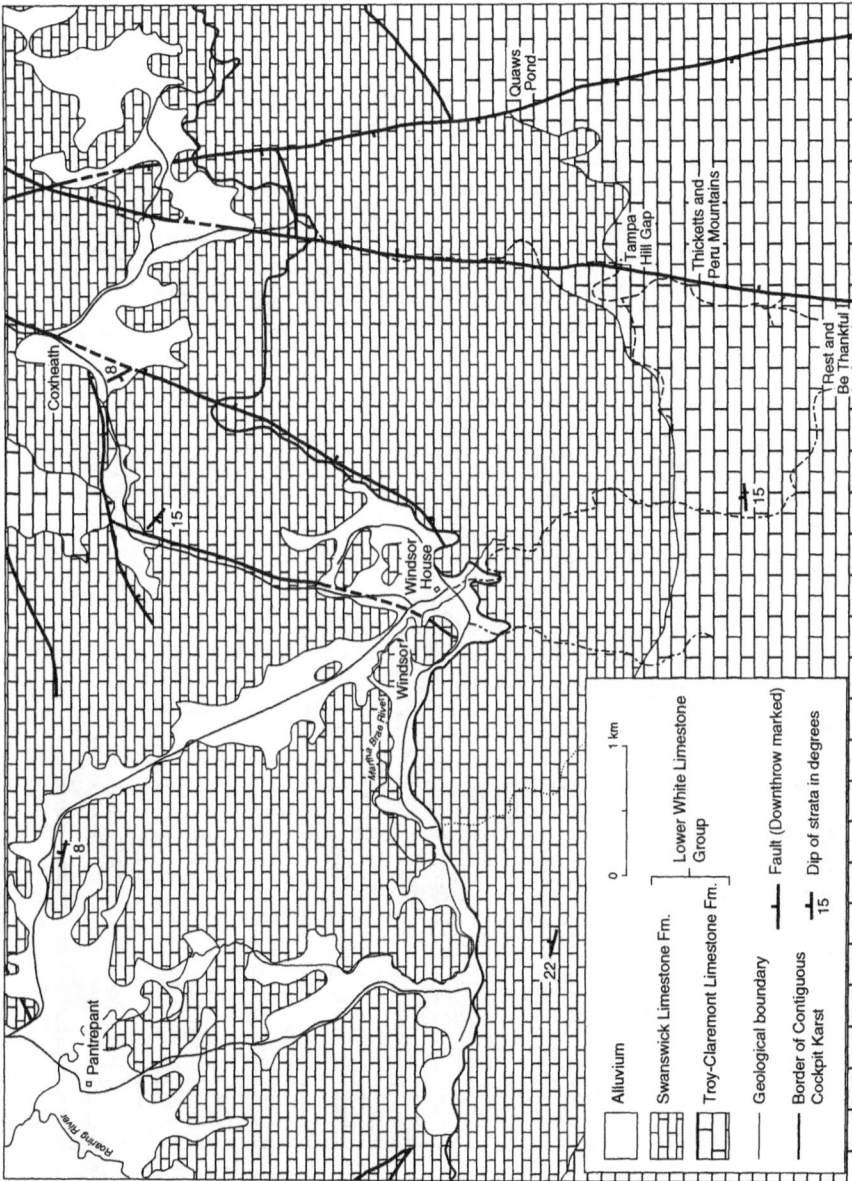

Figure 17.2   Geology of the study area

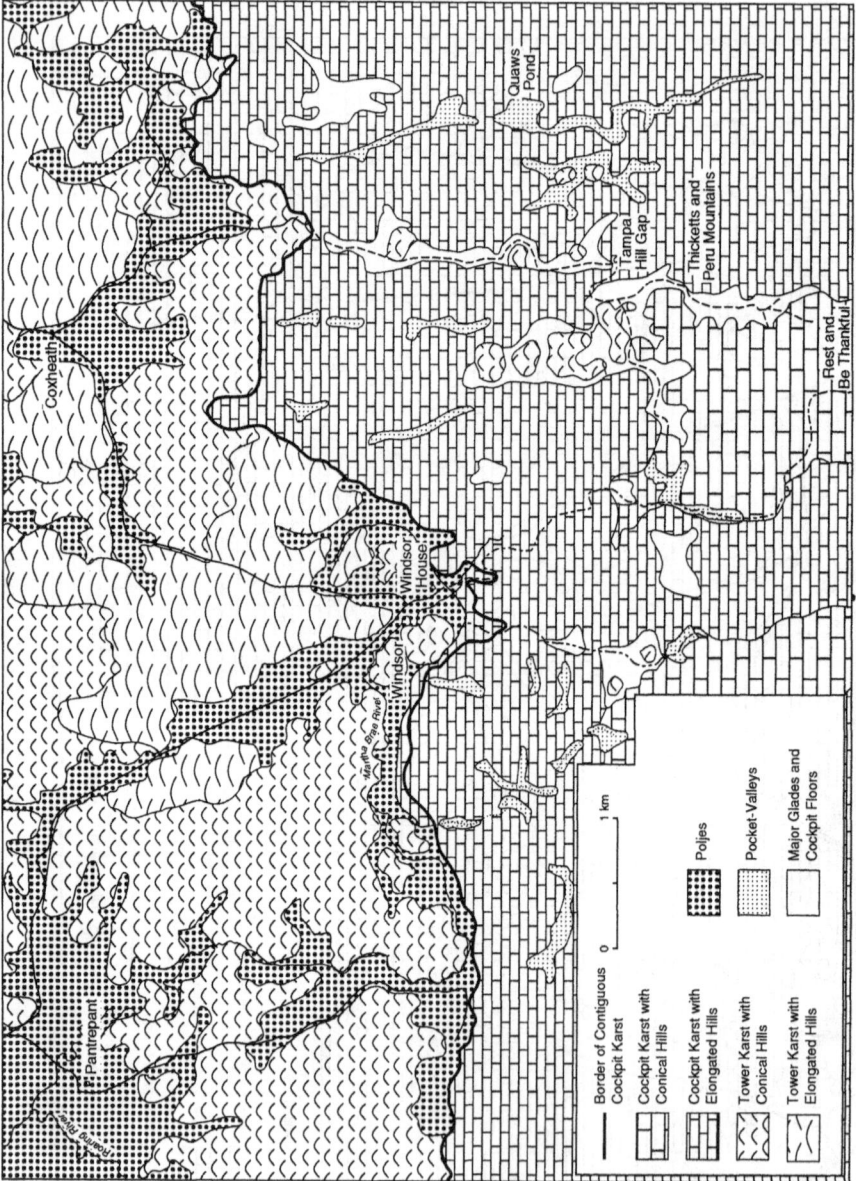

*Figure 17.3* Geomorphology of the study area

Border of Contiguous Cockpit Karst

Cockpit Karst with Conical Hills

Cockpit Karst with Elongated Hills

Tower Karst with Conical Hills

Tower Karst with Elongated Hills

Poljes

Pocket-Valleys

Major Glades and Cockpit Floors

0    1 km

karst and poljes. In the latter zone, agriculture is located on the flat land and remnant forest on the tower karst, although some lower slopes have been cleared for farming.

It was the significance of this dramatic juxtaposition of two quite different landscapes and environments which was the focus of the field research. All the encroachment trails (mapped in Figure 17.4 and described below) penetrated the forested cockpit karst from the settled areas of tower karst and poljes. On the other hand, the perceptions and attitudes towards the environmental, ecological and farming conditions in the two contrasting areas were investigated in the farm survey.

## Characteristics of Small Scale Farming

A total of 88 small farmers were interviewed in and around the rural communities of Sherwood, Content and Windsor, using purposive sampling methods. The study area falls within 5 census enumeration districts whose combined population in 1982 was 1,826 – slightly up from the 1970 figure of 1,610. All of the farmers lived in and farmed the area defined above as tower karst and poljes. Most of the farmers in the sample fell, typically, into the older age groups; 61 percent of the sample were over 50 years of age, and 43 percent over 60, whilst only 3 percent were under 25, and 17 percent under 35. Most of the data reported here on cropping systems relates to agriculture conducted in the area of tower karst and poljes, outside the forested cockpits. However, a small number of farmers who were interviewed actively farmed one or more plots deep inside the forested cockpit karst.

### Cropping Systems

The farmers are, in many ways, fairly typical of Jamaican farmers, not only in age. For example, about two-thirds of the sample were full-time farmers. They cultivate a wide range of crops, on fairly small acreages, and under difficult and modest circumstances. Yet they are remarkably adaptive in their survival strategies, exploiting the resources of a variety of topographic and ecological niches.

Generally, farmers with more than 2 or 3 acres (about 1 ha) of reasonably flat land grow sugar cane as a principal cash crop. It is collected by trucks and processed at the Long Pond factory. Coffee and bananas are also grown, but virtually all the farmers cultivate field crops, such as yams, dasheen, maize, sweet potatoes and cabbage, and tree crops like breadfruit, coconut, and avocado pear. Production of these crops is both for home consumption and as

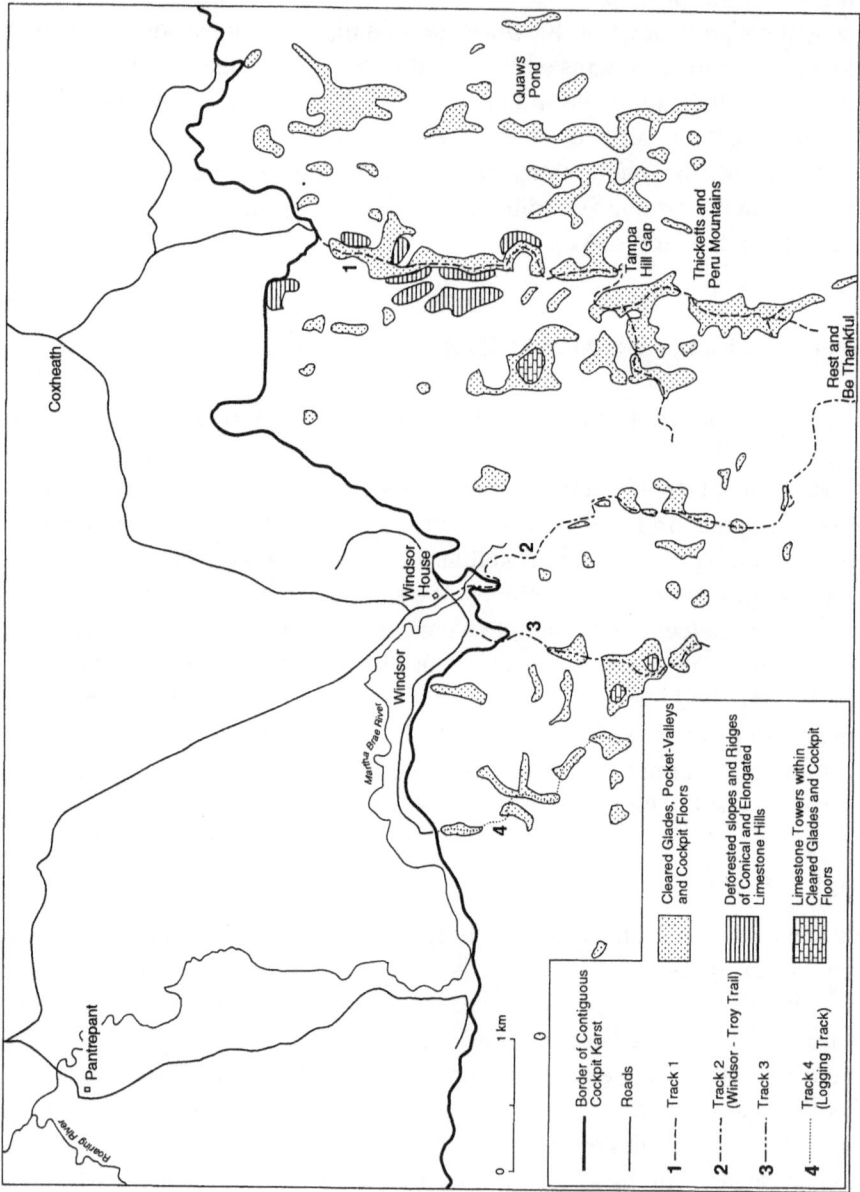

*Figure 17.4* Patterns of encroachment within the study area

cash crops for the domestic market. Falmouth is the principal market town, just less than 10 miles (16km) away on the north coast (see Figure 17.1).

Fallow periods, crop rotation and intercropping are ubiquitous techniques; while fertilizer is used principally for cane cultivation. Farmers are extremely knowledgeable about good and bad crop combinations and their explanations reveal detailed knowledge and skills in manipulating environmental variables like lowered temperatures (through shading). Fallow periods appear to be longer and more widespread than elsewhere in Jamaica.

Many farmers rear livestock, especially cattle and goats; a few were even identified as specialist cattle farmers. One individual had 45 cattle on 65 acres (26ha), and another small farmer used 10 separate pieces of land for grazing. Animal rearing is significant because many of the cleared glades in the forested cockpits are used for pasture.

Interestingly, farmers generally cited economic problems, especially marketing, rather than those relating to topography or land availability as their main problems. Further, a number of farmers gave detailed descriptions of how they were able to farm steep, rocky slopes; strategies like using "creeping" crops such as pumpkin, cucumber and yams which take advantage of soil pockets, and which spread over nearby stones and bare rock. For such farmers, steep slopes are not necessarily a severe constraint, once they have decided to undertake the arduous task of clearing a particular slope. In other words, farmers will rely on their ingenuity, adaptability and hard work to ensure some sort of return for their efforts. Whether they continue to cultivate the same hillside or abandon it within a couple of seasons is, of course, a critical variable in defining the extent of environmental degradation.

## Farm Fragmentation and Environmental Variability

Accurate data on land tenure in the study area were not available. Considerable tracts of land are the property of large or medium sized enterprises. The largest subdivision of the former Windsor estate is a property mainly in pasture and devoted largely to cattle farming. Kaiser Bauxite Company is an important landowner, having bought extensive areas of bauxite reserves in the parishes of Trelawny and St Ann in the 1950s and 1960s. A number of farmers living in the study area had been relocated from St Ann by Kaiser in the 1960s. Family land is common amongst small farmers, and some plots are owner occupied. But given the relatively large amount of land in the hands of bigger property owners, it is not surprising that the majority of small farmers interviewed needed to rent and lease land to survive, perpetuating the fragmented pattern of landholdings.

Table 17.1 indicates the high degree of fragmentation in the study area. The modal class of three plots per farmer is much higher than normally reported in small farmer surveys in Jamaica [McGregor & Barker 1991]. The 88 farmers in the sample utilized a total of 260 separate plots.

*Table 17.1*   Farm Fragmentation: Number of Separate Plots per Farmer

| Number of plots per farmer | 1 | 2 | 3 | 4 | 5 | 6 | 7 | 8 | 9 | 10 |
|---|---|---|---|---|---|---|---|---|---|---|
| Frequency | | 12 | 23 | 32 | 16 | 3 | 0 | 0 | 1 | 0 | 1 |
| Percentage of all plots | | 14 | 26 | 36 | 18 | 3 | 0 | 0 | 1 | 0 | 1 |

Note: *The farmer with 10 plots is a specialist cattle farmer*

Whilst the general pattern of land ownership is an important constraint on land availability, and thus a control on the fragmented pattern of land holdings, other factors are at work. Small farmers in the tropics deliberately cultivate scattered, fragmented farm plots to exploit different ecological niches and microclimates [Ibgozurike 1970; King & Burton 1982]. In the study area, there are contrasting environmental/ecological/climatological conditions over very short distances, especially between the forested cockpit karst area and the zone of tower karst and poljes. Farmers' perceptions and understanding of such environmental variability will influence where they farm and why.

Thus, in the survey, when farmers were asked whether land in the forested cockpits is good or bad for farming, responses confirmed accurate perceptions of environmental conditions there. Certain descriptions were encountered repeatedly. For example: the soils were more fertile; the weather cooler, with more moisture and rainfall; more protection from the sun; and higher humidity. As another example, the red bauxitic soils of the cockpit bottoms were frequently referred to as "rich" or "strong". Thus, farmers clearly understand that the microclimate within the forested cockpits, albeit only a few miles away from their homes, is different and represents a different range of conditions for farming.

Not surprisingly, a few farmers exploit environmental variability in farming conditions in order to spread their risks, and deliberately farm land in the forested cockpits, in addition to plots outside the forested area. Though few in number, these farmers regarded their best plots as those located in the forests, even in cases where they had to travel up to two hours on a donkey or a mule to reach them. In addition, several people mentioned that they occasionally searched old farming areas in the forests as a source for yam heads (used for propagation), because these yam heads were superior in quality. Only one farmer admitted to obtaining permission from the Forestry Department to cultivate a glade in the forested cockpits. She intercropped between saplings of blue mahoe planted by the Forestry Department. Further, she claimed to take care of the trees. This suggests that elements of one sensible strategy for land management are already in place, albeit in a fairly ad hoc, informal way.

Based on case interviews with those few individuals actively farming within the forested cockpits, it is clear that some are more sensitive to the environmental integrity of the forests than others. For example, one farmer claimed that he was careful to protect the forest when clearing bush. His conceptual distinction between bush and forest is interesting, as it reflects a degree of environmental sensitivity. It suggests that he is practicing genuine bush fallowing, cultivating plots for perhaps two or three years before "resting" the land for a longer period, whilst the plot reverts to bush. Such isolated bush fallowing, on a small scale and involving only a small number of individuals, is unlikely to have long-term detrimental effects on the forest. Whilst the above farmer was, apparently, in tune with his environment, a second individual who farmed within the forested cockpits, clearly, was not. He admitted he had bulldozed a section of forest for cattle rearing. The area had since flooded recurrently, but he did not agree that his own actions had affected the hydrological regime.

Considering the sample in general, virtually every farmer thought the forested cockpits offered some advantageous environmental conditions for farming. One farmer even insisted that rainfall was caused by trees on the slopes of the "high country", and their unrestricted removal would lead to less rainfall there. Farmers were able to generalize and lucidly make comparisons, and assign causal relationships between environmental variables and cultivation practices at different locations. Yet the majority of farmers in the sample do not farm within the forested cockpits, nor intend to in the foreseeable future, even when acknowledging the beneficial farming conditions within the forests. Their reasoning invariably points to the hard work required of the rough terrain, the limited amount of flat land, and perhaps most importantly, to *inaccessibility*. This latter point has critical implications for the management of the national park.

There was anecdotal evidence that the forested cockpits had been cultivated in the past; one lady claimed she had found old tools on her land (possibly of Maroon origin). Several farmers said their parents had farmed in the forested cockpits, often staying away from home for a week or more, although they themselves did not farm there. Two older farmers indicated that they had cultivated in the forest when they were younger, but said farming there was especially difficult given the terrain and inaccessibility, and was suitable for younger men.

## Geographical Patterns of Encroachment

Within the study area, the sharp contact between cockpit karst and the area of tower karst and poljes provides a physical barrier to extensive encroachment, due to the largely impenetrable nature of the steep cockpits and intervening conical hills (Figure 17.3). Encroachment into the cockpits is predominantly in the form of north-south linear zones along tracks following small pocket-valleys and glades which are frequently associated with major north-south trending faults (Figure 17.2). Accelerated weathering of the limestones along these zones has led to the development of relatively gently sloping elongated hills, with intervening pocket-valleys separated by small divides or cols physically more conducive to encroachment than the surrounding cockpit karst.

Thus there is a complex and variable pattern of encroachment. Neither does the invasion appear to be a systematic, one-way movement. Study of both available aerial photographs and of field evidence support temporal and spatial variations of encroachment and abandonment, with some former cultivated areas in glades and cockpit bottoms presently reverting to bush or in fallow.

Four main linear zones of encroachment into the forested cockpits can be identified within the study area (see Figure 17.4). The predominant pattern of invasion along each trail is one of exploitation of the linear floors and cockpit bottoms, though along the first zone (see below) the slopes and tops of the limestone hills are also partly cleared and deforested.

The first zone, to the south of Coxheath, has a well defined track (Track 1, Figure 17.4) extending into the forest to Tampa Hill Gap, Thickett's and Peru Mountains and onwards towards the heart of the Cockpit Country at Darwin's Gap. An extension of this track penetrates to the southern border of the Cockpit Country at Troy, so, in effect, significant encroachment has occurred along the entire length of this track, right across the Cockpit Country. A parallel track to Quaw's Pond has also been the site of agricultural encroachment. Both tracks mark the limits of a downfaulted block of White Limestone of the Troy/Claremont and Swanswick Formations, and follow clear topographical lineaments associated with the two fault systems.

The second zone contains a similar track (Track 2, Figure 17.4) extending southwards into the cockpit karst, south of Windsor House. It penetrates into the cockpit heartland as the present Windsor to Troy trail, occasionally used by hikers. The Windsor end of the trail follows a series of small pocket-valleys separated by steep karst towers and cones, the former being sites of agricultural encroachment which extend about 2.4km into the forested cockpits. Further penetration is made difficult due to topographical constraints; the cockpits become less contiguous, deeper and steeper, and also contain less basal soil infill. Consequently, the degree of agricultural encroachment is less marked than along Track 1, though east-west extensions of encroachment appear to connect the two areas and may be exploiting favourable topography controlled by major joint patterns within the limestones.

Thirdly, a smaller trail (Track 3) to the south and southwest of Windsor House, extends southwards into the cockpit karst and connects two or three small pocket-valleys together with a much larger cockpit floor. Encroachment into the cockpit area extends for about 1.5km, the final glade being terminated to the south by a steep headwall which appears to block further agricultural invasion.

Encroachment has also occurred to the west of Windsor House along a trail (Track 4) which probably leads to Wakefield Mountain and may exit on the southern margin of the Cockpit Country at Quick Step. Agricultural encroachment extends into the cockpits for about 1.4km, being constrained there by deepening and enhanced development of the cockpit karst.

Other minor areas of agricultural encroachment occur at the immediate margins of the forested cockpit karst, and other small glades and pocket valleys are exploited along "offshoots" of the major linear alignments.

## Types of Encroachment

The predominant types of invasion in the study area are small-scale farming and logging. The main crops grown are yam, corn, dasheen, banana and plantain on the cockpit and pocket-valley floors with minor extension onto the hills. Many of the cockpit floors and glades remain as pasture for cattle and goats. Logging operations involve both systematic clearance of the cockpit slopes and more selective removal of hardwood species leading to a thinning out of the rain forest cover rather than complete deforestation. The removal of saplings and branches of larger trees is also taking place in some localities for the production of yam poles.

Whilst some cockpit floors and glades are being actively farmed, others are seemingly abandoned or in bush fallow and overgrown with creeping vines, a further testimony to the complex and variable nature of the encroachment pattern. Indeed, some cockpit floors are minor sites of reforestation and at least partly under blue mahoe and Caribbean pine plantations. In places, there are mature food and fruit trees such as breadfruit, jackfruit and guava which are undoubtedly indicators of previous long-term occupancy. Much of the encroachment area must also have been used for illicit *marijuana* (ganja) cultivation in the past, though no evidence of this type of informal agriculture was encountered during fieldwork.

Track 1 has been the location of long-term access into the cockpit heartland, whilst the sheer scale of occupancy and invasion has resulted in the development of multiple land uses. The present land use is one of pasture for cattle and ground provisions cultivation. Many of the slopes of the surrounding elongated limestone hills have been systematically cleared (since the 1961 aerial photographs were taken) for both logging and small-scale agriculture, though some of these locations are now ruinate and overgrown with ferns. Significant clearance and deforestation of the limestone ridge tops has also taken place here, which has not been observed elsewhere in the study area.

Deeper into the cockpit karst, logging is a widespread encroachment practice and is both a systematic and a large-scale enterprise. A similar sequence of farming and logging encroachment occurs along the parallel track towards the Quaw's Pond area, whilst the fertile glades, pocket-valleys and cockpit floors to the west of the main trail have also been subject to long-term occupancy and are presently being farmed.

Along the Windsor to Troy trail (Track 2), farming encroachment takes the form of banana and plantain stands in minor pocket-valley openings which are overgrown and abandoned, the sites reverting to bush and ruinate forest. The first large glade has been cultivated for an extended period, though no enlargement of the cleared area has taken place since 1961. Indeed, the glade appears to be in fallow at present. Deeper into the cockpits other major areas of clearance are also mostly in fallow or may have been at least temporarily abandoned apart from relatively recent clearance of the lower cockpit side slopes for yam poles, whilst mature breadfruit trees probably indicate long-term farming encroachment in the past.

Along Track 3, to the south southwest of Windsor House, evidence of partial clearance takes the form of saplings removed for yam poles. Some of the glades here have also been used for dasheen and banana cultivation. The main glade bottom along this track is replanted with Caribbean pine and blue mahoe trees which are some 5 to 10 years old. The presence of mature jackfruit trees also attests to long-term encroachment and utilization, though clearance remains largely unaltered since 1961.

The trail then leads into a large and topographically complex cockpit bottom, largely gently sloping but subdivided by three small karst towers. The entrance to the cockpit is only partially cleared as rain forest emergents are left in place, whilst much of the remainder of this part of the glade is ruinate having succumbed to invasion by creeping vines. More significant cultivation occurs in the central and southwest part of the cockpit floor along with small Caribbean pine and blue mahoe saplings; evidence of an ad hoc agreement between the farmer and the Forestry Department, whereby the presence of the farmer is tolerated in exchange for weeding and bushing the plantation.

The last fertile pocket-valley appears not to have undergone significant additional clearance since 1961. It is presently abandoned or in fallow as tall grass and weeds predominate.

The fertile cockpits and glade floors along Track 4, to the west of Windsor House, also seem to have been more extensively farmed in the past. Most of the glades have been abandoned or are in fallow. The primary function of the trail at present is for timber removal and cattle pasture on the floors. Some of the glades here have also been replanted with blue mahoe. It is seemingly the cockpits further along the trail that are coming under most pressure, some appearing to be much more open than on the 1961 photographs. Active removal of trees for timber is prevalent.

A complex sequence of encroachment and abandonment pertains to this track, in that the primary invasion was one of pioneer farming and cattle rearing, though it is presently utilized for the removal of hardwoods. Although the predominant practice is selective removal of trees for timber, some of the glade floors have been replanted with hardwoods and pine.

# Implications for the Cockpit Country National Park

## The National Park Boundary: Core Area and Buffer Zone

The impending designation of a national park raises the whole question of where, precisely, the boundary should be located. The question was of no great consequence in the past, and was avoided by the cartographic expedient of printing "The Cockpit Country" across the wilderness core, and on occasion, using the more forbidding topographic descriptors "District of Look Behind" and "Me No Sen You No Come".

Current proposals for the Cockpit Country National Park envisage a core area surrounded by a buffer zone. The concept has already been used for the Blue and John Crow Mountains National Park [Smith, this volume] and is basically sound. It has the advantage of focusing attention on the critical role of the borders of the Cockpit Country as sources of pressure on the forested cockpits, and should facilitate the incorporation of communities living in these border areas into the management plan for the national park.

For national park planners, delimiting a boundary for the core area of the park should prove easier along the northern edge. It has been demonstrated in this chapter that there is a clearly identifiable boundary between forested cockpit karst and the tower karst and poljes, and this boundary also has functional relevance in terms of resource use. However, determining a precise boundary along other sections of the perimeter may prove more difficult, as deforestation pressures are more severe and the geographical patterns of encroachment more complex.

## Stability and Integrity of the Forested Cockpit Karst

Much of the core of the Cockpit Country is Forest Reserve, presently managed by the Forestry Department, and is already designated as a Wildlife Sanctuary. It consists of 55,170 acres (22,327ha) of largely primary forest. There are 12 separate Forest Reserves listed within the regional environs of the Cockpit Country, although a single contiguous forest area forms about 74 percent of the total.

Eyre's data [1989] suggest that deforestation pressures are not equally distributed around the perimeter of the Cockpit Country. The southern boundary is under more severe pressure than the northern margins. It follows that localized studies are urgently required in order to investigate the nature of encroachment processes, as there may be significant differences in the type of pressures along different sections of the boundary, reflecting spatial variations in the pattern of deforestation. The authors are presently undertaking more extensive research around Troy, on the southern boundary.

Further, as the national park becomes a reality, the fact that the northern margin is much more accessible to tourist areas may contribute to differential pressures on the forest boundary. Such impacts may not necessarily be negative, given a proper system of resource management.

Despite the regional evidence, in our study area the forest boundary appears to be relatively stable, with no significant increase in the areas cultivated in the 30-year period since 1961. On the contrary, the geographical pattern of agricultural encroachment is historically complex; some areas having been cleared recently; and other glades and pocket-valleys having reverted to ruinate bush, or secondary forest, or appearing to be in grass fallow. It is quite probable that our study area is atypical; large tracts of land are owned by a few large/medium size landowners and this may have acted (inadvertently) as a "buffer" against wholesale encroachment by small-scale cultivators.

## Forestry and Farming Encroachments

The Forestry Department is a key player in the scenario for establishing a national park, since it is engaged in the selective and systematic removal of hardwoods for timber along some encroachment zones. Indeed, the creation of a logging trail for timber exploitation has a side effect in opening up new areas for farming by improving accessibility. Thus, a potential conflict of interest is possible if the remaining contiguous area of forested cockpits is to be maintained as a wilderness national park. The parameters of sustainable harvesting of timber need to be clearly identified and adhered to whenever the national park becomes a reality. For example, increased logging to a level whereby the rain forest is systematically removed from the conical hills as well as the cockpit floors and glades would be out of place in a protected and conserved area.

The Forestry Department is also engaged in minor reforestation along some of the cockpit floors and glades. Evidence has been cited above of farmers intercropping and maintaining small plantations of blue mahoe and Caribbean pine. This is a potentially innovative management strategy which could be extended and formalized as part of the management plan for the national park. However, the authors consider that planting Caribbean pine, a species which is not native to Jamaica, is of dubious ecological and aesthetic value, and is vulnerable to damage from strong winds when grown in pure stands.

Whilst the activities of the Forestry Department could be integrated into management of the national park, of concern are the activities of small private logging companies and the gathering of saplings for yam poles, which will prove much more difficult to monitor and regulate.

This research suggests that, in the study area, all accessible fertile cockpit floors are being, or have in the past been, utilized. Topographical conditions have inhibited extensive farming encroachment due to the relative inaccessibility of the remaining cockpit floors, and also to the lack of basal soil infill for cultivation. Further, it was demonstrated that many of the farmers living in the nearby communities do not intend to farm in the forested cockpits, partly because of the difficult terrain and inaccessibility. Thus, the forested cockpit heartland will probably not come under additional agricultural pressure from small farmers along this sector of the northern margin in the near future, due to the rugged nature of the terrain. We must stress that these conditions are probably very different to those that prevail elsewhere on the margins of the Cockpit Country, notably the southern boundary. However, pressure on forest lands for agriculture, in this area, could conceivably increase dramatically should one of the nearby sugar factories suddenly close down.

## Inaccessibility as a Conservation Strategy

The research presented here strongly suggests that maintaining the inaccessibility of the core area of the Cockpit Country, (that is, the remaining contiguous forested cockpit karst) appears to be critical to the success of the proposed national park. Along the more accessible trails, invasion into the forested cockpits is apparently at a more advanced stage, with slopes coming under pressure as well as the cockpit floors and glades. Along the less easily accessible tracks, only the glades have been utilized. To date, the slopes along such tracks appear to be relatively stable, with a near pristine rain forest cover, apart from the selective removal of saplings for yam poles and some mature trees for timber. Some smaller trails have been partly widened to accommodate the removal of timber. But this raises concern given the potential, not only for the accelerated clearance of hardwood trees, but in providing easier access to farmers.

A limited amount of small farming has been undertaken in the glades and pocket-valleys of the study area, for several generations. Tracks and trails have been subject to a complex and variable history of encroachment patterns and types, including abandonment of farming. These encroachments into the cockpit heartland need not be harmful to the integrity of the national park provided they are carefully controlled, limited in number, confined to the bottoms of the glades, and provided that the hillslopes are kept forested.

Indeed, at least two recreational attractions can be adduced from existing encroachment trails to remote farming areas/logging operations. They provide access to scenically beautiful trails for hikers. Also, the bottoms of many glades are, in effect, small open meadows that act as miniature terrestrial reservoirs for nature lovers. They are ideal habitats for bird watching, each with a dazzling array of butterflies, other insects and wild flowers on display. As such, they complement the surrounding rain forest environment by providing hikers with opportunities to encounter a variety of landscapes.

The original proposals for the national park envisaged the core as a wilderness area in which no trails would be permitted, whilst the buffer zone was to be designated for nature tourism, forestry, watershed protection and other sustainable uses. Later proposals seem to be moving away from the wilderness concept by proposing the development of several of the axial trails across the core. Based on this research, there are already a large number of secluded farming trails which exist in a variety of different ecological settings. It is argued, therefore, that the cutting of new trails through primary forest, with all their potential for accelerating encroachment, appears to be unnecessary, and even unwise.

In conclusion, it should be noted that Smith [this volume] indicates that the Cockpit Country is to become a national park in the next round of designated areas, and Eyre [this volume] has argued a more important role for the Cockpit Country, as a possible World Heritage Site. Thus, it may be anticipated that resource management issues with respect to the Cockpit Country are likely to become more important in the near future. Given the results presented in this chapter, it is clear that further research is needed. For example, this might include: a detailed analysis of the historical-geographical patterns of encroachment, and their ebb and flow; linking agriculturally related encroachment and deforestation to population pressure; and examining local people's attitudes, perceptions and uses of the forested cockpits and their potential involvement in the national park. At present, the database with which to make effective decisions regarding the management of a national park based on the Cockpit Country's unique habitat is incomplete.

## References

Aub, C.F. 1969. "The nature of cockpits and other depressions in the karst of Jamaica". *Proceedings of the 5th International Speleological Congress*, Stuttgart, M15/1-7.

Barker, D., & B. Spence. 1988. "Afro-Caribbean agriculture: a Jamaican Maroon community in transition". *Geographical Journal* 154: 198-208.

Day, M.J. 1979. "The hydrology of polygonal karst depressions in northern Jamaica". *Zeitschrift fur Geomorphologie*, suppl. bd. 32: 25-34.

Day, M.J. 1985. "Limestone valley systems in north central Jamaica". *Caribbean Geography* 2: 16-32.

Eyre, L.A. 1980. "The Maroon wars in Jamaica — a geographical appraisal". *Jamaican Historical Review* 12: 80-102.

Eyre, L.A. 1987. "Mapmaker extraordinary". *Scottish Magazine*.

Eyre, L.A. 1989. "Slow death of a tropical rain forest: the Cockpit Country of Jamaica, West Indies". In *Environmental Quality and Ecosystem Stability*, edited by M. Luria, Y. Steinberger & E. Spanier. Vol IV-A: 599-606. Jerusalem, Israel: Environmental Quality, ISEQS Pub.

Eyre, L.A. 1990. "Water resource conflict on the north coast: who gets what?" *Jamaica Journal* 22: 2-11.

Hall, D. 1959. *Free Jamaica: 1838-1865, An Economic History*. Aylesbury: Caribbean Universities Press/Ginn & Co. Ltd.

Igbozurike, M.U. 1970. "Fragmentation in tropical Africa: an overarated phenomenon". *Professional Geographer* 22: 321-25.

King, R.L., & S.P. Burton. 1982. "Land fragmentation: notes on a fundamental spatial problem". *Progress in Human Geography* 6: 475-94.

McGregor, D.F.M., & D. Barker. 1991. "Land degradation and hillside farming in the Fall River basin Jamaica". *Applied Geography* 11: 143-56.

Pfeffer, K.H. 1986. "Queen of Spain's Valley, Maroon Town, Jamaica: a cross-section of different types of tropical karst". In *New Directions in Karst* (Proceedings of the Anglo-French Symposium, 1983), edited by K. Paterson & M.M. Sweeting, pp 349-362.

Robinson, C. 1969. *The Fighting Maroons of Jamaica*. Kingston: Collins and Sangster.

Smith, D.I., D.P. Drew, & T.C. Atkinson. 1972. "Hypotheses of karst landform development in Jamaica". *Transactions of the Cave Research Group of Great Britain* 14: 159-73.

Spence, B. 1989. "Predicting traditional farmers' responses to modernization: case of a Jamaican Maroon community". *Caribbean Geography* 2: 217-28.

Sweeting, M.M. 1958. "The karstlands of Jamaica". *Geographical Journal* 124: 184-99.

Versey, H.R. 1972. "Karst of Jamaica". In *Karst: Important Karst Regions of the Northern Hemisphere*, edited by M. Herak & V.T. Springfield, pp 445-66.

Wadge, G., & G. Draper. 1977. "Tectonic control of speleogenesis in Jamaica". *Proceedings of the 7th International Speleological Congress.* Sheffield: British Cave Research Association, pp 416-19.

# INDEX

## A

Abary Conservancy, 240
Above Rocks Inlier, 164
Agricultural dualism: geographical
  dimensions of, 8
Agricultural systems: research into
  dynamics of, 205
Agroforestry: and soil erosion control, 206
Agronomic techniques: in development
  strategy, 205-206
Albedo: increase in, 191
Alternative tourism: ecotourism as, 64;
  and hotel ownership, 64
Ambient water temperature: and marine
  organisms, 33
Andesitic volcanics: in Wagwater Belt, 165
Andros: blue holes of, 35; Project, 36-38,
  43
Animal rearing: in Cockpit region, 281
Anthropogenic activities: and natural
  slopes, 148
Aquatic weeds: in MMA area, 240-241
Arawaks. See Lucayans
Arco: skull of, at Sanctuary, 43
Areal productivity, 117
Aruba, 78, 83
Atlantic storms: increase in, 136

## B

Bahamas, the: blue holes of, 11, 35
Barbados: beach erosion in, 21; beach
  recession in, 22; and coastal
  hydrodynamics, 11; East Coast
  geomorphic system, 225-231; and
  Physical Development Plan, 225; and
  Soil Conservation Scheme, 224; and
  tourism, 9

Barbados Light and Power Company Ltd.,
  21, 22, 23
Base saturation percentage: as indicator of
  soil fertility, 193
Beach accretion: in Brandons-Brighton
  Bay, 21; rate of, within groyne cells, 26
Beach erosion: manifestations of, in
  Barbados, 21
Beach profiles: of Brandons-Brighton Bay,
  24
Beach recession: in Barbados, 22; rate of,
  at Brandons-Brighton Bay, 24
Beach recovery: at Brighton, 26
Beach sediment budget: and beach
  building, 29
Belize: ecotourism in, 13, 66
Benjamin, George, 35
Bermuda: decline in tourist arrivals in,
  79-80; efforts to revitalize tourism in,
  80-81; future of tourism in, 84-85; as
  model tourist destination, 87; profile of,
  73-74; protection of environment in, 85;
  "soft tourism policy" in, 85; tourism in,
  74-76
Biodiversity: of Cockpit Country, 263-264
Blue holes: archaeological excavations of,
  36; of the Bahamas, 11, 35; formation
  of, 35-36; protection of, 44; public
  attention and, 44; skeletal remains in, 36
Blue and John Crow Mountains National
  Park (Jamaica), 249
Blue mahoe: planting of, in Cockpit
  region, 289
Blue Mountain Adventure Tours:
  establishment of, 256
Blue Mountain area: soil erosion
  measurement in, 191, 193

Bridgetown Port (Barbados), 21
British Caribbean Geography Seminar, 11
Buff Bay valley (Jamaica): landslides in, 165
Butler's Model, 13, 71-72, 85

**C**

Caiman population: in MMA region, 242
Cape Verde cyclones, 140
Caribbean: and environmental risk, 5-8
Caribbean pine: planting of, in Cockpit region, 289
Carrying capacity,5; at Brighton, 34; and ecotourism, 62; of islands, 87
Cataclastic zones, 172
Catchment scale: extrapolation from plot scale to, 194
Cation exchange capacity: of Scotland Soils, 219; of soils in Upper St Andrew, 193
Caves: in Jamaica, 262
Census of Population and Housing (Virgin Islands), 93
Central Inlier: as main watershed of Jamaica, 275
Channelization: and MMA project, 242
Charcoal production: at Man Kote, St Lucia, 52
CHARMS, 66
Climate change: improved modelling of, 205
Climatic data: review of Caribbean, 202
Coastal Conservation Unit, 21, 22
Coastal development: need for planning of, 33
Coastal drainage and irrigation: in Guyana, 14
Coastal flooding: and deforestation, 8-9; and land use practices, 9; in Speightstown, 7
Coastal hydrodynamics: changes in, in Barbados, 11
Coastal resource management, 11
Coastal zone degradation, 7
Cockpit Country (Jamaica), 14; Arawak sites near, 265; archaeological value of, 265; contribution of, to modern biological science, 262; definition of area of, 273; and economic viability, 268; encroachment in, 273; and endemic plant species, 263; ferns in, 263; fireflies in, 264; as forest canopy research facility, 268; frogs in, 264; geology of, 273-274; geomorphology of, 273-274; history of human use of, 275-276; maintenance of inaccessibility of, 289-290; and Maroon Wars, 264-265; *Noctilio leporinus* in, 264; official attitudes towards, 260-261; as PNA, 261; and potential for national park, 259; prickly pole palm in, 263; rainfall in, 274-275; reduction of rain forest in, 259; significance of, 259; swallowtail butterflies in, 264; *Swietenia mahogani* in, 263; threat to endemic features in, 263-264; underground karst features of, 262; as world class biological environment, 262; as world class geomorphological environment, 262
Cockpit Country National Park: boundary of, 287; fulfillment of preconditions for, 266-267; proposals for, 287
Community involvement: in park projects, 255, 258
Conservation: of endemic species, 267, 290; soil, 224
Constant Spring Filter Plant, Jamaica, 149
Construction industry: costs, in Virgin Islands(US), 103-104; decline in, in Virgin Islands(US), 92-93; size of, in Virgin Islands, 104; upsurge in, in Virgin Islands(US), 90
Contract rent: median value of, 96
Convergence: in East Coast geomorphic system, Barbados, 228
Corals: and temperature fluctuations, 33
Cost-benefit analysis: concept of, 117; and disaster mitigation, 111, 117; limitations on usefulness of, 121; methods of, 117-120; technical limitations to, 119; and "willingness to pay", 120
Cousteau, Jacques, 35
Cretaceous rocks, 164
Crop loss estimates: reconsideration of methods of, 115, 119-120
Cropping systems: in Cockpit region, 279, 281
Cruise ships: attempts to limit access of, 65
Cuba: and ecotourism, 66
Curaçao, 78, 83
Cyclone chronology data: reliability of, 125
Cyclone data series: construction of, 125; length of accuracy of, 131

Cyclone tracks, 125; changes in, 124, 134, 144

Cyclones: in Caribbean, 144-145; changes in frequency of, 134-135; explanation of patterns of, 141-145; fall in levels of, 136, 145; in Hispaniola and Puerto Rico, 132; historical patterns of, 13; increase in, in Caribbean, 140; influences on, 140; intensification of, to hurricane status, 134-135; and intensity variations, 134; in Lesser Antilles, 131-132; origins of, in West Indies, 136; patterns of, in Hispaniola and Puerto Rico, 132; patterns of, in modern period, 132-134; records of, in Caribbean, 125; spatial variations in patterns of, 136, 145; variations in, 131

**D**

Debt-for-nature swap, 257

Deforestation: in the Caribbean, 191; and coastal flooding, 8-9; of Cockpit Country, 276, 286, 288; in Jamaica, 191

Department of Housing, Parks and Recreation (US Virgin Islands), 105

Deposition: in Scotland District, 220

Development planning: basis of, in Caribbean, 46

Development projects: and the environment, 234-235

Development strategies: and environmental interests, 233

Diagenesis: model of, for carbonate platforms, 43

Disaster: definition of, 113; and economy, 114-115

Disaster insurance: as mitigation strategy, 117

Disaster mitigation: definition of, 113; issues concerning, 114-116; opposition to planning approach to, 117; strategies for, 116-117

Disaster relief: public sector in, 121

Dominica: botany tour of, 65; ecotourism in, 13; effect of Hurricane David on,115; and volcanic activity, 6

Dominican Republic, 6, 78, 83

Drainage: in Guyana, 234; projects in Guyana, 235; and technological change, 243

Duanvale Fault system, 273

**E**

Earthquakes: in the Caribbean, 6; and landslides, 148; in Nicaragua, 115; and rock falls, 148; in Upper St Andrew study area, 173

East Coast system (Barbados): geomorphological determinants of, 225-226; and land use change, 228-231

"Ecocolonialism", 66

Economic growth: in Virgin Islands, 92

Economy: contraction in, in St Maarten/St Martin, 81-82

Ecosystems: disruption of, in MMA project region, 242; offshore, and sedimentation, 152

Ecotourism, 61, 63; as alternative tourism, 65; in Belize, 66; in Cuba, 66; debate on, 66-68; development of, in Caribbean, 65-66; in Jamaica, 63-64; manipulation of, 66-67; and resource development, 65-66; scale of development of, 67

El Niño, 140-141

Encroachment: geographical patterns of, in Cockpit region, 284-285; need for studies of, in Cockpit Country, 288; types of, in Cockpit region, 285-287; use of trails as recreational attractions, 290

Endemism: of Cockpit Country flora and fauna, 263-264, 275

Environment: degradation of, in St Maarten/St Martin, 84; and enhancement of natural resources, 245; link between, and development, 245; need for policy directions regarding, 243; protection of, in Bermuda, 84-85; recognition of importance of, in Jamaica, 63-64

Environmental assessment: importance of, 34

Environmental chemistry, xiv

Environmental economics: discipline of, 235

Environmental issues: and drainage and irrigation projects in Guyana, 234; importance of education on, 245

Environmental laws: enforcement of, 14, 257-258

Environmental Monitoring and Control Unit (Guyana): problems of, 237, 239

Environmental organizations: in the Caribbean, 15

Environmental perception: farmers and, 205-206, 282-283
Environmental projects: in Windward Islands, 64
Environmental protection: involvement of local residents in, 64; need for, in Guyana, 244
Environmental science: training in, 243-244
Environmental stress, 8
Equatorial pressure trough: and changes in storm tracks, 200
Ergodic Hypothesis, 212
Erodibility: of soils in Scotland District, 215
Erosion control strategies: farmers' perception of, 205-206
Erosion: accelerated, 22; accelerated soil, 149; Gabion boxes and soil, 116; gully, 196, 215; net, and systems collapse, 197; reduction of, on Barbados coastline, 26; soil, 189-191, 198; wind, 223
Eutrophication, 55

**F**

Fallow periods, 206, 281
Farm fragmentation: in Cockpit region, 277-283
Farming encroachment: in Cockpit region, 288-289
Ferns: in Cockpit Country, 263
Flank margin model, 38
Food forest, 205-206
Forest reserve: designation of, in Cockpit Country, 271, 288
Forestry: and land use in Scotland District, 224
Forestry Act (Jamaica), 254
Forestry Department (Jamaica): and hardwood removal in Cockpit region, 288; and reforestation, 289
Forfar, Archie, 35
Fox's Bay: rehabilitation of, 53

**G**

Gabion boxes: and soil erosion, 116
General circulation models, 199
Geographical research: on the Caribbean, 10-14
Geography: and economic development, 4; environment and development, xiv, 3, 4; physical, and housing construction in

Virgin Islands(US), 103; and sustainable development, 5
Geological zonation: of landslides in Jamaica, 167
Geomorphic change: evaluation of, 211; susceptibility of Scotland District to, 227-228
Geomorphic hazards: and land use on Barbados East Coast, 223-224
Geomorphological activity: in the Caribbean, 190; estimation of relationship between, and land use, 227; in Scotland District, Barbados, 209
Global warming: threat of, to Caribbean, 8, 204
Government policies: and housing, 105
Grand Bahama: blue holes at, 36
Greenhouse gases, 199
Groynes: construction of, at Brighton, 26; and effect on beach stabilization, 26-27
Gulf of Mexico: and cyclone tracks, 136, 140
Gullies: in Scotland District, 215
Guyana: Agency for Health Sciences Education, Environment and Food Policy, 243; coastal drainage and irrigation in, 14; post-war development planning in, 233-234

**H**

Haiti, 78, 83; and land degradation, 7, 191
Hazard management planning: in Caribbean, 121-122
Hazard mapping, 171, 175-179
Hermitage reservoir (Jamaica): siltation in, 149
High angle faulting, 172
Hillside farming: and environment, 9
Hollywell Conservation Trust (Jamaica): establishment of, 256
Hollywell Recreational Park (Jamaica), 252
Home value structure: and home ownership in Virgin Islands (US), 95-96
Hope River: rock blocks in valley of, 157; suspended sediment in, 196
Hotel rooms: growth levels of, in St Maarten/St Martin, 82
Houses: cost of purchasing, in Virgin Islands (US), 104
Housing: availability of rental, in Virgin Islands(US), 102; owner occupied, in Virgin Islands (US), 94; reasons for high cost of, in Virgin Islands (US), 101-105;

rental, in Virgin Islands (US), 96; shortage of, in Virgin Islands (US), 90-91; subsidized, in Virgin Islands (US), 97; US policies and shortage of, in Virgin Islands (US), 101-102; vacant, in Virgin Islands (US), 97-98; value of owner occupied, in Virgin Islands (US), 94-95

Housing market: in Virgin Islands (US), 103-105

Housing survey: data collection methods of, 93-94

Housing units: increase in, in Virgin Islands (US), 92; projected demand for, in Virgin Islands, 105-106

Human activity: and geomorphology of Scotland District, 220-223; and land degradation, 198

Human resources: shortage of, in natural resource protection, 251

Hurricane Allen, 115

Hurricane Andrew, 6

Hurricane Charlie, 198

Hurricane David: effect of, on Dominica, 115

Hurricane Gilbert, 6, 255; and slope failure in Jamaica, 198

Hurricane Hugo, 6; effect of, on Virgin Islands (US), 90; and housing in Virgin Islands (US), 93

Hurricanes: and Caribbean island economies, 6; frequency patterns of, 132, 134; increase of, and SST, 200; rise in frequency of, in Jamaica in 1950s, 201; shifts in pattern, 13, 144-145

Hydrothermal alteration, 172

**I**

Inter-American Development Bank, 237

Intercropping, 9

Intergovernmental Panel on Climate Change, 199

International Union for Conservation of Nature (IUCN), 260

Intertropical Convergence Zone, 140

Irish Town (Jamaica), 170

Irrigation: schemes in Guyana, 234

**J**

Jamaica: caves in, 262; Central Inlier as main watershed in, 275; distribution of landslides in, 153, 156; Forestry Act of, 254; geological zonation of landslides in, 167; Hurricane Gilbert and slope failure in, 198; impact of landslides in, 149; landslide habitats in, 156-157; landslide zones in, 163-166; landslides in, 13; morphotectonic landforms in, 156; and national park model, 252; and national park system, 14; neotectonic landforms in, 156; reasons for landslides in, 147; and recognition of importance of environment, 63-64; and response mechanisms to landslides, 153; slope movements in, 150-151; soil erosion in, 14, 149, 190; systems collapse in, 197

Jamaica Conservation Development Trust (JCDT): and debt-for-nature swap, 257; and responsibility for national park system, 250

**K**

Kaieteur National Park, 244

Karst features: of Cockpit Country, 262, 274

Kingston, Jamaica: and earthquake risk, 6

**L**

Land authority schemes: and watershed rehabilitation, 198

Land degradation: in Caribbean, 189; in Haiti, 191; and soil erosion, 7; and systems collapse, 205

Land tenure: in Cockpit region, 281-282

Land use: change in, on Barbados East Coast, 228-231; geomorphic hazards in Scotland District and, 224; and geomorphological changes, 220; relationship between, and geomorphological process, 227; in Scotland District, 220

Landscapes, natural: modifications to, 8

Landslide habitats: in Jamaica, 156-157

Landslide hazard: assessment of extent of in Upper St Andrew, 170-171, 175-177, 181-184; zonation of, 171

Landslide hazard zonation maps. See Hazard mapping

Landslide risk: methods of evaluating, 174

Landslide susceptibility map: use of, 184

Landslide zones: features of, in Jamaica, 163-166; of Jamaica, 163

Landslides: in the Caribbean, 7; in Jamaica, 13; distribution of, in Jamaica, 153, 156; economic costs of, 152, 167;

geological zonation of, 157-162, 167; impact of, in Jamaica, 149; inventory of, in Upper St Andrew study area, 174; in Jamaica, and land use, 147; and overland transport in Jamaica, 149; perception of, in Jamaica, 152-153; prehistoric, in Wagwater Belt, 156; in Quaternary alluvial deposits, 157; reasons for, in Jamaica, 147; response mechanisms in Jamaica, 153; results of Upper St Andrew survey, 179-180; and road design, 184; triggering mechanisms for, 148, 149; in Upper St Andrew, Jamaica, 170; and water supplies in Jamaica, 149
Liguanea Plain: rock blocks in, 157
Linear regression model: and rent structure, 98-101
Lithosols: erosion of, 148
Littoral current, 27
Local advisory committees (LACs): activities of, 255-257; and interest in national parks, 255; and national parks in Jamaica, 252, 253
Logging: side effect of, in Cockpit region, 288-289
Long Island: blue holes in, 35-36
Low and Moderate Income Affordable Act (Virgin Islands, US): objectives of, 105
Lucayans: burial sites of, 36; and habitation of Andros, 36, 43

## M

Mahaica-Mahaicony-Abary (MMA) project: 237-239; aquatic weeds in area of, 240-241; case study of, 234; environmental management of, 237, 239; and increase in surface water, 242; pre-project evaluation of, 239-240; and survival of animal species, 241-242; and wetlands, 242
Mahogany Vale (Jamaica): bridge at, 255
Mangrove Cay, 36
Mangrove forests: survey of, 47, 52
Marigot, St Martin, 77, 82
Marijuana: growing of, in Cockpit region, 281
Marine park: establishment of, in Montego Bay, 63
Martinique, 7
Mass wasting: in Scotland District, 215-219

Mesoscopic faults, 172
Microclimate, 14; of Cockpit Country, 274-275
Migrant workers: in St Maarten/St Martin, 83-84
Millas, J.C., 131
Millbank Progressive Group (Jamaica), 256
Modified Mercali scale, 148
Montego Bay Marine Park (Jamaica), 249; zoning scheme in, 257
Montego Bay Marine Park Trust, 257
Morphotectonic landforms: in Jamaica, 156
Mortgage rates: in Virgin Islands(US), 104
Mt Pelée (Martinique): and *nuée ardente*, 7; volcanic activity, 6-7
Multinational companies: in tourism, 64

## N

National Landslide Management Programme: need for, 153
National Park Commission (Guyana), 244
National park system: efforts to establish, in Jamaica, 14; responsibility for, 250
National Park Trust Fund: establishment of, 251
National parks: education for users of, 254; enforcement of laws governing, 254; model for, in Jamaica, 252
Natural disasters: mitigation strategies for, 13
Natural events: and soil erosion in Caribbean, 198
Natural resource rehabilitation: and sustainable development, 55
Natural resources: legislative protection of, in Jamaica, 249
Natural Resources Conservation Authority (NRCA), 250; Act, 257-258
Nature Conservancy: and debt-for-nature swap, 257
Negril Chamber of Commerce: and efforts to limit tourism space, 65
Neotectonic faults, 163
Neotectonic landforms: in Jamaica, 156
Nevis: and Hurricane Hugo, 6; and tourism, 63
Newcastle Volcanics, 172
NGOs: and Cockpit Country, 260; and environmental protection, 15; and national parks, 251
*Nuée ardente*, 7

## O

Organic carbon: in soils of Upper St Andrew study area, 191
Overland flow, 215

## P

Palmer, Robert, 35, 43
Pan Caribbean Disaster Preparedness and Prevention Project (PCDPPP): objectives of, 112; problems of, 112-113
Park projects: sustainability of, 257
Phillipsburg, St Maarten, 77, 82
Physical Development Plan (Barbados), 225
Pic Macauya, Haiti: and watershed management project, 7
Planning Institute of Jamaica: and responsibility for PARC project, 250
Pocket-valleys, 274, 284, 285, 286
Political economy: and island environments, 8
Poljes, 274, 279
Portmore (Jamaica): and earthquake risk, 6
Precipitation: decrease in, in Caribbean, 204
Preston Lands (Jamaica): landslide at, 163
Prickly pole palm: in Cockpit Country, 263
Project Sanctuary (Bahamas). See Sanctuary Blue Hole (Bahamas)
Property damage: estimates of, 119
Protected Areas Resource Conservation (PARC) project, 14, 250; aim of, 250; implementation of, 251
Protected Natural Areas (PNAs): proposed system of, 261
Public Finance Authority (Virgin Islands, US), 105

## Q

Quaternary deposits: 166, 172; and liquefaction, 157
Queen of Spain's Valley (Jamaica), 274

## R

"Rabland": in Scotland District, 220
Rain forest: reduction of, in Cockpit Country, 259
Rainforest Reserve (Guyana), 244
Reef survey: at Brighton, 33
Rent: high cost of, in Virgin Islands(US), 98; linear regression model and structure of, 98-101
Rental market: in Virgin Islands(US), 102-103
Residential Construction Cost Index, 93
Resort cycles. See Butler's Model
Richmond Formation, 165, 172
Richter scale, 148
Rio Grande valley, 254, 256

## S

St Croix, 90, 91; housing costs in, 95
St Eustatius, 78
St John, 90, 91; housing costs in, 95
St Kitts: and Hurricane Hugo, 6
St Lucia: charcoal production in, 52; landslides in, 7
St Maarten/St Martin: decline in tourist arrivals in, 81-84; environmental costs of tourism in, 83; future of tourism in, 85-86; profile of, 73-74; setbacks in tourism in, 87; socio-economic costs of tourism in, 83
St Thomas, 90, 91; housing costs in, 95
St Vincent: disasters and economy of, 114-115
Sanctuary Blue Hole (Bahamas): archaeological significance of, 43; findings at, 43; protection of, 44
Saturation Index, 219
Scotland District (Barbados): change in landforms of, 231; drainage pattern of, 214; erodibility of soils in, 215; geology of, 212-214; geomorphological processes in, 14, 209; geomorphology and human impact on, 220-223; land degradation in, 191; potential use of, 224-225; recreational use of, 220; soil erosion in, 116; soils of, 214; susceptibility of, to geomorphic change, 227-228; topography of, 214
Scour: at Brandons-Brighton Bay, 24; formation of channel, 26
Sea surface temperature (SST), 140; average rises in global, 199-200; and hurricane frequency, 202-204
Seasonality: increase in, in Caribbean, 8
Sediment discharge: measurement of, 195
Sediment transport: thermal effluent discharge and, 26
Sediment traps, 191, 193-194
Sheetwash. See Overland flow

Site rehabilitation: and assessment of value of wetlands, 55; and resource management, 55; of wetlands, 47, 53-55
Skeletal remains: in blue holes, 36; of humans, in South Andros, 43
Slope failure: 219, 223, 224; causes of, 190; and Hurricane Gilbert, 198; in St Andrew, Jamaica, 170; and slope angle, 183-184; and soil erosion, 7
Slope movements: in Jamaica, 150-151
Small farmers: and deforestation process, 273
Small farming: characteristics of, in Cockpit region, 279, 281, 285
Smithfield Experimental Station, 7, 193, 194, 205
Soft tourism policy: in Bermuda, 85
Soil Conservation Division (Jamaica), 193
Soil Conservation Scheme (Barbados), 224
Soil erosion: causes of, in Jamaica, 149; and gabion boxes, 116; in Jamaica, 14, 190; and land degradation, 190; modelling of rates of, 205; options for management of, 206; rainfall induced debris flows and, 149; research into, 7
Soil erosion data: for Jamaica, 193
Soil formation: natural rates of, 196
Soufrière, St Vincent: and volcanic activity, 6
South Andros Blue Hole: and economic activity, 44
Speightstown, Barbados: coastal flooding in, 7; flood prevention methods, 116
Subtropical high pressure cell, 136, 140
Surface water: increase in area of, in MMA region, 242
Sustainability: approaches to, 60-61; definition of, 60; manipulation of, 66-67
Sustainable development, xiii, 62-65; and geography, 5
Sweeting, M.M., 262, 271
Systems collapse: in Jamaica, 198; in Scotland District, Barbados, 198

T

Tax incentives: in disaster management, 116
Temperatures, global: increase in, 199-200
Terrain evaluation procedures, 174
Thermal effluent discharge: from Barbados Light and Power Co., 22; effect of, on water quality, 28-33; impact of, on beach changes, 24-26
Time series analysis, 125
Top of Jamaica Blue Mountain Tours: setting up of, 255-256
Tourism: and Barbados, 9; benefit-cost sequence of, 70; in Bermuda, 13, 74-76; and economy in St Maarten/St Martin, 81-82; effect of migrant workers on, in St Maarten/St Martin, 83; efforts to revitalize, in Bermuda, 80-81; and environment, 9; environmental costs of, in St Maarten/St Martin, 83; expansion of, in Virgin Islands, 92; and experiments with corporate enterprises, 64-65; future of, in Bermuda, 84-85; and housing in Virgin Islands, 13, 105; and island ecosystems, 9; lack of development model of, 71; life cycle stages for, in Caribbean, 71-72; mass market style of, in Caribbean, 70; negative impacts of, 59; in Nevis, 63; opportunities for, in Caribbean, 62-63; in St Maarten/St Martin, 13, 77-79; socio-economic costs of, in St Maarten/St Martin, 83; sustainability of, in Caribbean, 11. See also Alternative tourism
Tourism construction: absence of controls regarding, in St Maarten/St Martin, 78
Tourism destination life cycle model. See Butler's Model
Tourism patterns: monitoring and control of, 66
Tourism promotion: short term, 70
Tourist arrivals: in Bermuda, 75-77, 79-81; in St Maarten/St Martin, 77-79, 81-84
Training: and development projects, 245; in environmental science, 243-244
Trap measurements: and soil erosion estimates, 193-194
Tropical Forestry Action Plan, 47, 52
Tsunami, 6
Turks and Caicos Islands: blue holes in, 35, 36

U

Uniform Building Code: for Caribbean, 116
Universal Soil Loss Equation, 195
US Weather Bureau, 125

**V**

Vector diseases: and irrigation projects, 242
Virgin Islands (US): discovery of, as tourist mecca, 91
Virgin Islands Finance Housing Authority, 105
Volcanic activity: in the Caribbean, 6-7

**W**

Wagwater: Fault, 165; Group, 172
Wagwater River, 149
Water hyacinth: growth and spread of, in MMA area, 240
Water quality: changes in, at Brighton, 22; threat to, in MMA project region, 241
Watershed rehabilitation: and land authority schemes, 198
Water supply: turbidity levels of, in Jamaica, 149
Wetlands: current status of, and development potential, 52-53; degradation of, 50, 52; as degraded

resource in Eastern Caribbean, 47; destruction of, in Barbados, 52; drainage of, in Guyana, 14; and economic development, 11, 52; impact of damage of, 50-52; and MMA project; 242; potential use of, 53-55; results of survey, 47, 51-52; survey of, 47
Wild Life Sanctuary: in Cockpit Country, 288
Woodford (Jamaica), 170
World Heritage Convention, 261
World Heritage site: Cockpit Country as, 261; criteria for status of, 261; site listing and conservation, 267

**Y**

Yallahs: landslides in River Valley, 165; Pipeline, 149; Plantain Garden Fault, 165
Yellow Limestone Group, 166

**Z**

Zans, V.A., 262

# Contributors

## Editors

**David Barker** is Senior Lecturer and Head of the Department of Geography, University of the West Indies, Mona. His main research interests are in agricultural geography and sustainable rural development, and in the geography of the Caribbean region in general. He is co-founder and editor of the journal *Caribbean Geography* and he also edits and produces the *Jamaican Geographer*, the newsletter of the Jamaican Geographical Society. He has published widely on Jamaica and Africa, and co-authored a school textbook on Caribbean geography. His field experience includes work in Jamaica, Kenya and Nigeria.

**Duncan F. M. McGregor** is Senior Lecturer in Geography and Director of the Centre for Environmental Analysis and Management in the Department of Geography, Royal Holloway, University of London. His principal research interests include soil erosion, land degradation and land use change in the humid tropics. Ongoing work includes soil erosion and risk assessment in the West Indies; land degradation and environmental policy in Southeast Asia (Thailand and Malaysia); and examination of the physical and chemical effects on soils of the clearance of rainforest for pasture (Roraima, Brazil).

## Contributors

**Rafi Ahmad** is Lecturer in the Department of Geology, University of the West Indies, Mona and coordinator of the Mona Disaster Studies Working Group. Since 1986, he has actively pursued research in landslides in the Caribbean, especially in relation to the geological and geomorphological evolution of landforms in the plate boundary zones. His other interests are neotectonics, environmental geology, and structural and metamorphic geology. Prior to joining the University at Mona, he was a lecturer in Geology at the Aligarh University, India.

**Kenneth A. Atherley** is Coastal Planner with the Barbados Coastal Conservation Unit and has research interests and experience in coastal geomorphology, coastal land use development planning and legislation, and geographical information systems. He is currently undertaking further postgraduate research with the Marine Resources and Environmental Management Programme (MAREMP) at the UWI Cave Hill campus.

**Peter R. Bacon** is Professor of Zoology at the St Augustine campus of the University of the West Indies in Trinidad, and previously was Senior Lecturer at UWI, Mona. His major research interests are in the ecology and management of tropical wetlands, particularly those of the Caribbean region. Subsidiary interests are in coastal resource management and development control – topics on which he has provided technical advice and assistance to a number of government and international agencies. At the UWI he lectures on aquatic sciences, coastal management and general zoology topics.

**Leo A. Brewster** is a marine biologist and is involved in monitoring and analysis of trends in reefs and other benthic communities. He has extensive experience in marine water quality and tar ball monitoring and in development of ecological standards and marine reserves.

**Jeremy McA. Collymore** is Director of the Caribbean Disaster Emergency Response Agency based in Barbados. He has held posts in the Department of Geography at the UWI's Mona and Cave Hill campuses, as well as within the Pan Caribbean Disaster Prevention and Preparedness Project in Antigua. His research interests are in environment and disaster management, and he has published in these fields and on small farming systems.

**Klaus de Albuquerque** is Professor of Sociology at the College of Charleston in South Carolina, USA. He has lived and worked in the Caribbean region and has done extensive research on a wide variety of topics including fertility, migration, crime, tourism development and agriculture. He returned to the Caribbean for academic year 1994 as Visiting Fulbright Scholar and Professor at the University of the West Indies, Cave Hill, Barbados.

**L. Alan Eyre** was co-founder of the Department of Geography the University of the West Indies, Mona, and former Reader in Physical Geography and is author of more than 100 publications. An environmental activist, his regional and international work has focused on the degradation of the tropical rain forest, tropical climatology, and shanty towns in the developing countries. Though now semi-retired, he continues his research and publication activities, and part-time lecturing at the Department of Geography, UWI. His current affiliation is Research Fellow at the University of the West Indies Marine Laboratory in Discovery Bay, Jamaica.

**Lesley France** is Senior Lecturer in Geography at the University of Northumbria at Newcastle, specializing in tourism. Her research has focused on the development and impact of tourism in parts of Britain, Spain and the West Indies. She has visited the Windward Islands, and in particular Barbados, to research this topic.

**Russell J. Maharaj** is Engineering Geologist with the Institute of Marine Affairs, Trinidad. He holds a BSc in geology and an MPhil in engineering geology, and specializes in landslides and slope stability problems, and geotechnical investigations of soils and rocks. He has conducted research on large rock avalanches, cut-slope stability, soil slope failures, and geotechnical properties of soils in Jamaica, Trinidad and Tobago, and Barbados.

**Jerome L. McElroy** is Professor of Economics at St Mary's College, Notre Dame, Indiana, USA. He has taught in Belize and the US Virgin Islands and has held a number of policy positions in the region. His research has focused on tourism development, migration, agriculture, natural resources policy and economic development.

**David J. Miller** is Lecturer in the Department of Geography, University of the West Indies, Mona. His research interests are in geomorphology, Quaternary palaeo-environments, soils and peatland ecosystems, environmental and geomorphic hazards, with field experience in southwest England, the Falkland Islands and the Caribbean. He has published in the areas of soil science, environmental hazards and Quaternary geomorphology.

**Frank L. Mills** is Associate Director of Research of the Eastern Caribbean Center, University of the Virgin Islands. Lecturer at the University of the Virgin Islands, he was appointed Director of the Caribbean Research Institute there, in 1987. He has conducted extensive fieldwork in St Kitts and Nevis and the US Virgin Islands, and has published several research papers on agriculture, migration, and housing. He has considerable experience in scientific survey sampling, and the conduct of population and housing censuses.

**Leonard A. Nurse** is Project Manager and Head of the Coastal Conservation Unit, Barbados. His research interests include beach geomorphological changes induced by human activities, and the impact of sea level rise on the shoreline ecology of tropical islands. He has also worked as a consultant on coastal problems in various Caribbean islands.

**Fatima Patel** recently graduated from the University of the West Indies, Mona. She has taught in Barbados and will begin postgraduate research at Mona in 1995 in the field of applied geomorphology management. She has field experience in Barbados (slope and coastal processes in the Scotland District) and Jamaica (effects of small farming in Cockpit Country).

**Alison J. Reading** is Senior Lecturer in the Division of Geography at Anglia Polytechnic University. Her research interests in the Caribbean include analyses of the frequency of tropical cyclones and investigations into the stability of tropical clay soils. Her empirical work has been based in Dominica and throughout the Eastern Caribbean.

**Neil E. Sealey** is Senior Lecturer at the College of The Bahamas in Nassau. Current interests include promoting a better knowledge of the Caribbean region through the provision of locally produced texts and educational materials. He has published five regional textbooks to date and is editor of *The Bahamas Journal of Science*.

**David C. Smith** is Executive Director of the Jamaica Conservation Development Trust (JCDT) and was formerly

Lecturer in the Department of Zoology, University of the West Indies, Mona. He has been involved in drafting and development of the plan for a system of national parks in Jamaica; in drafting proposals for the first debt-for-nature swap in the English-speaking Caribbean; and the development of the Environmental Framework for Jamaica under the Enterprise of the Americas Initiative. He has also published several academic papers in entomology.

**Rory P. D. Walsh** is Senior Lecturer at the Department of Geography, University of Wales, Swansea. His research interests are humid tropical geomorphology and hydrology; recent historical tropical climate change, especially rainfall, droughts and tropical cyclones; and Mediterranean soil erosion and hydrological processes. He has undertaken field research in the tropics in the Eastern Caribbean, the Sudan, Sarawak, and Sabah.

**Brian Wheeller** is Lecturer in Tourism at the Centre for Urban and Regional Studies, University of Birmingham. As Course Director for the Tourism Policy and Management Masters programme, his research centres on current attempts at mitigating the negative impacts of tourism. His particular area of interests are the emerging economies of Eastern Europe and, more recently, the Caribbean – particularly Jamaica and Cuba.

**Patrick E. Williams**, is Senior Lecturer and Head of the Department of Geography, and the Dean of the Faculty of Arts, at the University of Guyana. His research interests include regional investment and development, urban infrastructure investment and development, and investment and environmental policies. He has extensive fieldwork experience in Guyana.

www.ingramcontent.com/pod-product-compliance
Lightning Source LLC
Chambersburg PA
CBHW020656270326
41928CB00005B/141